International Law as World Order in Late Imperial China

Sinica Leidensia

VOLUME 78

International Law as World Order in Late Imperial China

Translation, Reception and Discourse, 1847-1911

By

Rune Svarverud

BRILL

LEIDEN • BOSTON
2007

On the cover: World order in China. The title of this map is "Partitioning China like a melon" and is reproduced in *E'shi jingwen* from a British newspaper. A Russian bear, an English dog, a French frog, a German snake, a Japanese sun, and an American crow represent the partakers in the partitioning of China. This partitioning of China is the result of the 1895 American-Japanese treaty, according to the editors of the *E'shi ingwen*. (*E'shi jingwen* 俄事警聞 15 December 1903)

This book is printed on acid-free paper.

ISSN: 0169-9563
ISBN: 978 90 04 16019 4

PRINTED IN THE NETHERLANDS

In memory of my mother, Åse Svarverud,
and my father, Leif Svarverud

CONTENTS

ACKNOWLEDGEMENTS

My research project on the intellectual history of international law in late imperial China would not have been possible without the initial kind support from The Research Council of Norway (Norges Forskningsråd). As a post.doc fellow attracted to this topic I was generously included in the research project "Modern Chinese Scientific Terminologies" headed by professor Michael Lackner at the University of Göttingen. In my work with translated texts and the corresponding terminologies of early international law translations from Western languages I am deeply indebted to the resources and working tools developed by that project and the very rich and energetic working environment made available to me through Iwo Amelung and Joachim Kurtz in Göttingen and Berlin.

The resources made available to me in Germany included access to good libraries and collections of relevant texts. Further research into the textual histories of these translations and the various sources for the discourse on international issues in late imperial Chinese periodicals was also facilitated through access to Chinese libraries and collections. In that work I have been assisted by the goodwill of a number of kind colleagues in China, among which I particularly would like to mention professor Bu Jian (卜鍵) (Chinese Academy of Arts), professor Li Guilian (李貴連) (Beijing University), professor Ma Jun (馬軍) (Shanghai Academy of Social Sciences), professor Shen Guowei (沈國威) (Kansai University), professor Wang Jian (王健) (North-West University of Politics and Law), professor Wang Yangzong (王揚宗) (Chinese Academy of Sciences), professor Xiong Yuezhi (熊月之) (Shanghai Academy of Social Sciences), professor Zhang Haipeng (張海鵬) (Chinese Academy of Social Sciences), professor Zhang Naigen (張乃根) (Fudan University) and professor Zou Zhenhuan (鄒振環) (Fudan University). I also want to express my gratitude to the University of Oslo, which has supported me with an excellent working environment, and to the staff at the university library, who at all times are prepared to do their utmost in obtaining obscure editions of texts published and deposited in far away places.

At the University of Oslo I have also been blessed by the generous supervision of Iver B. Neumann in finding my way through the literature on the history of international law, a field initially fairly unfamiliar to me. Last but not least, I wish to thank my anonymous reader(s) at Brill for very helpful and to-the-point suggestions and comments on the first manuscript for this book. Needless to point out, when this book still abounds in shortcomings and inadequacies, the responsibility is mine alone.

Beijing, July 2006

CHAPTER ONE

CHINESE WORLD ORDER: PERSPECTIVES AND FRAMEWORKS

China's foreign relations in pre-modern and early modern history have often been framed within one of two mutually exclusive and historically distinct structures of inter-state relations; the traditional tribute system of suzerain-vassal relations between the states of East Asia, and the "modern" or "Western" system referred to as international law interpreting states as sovereign and equal members of a larger international society. The topic of this book is distinctively how the latter of these, as a system of theories and practices of inter-state relations, contributed to a world-view, or maybe we may even refer to it as a cluster of world-views, by different groups of Chinese intellectuals in the latter half of the 19th century and the early years of the 20th until the revolution and the establishment of the Republic in 1911-12. The terms used here for delineating international law as a "modern" and a "Western" system of international relations seem to indicate that one envisions China passing through a historic transformation when the ancient modes of inter-state relations are exchanged for a "modern" structure and model for conducting and interpreting such relations. The process of transformation in the intellectual interpretation of international relations in general and China's role and membership in the community of states in particular was indeed for a large part a process of adopting terms and concepts from international law as a theoretical framework. I hope, however, in this book to be able to show that the native Chinese discourse on these topics involves far more both in terms of traditional and modern ideas and frameworks, both indigenous and foreign, than the simplistic idea of a dichotomy of incompatible and mutually exclusive interpretations of inter-state relations seems to indicate.

The adoption of the term "modern" brings to mind a transformation of the Chinese national orientation and identity in international relations from an ancient, "outdated", or even "redundant" system no longer viable in a "modern" age to a new and updated universalist system imported from abroad. Undoubtedly, to some intellectuals in late Qing China international law also appeared to be the universal system of international relations for the new age to come. The fact that international law was among the areas referred to as Western studies (*xixue* 西學) delineated this international system along with the "modern" and "Western" modes of thinking about the state and the nation in late Qing intellectual circles. Our perspective here, however, is not to impose such a unilateral interpretation of "modernity" and "Western" on the entire spectrum of contributions to the Chinese discourse on these questions. We shall also be careful not to impose the idea of a linear evolution from a traditional (Chinese) to a modern (Western) world-view onto the study of the reception of international law in China. We shall be aware of the pitfalls of Eurocentrism when approaching the question of how an evidently foreign, Western European and North American, philosophy of the state in inter-state relations is approached and interpreted in the Chinese intellectual environment. In early works on the flow of goods and ideas between the West and the East a Europe-centred interpretative framework has too often been called upon to understand the development and substance of the object to be studied.[1] The risk of doing this is even greater when addressing a topic involving the adaptation and interpretation of what initially is an intellectual and political framework developed in the European context and introduced into China as such. I concur with Kenneth Pomeranz and R. Bin Wong, however, that we cannot eschew "many of the most important questions in history (and in contemporary life)" for the simple fear that we either evoke the dangers of Eurocentrism or the "postmodern" fear of cross-cultural comparison altogether. "It seem much preferable instead to confront biased comparisons by trying to produce better ones".[2] I sincerely hope that this book may contribute to an understanding of how a distinctively Eurocentric system of perception was utilized to become the framework for an indigenous Chinese discourse on these issues.

---

[1] This tendency is most emphatically refuted in recent works on international trade and diplomacy; such as Hamashita 2003, Pomeranz 2000, Pomeranz&Topik2006, Toby 1991, Wills 1984, Wills 2005, Wong 1997.

[2] Pomeranz 2000, p. 8. See also Wong 1997, pp. 1-4 and Pomeranz&Topik 2006, pp. xi-xv.

The aim of this book is to show how international law was translated, interpreted and received in China as a theoretical framework for conducting international relations, and how a Chinese discourse on questions related to China's role and identity in international relations developed from and within the theories of international law. This book is not a contribution to the already voluminous literature on China-foreign relations and diplomacy. I hope instead to be able to describe the way international law was translated and interpreted in China, how the principles and theorems of international law were integrated with doctrines and perspectives from other systems of examining inter-state relations, and finally how the discourse on international law in China changed over time from the latter half of the 19th century to the last years of Manchu Qing rulership in the early 20th century. I shall look at the Chinese interpretative process as one native to China and avoid presenting the process as a mere gradual adaptation to international law and the demise of a traditionalist view on inter-state relations. This book will focus on the intellectual history of international law in China but will also bring to our attention perspectives on how the European community of states responded intellectually to China and East Asia adapting to international law. China applying the principles of international law evidently not only concerns China in her own world-view but indeed also involves the world-view of the Western family of nations in international law.

In this context we may introduce four distinguishable, though not mutually exclusive, modes of perceiving Chinese inter-state relations. The first may for simplicity be called the traditional Chinese world-view, often described in the framework of a tribute system with China serving as a suzerain where neighbouring states in East Asia paid tribute to China. A second alternative system of seeing and interpreting China's foreign relations is related to private trade, often operating contrary to many of the principles of conducting trade according to the tribute system. This system of trade is occasionally protected by various forms of treaties, thus to some extent identifying these relations within the framework that we may call positive international law. A third way of perceiving international relations very influential in late Qing China is to see the world as a stage of fierce international battles between groups, races and nations explained within the framework of the particular form of East Asian

Social Darwinism. A fourth perspective on international relations in China is interpreted within the framework of theoretical international law. The latter two of these frameworks will contribute to the main core of my analysis of the Chinese discourse in late Qing. Other perspectives on international relations in the late Qing discourse may also evoke ideas from Confucianism, Daoism and other sets of Chinese and European currents of ideas. These do not, however, substitute full sets of frameworks for interpreting international relations in China and are as such only contributing to the discourse in various subtle ways. The two former modes of framing Chinese international relations, being "traditional" in the sense that they may be positioned in Chinese history prior to the intellectual current of ideas flowing into China from the latter half of the 19th century, will be briefly discussed below as the intellectual frameworks that create the surrounding conditions for the discourse on international law to follow. Before we proceed to these questions, however, I wish to consider the questions of language, translation and interpretation of foreign intellectual goods in the native (Chinese) environment. If we want to avoid seeing this process of cross-cultural currents of ideas simply as one of challenge and response, as a process of one party being the actor and the other being acted upon, as one involving an original Western and a Chinese imitation,[3] the first question we have to address is that of translation. The principles and fundamental ideas inherent in international law as it was conceived and practised in the West in the late 19th and early 20th centuries were first translated into a Chinese language suited for the purpose, a language which then gradually took form as a medium for the discourse on these issues which followed among Chinese intellectuals. The language and terminology for interpreting international relations in the Chinese linguistic context must be addressed on their own terms and we shall be careful not to impose on our analysis the idea that terms easily translate from one language to another to yield in the target language a semantic entity equivalent to the one in the source language.

[3] See Hamashita 2003, p. 45

LINGUISTIC CHALLENGES IN SINO-WESTERN TRANSFER OF IDEAS

One of the major obstacles to the introduction of Western learning in 19th century China was the lack of a terminological basis in the Chinese literary language for such imports. The literary language was primarily a language for administration and the classical Chinese domains, such as literature, poetry, philosophy and politics. Western sciences and technology were in need of an entirely new lexicon in the Chinese language in order to convey their terms, their way of reasoning and their logic to a new Chinese readership. In addition, the nature of the Chinese language makes it very cumbersome to import phonemic loans from Western languages. Only early phonemic loans through the spoken Cantonese language, mostly related to merchant activities along the southern coasts of China, have survived the test of time and are still used in the daily language of standard Chinese.[4] Otherwise, phonemic loans tend to be short-lived, unwelcome, and most often replaced after a short time by other kinds of loans in the Chinese language. Most loans for these new domains would therefore have to be imported as semantic loans or loan-translations involving the process of selecting suitable translations in the first place, and, secondly, the process of modification and adaptation into the technical language within the relevant fields of learning.

But even then, when a new term is established, presumably as a translation of an imported term from the West representing one notion or concept in the source language, is that new term in fact an identical representation of the same notion, the same concept in the target language? It is of course not that simple. "One familiar way of producing knowledge about other people and other cultures is to construct the terms of comparison on the ground of perceived linguistic equivalence", as Lydia Liu formulates it.[5] There may be near equivalents between languages, especially languages and cultures in close genetic relationship. Between China and the West in the middle of the 19th century hardly any such relationships can be said to have existed. Any string of seemingly logical reasoning or cause-and-effect relationships in the one culture translated into the language of the other may have seemed entirely irrational, inconsistent, or even

[4] Masini 1993, pp. 13-15
[5] Liu 1995, p. 3

contradictory in terms. There is no necessary equivalency between terms and words in two different languages, even if the production of bilingual dictionaries produces and maintains that idea:

> The thriving industry of bilingual dictionaries depends on the tenacity of this illusion—its will to power. It is the business of this industry to make sure that one understand 'that languages are made up of equivalent synonyms.' The implication for cross-cultural comparison is that one relies on a conceptual model derived from the bilingual dictionary—that is, a word in language A must equal a word or a phrase in language B; otherwise one of the languages is lacking—to form opinions about other people or to lay philosophical grounds for discourses about other cultures and, conversely, about one's own totalized identity.[6]
>
> At a certain point, the crossing of language boundaries stops being a linguistic issue, for words are easily translated into analytical (often universal) categories in the hands of scholars who need conceptual models for cross-cultural studies... Perhaps, the crux of the matter is not so much that analytical categories cannot be applied across the board because they fail to have universal relevance—the impulse to translate is in fact unstoppable—but that the crossing of analytical categories over language boundaries, like any other crossing or transgression, is bound to entail confrontations charged with contentious claims to power. To be sure, universality is neither true nor false, but any intellectual claim to it should be rigorously examined in the light of its own linguistic specificity and sources of authority.[7]

Cross-cultural transfer of analytical and theoretical categories, such as the categories involved in international relations and international law, were not merely linguistic issues. In the hands of missionaries and translators, such as Martin and Fryer, the zeal to transgress the cultural boundaries through linguistic means was indeed very strong, as we shall see in the subsequent chapters. They must themselves have been aware of the claims to power involved in their undertakings. However, at that point in Chinese history the confrontation between China and the West was already a fact, and the translingual crossing and transgression of boundaries involved in the translation of works and terms for international relations may have appeared as no more than an aid on the Chinese side for bridging the gap between categories. The West had inevitably transgressed the boundaries in physical terms

[6] Ibid., p. 4
[7] Ibid., pp. 6-7

and China's hope, in the eyes of these zealous missionaries, was to mentally adapt to the seemingly universal categories of international law. Then, and only then, could China anticipate a claim of power to confront the West. The missionaries had a partial success in this respect in the latter half of the 19th century. However, the most successful and lasting Chinese adaptation to the analytical categories of the West did, in reality, take place through the mediation of the Japanese Meiji culture of modernisation in the early 20th century.

Only through adaptations and long term contacts may two languages come to share more of a common conceptual framework for communication and comparison. In the case of China and the West the terminological adaptation came to take place almost entirely on the Chinese side and on Western terms. Gradually the terms and notions from the West, in everyday life as well as in social, political, human and natural sciences, were translated and adapted to the Chinese language, in some cases without much confrontation and negotiation, while in other cases only through prolonged processes which may on the surface seem to have come to an end with the massive production of bilingual dictionaries and a seemingly general acceptance of universality. On closer scrutiny, however, we often find that seemingly universal categories and equivalence in terms and words in fact involve conceptually related but not universally overlapping semantic and conceptual fields for particular terms. "Modern Chinese words and concepts as well as those from the classical language, which are increasingly mediated through modern Chinese, often present hidden snares, even though on the surface they seem relatively transparent."[8] The most frequently quoted examples of such categories are the conceptual and linguistic relationships between the notions of 'rights' and 'power', of *quanli* (權利) and *quanli* (權力), the notion of 'civil rights' compared to the Chinese term *minquan* (民權), the connotations of the term *wenhua* (文化) in Chinese as compared to the English seemingly equivalent 'culture', the Chinese term *minzhu* (民主) as opposed to the notion of 'democracy' in the West, and the conceptual differences between 'freedom', 'liberty' in the West and the term *ziyou* (自由) in Chinese.[9] The Chinese discourse on

[8] Ibid., p. 17

[9] Svarverud 2001; Liu 1995, pp. 33-36, 239-256; Liu 1999; Wang, Gungwu 1991; Svensson 1996, p. 85; Angle 2002; Fang Weigui 1999; Wang Jian 2001, pp. 220-229; Li Guilian 1998b; Xiong Yuezhi 1994, pp. 692-693; Xiong Yuezhi 2001; Xiong

sovereignty, on power and the struggle for national survival discussed in the chapters below will also bring to the surface some of the fields of meanings where the universality of categories may be contested in the context of late Qing China.

THE TRIBUTE SYSTEM AND THE TRADITIONAL CHINESE WORLD ORDER

My claim in this book is that international law gradually became a new system of reference for the discourse on international relations and China's international position in late Qing China. This contention evokes the idea that this new framework challenged one or more already existing ways of accounting for and recognising China in a community of states, as claimed at the outset of this chapter. The most immediate response would maybe be to argue that international law defining China as a nation among equal and sovereign nations in the international family of nations fundamentally counters a traditional way of defining China as a suzerain in an unequal relationship to its East Asian and other Asian neighbours in the tribute system.[10] If we are to make such a claim we will first have to scrutinize this system as one of defining Chinese inter-state relations, and we shall have to address the question of how practice in trade and diplomacy in fact corresponds to this framework of East Asian international relations.

The abolition of the tribute system became a point of controversy between China and Europe when European nations sought to expand their markets in China in the early 19th century. The argument on the part of the Europeans was that the tribute system treated different principally "equal" nations on an unequal basis in their conditions for trade. To contemporary Europeans claiming the liberty of man to engage in the free trade of goods across the globe the ritualistic and inhibited way of trade conducted between China and her trading partners seemed ridiculous in its form and constrained in its implications. The demand that China should be forced open to trade on an equal basis defined through the signing of bilateral treaties appears to fundamentally challenge the principles of age-long Chinese foreign relations. We shall later address the question whether or not

---

Yuezhi 2002, pp. 1-25; Wang Jian 2001, pp. 221-229, 247-248, Yanabu 2005

[10] A claim explicitly made by Fairbank in Fairbank (ed.) 1968, pp. 4-5

this system of bilateral treaties was entirely unknown in China in the early 19th century. First, however, I shall attempt to outline the main fundamentals of the ancient Chinese tribute system.

Economic gain was not the main purpose of the Chinese tribute system. China was to a large extent a self-sufficient economic unit and tribute trade was embedded in political and social practice rather than for the purpose of economic gains or for the import of much-needed foreign goods. Trade was a part of the Chinese world order. That world order was not construed on the basis of sovereign parties conducting intercourse on an equal footing. The Chinese world-view was one perceived as made up of concentric circles of relationships to the Chinese emperor, the son of Heaven. China saw her civilization as universal and the Chinese emperor as representing all humanity before Heaven. To China foreign nations did not constitute sharply separate states with clear boundaries keeping them apart from China. Rather, the world around China was construed as states or peoples with various degrees of commitment to Chinese customs and relations with her civilization. In their book *The World that Trade Created* Kenneth Pomeranz and Steven Topik have described the relations between the Chinese emperor and his subjects as forming four such concentric circles. The first of these circles consisted of those subjects directly ruled by the emperor and his officials paying compulsory tax to the emperor. The second circle consisted of those ruled by and living under the partially assimilated native chiefs or kings situated in the vicinity of Chinese civilization but still partly living under their own sets of rules and laws. Representatives of these peoples would pay regular tribute to the Chinese emperor, while private trade with almost any articles was encouraged as well. The third circle comprised less assimilated rulers and kings paying tribute to China less frequently and private trade was subject to more restrictions and limitations. The fourth and outermost circle of peoples or states around the Chinese civilization paid no tribute to China in any formal or informal way, and has often traditionally in China been referred to as 'barbarians'.[11]

---

[11] The term 'barbarian' (*yi* 夷) became a topic of political controversy in late Qing relations between China and the West. What I refer to here is the way these civilizations were perceived distant from the cultivated Chinese and thus found to be uncultivated in the Chinese context. I do not imply that the term used in China in pre-modern times involves any evolutionary perception of the difference between peoples or nations. For an inquiry into the use and ban of the character *yi* in late Qing China see Liu 2004, pp. 31-69.

They conducted no direct trade as part of the Chinese tribute system. Their trade was therefore either limited to one or two specific border cities or they would have to conduct their trade as a part of the tribute trade of another state.[12] The limitations on trade with the latter group was the attitude of the Chinese that was contested by the European nations when they claimed their rights to open up Chinese ports to foreign trade on an "equal" basis in the first half on the 19th century—leading to what is commonly referred to as the "unequal treaties", such as the Nanjing 1842 treaty with Britain. The European nations were expanding eastwards, bringing with them their terms for inter-state relations: "While Europe was expanding outward overseas and across the steppes, the states of the European system were also working out, by trial and error, an elaborate and remarkably successful international society. Two fundamental principles which determined the rules and institutions of that society were that all member states were to be regarded as juridically equal and that their sovereignty was absolute."[13] The equality of trade and diplomatic relations in the European sense referred to the relations between states in Europe and did not normally include non-European states in their relations with Europe. Hence, the arguments and demands for equal trade based on the principles of international law did not initially include China, resulting in unequal treaties setting the framework for trade and diplomacy between China and the West.

The trade and ritual of this tribute system confirmed the unequal relations between China and her neighbours where China played the role of the suzerain. The foreign representatives presenting tribute to the Chinese emperor were subject to a set of procedural formalities ritually symbolising the superiority of the Chinese emperor and the inferiority of the emissary, also in the cases when the visitor was a king himself.[14] The goods presented to the Chinese emperor were often exotic goods from the country of origin and were more of symbolic value than of any use to the Chinese. In return the Chinese emperor presented gifts representing the core values of Chinese

---

[12] Pomeranz&Topik 2006, pp. 11-14. See also Fairbank (ed.) 1968, pp. 1-4; Wills 2005, pp. 272ff; Wong 1997, pp. 153ff

[13] Bull & Watson 1992, p. 23

[14] Even if foreign embassies, in particular the European embassies, often neglected or ignored the implications of Chinese suzerainty involved in the ceremonials. (Wills 1984, pp. 177ff)

civilization, such as Confucian books, musical instruments, silk, porcelain etc. These gifts served as symbols of loyalty and submission to Chinese civilization in their home countries. At the same time, the admission of private trade in correlation with the tribute missions was largely exploited by many of the tribute states. Merchants often accompanied these tribute missions to Beijing, and we even find that gifts from the Chinese emperor were recycled on the Chinese market, giving the foreign merchants cash to purchase other goods on the Chinese market. "So the tribute system—which so clearly subordinated economic gain to other priorities—at the same time helped define a vast common market, giving it its currencies, defining tastes that helped create markets worth producing for, and creating standards by which its elites recognized in each other the peoples they could deal with without either lowering themselves or running too many risks of default."[15] The tribute system defined the world and China's relationship to foreign nations according to an unequal system of proximity to the Chinese cultural sphere. On the other hand, it facilitated the creation of a market for trade among equals. The clashes between China and the West over trading rights may well be explained by the fact that the West was excluded from the opportunities that the tribute trade could have given them. They attacked the "inequality" of the tribute system and forced China into inter-state relations based on the "equality" of formal treaties, while in fact what they really may have wished for was the opportunity to take part in the private trade under the tribute system.

The system of tribute and diplomacy described above is, needless to point out, a gross simplification of an elaborate system of trade and diplomacy practised in China from the Tang dynasty and into the early 20th century.[16] For our case it may serve as a system of reference and as a framework for understanding the context of the introduction of

---

[15] Pomeranz&Topik 2006, pp. 13-14

[16] This system representing the Chinese bureaucratic way of handling their foreign relations may, however, only be traced back to Ming times. (Wills 1984, p. 173)

The system we here refer to as the tribute system was indeed not a static framework for structuring and managing Chinese foreign relations throughout history but rather a system under constant change and adaptation, and may hence generally more accurately be referred to as the traditional Chinese world order. For fascinating accounts and studies of the various workings of this world order from pre-Qin times to Chinese international relations in the 20th century see the different contributions in Fairbank (ed.) 1968. For accounts of the international relations of the Chinese empire one may also consult Morse 1971.

bilateral treaties between China and the Western nations and as an intellectual framework forming the background for the introduction of international law as a set of theories defining inter-state relations in terms of equality and sovereignty in late Qing China. It should, however, at this point also be emphasized that the tribute system was not a formal and rigid system defining Sinocentrism as a basis for all foreign contacts throughout the history of the Chinese state. A number of studies on the mechanisms of Chinese international trade and diplomacy reveal that the Chinese court conducted their foreign relations on a much more flexible basis with larger fluctuations over time that what the introduction above has suggested.

Chinese Trade as Diplomacy

Studies of the foreign relations of the early Ming dynasty reveal that trade was conducted basically according to the tribute system that we have discussed above, indicating that the tribute system defined China in her relations with foreign countries at that time. By the 16th century, however, trade was gradually also being conducted outside of the tribute system. Trade in Central Asia as well as maritime trade relations with Europe were conducted without reference to the tribute system. John E. Wills argues that much of the maritime trade during the Ming was in fact directed towards avoiding dangerous contact with the foreigners rather than maintaining a ritual of Chinese superiority. "The two goals were not incompatible, but neither were they identical."[17] The institution involving foreign embassies paying tribute and conducting trade at regular intervals and with a set of strict rituals according to their intimacy in relations with the Sinocentric world determined the formal Chinese world-view in a cultural and political sense. Trade, on the other hand, together with the defensive measures against the foreign dangers, was at the same time gradually forming an alternative Chinese way of dealing with foreign nations and of negotiating a position for China in the world (of trading relations). This system of trade and foreign contacts was to some extent taking place outside of central Chinese control. But for a large part it also became an integrated part of Chinese foreign policy during

[17] Wills 2005, p. 24

the Ming. The tribute system was thus not the only way to conduct foreign relations in Ming China.

The Manchu Qing conquest brought about a disruption of the tradition of contempt for trade and foreigners. The Manchus were themselves foreigners in China and they had less reverence for the age-old Confucian refutation of commercial activity. The tribute system became less important in the early Qing Chinese diplomatic orientation towards foreign countries and trade seems to have been more appreciated for its economic value to China than was the case during most of the Ming. When trade met with severe restriction during the Qing it was usually out of security and/or domestic concerns, in particular related to Japanese piracy and the Zheng (Zheng Chenggong or Koxinga) regime on the coast of Fujian, rather than because of the ritualistic order of foreign relations defined in the tribute system. In diplomatic conduct and negotiations, however, the traditions of the tribute system could still be seen in operation. Wills has shown that in the 1662-1664 cooperation between the Qing and the Dutch in their attacks on Amoy and Quemoy the Chinese implicit understanding of their superiority hampered the negotiations regarding the Dutch reward for their aid in these campaigns. The Dutch considered the reward to be subject to negotiations between equal and sovereign states, while the Qing saw this to be a matter of favour to be bestowed on the Dutch by the emperor at his will. The controversy over the magnitude of the reward was not so much an explicit conflict of interests between the two parties as it was an implicit divergence caused by the different principles for conducting foreign relations. "Such conflicts of assumptions sometimes posed as grave obstacles to limited cooperation for the attainment of limited common goals as did the more explicit conflicts of ideologies of international relations in nineteenth-century Sino-Western relations; an explicit conflict could be recognized and temporarily set aside, but an implicit and unconscious one could not."[18]

In 1684-1685 Qing abandoned altogether the link between diplomacy and trade in Sino-Western relations and began regulating this trade purely for economic ends, which led to relatively peaceful trading relations between China and the West for more than a

[18] Ibid., p. 58

century.[19] Trade between China and the West had no longer any strong political implications. Ideas of cultural and political superiority on both sides could live on unaffected by trading activities. It was only after 1790 that the differences implicit in the two diplomatic traditions surfaced again. A much more self-confident Europe demanded further opening of China to trade and the implicit conflicts between the two traditions were forced into the open. China was not aware of what she was up against in the century to come, not in terms of the principles of the Western diplomatic tradition, nor in terms of the power of the Western ships and cannons. Basing their negotiations on the formal ideas of equality of sovereign nations and referring to international law in their conduct of diplomacy, the Western nations imposed (unequal) treaties and international law on China by force. China on the other hand was reinforced in her references to the tribute system when dealing with the West. "It is most obvious that the diplomatic traditions of the two sides had been formed in different environments, and each side approached these relations with expectations and habits that were rational in their usual environment but irrational here."[20] The result was that China was formally but against her own will introduced into the scope of international law during the 19th century. The tribute order of East Asia was, however, not entirely discontinued as soon as the ideas of treaties subsumed under international law were introduced as a system of relations between states.

In his article "Tribute and Treaties—Maritime Asia and Treaty Port Networks in the Era of Negotiation, 1800-1900"[21] Takeshi Hamashita has discussed the development of diplomacy between the states in East Asia during the 19th century. He argues that the era is dominated by negotiations and may be characterised as a period when both the ancient tribute system and the foreign treaty system were in operation in these relations. From a perspective of diplomacy we may say that China was maintaining relations with her neighbours based on the age-old tribute system, while simultaneously also conducting diplomacy in the East Asian region based on negotiations and the principles of treaties. Trade was again subsumed under the sphere of

[19] For an analysis of the Japanese policy towards the exterior world during the Tokugawa period see Toby 1991.
[20] Wills 2005, p. 267
[21] Hamashita 2003

diplomacy but on terms different from that of the previous centuries. China's role and identity in international relations was again changing.

Hamashita has specifically described the internal relations in East Asia in his article and found that the changing international climate in the region was initiated by the waning of Manchu Qing power. Qing was severely weakened both in her internal relations with peripheral and minority regions, in her relations with her former tributary states and through the increased strength of her more distant trading partners. This weakness of central authority and the principle laid down in the treaties that trading rights could be obtained through negotiations were utilized by other East Asian countries in their relations with China. Hamashita argues, however, that the tribute system was not dead. On the contrary, these two systems, one originating in the East and one in the West, were both in operation in inter-state relations in East Asia in the 19th century: "The concepts of East and West did not spatially overwrite one another, but rather it can be said that the tribute concept, that is the concept of a hierarchical order, remained primary, with the treaty relationship subordinated to it."[22] Treaties between China and Ryukyu, Japan, Korea were modelled on the treaties concluded between China and the West but were clearly taking into consideration the historical tribute relations in their intentions and implementations. Often these historical relations were even explicitly expressed in these treaties. During negotiations, however, all parties used European and American legal and diplomatic advisors.[23] The active way of applying these two systems for particular purposes in East Asian relations indicates that we should not look at Asia in a simple challenge-response perspective, which has often been the case in studies of East-West relations. Rather than seeing the East Asian region as a respondent to the Western challenges, Hamashita argues that what we observe in the international relations, diplomacy and trade in East Asia in the 19th century are "the indigenous sources of Asian modernisation".[24] The Sino-Japanese war 1894-95 ended the period of negotiations discussed by Hamashita and marks the beginning of an era of Japanese influence in East Asia. The task of identifying and defining China's role and position in the international order of states was not over. A new era of

---

[22] Ibid., p. 24
[23] Ibid., p. 26
[24] Ibid., p. 47

intellectual discourse on these questions commenced when the diplomatic era of negotiation ended. As I shall argue in this book, the discourse on China in international relations entered a new phase with the Sino-Japanese war. International law and the principles of sovereignty and equality of nations became important elements in that discourse. The tribute system was no longer a framework exploited for establishing a Chinese international identity. Other elements in the Chinese tradition, such as Confucianism and Daoism, together with other disciplines of the Western sciences, most notably Social Darwinism and evolutionary theories, were incorporated into or contrasted with the fundamental principles in international law in the intellectual negotiation of China's place in the world of states. Yet another Chinese world-view was forming. The perspectives on Chinese world-orientations discussed above all relate China to the world through diplomacy and trade. My perspective here, however, is focussed on the intellectual discourse on China's place and position in the world. I endorse Peter C. Perdue's caution against "an exclusive focus on foreign trade as the engine of inter-state relations and economic development", in particular in late Qing China.[25] His perspective is "A Frontier View of Chineseness", mine is "an international law view of Chineseness".

INTERNATIONAL LAW AS WORLD ORDER

China in the world order was very much formed and formulated by the experiences of the Sino-Japanese war. In a broad sense China's relations to the outside world became much more complex by the end of the 19th century as areas of what earlier had been referred to as Western learning were becoming an integrated part of China's own solutions and keys to a wide array of political, social and legal challenges. Western learning was no longer alien to China. Above we have pointed out the misconstruction of seeing 19th century Sino-Western relations in a simple challenge-response perspective. That point cannot be overstated for the intellectual developments in China in the early 20th century. China was no longer responding to the challenges from the outside world but was gradually entering that

[25] Perdue 2003, p. 60

world on her own conditions and terms. The Chinese education system was subjected to radical changes incorporating Western social and natural sciences into the curriculum. China was negotiating her own political system on the basis of imported ideas of governance and administration. The traditional law system of China was challenged by Western legal standards leading to indigenous reforms in China's own legal system. Nationalism and the concept of the citizen were exploited as a means towards making Chinese society and the nation more congruent and suited for survival in the conceived international Darwinian struggle for survival. Revolution was seen by many intellectuals as the only way to fundamentally challenge the aristocracy and nepotism of Manchu China. Also Chinese anarchism became part of an international anarchist discourse. Individualism was introduced as a means of interpreting a liberal role of the individual in society. Hobbes, Rousseau and Kant were introduced in order to exploit the political relations between man and society, and Western liberalists were called upon to refashion the way economics were construed in China. The Chinese role in these negotiations and changes was not that of a passive respondent to Western challenges. The solutions and discourses on China's questions were her own, often more conditioned on what was taking place in Japan than on the direct challenges from the West. The questions facing China in the preceding century had to a large extent been seen as the challenges imposed on China from abroad. Now, the major challenges appeared to be China's own internal problems and the West became a part of the solution. China was indeed entering the larger world on her own conditions and was formulating a new interpretation of her role in the world of nations. My claim is that international law became one of the most important frameworks for Chinese intellectuals and officials in their discourse on China in the world after the Sino-Japanese war. China utilized international law as a perspective for renegotiating China in the community of states, while international law seen from the perspective of the West responded to China's call by incorporating China into the European discourse on international law and international relations. The development of this discourse in China was not linear but the tendency is clear—China was entering the world on the terms of international law. With this claim I do not refer to China and relations to the world from the perspectives of diplomacy and bilateral treaties. I refer here to the intellectual discourse on China in the large family of nations. That Chinese world-view is the topic of this book. John K. Fairbank claimed in the introduction to his edited volume entitled *The Chinese World Order: Traditional China's Foreign Relations* in 1968 that: "Modern China's difficulty in adjustment to the international order of nation-states in the nineteenth and twentieth centuries has come partly from the great tradition of the Chinese world order. This tradition is of more than historical interest and bears upon Chinese political thinking today."[26] I shall not attempt to challenge this bold assumption by arguing that the Chinese traditional world order was abandoned altogether as a framework for reference in Chinese international relations in the 19th and 20th centuries. Rather, I intend to show that international law became a new framework for such orientations and that this framework was exploited in many different ways to challenge traditional Chinese international orientations. A new Chinese world-view was forming on this platform in the late 19th and the early 20th centuries.

Chapter 2 will introduce international law as a discipline formed by diplomacy and a legal-political discourse in the West. The main purpose of this chapter is to outline the main features of the discipline as an intellectual framework that was introduced into China from the middle of the 19th century. This chapter will also look into the way in which China in terms of diplomacy and international politics was drawn into the framework of international law on the "unequal" conditions offered by the European theories of relations between equal, sovereign states. Finally, chapter 2 will also present the ways in which China was perceived within the scholarly field of international law when she gradually entered the international society on the terms conditioned by international law.

In chapter 3 we shall explore the process by which international law was translated as a discipline of Western learning into China before the Sino-Japanese war 1894-95. The main purpose of this chapter is to analyse the language and the textual conditions for the introduction of this discipline between the first translation of a short text into Chinese in the 1840s to the large volumes of texts on international law translated by the two main branches conducting such translations in Beijing and Shanghai in the 1880s and 1890s. These texts and the way that international law was translated and introduced

---

[26] Fairbank (ed.) 1968, p. 4

in these texts formulate the intellectual basis for the burgeoning discourse on international law in China discussed in chapter 4.

In chapter 5 we shall examine the ways and the language of the translations of international law into China after the 1894-95 war with Japan. Early in the 20th century the experiences of Chinese students in Japan started to influence the "market" for these translations and subsequently also the discourse on related questions. The final chapter 6 will address the wide array of contributions to the discourse on international law in early 20th century China. In this chapter I intend to show that Chinese intellectuals on a broad basis utilized the system of inter-state relations then known as international law through a wealth of translated texts in order to re-interpret China in her international position. I shall endeavour to show that China was not passively responding to the international challenge posed from the West but in an active fashion created an indigenous space for China in her international relations. That space for an early modern Chinese interpretation of the world order was not infused with one straightforward and unilateral perspective on China in the world. Rather, it was filled with a wide range of perspectives on China partly drawing on international law and partly on other frames of reference. The main period for the discourse analysed in this chapter is between 1895 and the 1911 revolution. Most of the roots of a modern, Chinese intellectual discourse on China in the world may be found in its early phase in the periodicals of this period. A study of this discourse beyond the establishment of the Republic is outside the scope of this humble contribution to an understanding of China's place in the world.

CHAPTER TWO

INTERNATIONAL LAW AS DISCIPLINE WEST AND EAST

In the Chinese discourse on international law, international theory and international relations we find a general assumption that international law is a Western discipline among other fields of Western studies, introduced into China as a theoretical branch of learning from the middle of the 19th century. International law appears in this Chinese context to be a comprehensive system of regulations and laws that orders the relations between states in the West. China had for centuries lived by other principles regulating her inter-state relations, as we have discussed in chapter one, and international law and the Western discipline of international theory were introduced as a "modern" alternative to the Chinese tradition, a new way of perceiving China as a nation among nations. This concept of international law is of course to some extent accurate since the discipline of international law has grown out of the European historical context and refers to the diplomatic tradition, the discourse on inter-state relations and the system of treaties and inter-state relations in the European system of states. On the other hand, international law is to be sure not a very precise or a complete system of laws and theories regulating these relations. Rather, it is a discipline and a system open to negotiation and to new members in this family of states, also members from the non-European community of states. China was in a pragmatic sense introduced into the sphere of international law by the forceful introduction of bilateral treaties between the West and China. The intellectual history of international law in China refers, however, not to the system of treaties but to an indigenous Chinese process of intellectually applying these principles to China and her environment and hence negotiating a space for China in this family of nations. The main purpose of this book is to study the introduction of this Western discipline into China in the last part of the Qing dynasty and subsequently to analyse how the theories of international law as a Western discipline are integrated into the discourse on Chinese international relations. As we shall see, the notions of sovereignty, balance of power, neutrality, national rights and duties, possession and jurisdiction of land, right of self-protection, the relations between civilised and barbarian, between Christian and non-Christian peoples, and the struggle between races were all central elements in the reception of and discourse on international law and international relations in China in the late 19th and early 20th centuries. These concepts, and their theoretical and pragmatic implications, were all developed and historically rooted in the international context of Europe from ancient Greece and hence conceptually alien to the Chinese setting of late imperial times. The introduction of these ideas into China involved a process which belonged to China alone and contributed to a changing Chinese intellectual orientation in international affairs. In this chapter I shall bring to our attention the nature and history of international law as a discipline, how China was introduced into this system of positive international law and how China was understood and recognized in this system of international relations seen from a European or Western perspective. This introductory chapter will subsequently direct our attention to the intellectual process of translation, introduction and reception of international law, and the relevant discourse on these questions in China in the following chapters.

INTERNATIONAL THEORY

The disciplinary domain of international thought, or international theory, in the West is historically instituted in the more generally recognized theoretical discipline of politics, political theory or political science. The theoretical aspects of international thought and international relations are intrinsically linked to the theories of political thought and political philosophy. Attempts to establish international theory as an independent discipline outside of political theory have, however, moved these two sub-disciplines of politics into two distinct universes of discourse.[1] It may indeed be questioned whether there exists a separate discipline of international theory, a science of speculations about the society of states, or the family of

[1] Boucher 1997

nations, apart from political science, the science of speculations about the state. Considerations on international theory have been comprehended under international law as "an amalgam of formulae, jurisprudence, political speculation and recorded practice".[2] Wight, in his article "Why is there No International Theory?", holds that in contrast to political theory, which is generally accessible as a discipline, "international theory, or what there is of it, is scattered, unsystematic, and mostly inaccessible to layman. Moreover, it is largely repellent and intractable in form. ... I believe that it can be argued that international theory is marked, not only by paucity but also by intellectual and moral poverty."[3] He has also found the two discourses of political and international theory principally different in nature: "Political theory is in direct relation with political activity ... But international law seems to follow an inverse movement to that of international politics. When diplomacy is violent and unscrupulous, international law soars into the regions of natural law; when diplomacy acquires a certain habit of co-operation, international law crawls in the mud of legal positivism."[4] Wight is tempted to answer the question raised in his article adversely, that there is no international theory except for what may be called philosophy of history. The reason, he concludes, is that "all theorizing has to be done in the language of political theory or law." These are, according to Wight, "the theories of the good life. International theory is the theory of survival."[5] It may be contested whether international theory merely is the theory of survival. International law certainly stems from the practice of international relations in time of conflict and war but embodies also speculations about the normal peaceful order between the subjects of international law. Wight's main point, that there is an insubstantial foundation for theoretical speculations in international theory apart from political theory is, however, valid and significant. Speculations about international relations are invariably confined to the discourse of either political theory on the one hand or to diplomatic practice on the other. International law is commonly conceived as interplay between these two. In the Chinese case international law as diplomatic practice was indeed known prior to the

[2] Wight 1966, pp. 17-18
[3] Ibid., p. 20
[4] Ibid., p. 29
[5] Ibid., p. 33

introduction of international law as a theoretical discipline. One of the reasons for the lack of a theoretical discipline apart from political science may also be rooted in the uneasiness with the anarchy of the international system, as Hedley Bull has characterized it:

> The feeling of unease about the system of sovereign states is a deep-rooted one in Western thinking about international relations. It exists not only among those who explicitly espouse the elimination of the system, but also where we might least expect to find it, in the pronouncements of the servants of sovereign states themselves, by whose daily acts the system is preserved.[6]

Apart from the theoretical discipline of international relations based on political theory, if indeed there is such a theory, the present international order and international law in operation may be conceived as an order established and ruled by a legal order similar to municipal law upheld by the law-making bodies established by constitutional law. The sources of these two "legal" systems should, however, not be confused. Whereas the law-making machinery within a state is established and upheld by the principle of supremacy of the constitutional body, the international legal order between states is not based on similar sources. Formal sources guiding all the members of the international community do not exist in international law. One may say that custom, thus the existing agreements and practice of relations between states, is the ruling principle in international law. General constitutional principles apply only to the extent that each and every sovereign state adheres to these principles. What matters is in fact only the existing particular rules and agreements established between two or more states.[7] Needless to say, there is no super-national organ governing the general principles of international law or sanctioning actions outside the bi- or -multilateral agreements established between sovereign states, as illustrated by Andreas Osiander: "There is, in international politics, no strong central authority capable of laying down, and enforcing, the rules that international actors will follow."[8] Hedley Bull has termed this lack of supremacy in international law an anarchy in international relations: "Whereas men in each state are subject to a common government, sovereign states in their mutual relations are not. This anarchy it is

---

[6] Bull 1966, p. 36
[7] Brownlie 1998, pp. 1-30
[8] Osiander 1994, p. 2

possible to regard as the central fact of international life and the starting point of theorizing about it."[9] Osiander has focused on the structure and the conditions securing the stability of the international community. He argues, somewhat contrary to Bull, that order rather than anarchy rules the arena of international relations: "[A]lthough, in the international sphere, there is no supreme political authority overarching the individual actors, the international system is not characterized by disorder—it has a structure, which is normally quite stable."[10] He describes the structure of the international system as: "the number and the identity of the international actors, their status vis-à-vis one another, and the distribution of territories and populations between them."[11] He further argues that because of the conspicuous nature of conflict and war, little focus has been attached to the structure of the stability of the system. Because the international system is without a physical reality and hence is a construct of the mind, it rests on shared and rather complex assumptions. They may seem stable because of the pervasiveness of such common assumptions, being the basis for the notion of self and other from the early tribal societies onwards. These assumptions have been the basis for the international[12] order from early human history but also the cause of international strife and hostility. But these assumptions are never axiomatic and are to some extent arbitrary, and may hence also be "deconstructed". "There will be stability in the international system if the principle assumptions on which the system is founded do not clash. There will be less stability if they do."[13] Osiander's analysis of the international system from the Peace of Westphalia to the present is hence "concerned primarily with a type of assumption which I will call structural principles. There will be less emphasis on another type of assumption, which I will call procedural rules. Structural principles are assumptions that influence the three basic aspects of the structure of the international system ... Procedural rules influence the way that relations between the actors are conducted. The structural principles are more important to the stability of the international system than the

[9] Bull 1966, p. 35
[10] Osiander 1994, p. 3
[11] Ibid.
[12] Using the term 'international' in a very broad sense certainly not constricted to the Jeremy Bentham term but rather in a sense of intercourse between social groups of different sizes.
[13] Osiander 1994, p. 5

procedural rules."[14] Another decisive factor in international stability is the consensus in the system. "It is nothing other than the sum of the structural principles and of the procedural rules that form the object of a consensus among the international actors."[15] The structural principles of the system prevent behaviour that would disrupt the system. Therefore it operates largely unnoticed when there is stability in the system. The system is stable when there is sufficient conformity with the structural principles in the system, a conformity that in the long run must be voluntary. If these requirements are not fulfilled conflict will arise, a situation that in turn will lead to modification of the system.[16] These modifications of the structural principles are usually the results of major wars and other large-scale conflicts among the actors in the system.

Despite the focus on structural principles and procedural rules in the study of international relations, stability and disorder, there has for centuries, in the European historical context, been a debate on the guiding and universal principles for international conduct among so-called civilised nations. These principles are primarily deduced from international treaties and agreements, in particular some of the epoch-making international agreements following major European wars since the 16th century[17] but raised to a philosophical level above the structures and practices of the international system. These principles were recognized as expressions of the legal conscience of civilised people since they were agreed upon by the various (Christian) nations in Europe in the renaissance. The idea of a natural law common to all civilised humans did potentially give international law a foundation in political thought in particular and in philosophy in general. Hence, in addition to the primary sources for international law being the practice and custom of international intercourse, international law as such was, from its birth as a theoretical discipline, linked to the philosophy of politics, to European ideas of natural law, natural rights, sovereignty (of individual and states), liberalism, and last but not least the history of European expansion. The writings by political philosophers and publicists stipulating the general civilizing

[14] Ibid.
[15] Ibid., p. 6
[16] Ibid., pp. 6-11
[17] The Peace of Westphalia 1648, The Vienna Conference 1815, The Hague Peace Conferences 1899 and 1907, The Paris Conference 1919-20.

principles in international conduct have again been the object of analysis within international legal practice, in particular in cases of international legal disputes in both tribunals of arbitration and national courts. These two aspects of international law, the disciplinary domain of international thought and the functional domain of international practice, are consequently closely inter-linked and also linked to the discipline of political thought and politics.[18]

China, as well as most of the non-Western world, had been outside the scope of international law precisely for these two reasons. The disciplinary domain of international thought in the European sense was entirely unknown to China prior to 1847, as we shall see later. It may be argued that the functional, or pragmatic, domain of international conduct did not include China until she signed treaties with Russia in the 17th and 18th centuries and with most of the European nations in the middle of the 19th century. China had also a long tradition of diplomacy with the nations trading in China, both Asian and European, as we have discussed in chapter 1. This kind of diplomacy without permanent diplomatic envoys is, however, not subsumed under the main theories of international thought. China only established diplomatic relations with permanent embassies in the latter half of the 19th century. Hence, the process to take place in China, if she was to be included into the sphere of international relations on the conditions of international law, was two-fold; She would have to adopt the theories and practices prescribed by international law, and in addition she would have to make the system referred to as international law as a theoretical discipline inscribe China into its discourse. This book is focussed on the processes of intellectual adaptation of international law as a theory in the Chinese discourse and does not engage in a study of diplomacy and diplomatic relations. In this chapter we shall, however, briefly also look into the way China did enter international law from the perspective of treaties, permanent diplomatic embassies, and how China was conceived in the Western discourse on international law in the East Asian context.

[18] Preiser 1984, pp. 126-132

THE EARLY INTERNATIONAL SYSTEMS

The early history of international thought in the West is usually traced back to a relationship between five independent states of equal rank guided by some sort of law and inter-state regulations in the ancient Near East from the 15th century BC to around 1200 BC. In particular, the international relations of the Hittite Empire are well documented.[19] After this presumed well-organized order collapsed, we know of no documented international order before the inter-state system of ancient Greece, hence between the various city-states (*polis*) of the Greek world in 6th century BC. In this ancient Greek order one may detect an inter-state order based on a sense of duty for each actor to participate in common sanctions against disturbers of peace. On the other hand, it may be argued that this order was in fact an order within one national group[20] and on a relatively small scale. The main point here is, however, the existence of a legal structure regulating the relations between equal actors.[21] It has also been suggested that a coexisting system of international order existed in ancient China. Evidence for the existence of such a system in China is, however, vague. Historically there is no link between this presumed ancient Chinese order and later Western international law since it is usually agreed that any such legal order of inter-state intercourse in China, if it ever existed, was disrupted by the unification of the central Chinese plain under the first emperor of Qin in 221 BC several centuries before any documented direct contact between the Roman and the Chinese empires. Similarly, the history of the European international system took a comparable turn in 168 BC when Rome's last two recognized independent and equal states were subjugated and a system of relations between equal states ceased to exist in Europe. From 338 BC onwards a distinguishable international order of equal states under the Roman Empire was in operation. Also after 168 BC some sort of an international order continued to exist under Roman supremacy. But the apprehension of relationships between equal and independent actors of this international system did no longer prevail. The transitional period from antiquity to the Middle Ages in the West was

[19] Ibid., pp. 133-134

[20] If indeed national entities may be said to be historical, biological or sociological realities.

[21] Preiser 1984, p. 135

characterized by peace treaties and armistices but there existed no international order of relations conducted among its actors according to generally accepted law and equality. During this period also Islamic theory of international relations began to influence the European continent. Islam influenced the way in which states entered into alliances and sent missions dependent upon their faith; relations between Muslim states and non-Muslim states were conducted differently from relations between Muslim states.[22] It was, however, the doctrines of the Fathers of the Christian church that started to influence the direction of international thought in the ages to come.

Jus Gentium of the Middle Ages

The Middle Ages experienced great changes in the international order of the West. At the beginning of the 9th century the European continent was dominated by a small number of powerful states, although not as universal in their dominance as the Roman Empire had been. By the 14th century these great empires had largely disintegrated and been replaced by a number of smaller states retaining an equilibrium of power and influence. The small-scale international order of the early Middle Ages had been replaced by a system of equal states with a basic structure much similar to the modern system of international law and order in Europe.[23] One of the main early events in this process of national separation between different cultural and linguistic groups on the European continent is the disintegration of the Frankish Empire and the subsequent Treaty of Verdun in 843. In China the great empires reigning at the beginning of our era, the Qin dynasty (221-206 BC) and the consecutive two Han-dynasties (206 BC-220 AD), had also disintegrated and a number of smaller states aspired to regain cardinal authority and rule the Chinese empire under one dynastic clan to re-establish the former golden age. The multi-state system on the Chinese continent did have the potential to develop into an international order between equal states consisting of relatively homogeneous national, cultural and linguistic groups. Different factors, however, led China in a different

[22] Ibid., pp. 139-143
[23] Ibid., p. 143

direction. Of the most decisive factors the Confucian examination system is perhaps the most important, a system of recruiting civil servants by securing common allegiance to one literary and historical tradition and a common writing system bridging the regional linguistic differences. The most decisive factor distinguishing China from Europe of the Middle Ages was, however, the establishment of a new grand supra-"national" Chinese empire with the Sui, Tang and Song dynasties between the 6th and the 13th century. The tribute system of inter-state relations was established between China and her neighbouring East Asian states during the Tang, a system that secured an exceptionally stable system of inter-state interaction under the suzerainty of China for centuries to come. An international order growing out of necessity, such as between smaller states in Europe, was superfluous in and around the unified and influential Chinese empire in East Asia.

"[F]ar from constituting a system of independent political associations, the defining feature of Medieval Europe was the decentralization of political authority."[24] The smaller states of Europe in the early Middle Ages were by no means fully-fledged, territorially self-contained sovereign states. The idea of a single powerful empire ruling the continent only weakened towards the end of the Middle Ages, and only then did the states develop towards independent, autonomous entities between which the modern system of international law could gradually evolve. The final collapse of the Western Frankish Empire with the death of Henry VI in 1197 led to the creation of a system of European states developing from the earlier mainly feudal kingdoms into autonomous states through the course of the 13th century. The development of these autonomous states was also made possible by the weakening of the secular power of the Papacy. The Papacy's idea of a single European Christian empire disintegrated with the growing hostile relations between Christian states, and between Christian and Muslim states. This, in turn, resulted in a secularization of the states where the leaders claimed God's authority as rulers of single states, whereas they had formerly conceded this divine authority to the Emperor and the Empire.[25] The effect of this growing autonomy of single states in the High Middle

---

[24] Holzgrefe 1989, p. 11
[25] Preiser 1984, pp. 143-144

Ages was also that agreements and international treaties were established between states, between Christian as well as Islamic states, in a fashion that corresponds to the modern system of international law. The participating subjects of the international order at this time were not confined to a small number of major states but included also minor states, all which could establish treaties and alliances with larger states on an equal footing. The law as such was "based on the precepts of Roman law applied to the individual members of the communities that accepted them. In the Middle Ages, the modern distinction between domestic and international law was therefore unknown. Law was either peculiar to one community (*jus civile*) or common to many (*jus gentium*)."[26] Holzgrefe has pointed out that the modern notion of public international law is fundamentally different from the legal operation of the Middle Ages:

> [T]he relations between the fragmented sovereignties of Medieval Europe were regulated not by public international law, but by *jus gentium*. The difference between these two types of law lay mostly in the fact that the sovereign state is the subject of the former, while individuals were the subjects of the latter. The evolution of modern public international law thus involved the replacement of individuals by sovereign states as the principal subjects of international law.[27]

In the late Middle Ages the European international system was further consolidated and the sovereign power exercised by the rulers of these states was strengthened also by the writings of theorists. The 15th century also witnessed the development of two practices that later became central to international order; the sending of permanent diplomatic missions abroad and the legal requirements for the acquisition of territories overseas.[28] In both ancient Europe and ancient China the management of international relations had been upheld through extraordinary envoys for particular cases. The concept of accepting permanent representatives of foreign states on its own territory must have appeared dangerous to the hosting party in both these two worlds. In China the tribute system of international relations was retained with missions from the tributary states arriving in the Chinese capital at regular intervals paying tribute to the Chinese emperor. This system preserved for a long time the status of the

---

[26] Holzgrefe 1989, p. 14
[27] Ibid., p. 19
[28] Preiser 1984, p. 148

hierarchy through which the different tributary states were identified and treated by the suzerain in the Chinese universe. Only after China was coerced by the Western powers into letting permanent foreign missions reside in thc capital in the 1860's did China accept in practice this notion of reciprocity on an equal footing in international relations. This was one of the most disturbing blows to the traditional Chinese world of international relations during the course of a changing international orientation in China in the second half of the 19th century. In Europe the practice of sending permanent missions abroad started between the city republics in Italy in the middle of the 15th century. For these militarily weak republics permanent envoys became their only possible means of retaining diplomatic stability. This system later expanded and developed into the modern system of permanent diplomatic missions. A number of treaties between independent states in the 15th century involving the recognition of the acquisition of territory overseas necessitated papal protection. Through the practice of the legal title based on enfeoffment by the Church established through these instances, a recognized set of legal requirements for the acquisition of territories overseas was established.

THE INTERNATIONAL SYSTEM OF THE SPANISH AGE AND THE FIRST THEORIES OF INTERNATIONAL RELATIONS

In the history of international law the period between 1500 and 1648 is often referred to as the "Spanish Age" because of the Spanish influence on all procedural and theoretical developments in the international order on the European continent. The Spanish Habsburg Empire brought extensive new areas in the eastern parts of Europe into the sphere of its international order and hence brought about a considerable expansion of the community of states in the European international community. The immense power of this empire also instigated a new development in the practice of the law of nations. Where smaller states earlier had joined together to counteract more powerful states, the principle of balance of power now began to form as the fundamental principle in how to retain a diplomatic and military balance between states regardless of size and military power. This principle of balance of power became the main foundation of international order in the centuries that followed and to a large extent laid down the foundation for the modern international system. At the time of the Spanish Habsburg Empire this practice was, however, only in its infancy as the principle of inter-state relations.[29] The most important contribution to later international thought in this period was brought about by the growing respect for learning in general and for political theory and the theories of constitutional and international law in particular. The development of international thought cannot be discussed without including the influential political theories of Niccolò Machiavelli (1469-1527). The main argument in Machiavelli's writings with respect to international theory is the prominence he places on maintaining a state as an end in itself. He argues that a state being in a conflict between moral and treaty obligations on the one hand and internal measures to maintain power or to preserve the state against an external enemy on the other hand, must always opt for the latter. In plain terms this means that international treaties and obligations may be maintained only if they do not go contrary to the internal interests of the state. In this way Machiavelli positively prescribed a practice that had been observed in international custom but never before permissible in theoretical terms. The principle of regarding a strong and sovereign state as an end in itself was later referred to by Francesco Guicciardini (1483–1540) as Reasons of State (*raison d'etat*). In contrast to Machiavelli's disregard for the reasons of law we find that the lawyer Jean Bodin (1530-1596) argues that the sovereignty of a state is defined both in its internal and its external relations. This means that although Bodin adhered to the doctrine of social contract in a state's internal affairs, he claimed that a state could not disregard its legally binding international obligations if that state wished to preserve its external qualifications as a sovereign state. Where the law for Machiavelli had its justification only when it could be exploited for the purpose of politics, for the lawyer Bodin laws are binding on all involved parties regardless of the political circumstances.[30]

The late scholastic school was also flourishing during the Spanish Age. The most prominent representatives of this school are the Dominican Francisco de Vitoria (ca. 1483-1546) and the Jesuit

[29] Ibid., p. 149; See also Butterfield 1966
[30] Ibid., pp. 150-151

Francisco Suárez (1548-1617). They developed the scholastic understanding of the law of nations and inter-state relations where the question of the relationship between European and non-European civilisations for the first time became the focal point of the law of nations. In the history of international thought Suárez is primarily known for his interest in the question of natural law. He separates the law of nations from natural law when he argues that only the normative force and not the content of the law of nations is derived from natural law. The natural law principle of keeping faith with one's agreements is the normative force that makes the content, the legally binding rules, of the law of nations attainable.[31] Suárez was also the first to make a clear distinction between laws that regulate the relations between sovereign states (*jus gentium inter se*) and the laws common to a number of states (*jus gentium intra se*). Only the former is *jus gentium* in its proper sense, he argued. Since his concept of *jus gentium* was based on natural law, his apprehension of the law of nations was, however, in this respect not fully consistent with the modern notion of public international law.[32]

In late 16th century Europe there were two distinct traditions with regard to ideas on war and peace; the scholastic, or theological, tradition discussed above, and a tradition that is usually referred to as humanist or oratorical.[33] In the same way as the scholastics, the humanists did not oppose war per se. The debate between the two traditions was rather focused on the range of justifications for war. The most apparent of the controversial points was the question of pre-emptive strike. Contrary to the arguments on the just causes of war held by the scholastics, Alberico Gentili (1552-1608) argues that fear of aggression or ill intention of another party is sufficient reason for making a pre-emptive strike.

The development of the law of nations in the Spanish Age was determined through changes in the state system of Europe but also to a large extent through the writings of these political theorists, lawyers and theologians. Perhaps the single most important person for the theoretical development of international law in this period is the Dutchman Hugo Grotius (1583-1645), who lived at the very end of the Spanish Age, at the time after the Renaissance and the revival of

[31] Ibid., pp. 151-153; See also Tuck 1999, pp. 73-75
[32] Holzgrefe 1989, p. 21
[33] Tuck 1999, p. 16

ancient scholarship. He represents very much the new ideas of humanism as their first exponent in international theory, even if he lived just before that milestone in international events in Europe, the Peace of Westphalia in 1648. He stands very much in a previous age contemplating and writing for the international law of the times to come. Many of his views of the principles of international relations are indeed new, but his notion of international law is, it may be argued, still based on the medieval apprehension of individuals as the principal subjects in *jus gentium* even when defining *jus gentium* as: "that body of law concerned with the mutual relations among states or rulers of states".[34] Grotius participated in debates on a number of important issues of international relations, such as the freedom of the seas, the issue of permanent diplomatic missions and neutrality, which were also among the most contested and debated subjects in international law in the international discourse in China in the late 19th and early 20th century. Grotius' main contribution to the theories of international law, however, lies in his comprehensive discussions of the theories of international law as such, which is presented in his famous *De Iure Belli ac Pacis*[35] first published in 1625.[36] In this work Grotius is able to isolate international law from other parts of law and thus establish international law as a separate area of science. For this Grotius is often referred to as the father of international law,[37] and his work has for centuries been regarded as the primary textbook on international law.[38]

THE 1648 PEACE OF WESTPHALIA AND THE BEGINNING OF A NEW INTERNATIONAL ORDER

The Spanish Age ended with the peace treaty signed in Westphalia in 1648. During the period between the peace treaty of Westphalia and the Vienna Congress in 1815 European international order expanded beyond the European continent into the Asian and American

[34] Holzgrefe 1989, p. 21
[35] Curiously enough this work has never been translated into Chinese, neither during the early period of international law translations discussed in this book, nor in the 20th century up to the present.
[36] With a second edition in 1631
[37] Discussed and contested by Holzgrefe 1989, p. 22
[38] Preiser 1984, p. 155

continents, encountering and involving entirely new questions and traditions. China was for the first time brought into contact with the expanding European nations bringing both Western mercantile and spiritual goods to the East Asian continent. The importance of Sino-Western contacts in this period before 1815 is, however, not of the same significance for the disseminating of international order as the European contacts with South and South-East Asian states.

The Roman Empire was no longer more than a confederation of states after the Reformation. The political consensus under the Emperor in Germany was indeed very weak, and the main threat to European stability was the opposition between Catholics and Protestants. The Emperor, being a Catholic, and his ally, his Habsburg relative the King of Spain, tried to increase power and oppose the Protestant elements of the Empire. The Protestant princes and free cities formed an alliance in 1608, and the Catholics counteracted in the same way the year after. The growing absence of consensus in the European system of structural principles and the breaking down of the European political balance caused other non-German actors to intervene on the side of the Protestants in the conflict against the Catholics and the Emperor. Both Danish and Swedish, and finally also French troops (in spite of being a Catholic power) intervened against the Habsburgs. A century of religious wars in Europe reached its climax with the 30 years of war between 1618 and 1648 where none of the two sides in the conflict won any major advantages. "The issues being fought over became somewhat obscured as the conflict developed its own dynamic. In the absence of any workable international consensus it fed on itself. To promote such a consensus was the daunting task of the assembly that, after many delays, assembled at Münster and Osnabrück in Westphalia in 1644."[39] The war terminated with the Peace of Westphalia in 1648 where around 300 members of the Roman Empire in effect achieved status as sovereign states. The peace agreement granted these states rights to enter into alliances with other states as long as these were not directed against the Empire. All foreign policy on behalf of the Empire required the consent of the member states, hence drastically reducing the authority of the Empire. France became the major power in Europe and French replaced Latin as the language of diplomacy. The peace treaty of 1648

[39] Osiander 1994, p. 17

involved most states on the European continent and established rules for international conduct that were followed until 1815. This meant that the international order of Europe was based on states that in practice operated as sovereign actors conducting their international relations according to a system of rules and principles vested in the Westphalia treaty. These rules and principles included; the observation of treaties, negotiation by peaceful means, mediation or arbitration by a third party, war without a just cause is illegal, the treaty states should jointly stand up against a disturber of peace etc.[40]

One of the maxims of the international order in Europe after 1648 is the principle of balance of power.[41] As Verosta argues, a balance of power is in fact a political balance of power, "since the politics of foreign policy are always power politics". He argues further: "The political balance of power of a particular region is not a rule of international law, but it is one of the political and sociological bases of international law in the State system of a given region and at the same time a maxim of foreign policy."[42] The politics of the balance of power continued to change the structure of alliances, coalitions and power-politics between states in Europe and did not end the inclination to warfare for the renegotiation of territorial rights. But the treaty of 1648 had in the history of European power politics established a new international order on the European continent that has continued to fashion the basic structures of the modern system of international relations.

THE INTERNATIONAL ORDER 1648 TO 1815, AND THE FIRST CHINESE ENCOUNTERS WITH THE INTERNATIONAL ORDER OF THE WEST

The new era in European international relations that began with the Peace of Westphalia in 1648 ended with the Napoleonic wars and the Congress of Vienna in 1815. When the Spanish Habsburg King Charles II died in November 1700 without an heir the major European powers disagreed over the Spanish succession to the French Bourbons or to the German Habsburgs. In both cases it would change the balance of power in Europe. For Louis XIV the future of French

[40] Verosta 1984, pp. 160-161; Osiander 1994, pp. 16-17
[41] Butterfield 1966, pp. 139ff
[42] Verosta 1984, p. 162

dominion was at stake, while the rest of Europe feared French hegemony. The controversy ended in declarations of war in 1702 between a Hague Alliance and France and lasted with protracted hostilities until 1714. French dominance in Europe reached its height under Napoleon's struggle for hegemony for France from the late 18th century. A coalition of European states finally brought an end to the French supremacy during the Napoleonic wars and a much smaller German Confederation succeeded the French in 1815. The Westphalia international order in Europe was terminated and a new balance of power was established with the Congress of Vienna in 1815.[43]

Many important developments in international law are a consequence of the history of this period. The increasing need for diplomacy and permanent diplomatic missions in foreign states gave rise to the 3 classes of diplomatic representatives; ambassadors, envoys and chargés d'affaires. Consuls and consulates became an important institution for the protection of national trading interests in the era of mercantilism and capitalism. These institutions were also vested with consular jurisdiction over their own nationals on foreign territory. The principle of consular jurisdiction and extraterritoriality became a sensitive issue in the relationship between Chinese authorities and the consular corps in the Chinese trading ports, in particular in Shanghai. Increasing trade also brought the area of commercial treaties into the domain of international law, and in some areas this trade also included the trading of humans—slaves.

China's early encounters with European international law were in the form of commercial and peace treaties. It has been proposed that China came into contact with international law during this time through Jesuit missionaries in the middle of the 17th century. It has been claimed that Martin Martini (1614-1661) translated the work *De legibus* (1612) by Francisco Suárez into Chinese. This claim has, however, never been sustained by textual evidence. It has also been held that international law was referred to in the negotiations between the Dutch and Chinese officials in the 17th century, but then only in a unilateral fashion since these principles were entirely unknown to the Chinese at the time.[44] In the late 17th and the 18th century China signed two treaties with Russia, in 1689 the treaty of Nerchinsk and in

[43] Ibid., pp. 166-171

[44] Tian Tao 2001, pp. 16-17; Li Zhaojie 1999, pp. 77-79; Wills 2005, pp. 267-268

1727 the treaty of Kiakhta with a supplement in 1768.[45] The former included extradition of criminals and mutual rights to trade, while the latter also involved the right of sending permanent missions, an exceptional and singular early case of the application of the principles of European international law in the Chinese context.[46] In fact, two Jesuit representatives, Jean Francois Gerbillon and Thomas Pareira, accompanied the Chinese negotiators and served as interpreters and supervisors in the negotiations with the Russian representatives. To what extent Gerbillon and Pareira knew international law and made active use of it in the drafting of the treaty texts is not known in detail. From their notes, however, it seems that some of the principles of European international law were in fact applied in the meetings between the two parties. It also appears that the Chinese representatives set aside the traditional view on China's inter-state status and treated the Russian delegates as equal partners in the negotiations.[47] More generally, however, these treaties did not have any immediate consequences for China's international relations beyond the direct implications of the regulations stipulated in the agreements. The same is the case with an incident in 1804 where the term 'international law' was used in an official document sent to Chinese authorities in a dispute between England and America regarding the right to search foreign vessels in Chinese waters. The terms and conditions of international law were, undoubtedly, unknown to Chinese authorities at this time and none of these incidents had any lasting effect on the introduction of international law in China.[48] In addition China was also involved in diplomacy with European nations related to trade during this period. As John E. Wills has shown, however, this form of diplomacy was conducted on traditional Chinese principles for diplomacy on the Chinese side, as well as on Western principles on the European side—often resulting in frustration on both sides.[49]

Private international law saw also some developments in this period. By private international law, or conflict of laws as it is also termed, is meant the international resolution of problems resulting

[45] Chen 1966; Mancall 1971
[46] Verosta 1984, p. 172
[47] Tian Tao 2001, pp. 17-20; Li Zhaojie 1999, pp. 79-82
[48] Tian Tao 2001, pp. 20-22
[49] Wills 2005

from the diversity of different sets of national laws and courts in certain international matters. The practice of issuing *lettres de marque* (letters of reprisal) was a means of avoiding the escalation of a minor private affair to a national level. A letter was issued by which a person was permitted to claim goods of a state where he had suffered damage and been unable to obtain compensation. These acts were accepted in time of peace and not regarded as a warlike action. International law in time of war also developed in a humanitarian direction. Military agreements included exchange and release of prisoners of war, treatment of wounded and sick enemies, terms for surrender, and the exemption from seizure of hospitals.[50]

By the 18th century the practice of international law had developed away from the theories of the scholastics and in the direction of humanism. Hugo Grotius was in the early 17th century still working in the tradition of the scholastics in his writings, even if he went far in establishing the theories of international law separate from theology. With the development of humanism after Grotius apart from theology, the secularized interpretation of natural law represented a system of rules and values vested in the individual and based on philosophical deliberations. The fundamentals of the international system of states were based on the same values, deducing rules of natural law for cooperation between states from the natural law of the individual in this humanitarian spirit. The result was that the natural state of the relationship between states was gradually interpreted as one of peace and not of war as we shall see. War was no longer seen as a means of asserting that all members of the international community upheld the same principles of justice vested in the correct faith but only as a means of enforcing the law or for self-defence. The writings of this period fall into two main categories. First we have a large body of treaty collections collated in the spirit of the Enlightenment. Among these the largest collection of its kind is the *Recueil des traités*[51] edited by Georg Friedrich von Martens (1756-1821) and his nephew Karl von Martens (1790-1861). Karl von Martens is of particular interest in this context because of his later role in the introduction of diplomatic conventions and traditions, much in the same spirit of the Enlightenment, when one of his texts was translated into Chinese in

[50] Verosta 1984, pp. 166-167
[51] Published 1791-1801

1876. The other category of writings is represented by political philosophers and publicists.

Thomas Hobbes (1588-1679) has contributed one very important element to modern international law theory. Where Grotius lacked a clear distinction between the community of sovereign states and the community of mankind, and hence maintained that individuals are the primary subjects of *jus gentium*, Hobbes established this distinction in his writings. For Hobbes the laws that regulate the relations between states are distinct from the laws of men, both derived from natural law. Hobbes saw Europe as composed of sovereign states internally governed by civil law and externally governed by public and private international law. The Christian foundation of the European international community was substituted by what we may recognize as the modern European state system.[52] Hobbes was early associated with and under the direct influence of Francis Bacon (1561–1626), who advocated the idea that the natural condition of man is a state of war of every man against every man. Bacon favoured a pre-emptive strike on grounds of fear, and Hobbes advocated a "plea for the right of self-preservation even if the agent had endangered himself by his own unjust conduct, which goes well beyond what was commonly believed even by advocates of war".[53] Hobbes is commonly described as advocating a harsh theory of natural law:

> For Thomas Hobbes (1588 to 1679) in his *Leviathan* (1651) the natural state consisted in the war of all against all, which could only be transformed into a strict order by command of the sovereign. As the sovereign has no one above him, the "law of the stronger" continued to prevail in international relations. Baruch Spinoza (1632 to 1677) expounded a similar theory.[54]

Indeed, these extremely pessimistic views on humankind have been seen as presenting a theory in line with the later theories of social Darwinists. "The exponents of natural law and rational Enlightenment had, however, a more optimistic view of mankind and attempted to construct a peaceful order..."[55] These were also among the most influential interpretations of international law when the discourse on Chinese sovereignty and self-preservation, on the survival of the fittest

---

[52] Holzgrefe 1989, pp. 21-22
[53] Tuck 1999, p. 127
[54] Verosta 1984, p. 174
[55] Ibid.

and the struggle between races, gained momentum in China in the late 19th and early 20th century, as will be discussed in the following chapters.

There is one apparent problem with the Hobbesian theory of international relations. If the natural state of affairs between states is a war-like condition which may only be brought to order by a common sovereign, how then is the observable relative order in international relations to be accounted for? Samuel Pufendorf (1632-1694) refuted Hobbes' idea that international order could only be established by a common power. He disproved Hobbes' idea that individuals as well as states are in a state of nature where the law of the stronger prevails and that the struggle may only be resolved by a common sovereign. Pufendorf claims that there exists a sovereign God who has declared to humankind what is profitable and what is not. Profit is hence not to be brought about by human struggle for the conversion of interests into rights but is preordained by God himself. Whereas Hobbes' "insisted on the savagery of the state of nature, governed by nothing more than the bare search for self-preservation", Pufendorf argues that "a state of nature could be a state of peace and self-improvement, since the men concerned would be led by God to seek a wider range of 'utilities' than mere self-preservation."[56]

Charles-Lois de Secondat Montesquieu (1689-1755) is not primarily renowned for his contributions to international theory. Tuck argues, however, that *De l'esprit des lois*[57] contains explications of the conjunction of the two apparently contradictory theories of human sociability and the search for self-preservation. Montesquieu's critique of Hobbes is that the state of nature in which individuals find themselves is that of sociability, while only nations find themselves in a state of war. "The state of war between nations, Montesquieu argued, was one in which quite far-reaching rights of war were permitted, including (notably) a right to make pre-emptive strikes out of fear."[58] There was, however, in his view, no principal difference between these two realms, only different degrees of fear and

[56] Tuck 1999, p. 150

[57] *De l'esprit des lois,* first published in French in 1768, was translated into Japanese from an English translation (*The Spirit of Laws*) and published in Japan in 1875. The Japanese edition was the basis for a Chinese translation by Zhang Xiangwen (張相文), published with the title *Wanfa jingli* (萬法精理) in Shanghai by Wenming shuju (文明書局) in 1905.

[58] Tuck 1999, p. 186

sociability. Inter-state relations are much more than inter-personal relations governed by fear, because they lack the sexual attraction that exists between individuals and which forms attachments between them. There are certainly strong Hobbesian elements in Montesquieu's appraisal of the situation on the international arena. But to a larger extent than his predecessor he admits to elements of sociability also in international relations.[59]

Christian Wolff (1679-1754) went further than Montesquieu in appraising the sociable elements in the governing of international relations and hence his theories resemble the theories postulated by Pufendorf. Wolff claimed that a state of nature, including the relations between individuals as well as between nations, is sociable in character. The essence of this sociability was common good and mutual aid among humans. What distinguishes Wolff's theories from Pufendorf's is that he claims that the common good may only be secured through a common governing body called a 'supreme state'. Wolff's theories "in fact presupposed that the relations between states were designed to fulfil the desires of their individual citizens".[60] By this manoeuvre he was in fact able to construe international law as genuine law secured by an international supreme organ and operating with the object of implementing natural sociability. Wolff was cautious to emphasis that his claims to international sovereignty of the supreme state were in fact not to be visualized as a universal monarchy. The sovereignty of the supreme state would only be limited to those things states willingly recognize as belonging to this supreme sovereignty. Wolff went in fact strongly against intervention by one state in the affairs of another and hence also against the activities of the European commercial empires. The only form of international punishment that Wolff supported was against a nation that delights in war as such. He argued strongly against the Grotian principles of war against native peoples.[61] In line with his theory of non-intervention against foreign states Wolff, along with his teacher Gottfried Wilhelm Leibniz, took an unusual interest in non-European peoples and cultures, in particular the Chinese, and was instrumental in introducing Chinese morality and philosophy to the Europeans.[62]

---

[59] Ibid., pp. 184-187
[60] Ibid., p. 188
[61] Ibid., pp.187-191
[62] See for instance Ching & Oxtoby 1992 and Perkins 2004

Surprisingly, the first theories of international relations to be known to the Chinese were not the potentially affirmative theories on China's behalf that Wolff represented but the much harsher theories of international relations from one of his adversaries, Emmerich de Vattel (1714-1767). Vattel worked from the theories presented by Wolff but arrived in many respects at quite contrary conclusions with regard to the principles of inter-state systems. Vattel argued against the idea of a supreme state and for the independence of each and every nation. In line with Pufendorf Vattel perceived of the natural society where mutual aid and a common good represent the ultimate end as extending also to the society of nations. "Hence the end of the great society established by nature among all nations is likewise that of mutual assistance in order to perfect themselves and their condition."[63] Having established this basis for international relations, he introduced two qualifications; (1) Sovereign states are much more self-sufficient than individual men, and mutual assistance is hence less necessary and frequent. (2) The care for a nation's safety calls for much more reserve in giving assistance than is the situation for individuals. These qualifications lead to implications for his international theory quite contrary to Wolff's. Where Wolff only acknowledges the right to war against a foreign state in cases of those who delight in waging war as such, Vattel favours war against any potential hegemonic power (which of course could have been interpreted positively on China's behalf).

In spite of his arguments against a supreme state Vattel sees the international system of Europe as one integrated system of mutual interests like those of one republic where all members "unite for the maintenance of order and the preservation of liberty. This is what has given rise to the principle of balance of power."[64] Vattel argued in line with Wolff that native peoples have the right to the land they occupy. But he qualifies this argument in favour of colonization of the American continent by the claim that the tribes on that continent had no right to keep the entire, vast continent to themselves. The chief argument is that only peoples who have cultivated their fertile land have the right to that land, while those who disdain the cultivation of their soil, live by plundering and fail in their duty towards themselves,

---

[63] Introduction to Vattel *Le Droit des Gens* quoted in Tuck 1999, p. 192
[64] Chapter 3 in Vattel *Le Droit des Gens* quoted in Tuck 1999, p. 194

are to be treated as beasts of prey.[65] We may assume that he would have classified the Chinese nation not as a plundering tribe but as a cultivating people, had China at this time been a part of the family of nations.

Vattel was criticized for construing the laws of the international society in line with the power politics of his time. Immanuel Kant implied in his criticism that Vattel never saw beyond power politics in his descriptions of international relations and that international law in Vattel's interpretation justifies the power game of states. Vattel has never been seen as a great intellectual capacity and innovative thinker in international theory. On the other hand, his way of describing international law in line with the realities of international politics, and by writing in a lucid and easily understandable manner, made *Le Droit des Gens* eminently popular and widely read in the late 18th and early 19th century. "It filled a clear gap as an elevated manual of diplomatic practice written by a professional international lawyer when, for the first time in European history, such a phrase had begun to take on meaning."[66] Hurrell has, however, also argued against this simplistic portrayal of Vattel. He has convincingly argued that Vattel "is far more than a complacent and simple-minded exponent of state liberalism or legal individualism. Vattel stands as one of the abidingly important 'classical theorists of international relations' because of his attempt to hold law, morality and power politics together. He remains the locus classicus for a limited conception of international society in a world where might rather than right will all too often predominate, in which pluralism and the respect for diversity have a moral value, but in which there are also moral bonds that stretch between states and across societies."[67]

CONSOLIDATION OF THE 19TH CENTURY ORDER OF INTERNATIONAL PRACTICE

The period after the 1815 Vienna Congress is characterized by the practice of international law setting the course for theoretical deliberations on international law. The writings on international law in

---

[65] Tuck 1999, pp. 191-196
[66] Hurrell 1996, p. 248
[67] Ibid., p. 251

the 19th century are primarily based on the customs, treaties and diplomatic practice in international relations, and hence "[t]he new feature of the writings on international law of this time is the decline in abstract discussions of principle in favour of consideration of State practice. State practice enters the literature and dominates it, while natural law speculations disappear."[68] The practice of international law, on the other hand, became to a larger degree than before codified and international relations were conducted on a more sound and regular legal basis. This meant that the practice and theories of international law came much closer to each other than had been the case in the 17th and 18th centuries. Scupin sums up the history of this period as follows:

> The history of international law at the beginning of the 19th century is not so much the history of principles of law as an account of the law applied in practice at the time.[69]

The 19th century also saw the rise of the idea of the nation state, which again altered the map of Europe and changed the European order of states established by the Vienna Congress. It also had certain implications for international law but not to the extent that Italian international lawyers predicted in the middle of the century. G. D. Romagnosi and G. Mancini claimed that the nationalist principle would completely transform the law of nations, that international law had to take this into account, and that the effect would be that changed relationships between nation states would inevitably lead to more peaceful relations. Mancini argued that a nation has certain natural rights akin to the human rights of the individual and that these would have to be taken into account in an entirely new international legal order. His predictions did not turn out to be right. The formation of nation states in Europe had certain implications for international law, such as with regard to the rights of option of nationality and the right of self-determination among religious or cultural minorities. The idea of a nation state embodying the rights of natural peoples has, however, not as such entered international law as a principle.[70]

Another prominent feature of this period is that the European international order was fully brought out of the European context and

[68] Scupin 1984, p 181
[69] Ibid., p. 179
[70] Ibid., pp. 189-191

into non-European cultures and areas, often through the employment of force. The latter was certainly the case in East Asia where both China and Japan, in very different ways, were directly exposed to and responded to the expanding European order of the day. The British-Chinese Nanjing treaty of 1842 was followed by a number of other "unequal" treaties coerced on the Chinese court by military and economic means throughout the last decades of imperial Chinese history, gradually expanding foreign trading, political, legal and diplomatic rights on the conservative Qing Manchu administration. Immanuel Hsü for this reason has called the period from 1858 to 1880 the diplomatic phase in China's entrance into the family of nations.[71] Japan was much more efficient in adapting to a new world order and made use of these maxims and practices for securing a Japanese membership among states in the expanding world community. China was eminently more resistant to including international law as the guiding principles for conducting foreign relations, as we shall discuss in some more detail later in this chapter.

In Europe a number of institutional innovations characterize the period demonstrating the pragmatic approach to international law and the consolidation of its practice. These institutions were not international institutions in the legal sense. But they did mean that the practice of international law gained a more stable status and were thus instrumental in securing an international environment changing and developing much more slowly than had been the case during the earlier stages of the development of international law. The first of these institutions is the establishment of the Holy Alliance by the leading powers soon after the Vienna Congress in 1815. The motivation for establishing this institution was to give the new European alliance Christian religious legitimacy. In order to secure cooperation between the states in Europe a number of other international organizations were set up. These include institutions for cooperation in traffic on the great rivers, for telegraph, postal and later radiotelegraphic, communication, for cooperation on customs and tariffs, for international protection of industrial property, literary and artistic works etc. Also organizations for humanitarian purposes were established and invested in an international agreement, such as the Geneva Red Cross convention from 1864 and 1906. Also associations

[71] Hsü 1960

for the furtherance of international legal science, the Institut de Droit International and the International Law Association, were established in 1873. These two organizations do not have status as international legal bodies, although they have occasionally been consulted by courts and tribunals.[72] A publication by the Institut de Droit International entitled *Les Lois de la Guerre sur Terre* published in French and dated 1880 attempted to codify the rules of land warfare. Its Chinese translation was published in Beijing in 1883. Further evidence for the stabilization and consolidation of international law in the 19th century is the institutionalization of a number of important features in international law. These features include: permanent neutrality, intervention as a means to maintain established conditions, intervention to avert threats to the human rights of a state's own subjects, procedures for the recognition of a new state and other subjects of international law, the right of asylum for those suffering political persecution and the right to refuse extradition of political offenders.[73]

The writings on international law in the 19th century were, as mentioned above, void of theoretical deliberations on natural law, the just causes for war and the theological foundation in international law. Books were written by diplomats and lawyers and their writings reflect their practical approach to international legal questions. Of great importance for our purpose is that a number of these were the works on international law which formed the first basis for the introduction of the principles of international law into China. The writers and authors mentioned here are therefore only those who are of particular interest for the Chinese case.

The American Henry Wheaton (1785-1848) had worked as a diplomat in Europe and wrote his work *Elements of International Law*[74] as an empirical compilation on international law based not so much on the practice of American international politics as on European diplomatic relations. His *Elements* was the first complete work on international law to be translated into Chinese, published in Beijing in 1864. Theodore Dwight Woolsey, an international law professor at Yale, had a much more pedagogical approach in his publications. He is particularly famous for his writings on warfare during the American Civil War. His work *Introduction to the study of*

---

[72] Ibid., pp. 191-193
[73] Scupin 1984, pp. 181-184
[74] Published 1836

international law: Designed as an aid in teaching, and in historical studies first published in 1860, was translated into Chinese and published in Beijing in 1877. The British Sir Robert Phillimore (1810-1885) wrote a long and didactic explication of the practice of international law entitled *Commentaries upon International Law* in 4 volumes.[75] His work was the first comprehensive British work on international law to be available in Chinese translation when it was published in the late 19th century in Shanghai. Of the continental European writers of this time to reach China, the Swiss Johann Caspar Bluntschli (1808-1881) is the most prominent. His work does not approach the question of international law from a purely pragmatic point of view. His position is much more of a political scientist, a position which also exercised much influence in the German interpretation of international law as well as in political philosophy in both Japan and China. His influential *Das moderne Völkerrecht der civilisierten Staaten als Rechtsbuch dargestellt*, first published in German in 1868, was translated into Chinese and published in Beijing in 1880. Another influential German work of this same period to be published in Chinese is Franz von Liszt's (1851-1919) *Das Völkerrecht: systematisch dargestellt*, published in German in 1898 and in Chinese translation in 1903.[76] The process of translation, its language and the influence of these and other texts on the discourse in China will be the topic of the succeeding chapters.

THE END OF THE PERIOD OF CLASSICAL INTERNATIONAL LAW

The hostile environment in the Western world at the end of the 19th century was not a fertile ground for the development of trade. That is one of the reasons why Russia called for a peace conference in 1899. The conference led to the establishment of the Permanent Court of Arbitration with its bureau at The Hague. The conference also observed the need for positive codification of certain areas of international law. The result was a number of conventions and declarations dealing with the law of land warfare, sea warfare and the peaceful settlement of international disputes. A second conference

[75] Published 1854-1861
[76] Scupin 1984, pp. 196-198

was convened in The Hague by the American president Theodore Roosevelt in 1907 to discuss mainly the same problems of common concern. The matters discussed in these conferences were all of a very important nature for international peace. All specific disputes and controversies between individual states were, however, shunned in the discussions. The result was that the conclusions of the conferences were of a too general nature to have any real effect on the international situation. In particular the elevation of the principles of inviolable and unimpaired sovereignty of individual states effectively debarred the conferences from reaching agreements which could settle disputes over conflicting interests between states. A Naval Conference convened in London in 1908-09 in an attempt to revitalize the conventions of the last Hague conference on the law of maritime warfare and with a view to establishing an international prize court. But the attempts were aborted when the British House of Lords rejected the ratification of the convention. Other attempts at reconciling the conflicting interests in Europe at the beginning of the 20th century also failed and the outbreak of World War I in 1914 was a fact. Scupin concludes that: "The political events which led to the outbreak of World War I added nothing to the existing institutions and functions of the law in the international field. None of the States could be condemned by history because the war began with formal declarations of war in accordance with the traditional classics of war."[77]

The Hague Conferences initiated a new phase in the debates on international law, in spite of, or maybe precisely because of, the failure of the conferences in attaining progress in the establishment of international peace. "The effect of the Hague Peace Conference of 1899 was felt less in the practice of the law than in the everyday discussions of legal opinions. The proponents of State sovereignty of the old school, including those who denied the existence of international law, stood face to face with those who favoured the development of international law into as complete a system of world law as possible. The theoretical treatment of the basic doctrines of international law was not much affected by this debate, however."[78] These developments of the debates on international law after the turn

[77] Ibid., pp. 199-203
[78] Ibid., p. 198

of the century had, however, no implications for the introduction and debates on international law in China before 1911, which is our focus in this study.

In the European international system World War I brought the international actors together again to lay out a new foundation for international order in the Peace Conference of Paris 1919-1920. The map of Europe changed yet again and entirely. Self-determination became the accepted criterion for membership in the international system. The great-power principle of the Vienna Conference, which never had been acknowledged by more than tacit consent, was no longer accepted after World War I, thus contributing to the failure of the 1919 settlement and the international policy of the 20s and 30s. The principle of national self-determination took over from the balance of power principle in the determination of boundaries.[79] Because of World War I and during the Paris Conference new actors were formally brought into the family of nations. One of these was China, and the Paris Conference became a landmark in Chinese history because the negotiations granted Japan concessions on Chinese territory. This was the first time China took part in a conference of this kind, one of the cornerstones in the history of international law, which demonstrates that China had thus become an actor in the international system. On the other hand, the disturbing results of the negotiations as they were felt in Beijing did not leave the Chinese with an affirmative perception of international law. That chapter in China's reception and adjustment to European international law is, however, beyond the scope of this book.

The international changes taking place in the Western world, both in terms of practice and in theoretical deliberations, did not have any major impact on the international relations of China before the middle of the 19th century. When, however, China came into closer contact with the expanding West after 1840, the entire universe of terms and conditions in Western international relations was introduced to China both in the form of bilateral treaties and some 20 years later as a theoretical system of inter-state relations. Both these aspects of international law as they were introduced into China prompted discourses on China's status and relations in international terms. The practice of China's international relations and her diplomatic practice

[79] Osiander 1994, pp. 318, 324, 331

after 1840 have been thoroughly described by others and is not the object of this study. The succeeding chapters shall rather make an effort to describe and analyse the introduction of the theories of international law and the subsequent discourses on China's status, role, position and conditions in her relations with friend and foe.

However, before we probe into the process of the introduction of international law as a discipline and a discourse on China in international law I shall briefly turn our attention to the way in which the West conceived of China as a partner in international relations. China had been introduced into the sphere of treaties and diplomacy on European conditions and terms, and hence as a member in the family of nations. Her membership was initially based on terms regarding her as a non-European, non-Christian, semi-civilised member of that community and only conferring upon her treaties on unequal terms. Equality in inter-state relations was only conferred upon civilised nations adhering for instance to the European sense of civilised warfare. As we have discussed above, the recognition of China as a full, equal, sovereign member in this family of nations is not solely a matter of a formal application of and adherence to treaties and the practice of diplomacy according to European standards. More importantly, membership depends on the Western nations tacitly accepting the new member on terms involving the degree of civilization, the practice of what is understood as human warfare etc. on the part of the "applicant". The way international law was interpreted in China had indeed major implications for the Chinese world-view, as we shall discuss later. International law as such was, however, also influenced by the way the nations of East Asia in general, and China in particular, commenced on a road to the implementation of and adherence to the standards of international law. China was changed by international law but international law was indeed also gradually influenced and changed by China.

THE WESTERN DISCOURSE ON INTERNATIONAL LAW IN THE EAST

In present international works on the principles and history of international law China and other nations in East Asia are included as full members of the international community and the applicability of the principles of international law in the East are not questioned in modern legal scholarship. The relevance of human rights in China, her membership in the security council of the UN, and China's role in questions of international co-operation are no longer in question in these texts.[80] J.H.W. Verzijl describes, in an article from 1955, the process of non-European states entering the international community and accepting the terms of the European international system as similar to obtaining a "free ticket" to a world order painstakingly established over centuries by the European members:

> All that the newcomers to the international community have in fact done—which was, as far as that goes, the almost inevitable consequence of their entering into a community long since more or less integrated—was to adopt *en bloc* the traditional law of nations as it had developed throughout the course of Western European history and to embody it in their treaties, their prize laws and their neutrality declarations, their diplomatic protocol and in the argumentation used in their diplomatic notes and in their international claims. As did Turkey since its admission to the "European Concert" in 1856, as did China and Japan after having been forced into regular contacts with the western world in the last quarter of the nineteenth century...[81]

The *Encyclopedia of Public International Law* has included China and the Far East as parts of the international order in their current introduction to the order of international law.[82] The West has, according to this standard introduction to the history of international law, readily accepted China, Japan and other states traditionally outside the Christian cultural sphere into the world community of states:

> After the removal of the psychological obstacles, there was no further resistance to the expansion of the international law of Europe into the international law of the world, which had begun in the Middle and Far East.[83]

Gerrit W. Gong has described the process of adaptation to international law as a very painful process for China, which indeed in many respects it was. His main focus is the process from the "unequal" Nanjing treaty of 1842 to the abrogation of extra-territoriality in 1943.

---

[80] Western scholars, such as Jerome Alan Cohen, Hungdah Chiu, Jean Escarra, Immanuel C.Y. Hsü, E.R. Hughes and others have engaged in questions pertaining to Chinese politics, international relations and international law in modern politics.

[81] Verzijl 1955, p. 145

[82] *Encyclopedia of Public International Law* 1984, vol. 7, pp. 171-173, 215-222

[83] Ibid., p. 186

> In their initial and deepest emotional sense the 'unequal treaties' represented a cultural humiliation for the Middle Kingdom, the shattering of China's tradition of cultural superiority by Western 'barbarian' powers which were not only China's military superior, but which tacitly and explicitly asserted the superiority of their standard of 'civilization' over China as well.[84]

Nonetheless, China was also to accept the terms and adhere to the conditions of the international law of the 'barbarian' powers and became a nominal full member of the international community from 1943: "... China's perception of 'unequal treaties' evolved as China gradually became a sovereign and 'civilized' member of international society. By 1943 this transition was at least nominally complete."[85]

Indeed, in 1943 China understood her international relations as a sovereign and equal member of the international community of states and she was accepted as such by the larger community of states. The Western discourse on the position and role of China in international relations was gradually evolving from 'barbarism' to 'civilism' from the late 19th century. That is the focus of the following short exposition on the perception of China in the theoretical framework of international law.

China in Western international law before 1895

China did not figure in Western theoretical writing on international law to any substantial degree before 1895. The treaties entered into with China were generally regarded as parts of international law. But the assumption that there was a fundamental difference in the degree of civilisation between the West and China, and a general distrust in the Chinese juridical system, together with a general unwillingness to let China join the family of nations, defined China as outside the theoretical framework that the West referred to as international law. She was only admitted recognition as a semi-civilised member and as such subject to treaties and diplomacy on unequal terms. It was the juridical and jurisdictional system in the treaty ports in China that occasioned Western writers on international law to engage in the early debate on China and her place in international law. The core question

---

[84] Gong 1984, p. 183
[85] Ibid.

was the general distrust of the Chinese native juridical system and an unwillingness to let cases involving criminal acts or interests of expatriates be tried according to Chinese law in a Chinese court. The system referred to as extraterritoriality, where foreign nationals residing in the foreign concessions in China were subject to the laws of their native country and to the proceedings of their own consular courts, needed a theoretical justification in international law. Wheaton's *Elements of International Law* refers to the 1844 treaty between the US and China when introducing this system in China:

> By the treaty of peace, amity and commerce, concluded at Wang Hiya, 1844, between the United States and the Chinese Empire, it is stipulated, art. 21, that "citizens of the United States, who may commit any crime in China, shall be subject to be tried and punished only by the consul, or other public functionary of the United States thereto authorized, according to the laws of the United States."[86]

The system was in operation in a number of countries in a situation resembling China's, such as Egypt, Turkey and Japan, all areas outside the Christian sphere of civilisation. The difference in moral standards and the more advanced legal culture of the Christian world was used as the theoretical justification for this design, as described by Theodore Dwight Woolsey in his *Introduction to the Study of International Law*:

> Exemption from local jurisdiction has been granted to foreigners from Christian lands, resident in certain oriental countries; the reasons for which lie in the fact that the laws and usages there prevailing are quite unlike those of Christendom, and in the natural suspicion of Christian states that justice will not be administered by the native courts, which leads them to obtain special privileges for their subjects. The arrangements for this purpose are contained in treaties which have a general resemblance to one another. … The same system in general has been followed in the treaties of Christian states with China, of which that made by the United States in 1844 … may serve as an example.[87]

These nations all had their own particular systems for managing their inter-state relations prior to their exposure to contact with the Christian world. However, the "recent intercourse between the Christian nations in Europe and America and the Mohammedan and Pagan nations of Asia and Africa" compelled the latter to "renounce

---

[86] Wheaton 1855, p. 166
[87] Woolsey 1875, p. 68

their peculiar international usages and adopt those of Christendom".[88] Through intercourse between the West and the different nations in Asia and Africa the latter were brought "within the pale of the public law" of the Christian nations in Europe and America. In the case of "the recent diplomatic transactions between the Chinese Empire and the Christian nations of Europe and America, in which the former has been compelled to abandon its inveterate anti-commercial and anti-social principles, and to acknowledge the independence and equality of other nations in the mutual intercourse of war and peace",[89] China was also brought into the framework of international law. The main perception of this process in these early Western deliberations is that China is brought to abandon her former "anti-social" views on inter-state relations and that she will have to acknowledge the equality and independence of other nations—equality and independence on terms set by the Western world, however. The anti-social, anti-commercial, pagan morals and peculiar views on inter-state relations among the states of the Orient compared to those of the Christian world were understood as due to a difference in religious and cultural standards. These perspectives are particularly transparent in the writings of Jan Helenus Ferguson (1826-1908), who served as Dutch ambassador to China from 1872 to 1894. Upon his return to Holland he wrote a practical guide to international law, *Manual of International Law: for the use of navies, colonies and consulates*.[90] In 1890 he published a book in French on the juridical system and extraterritoriality in China entitled *Juridiction et Exterritorialité en Chine*. The main purpose of Ferguson's work is to introduce the particular juridical problems and solutions arising from the fact that Christian nationals reside and trade in a non-Christian society. In order to explain and justify the system which was practised by the consular courts and the Mixed Court in the foreign settlements in China, Ferguson brings up the essential question regarding the application of laws in cases when different civilisations are involved with entirely different views on the nature and role of man in society. According to Ferguson Christian ethics and interpretation of human nature represent a more advanced form of civilisation than non-Christian societies like the Chinese. Hence, when China now has

[88] Wheaton 1855, p. 20
[89] Ibid., pp. 21-22
[90] Published in 1884 and later translated into Chinese in 1901

come into contact with the West and is engaged in commerce and diplomacy, and conflicts of law arise, it will necessarily be the more advanced system that presides over the less advanced. Therefore, in the general intercourse between states like China and the West the Christian framework for such intercourse referred to as international law will have to serve as the basis. That is why consular courts practising the laws of their native countries have to be protected under the system of extraterritoriality.[91] These were the fundamental and systemic perspectives on the application of international law in China from a Western perspective prior to the Sino-Japanese war 1894-95.

Even by the time of the Sino-Japanese war in the late 19th century the West did not express much trust in China as a partner in international law. In William Edward Hall's *A Treatise on International Law* published in 1895 the general European attitude towards China is made explicit:

> Tacitly, and by inference from a series of acts, states in the position of China may in the long run be brought within the realm of law; but it would be unfair and impossible to assume, inferentially, acceptance of law as a whole from isolated acts or even from frequently repeated acts of a certain kind. European states will be obliged, partly by their sense of honour, partly by their interests, to be guided by their own artificial rules in dealing with semi-civilised states, when the latter have learned enough to make the demand, long before a reciprocal obedience to those rules can be reasonably expected. For example, it cannot be hoped that China, for a considerable time to come, would be able, if she tried, to secure obedience by her officers and soldiers even to the elementary European rules of war.[92]

In his 1895 publication *The Principles of International Law* Thomas Joseph Lawrence refers to the requisites for the position of Japan and China, along with other non-European states, as "admitted to participate in the advantages of the public law of Europe" after the Treaty of Paris in 1856:

> A further requisite is that the state to be admitted shall be to some extent civilized after the European model; but the exact amount of civilization required cannot be defined beforehand. Each case must be judged on its own merits by the powers who deal with it; and it is clear that they would not admit a state into their society if they did not deem

[91] Ferguson 1890, pp. 7-11
[92] Hall 1895, p. 44

> it sufficiently like themselves in organization and ideas to be able to observe the rules they have laid down for their mutual intercourse.[93]

Both China and Japan were entering the European society of nations in international law on probation with a "free" ticket to an already well established and highly civilised system of international conduct. They would have to prove their loyalty and ability to observe the laws of war and intercourse laid down by the Europeans. They would have to live up to the Western standards of civilisation. Did they stand the test? The Sino-Japanese war gave Europe a preliminary answer to this question.

China in Western international law 1895-1905

In a fashion parallel to the way that the Sino-Japanese war in 1894-95 changed the Chinese native discourse on international law and China's international relations, as we shall see later, it also had a lasting effect on the international identity and image of China in the world community. The main area of interest in Western international law writings on China was no longer only the questions of jurisdiction and extraterritoriality that had troubled the Western powers in China before 1894.

The war in the East and its implications for international law prompted international law publicists to deliberate the role of China and Japan in international law also prior to the outbreak of hostilities in 1894. Thomas Erskine Holland, in his work *Studies in International Law* published in 1898, has dedicated a chapter to the topic "International Law in the War between Japan and China". We detect already in the opening passage the general sense of positions in the world community that the war has brought to China and Japan: "The great war in the East has lasted not quite ten months. It has destroyed the reputation of one Empire, and made that of another."[94] Holland initially raised the question of the general applicability of the principles of international law in the East:

> Are China and Japan, with reference either to one another or to the Powers, subject to the duties which are recognized as subsisting

---

[93] Lawrence 1895, p. 84
[94] Holland 1898, p. 112

> between the States of Europe? We come here upon a large question, no less than the essential character of International Law, and the sphere of its operation.[95]

The law of nations was the law of Christendom before the Reformation. Gradually, however, the "Oriental races" were brought into the "law or "concert" of Europe", starting with the formal admission of the Ottoman Empire through the Treaty of Paris in 1856. The treaties with China and Japan made them into newcomers "belonging to the charmed circle, though, perhaps, as admitted to it only on probation. Such might seem to be the position of Japan; but such could hardly be said to be the position of China; for China is far behind Japan in readiness to assimilate the ethical ideas of the West, or to enter into the network of treaties which so much facilitates the social life of the world."[96] "Antecedently to the war, therefore, we should have said that Japan was admitted on probation, while China was only a candidate for admission, to the "Family of Nations"."[97] Holland clearly shows the changing European attitude towards China, and Japan, as a result of the war in the East. Whatever reputation China may have had in international law before the war, although not much was written about it, her name in international relations was rapidly deteriorating after 1895, in particular compared to that of Japan. Holland has studied events and proceedings of the war; the declaration of war, the conduct of warfare, and the quasi-friendly transactions that occur between enemies at war, and found that Japan generally adhered to the principles of civilised warfare, while China did not. In particular, "with reference to the conduct of warfare, China has not accepted the customs, nor has she bound herself by the express conventions, which prevail among civilized nations." On the other hand, the "conduct of the operation of war by the Japanese seems to have been in accordance with the best European practice", with one single exception,[98] Holland's review of the procedures and development of the war causes him to conclude:

> Japan, apart from the lamentable outburst of savagery at Port Arthur, has conformed to the laws of war, both in her treatment of the enemy and in her relations to neutrals, in a manner worthy of the most civilized

---

[95] Ibid., p. 113
[96] Ibid., pp. 113-114
[97] Ibid., p. 115
[98] Ibid., p. 116

> nations in Western Europe. China, on the other hand, has given no indication of her acceptance of the usages of civilized warfare; and, although she was prepared to exercise the rights conceded to belligerents against neutral commerce, took no steps, by establishing prize courts, to secure vessels engaged in it from improper molestation. ... [T]he Chinese have adopted only what I have already described as the rudimentary and inevitable conceptions of International law. They have shown themselves to be well versed in the ceremonial of embassy and the conduct of diplomacy. To a respect for the laws of war they have not yet attained.[99]

China has obviously not accentuated her reputation as a civilised and humane nation in warfare during these hostilities. Holland has made very clear the position and reputation China had in international relations when she was entering the 20th century. Other writings from the same time confirm Holland's perspectives as the general attitude among international law scholars in the West. In his article "China und das Völkerrecht" published in October 1900 Georg Jellinek, professor of international law in Heidelberg, accords with the conclusions reached by Holland.[100]

Japan had won the war, and the Japanese had won themselves a good reputation in international relations. It is, however, pertinent to ask whether or not this war also was a war of the "media"—the Western media for deliberating on conduct and usages in time of war being the publishers and scholars in international law in the West. Through which media and publications were the perspectives of Holland, Jellinek and others on the conduct of warfare in East Asia formulated? Were both Japan's and China's perspectives on the war presented in the Western media at the time? Were there any particular relations between scholars of international law that helped promote the Japanese perspectives on the war and not the Chinese?

There are simply no Western publications from the Chinese perspective on the war in the East or on the position of China in international relations in general.[101] The Western market for perspectives on the rights and wrongs of the war of the East was entirely left for the Japanese to utilise and shape. The perspectives

---

[99] Ibid., pp. 128-129

[100] Jellinek 1900

[101] The only possible exception is Arthur Desjardins' article "La Chine et le Droit des Gens" published in 1900. The text is, however, very critical of the Chinese role and image in international relations.

were formulated and promoted both by Japanese scholars and by Western scholars furthering the ideas that Japan was successfully accepted into the family of nations by the end of the 19th century. Alexander Freiherr von Siebold had personal experience from years in Japan between 1859 and 1887 and wrote an introduction to Japan's entrance into European international law entitled *Der Eintritt Japans in das europäische Völkerrecht* published in Berlin 1900.[102] His main argumentation is that Japan had long endeavoured to enter the international family of nations, and by 1900 "Japan ist nun der erste aussereuropäische Staat, dem es nach jahrelangen Bestrebungen gelungen ist … von den Westmächten die Anerkennung der vollen völkerrechtlichen Rechte zu erlangen."[103]

von Siebold was, however, not the most prominent figure in promoting Japanese perspectives on the position of international law in the Far East. Takahashi Sakue (高橋作衛) (1867-1920) was one of Japan's most prominent international law specialists in the early 20th century, with a degree from Europe and with ample experience from the handling of Japan's international questions, in particular the Sino-Japanese war. He became acquainted with a number of European scholars on international law, of whom Thomas Erskine Holland became the most important in this context. We have discussed Holland's interpretations of the Sino-Japanese war in the light of international law and found him to be inclined to accept Japanese perceptions of justice and rights during the hostilities. One of the occasions for this is most likely the ties between himself and Takahashi. Takahashi had been directly involved in the war on the Japanese side and he was well versed in the European terms and conditions in international law. He published in Western languages and had, so to speak, the perspectives on the proceedings of the Sino-Japanese war in the Western media to himself. Indirectly, the reason for Holland's inclination towards the Japanese interpretations of the war is that Takahashi's interpretation was the only one available in a Western language.

Takahashi Sakue published extensively on international law and international relations in Japanese, several of his works also being translated into Chinese. Takahashi was hence important for the

---

[102] By the Japanese publisher Verlag von Kisak Tamai (玉井喜作)
[103] von Siebold 1900, p. 2

introduction of international law into China in general after 1904. He wrote three publications in English published between 1898 and 1908.[104] Two of these represent the main Japanese contributions in the West to the interpretation of the war between China and Japan, and not just by any observer of the belligerent actions. Takahashi served as legal adviser to the Japanese fleet and interpreter to the Japanese forces in Port Arthur during the war. He was also assigned to compile the official Japanese history of naval warfare during the Sino-Japanese war.[105]

The main purpose of his 1898-99 works was to make inquiries into some of the cases involving prize law, as a part of international law, pertaining to instances during the war between China and Japan. Of the hundreds of such cases occurring during the war "at present only a few of these are known to the world. I am not surprised that such important matters should still remain in such a condition, for accounts of them are kept in the archives of the Far East, and no opportunity has been given for their introduction to the Europeans on the other side of the world. It seems a matter of regret that those facts should be kept any longer in obscurity. Fortunately I had exceptionally favourable opportunities to examine these occurrences during the war, and at the close of hostilities I was also commissioned to compile all these matters in the official history."[106] Takahashi is acting as an agent of the Japanese government in these matters, and his presentation of these matters to the "fortunate" European readership eventually getting access to these "accounts" is at best biased. The perspectives of the just cause on the Japanese side in the war, as presented by Takahashi, was not balanced or countered by a Chinese presentation of these cases because of the lack of any such resources available in a European language: "It was the earnest intention of the Japanese Government to do everything in accordance with International Law."[107]

---

[104] These are; an article with the title "The Application of International Law During the Chino-Japanese War" published in the *Law Quarterly Review* 1898, a book entitled *Cases on International Law during the Chino-Japanese War* published during his time in London in 1899 and translated into German the following year, and a book on the Russo-Japanese war entitled *International Law applied to the Russo-Japanese War, with the Decisions of the Japanese Prize Courts.*

[105] Takahashi 1898, p. 405

[106] Ibid.

[107] Ibid.

The matters pertaining to maritime international law during the Sino-Japanese war were extensively treated by Takahashi in his book published in 1899. Similarly, all cases pertaining to the Japanese army and its actions in the war are treated in an article entitled "La guerre Sino-Japonaise au point de vue de droit international" co-authored by Ariga Nagao (有賀長雄) (1860-1921) and Arthur Desjardins (1835-1901) in 1896.[108] Ariga was, like Takahashi, himself directly involved in international legal interpretation of the Sino-Japanese war on behalf of the Japanese government. The main contribution of these two gentlemen in their presentation of the Japanese perspectives on the justice of the war is their affiliation with Western scholars on international law, Ariga with Desjardins in Paris and Takahashi with Holland and John Westlake in England. Holland demonstrates the way Takahashi's arguments have had an impact on the European interpretation of the situation in East Asia:

> The war was conducted on the part of the Japanese with an anxious desire that their forces should conform to the highest standards of loyalty and humanity; and it was to secure this object that, while a law Professor at the Military College, Mr Ariga, was attached to the troops on land. Mr Takahashi was sent from the Naval College to advise the fleet. ... Mr Takahashi's narrative is always clear, and his arguments are, as a rule, convincing.[109]

Westlake has, in the introductory chapter to one of Takahashi's works, clearly demonstrated the changing image of Japan after the war, from an oriental state outside the European scope of international law to a state abiding by these laws and customs:

> Japan presents a rare and interesting example of the passage of a state from the oriental to the European class. By virtue of treaties already concluded with the leading Christian states of Europe and America she will shortly be freed from the institution of consular jurisdiction, and in her recent war with China she displayed both the disposition and in the main the ability to observe western rules concerning war and neutrality.[110]

Japan had won the war against China, both during the military hostilities and through the media. The war between Japan and China had indeed "destroyed the reputation of one Empire, and made that of

---

[108] See Qi Qizhang 2001, introduction p. 8
[109] Takahashi 1899, p. vi
[110] Ibid., p. xvi

another". Japan had won herself acceptance into the theoretical framework of European international law. China had won herself a loathsome reputation in international relations.

China in Western international law after 1905

The Russo-Japanese war in the northeast of China had in 1904 occasioned China to declare neutrality in the ongoing hostilities. The neutral position of China in the conflict was internationally interpreted as yet another sign of China's international weakness, as commented upon by T. J. Lawrence in his book *War and Neutrality in the Far East*[111] when referring to areas in south-western Manchuria reoccupied by Russia: "Doubtless this reoccupation was a wrongful act. Had China been a strong neutral she would have prevented it, as she had every right to do."[112] In the book entitled *International Law as Interpreted during the Russo-Japanese War* by F. E. Smith and N. W. Sibley a similar portrayal of China is found, describing the situation in China as "the curiously artificial situation created by the partial neutralization of China by the belligerents". Japan, on the other hand, and in stark contrast to the Russian actions in the war, is pictured as a loyal servant of international law:

> Throughout the war her (Japan's) attitude has been one of intelligent correctness, "giving nothing away" in the current phase, but taking no liberties with accepted international practice.[113]

Through the use of Ariga Nagao and Takahashi Sakue as advisers and through strict observance of the principles of international law Japan had done an excellent job in creating an image of an ardent subordinate to the European norms for an international order through the two wars in the Far East.

---

[111] Published in June and September 1904

[112] Lawrence 1904, p. 291

[113] Smith & Sibley 1905, p. 8; Amos Shartle Hershey, in his book *The International Law and Diplomacy of the Russo-Japanese War* (1906), draws a similar picture of the anomalies of the Chinese neutrality in the chapter "The Hay note and Chinese neutrality" (pp. 246-268). The Chinese signs of military and administrative weakness is equally discouraging to Hershey. He is, however, more inclined to argue in favour of the Chinese position in the war. Hershey to a large extent blames Russia for China's weakness and difficulties in maintaining her neutrality (Hershey 1906, p. 268) and recognizes China's (feeble) efforts to abide by international law.

The main contribution to the sustained righteous image of Japan in the Russo-Japanese war is the work *International Law Applied to the Russo-Japanese War* by Takahashi, published in London in 1908. Together with Dr. Terao and Dr. Namamura, Takahashi was commissioned by the Japanese department of foreign affairs to make certain investigations and supervise the Japanese government during the course of events in the war. Again, we find that Takahashi, as was the case in the Sino-Japanese war, served the cause of the Japanese government during the war, and his publication represents the justification of Japanese manoeuvres and tactics in the war. Nevertheless, his book is the most authoritative interpretation of the war in terms of international law in any Western language.[114] It would not be an exaggeration to claim that Takahashi formulated Western opinion on the rights and wrongs of the war. For instance, in the justification of the Japanese occupation of Manchuria and the legal foundation for belligerent actions between Russian and Japanese troops on Chinese territory, Takahashi writes:

> Manchuria was under the sovereignty of China, which was neutral during the Russo-Japanese War, and hence Manchuria was neutral territory. But before the outbreak of war, Manchuria was occupied by Russia, and was entirely under her authority. The expulsion of the Russian troops from the three provinces of Manchuria was the principal object of Japan in beginning of the war, which was carried on *de facto* in Manchuria. Thus Manchuria came to be occupied by the Japanese, who drove out the Russian troops. Taking these facts into consideration, it might be said that the occupation of Manchuria was a unique case, different from what is called military occupation of hostile territories in International Law. But the fact that China recognised a portion of her territory as the area of fighting implies that her consent to military operations by belligerents in her own territory was given. And as a form of military operation, the act of occupation is naturally included in this recognition.[115]

Takahashi shows also full confidence in the benefits for the Chinese inhabitants in Manchuria of the Japanese administration:

---

[114] The only possible exception would be Hershey's 1906 work published two years earlier than Takahashi's. Hershey is, however, very careful not to portray any of the involved parties in an unfair way, and praises both Japan and Russia for their civilised and humanitarian ways of wartime conduct. (Hershey 1906, p. 294)

[115] Takahashi 1908, p. 250

> As many of the Chinese were desirous to learn Japanese, the language was made one of their lessons, and was taught by the Japanese teachers. ... They (the Japanese military administrators) showed to the people their dignity at one time and their tenderness at another as occasions occurred, and the Chinese people were delighted with the administration.[116]

China's position and the consequences of the war on China were presented to the West through the interpretation of one of Japan's legal supervisors in the war. China was not yet in a position to utilise international law and the rights of neutrals to ward off the consequences of the current crisis of international identity. China was deemed too weak and too disloyal to the principles of international law for her interests to be protected through international law and to be regarded as a civilised member in the family of nations. Japan and Takahashi had the upper hand in defining the rights and wrongs of the power play in East Asia.

China from obscurity to distrust in international matters

Through the Sino-Japanese war China was drawn into the sphere of theoretical international law mainly because of Japan's application of and adherence to its principles. The West interpreted China's role in international relations against that of her war enemy Japan. International opinion turned its sympathy towards the civilising project of Meiji Japan and China seemed less compatible with the civilised West than ever before. China appeared weak, out of line with international conduct and not to be trusted as a partner in international affairs. Internally China was wavering with regard to the application of the principles of international law. Externally she was distrusted. During the Russo-Japanese war China attempted to make use of principles laid down in international law to secure her rights in Manchuria and to maintain an idea of Chinese national sovereignty. But Japan had an upper hand in the Western discourse on these matters and China again appeared incapable of handling her own international affairs.

China had entered the sphere of international law in a more active fashion in the early 20th century but her membership was still

[116] Ibid., pp. 259-260

perceived in unequal terms by the larger community of states. China was a de facto member in international law through her practice of diplomacy, through her history of bilateral treaties and through her application of terms in international law on a number of occasions. Seen from the perspective of the core members of the international family of nations in international law, however, she was only accepted as a semi-civilised and partial member in the international community. China had abandoned her former tributary perspectives on her international relations for all practical and theoretical purposes by the early 20th century. The community of states operating according to international law had, however, not yet accepted her as a proper member of their society. This historical and intellectual setting was the basis for the discourse to take place in China in late Qing aimed at negotiating a new identity for China in the international family of nations. In the following chapter we shall first look into the intellectual history of texts and language for this discourse, and subsequently we shall analyse the discourse in China as it developed in terms of international law and international theory in the late 19th and early 20th centuries.

CHAPTER THREE

THE EARLY INTRODUCTION OF INTERNATIONAL LAW: TRANSLATIONS AND LANGUAGE

In chapter two we have introduced China into the framework of international law from the perspective of its practical, or procedural, implications. China was, for all practical purposes, gradually entering a membership in the world order of international law in the 19th century, though not as a very active member utilizing the system for her own benefit. China was coerced into its structure and only by the early 20th century did she actively and on a more comprehensive scale apply principles in international law to her own conduct of inter-state relations. As we have seen above these first attempts at conforming to its procedural rules were not immediately accepted as China's membership application into the family of nations, while Japan was much more successful in this respect. In the following we shall approach the core questions in this book, namely the introduction and reception of the theoretical, the structural, principles of international law in China. We shall analyse the process by which the theories of international law, as deliberated and practised in Europe at this time, were introduced by the use of the Chinese language, printed in China and hence made available to a Chinese readership. This gradual process started as an immediate effect of the Opium war. The expansion of that process into a theoretical basis for a Chinese national discourse on sovereignty and equality as a basis for an alternative Chinese world-view was, however, delayed for several decades. The process only accelerated parallel with the effects caused by the late 19th century Sino-Japanese war, as we shall discuss later. This chapter will consider the texts and their language for the early Chinese introduction of international law prior to that war.

In order for the new world-view to take shape in China based on international law as a foreign discipline, the theoretical basis in texts would need a technical language to serve as a vehicle for conveying the ideas and theories of international law. The written Chinese language of late Qing was not immediately adaptable to its new domain.

THE LANGUAGE OF QING CHINA AND EARLY LANGUAGE CONTACTS

The literary standard of the Qing dynasty was the language referred to as Baguwen (八股文) established through the standard Confucian canon, such as the *Four Books* (四書) and the *Five Classics* (五經), and maintained through the civil service examination system. The spoken language did not have any status in the examination system or in classical learning as such in China. The only area where such a medium was needed was in the administration, for which purpose an administrative norm for a spoken *koinè*, Guanhua (官話), was adopted. This norm was only partly a national norm as the different local and regional variants of this language of administration were influenced by the various local languages and dialects. The written literary standard Wenyan (文言) and the oral standard or standards Guanhua were very different in function and form in late imperial China. They were both artificial in their remoteness from the spoken forms of the language areas in China, and only Guanhua in its various regional variants had certain affiliations with the spoken language. Wenyan had retained many lexical and syntactical features of the Chinese language of the pre-Qin and Han periods more than two millennia before the Qing period and was used mainly for administrative and literary purposes, being as such an alien language to most Chinese in the 19th century. It was, however, the only medium by which new learning could be introduced into China. There existed also a written tradition and norm for certain kinds of popular literature called Baihua (白話), *lingua clara*. This tradition developed into a medium for a growing number of communicative domains in early 20th century China, in social and political discourse, in fiction, in poetry etc. Gradually also the new domains for Western sciences adapted the Baihua norm as its basis. In late Qing, however, the lexical innovations for new learning took place within the framework of the Wenyan norm, and only later was this lexicon of new learning taken over by the new Baihua medium.

The impact from Western languages was insignificant in China before the 19th century: "Over the centuries the contacts between

China and the West had very little impact on the languages of the Chinese empire. Indeed, prior to the XIXth century, very few Chinese had undertaken any formal study of western languages, although some Westerners had already shown interest in the Chinese language."[1] In the 17th century a number of Jesuit missionaries stationed in China, such as Matteo Ricci and Giulio Aleni, wrote works on geography and technology in Chinese. For this purpose a number of neologisms for technical terms in these fields were coined. These works constituted the only sources on the West in Chinese for centuries. They were kept in the imperial archives but were not generally accessible or exercising any impact on the Chinese language, neither Wenyan, Baihua or Guanhua. Trade was an area of early Chinese-Western contacts where the use of language as a means of communication was much needed. In the 16th century Portuguese merchants established trading ports and founded the colony Macao in 1557. These merchants did not know any Chinese and their Chinese partners did not know any Guanhua. In addition, in contrast to the missionaries who were regarded as valuable to the Chinese and hence integrated into Chinese life, the merchants were kept separate from the Chinese people in the trading ports of Macao and Canton. All transactions between Chinese and the foreign merchants were conducted in a *lingua franca* known as *pidgin*. This language was built on Chinese syntax and composed of Portuguese and Chinese words with the addition of terms and expressions from other languages in the trading areas in South and South-East Asia. Gradually, as the British influence in these trading routes grew, more and more terms in *pidgin* were exchanged for English words. Foreigners were not allowed to study Chinese.

The situation changed in the early 19th century when the British Protestant missionary Robert Morrison arrived in China and secretly studied Chinese for missionary purposes. Morrison published bi-lingual dictionaries, translated the Bible and published a monthly magazine in Chinese. He seems, however, to be one of the very few Westerners who did learn Chinese and were able to communicate in Chinese prior to the Opium war of the 1840s. Most other merchants and missionaries were confined to *pidgin* in their communication with the Chinese and all official communication between China and the

[1] Masini 1993, p. 5

West took place through Chinese interpreters.[2]

Before the middle of the 19th century only very few sources in Chinese on the West had been added to the early Jesuit works left in Beijing. These included a small number of travelogues and reports from travels in Europe and South America. Foreign terms and names are invariably rendered by phonemic loans in addition to some of the terms coined by the early Jesuits. After the Opium war the need for more extensive knowledge of the West was apparent in China and a number of projects to accommodate this need were launched, the most influential being the *Haiguo tuzhi* (海國圖志) and the *Yinghuan zhilüe* (瀛環志略).

Lin Zexu (林則徐) (1785-1850) was appointed Imperial Commissioner and sent to Canton in March 1839 to solve the opium issue. As we know Lin did not have much success in his political task in Canton. A more lasting effect of his endeavours is, however, the material that he collected and translated in order to learn about the foreigners. Much of the material was collected in Macao and Canton where newspapers, such as *Canton Register*, the *Chinese Repository*, and the *Canton Press*, were published in order to inform people in Europe about the situation in Guangdong and the Western merchants and missionaries in Canton and Macao about events in their home countries. These papers served as valuable material for Lin and his interpreters, who used this material in their strategies for controlling the foreigners in Canton, and also as more general preparations for a better Chinese knowledge of countries overseas. "Lin's ultimate goal was knowledge of the West, not to satisfy his own intellectual curiosity, but to enable China to prepare an adequate response to the foreign threat."[3] After Lin was unable to continue his work the material was handed over to his friend Wei Yuan (魏源) (1794-1856) who continued collating new material and published this in 1844 as an anthology with the title *Haiguo tuzhi*. The publication became very popular and was expanded and republished several times during the latter half of the 19th century. Federico Masini has concluded that it is difficult to establish exactly when a new term was used in Chinese for the first time, since there are very few sources on the lexicon of foreign terms prior to the *Haiguo tuzhi*. Additionally, the *Haiguo tuzhi*

[2] Ibid., pp. 8-15
[3] Ibid., p. 21

was borrowing heavily from other earlier sources and may not have been instrumental in itself in coining new terms for new ideas. Rather, the lexicon of the *Haiguo tuzhi* "can legitimately be considered representative of the lexicon of the period and useful, therefore, for studying the early influence of western languages on Chinese, and especially on (sic!) Chinese lexicon."[4] Masini has found that the *Haiguo tuzhi* contains many phonemic loans, loanwords that have proven unstable in the Chinese language and often exchanged for semantic loans or loan-translations during the course of time. A few semantic innovations representing new ideas in the Chinese language may, however, be found in *Haiguo tuzhi*, such as *gongsi* (公司) for 'company', *xinwen* (新聞) for 'news', *xinwenzhi* (新聞紙) for 'newspaper' *guohui* (國會) for 'parliament', *maoyi* (貿易) for 'trade', *huoche* (火車) for 'train', *wenxue* (文學) for 'literature', *falü* (法律) for 'law' and *zhengzhi* (政治) for 'politics'. These words may not have been coined for the *Haiguo tuzhi* particularly but were certainly disseminated throughout China through the popularity of this work. In addition, the *Haiguo tuzhi* was also very popular in Japan and some of these terms may have come into circulation in Japan through this work.[5]

The *Yinghuan zhilüe* is different in nature compared to the *Haiguo tuzhi*. The *Yinghuan zhilüe* is written by one single man, Xu Jiyu (徐繼畬) (1795-1873), and is almost exclusively based on Chinese sources, while the *Haiguo tuzhi* is compiled from many different sources, many of which are Western. In contrast to Lin Zexu and Wei Yuan, Xu Jiyu has more systematically approached the problem of terms and name translations and has adopted loan-translations as his main policy when rendering Chinese terms of foreign origin. "Xu Jiyu's preference for loan-translations was not purely coincidental. In the introduction he actually addressed this particular issue, indicating that "the names of foreign places are the main problem". He has also explained that the lack of consistency between Chinese and western sounds had resulted in several transcriptions being invented for the same foreign terms."[6]

With these early works on overseas matters and foreign countries the editors and translators met the first challenges when introducing

---

[4] Masini 1993, p. 28
[5] Ibid., pp. 27-30; See also Liu 1995, pp. 34-35
[6] Masini 1993, p. 32

entirely new concepts into China through the Chinese language. The real challenges in introducing Western knowledge was, however, yet to come. Only with the first systematic attempts to translate and introduce Western sciences, hard sciences as well as social and human sciences, the task of suggesting and establishing lexica of technical terms for these new areas of knowledge became a vital and all-important undertaking. That process was in many respects a particularly Chinese undertaking. On the other hand, the process taking place in China in this respect cannot be separated entirely from a parallel process taking place in Meiji Japan. In general, the first Chinese translations and descriptions of the West were exported to Japan and had a terminological influence on the modern Japanese lexicon. Later, the process of translation and adaptation of Western sciences took place in Japan under Japanese conditions, using Chinese characters (*kanji* 漢字) to coin new terms for new knowledge in Japanese. In China, throughout the 1870s, 80s and most of the 90s, the process of translating new ideas from the West was seemingly not influenced by the parallel process in Japan. When Chinese students started to study in Japan from the middle of the 1890s, however, the Meiji Japanese lexicon based on Chinese characters was a major source for new terms in early 20th century China.[7] Since some of these terms originally had been coined, or at least used in a different meaning, in China, brought to Japan and used with a new semantic content, they were returned to China as return loans. Generally the return *kanji* loans from Japan may be divided into three categories; 1) Two-character compounds found in pre-modern Japanese and not in classical Chinese imported into the Chinese lexicon with their modern Japanese meaning 2) Classical Chinese words infused with new meanings in Japan and imported back to China with this new semantic field added 3) Modern Japanese *kanji* innovations with no equivalent in Classical Chinese or in pre-modern Japanese imported to China with the modern Japanese semantics.[8] Masini has made an overall

---

[7] Linguists have identified more than 1000 neologisms in the Chinese language to be loans from Japanese *kanji* translations. (Liu 1995, pp. 17-18) A statistical survey of such words in the recently published etymological dictionary of modern Chinese *Jin-Xiandai Hanyu Xinci Ciyuan Cidian* (2001), based on the research by Huang Heqing (黄河清), Xu Wenkan (徐文堪) and Yao Dehuai (姚德懷), would most probably yield an even higher number of Japanese *kanji* translations in modern Chinese.

[8] Liu 1995, pp. 32-33

survey of the process of forming a modern Chinese lexicon between 1840 and 1898, leaving out the period of massive influx of Japanese terms into China from the end of the 19th century.[9] My purpose in this chapter is in addition to look at the translations of texts on international law as theoretical sources for the discourse on international questions in China, also to analyse the development of a technical language and the terminology with which international law was introduced into China. As will become obvious in the chapters to follow it is indeed impossible to see the process of intellectual transfer of ideas entirely separate from the process of language adaptation. As discussed in chapter 1 we need to be careful not to impose on a field of learning the idea that words translate as exact semantic units between languages as they do in bilingual dictionaries.

THE FIRST ATTEMPTS AT A CHINESE TRANSLATION OF INTERNATIONAL LAW[10]

China's first exposure to the discipline of international law is intimately related to her first brutal encounters with an expanding Europe in the later 19th century. It was going to take a long time before international law as a theoretical discipline as well as the organising structure of international relations in the West would dawn on China in all its details and with all its principles—and correspondingly be forged into a framework for interpreting China in her international relations from within. The first attempts at a translation of a text on international law paved in some respect the way for the translations and reception of international law to take place in the coming decades. In the 1840s a small group of dedicated officials engaged in the pressing issues of China's relationship with an

[9] Masini 1993

[10] This subchapter on Vattel in *Haiguo tuzhi* is an abridged version of Svarverud 2000. The following sources are consulted: Angle 2002, pp. 104-107; Barnett 1970; Britton 1966, pp. 30-34; Chang 1950; Chiu 1967; Covell 1978, p. 145; Hsü 1960, pp. 123-125; Hughes 1968, pp. 61, 222; Katô Shûichi & Maruyama Masao 1996, pp. 381-382; Li Guilian 1998a, p. 9; Li Zhaojie 1999, pp. 82-96; Masini 1993, pp. 22, 26, 30, 47; Spence 1969, pp. 34-56; Stevens, George B. 1896; Tian Tao & Li Zhuhuan 2000, p. 355; Tian Tao 2001, pp. 23-33; Wang Jian 2001, pp. 93-113; Wang Tieya 1998, pp. 375-377; Wang Weijian 1985, pp. 58-67; Xiong Yuezhi 1996; Zhang, Jingcao 1992, pp. 264-270; Zou Zhenhuan 1996, p. 55.

expanding Europe made a daring attempt at translating excerpts from a French/English text on such issues. Another 20 years was, however, to pass before the intellectual environment in China was sufficiently open to Western studies as a theoretical foundation for deliberations on China's own issues and concerns. The schools and traditions for translating social sciences in general and international law in particular from the 1860s do not owe a great deal of their vocabulary or perspectives to the circumstances revolving around the international issues introduced at the time of the Opium war. The first translation of a text on international law into Chinese, published in the *Haiguo tuzhi*, may be interpreted as a daring and, from a linguistic perspective, very interesting, although partly futile attempt to initiate Chinese introduction of the principles of international law.

Lin Zexu had been sent to Canton in 1839 to deal with the growing problem of opium trade and addiction, the controversy that evolved into the Sino-British Opium war. To meet the foreigners on their own terms and comprehend their language of reasoning Lin started collecting material for a compilation of translations of overseas matters, finally completing an anthology on the four continents entitled *Sizhouzhi* (四洲志), a partial translation of Hugh Murray's *An Encyclopaedia of Geography*. As Lin did not succeed in having his work or any of his material published before he fell into disgrace after his failed mission to Canton, he handed over the translated texts and his material to Wei Yuan in 1841. Wei continued Lin's work enlarging the *Sizhouzhi*, including substantially new material, general information on the history and political systems of foreign countries, maps, articles and drawings and descriptions of cannons and other Western technological devices. Finally, in the summer of 1844 the first 50 volume (*juan*) edition of Wei Yuan's *Haiguo tuzhi* was published in Yangzhou. The *Haiguo tuzhi* became very popular, and an enlarged edition in 60 volumes of this influential work came out already in 1847. In 1852 a 100 volume edition was printed, and finally in 1895 the 125 volume edition was published. Wei Yuan explicitly argues in this text for the importance of understanding the foreigners through translations of foreign texts in order to subjugate the foreign barbarians,[11] and explains that the *Haiguo tuzhi* is compiled for that

[11] *Haiguo tuzhi* (1880), *juan* 2, pp. 4b-5a

specific purpose.[12] Some passages from a text on international law must have been introduced into the *Haiguo tuzhi* for the same reason.

Lin himself could not speak or read any foreign language and had to depend on the skills of his assistants. Yuan Dehui (袁德輝) had served as imperial interpreter in the Colonial Office, Lifanyuan (理藩院), in Peking and joined Lin's staff in Canton in 1839.[13] It was most probably through Yuan Dehui that Lin's attention was brought to the English translation of Emmerich de Vattel's influential work on international law entitled *Law of Nations*.[14] The first medical missionary to China, the American Peter Parker (1804-1888),[15] was asked by Lin Zexu to give a prescription for the cure of opium smoking. Through Parker's knowledge of the Chinese language he was at the same time furnished with a few passages from Vattel's work for translation. Lin Zexu and his staff of interpreters also knew Parker because he had established the English language periodical *Chinese Repository* in May 1832,[16] from which Lin gained much of his knowledge of Western affairs. Lin Zexu approached Parker and requested his assistance to cure his hernia. In Lin's case history from 1839 Parker refers to Lin's request for a translation of a few passages from Vattel's text:

> His first applications, during the month of July, were not for medical relief, but for translations of some quotations from Vattel's Law of Nations, with which he had been furnished: these were sent through the senior hong-merchant; they related to war, and its accompanying hostile measures, as (sic!) blockades, embargoes, &c.; they were written out with a Chinese pencil.[17]

Vattel's text was originally written in French with the title *Le Droit des Gens* and published for the first time in 1758. The first English translation, *Law of Nations*, appeared in 1759. The Chinese translations by Yuan and by Parker appear both too have been based on the English translation.[18] The choice of topics fell naturally on

[12] Ibid., preface pp. 1a-1b

[13] For more biographical information on Yuan Dehui see Wang Weijian 1985, pp. 60-62. See also Masini 1993, pp. 18-19

[14] Chang 1950, p. 1430

[15] For biographical information on Peter Parker see Spence 1969, pp. 34-56 and Wang Weijian 1985, pp. 58-60

[16] Masini 1993, p. 22 n54

[17] Chang 1950, p. 1428

[18] Most probably the 1833 Joseph Chitty edition; See also Wang Weijian 1985, pp.

international regulations of commerce, restrictions on allowing foreigners to enter a country and conventions for the rights of nations to wage war. All these represented urgent issues for China on the verge of a military conflict with Britain over the opium trade. Wei Yuan's anthology on foreign affairs in 50 volumes published in 1844 did not include the translated passages from Vattel's text, which were only added to the anthology in the 1847 60 volume edition.

As I have argued in more detail elsewhere we may assume that Yuan Dehui in some way or another had come across Vattel's text and found it suitable for translation on the matter of international law.[19] Yuan may himself have been given the task of translating the text passages on commerce, foreigners and war but found it difficult in a Chinese language not yet equipped with a terminological apparatus for translating Western concepts in international law. He presumably consulted Parker and had him translate the most difficult parts of Vattel's passages by transcribing certain parts of the text and passing them on to Parker. He later reworked Parker's language of the translated passages into what he would consider a more smooth and comprehensible Chinese. It appears from a comparative study of the Vattel translations in *Haiguo tuzhi* that Parker's translation may not have been intended for publication. Parker's text was most probably only meant as a basis for Yuan Dehui's translation. That will have been the reason why Parker mentions in Lin Zexu's case history that he was only furnished with a few hand-written passages from Vattel's text, not the book or text proper. Because of the very differences in their ways and terms of translation the editors of the 1847 edition of *Haiguo tuzhi* may have misunderstood the purpose and content of these texts and published what in reality are two different versions of the same texts from Vattel. Yuan Dehui must have been the predominant figure in this first attempt to introduce Western concepts and terms on international law to the Chinese, and Parker was only doing Lin Zexu a favour when he translated these few passages, altogether unaware that his translation would later be published in the *Haiguo tuzhi*.

The political situation in China after the first Opium war was not favourable to the introduction of international law in China. The

---

62-63

[19] Svarverud 2000

translations from Vattel's text did not gain much influence in China during the decades following their publication in 1847. W.A.P. Martin had initially intended to translate Vattel's entire texts into Chinese in the early 1860s but does not make any reference to Yuan and Parker's translation on that occasion. When Martin translated the first major text on international law in 1864, he did not follow the works of Parker and Yuan. As we shall see below, Martin's vocabulary on international law was introduced and came into current usage in China only after Martin's translation had been retranslated into Japanese. Parker and Yuan's translations are thus primarily interesting because of their originality and the innovative spirit shown by the two translators, and not because of their impact on the later language and logic of international law in China. The first major impact of the terms and conditions of Western international law on the Chinese may be ascribed to the American missionary and translator William A.P. Martin. Before we discuss the large-scale project of international law translations by Martin and his staff, however, we may want to take a look at some of the linguistic specificities of the Vattel translations.

Chang Hsi-t'ung has discussed these two translations briefly in an article in the *Yenching Journal of Social Studies* in 1950 and drawn the conclusion that except for the difference that Parker's translation is relatively more "vitiated by foreign phraseology", both translations are misleading. Immanuel Hsü has, in his book *China's Entrance into the Family of Nations*, concluded along the same lines regarding the general impression of the language of the two translations: "The translation was not literal but paraphrastic, and the translator's comments were in a labored and unliterary style, which is a travesty of Vattel's perspicuity." [20] For Yuan Dehui's translation of Vattel specifically Chang Hsi-t'ung has delivered only two generally harsh and depreciating conclusions; "entirely miss the mark" and "almost gruesome". Otherwise Chang tends to be particularly troubled by Parker's attempt to render the logic of Western international law into Chinese and terms Parker's language: "... a mockery of Vattel's precision and clearness, and a few notes to make it more intelligible only serve to increase the confusion. One is forced to conclude that Parker did the work by himself, without seeking counsel from any

[20] Hsü 1960, p. 123

Chinese."[21]

I tend to agree that these Chinese translations of Vattel's text are inadequate and crude summaries of Vattel's lucid and well-formulated language—judged by the standards of the Chinese language of the 20th century. It would, however, be useful to raise the question as to with what kind of linguistic devices these passages were translated in 1839. One may find that Parker's language is deficient in conveying the lucid formulations of Vattel and that Yuan certainly turns Vattel into arguments that the author himself would barely recognize. I believe, nevertheless, that these two texts should be taken seriously as historic attempts to convey the logic of some aspects of Western international law in Chinese and should be approached accordingly.

The two translators were facing the arduous task of introducing an altogether unfamiliar matter to a Chinese readership in a language not yet equipped for this purpose. The two translators had no established standard or model to adhere to and consequently had to fashion ways of conveying the terminology and philosophy in international law cross-culturally from the West in a Chinese linguistic context. Rather than judging the translations by Parker and Yuan by Chang Hsi-T'ung's contemporary literary and linguistic standards, I embrace the conclusion drawn by Wang Weijian:

> Because the works of Western international law had only recently been introduced into China, the establishment of appropriate translations of specific terms in legal studies was a question which couldn't be fully solved by Parker and Yuan Dehui. Even at the time when W.A.P. Martin translated H. Wheaton's *Elements of International Law* more than 20 years later the question of terminology still remained a problem. In spite of the fact that they merely translated a small number of text-passages, the challenging nature of their work should be appreciated. If one, in addition, also takes into account the influence of these translations on Lin Zexu's struggle against the foreign aggressors and his determination to handle the relationship between China and the outside world, these two translations may be conceived as an even greater and more favourable achievement. Seen from the perspective of communication and exchange between Chinese and Western philosophy and culture, the historical significance of the translation of Vattel's work on international law instituted by Lin Zexu cannot be ignored.[22]

---

[21] Chang 1950, p. 1429

[22] Wang Weijian 1985, p. 66

It has been suggested that the *Haiguo tuzhi* established neologisms within certain disciplines, even if this is not altogether a prominent feature of the anthology. Then what is the case with regard to Vattel's text? Was it necessary for Parker and Yuan to introduce neologisms or did they carry out their translations by applying already established terminological and conceptual categories in the Chinese language? In order to approach this question a set of basic terms and formulations in the relevant Vattel passages has been extracted and their equivalents in the two translations have been identified for comparison.

Key terms and formulations in Vattel's text:[23]

Terms and formulations	Parker	Yuan
right	reformulated	道理(權)
preservation of rights	reformulated	保全自己道理
prosecute our right	應有此事	伸吾之道理
complain	告訴委曲	心懷怨恨, 含怨, 有怨
not founded on any reason drawn from the welfare of the state		將本求利
law		律例
respect the law		omitted
carried out in the name of the public power	所事皆出于公	omitted
acts in the name of society at large		omitted
nature gives man a right to employ force	(人人皆欲戰)	自然可以有用武之道理
checks every attempt to do ourself justice with our own hands		禁止我們私自所欲伸之義理
the right of judging whether the nation has real grounds of complaint		有何怨的道理
(law of) nature	性理之常	妥當道理
nature has given man right...	天理	天性所賦之理
body of the nation		omitted
will of the nation		omitted
justice		義理, 理
principle	事	道理
fanatics	匪盜	迂儒
constitution		例制
parliament	大臣	巴厘滿衙門會議

The table above presents the results of this study, where blanks in Parker's column indicate that these terms and formulations found in

[23] For a detailed comparative analysis of the three texts, Vattel, Parker and Yuan, see appendix in Svarverud 2000

sections of Vattel's text are not translated by Peter Parker, only by Yuan Dehui. The annotations "reformulated" and "omitted" refer respectively to cases where Vattel's passages have been reformulated to the extent that there is no longer any correspondence between the precise terms and to cases where entire passages have been omitted. We may from this material conclude that Parker did not omit formulations central to the intention of the relevant passages. He avoided creating neologisms and reformulated passages when he found the Chinese language insufficient as a tool for the purpose. Yuan, on the other hand, created a small set of neologisms for the purpose of conveying these matters to his readership. These are primarily *daoli* (道理) as a translation of 'rights'[24] and *yili* (義理) for 'justice'. When these neologisms and a traditional set of terms and formulations failed to convey the essence of the workings of international law, Yuan tended to omit entire passages.

Yuan has applied already existing combinations of characters from the established literary language and infused them with the semantics of these important concepts in Western international law. These semantic neologisms created by Yuan were not taken up by W.A.P. Martin two decades later when Wheaton's text was translated. Nor did any of these neologisms from the Vattel translation ever become current in the Chinese language, indicating that Yuan's translation never became very influential. The same preliminary conclusion may be drawn with regard to Parker's translation and the entire chapter on international law in *Haiguo tuzhi*, as also suggested earlier.

The difference in the two translators' use of neologisms is, however, not the only and most prominent distinction between these two texts. Their individual differences become more transparent when we investigate the techniques with which these two translators convey the logic and internal argumentation in Vattel's international law. The impression that Parker's text is more characterized by Western phraseology, as Chang Hsi-t'ung concluded, may in fact not be

[24] Masini refers to Yuan Dehui's translation of 'rights' as *daoli* and claims also that Parker has rendered the same notion with the Chinese equivalent *li* (例). (Masini 1993, pp. 30, 47) Since the term *li* is only applied *once* out of eight occurrences of the term 'rights' in the passages translated by Parker Masini's conclusion seems misleading. There is no evidence for Parker introducing *li* as a technical term for 'rights'. The one occurrence of *li* in Parker's translation may in this passage be understood as 'regulation', parallel to *li* in Parker's translation of the title of Vattel's work *Geguo lüli*.

attached to his translation of terms and formulations but rather to his use of Western syntax and an adherence to Western argumentative techniques. Parker's language of translation seeks to follow the English juridical language with regard to complexity and accuracy. Lacking certain central terms in the current Chinese language, he reformulated the passage without diverging from the logic of the original argumentation. Yuan, on the other hand, polished and shortened Parker's text to peel away all the "cryptic" Western phraseology and replaced it with plain and straightforward Chinese sequences of arguments supported by additional use of terms from a traditional set of Chinese values.

The translation of the first passages in the section on war may illustrate the way in which Yuan found Parker's translations incomprehensible for a Chinese readership and subsequently reformulated and simplified the text. The text in Vattel begins with the passage: "War is that state in which we prosecute our right by force."[25] Parker strives to express the logic of "prosecution of rights" without an appropriate terms for it. He has reformulated the sequence, tentatively translated back from Chinese as follows: "War is that matter we are entitled to when we have no other way than to apply force."[26] Yuan has made use of his term for 'rights', and the verb *shen* (伸) meaning to extend, to simply translate the sequence: "War is employing force in order to extend (*shen*) [one's] rights (*daoli*)."[27] Following this pattern, Parker continues into the next passage where the problems of making this technique transparent for a Chinese readership becomes greater. Vattel's text runs as follows: "Public war is that which takes place between nations or sovereigns, and which is carried on in the name of the public power, and by its order. This is the war we are here to consider:—private war, or that which is carried on between private individuals, belongs to the law of nature properly so called."[28] If we attempt to translate Parker back into English we may comprehend the difficulties a Chinese reader would have had in 1847 trying to grasp the essence of rules for international war: "War may be divided into public and private war. [Public war] may take place between nations or between two sovereigns. That which takes

---

[25] Vattel 1863, p. 291
[26] *Haiguo tuzhi* (1847), *juan* 52, p. 18b
[27] Ibid., p. 20b
[28] Vattel 1863, p. 291

place all originates in the public, and the military authority also originates in the public. This is it. [Private war] is enmity between two individuals, which belongs to the law of nature. This is what it is called."[29] Again Parker is hampered in his translation by the lack of terms and suitable discursive tools. The passage: "Public war ... carried on in the name of the public power, and by its order" makes it clear that he lacked the instruments for describing the fact that a war may be "carried on in the name of the public power". Yuan has not been able to get any sense out of Parker's 'rambling' and has created a short summary where Vattel's intention is entirely lost: "There is public and private war. Public war is when two nations engage in military action. Private war is when two families harbour resentment. This is the appropriate principle."[30]

One may claim that Vattel certainly loses his lucidity and preciseness in Yuan's translation. But he seldom diverges far from Vattel's presumed intention with a passage when he has access to Parker's translations. However, when he continues to translate passages and sections not based on Parker's work he seems to be easily drifting off into arguments hardly recognizable in Vattel's original. One may even have to question Yuan's intentions in some of these cases—is he in fact twisting Vattel's text as a device to make the text comprehensible to a Chinese readership or is he consciously changing the meaning of Vattel's text? I will illustrate this with one of the most prominent cases in this text.

In the section on commerce Vattel discusses the right of every nation to prohibit the entrance of foreign merchandise, passages treated by both Parker and Yuan in fairly accurate translations. Vattel then goes on to discuss cases where the nation affected by this prohibition is convinced that when the prohibition "was not founded on any reason drawn from the welfare of the state that prohibited them, she would have cause to consider this conduct as a mark of ill-will shown in this instance, and to complain of it on that footing." "But", as Vattel continues, "it would be very difficult for the excluded nation to judge with certainty that the state had no solid or apparent reason for making such a prohibition."[31] This would have been a promising argument for China and Lin Zexu taken from a Western

[29] *Haiguo tuzhi* (1847), *juan* 52, p. 18b
[30] Ibid., p. 20b
[31] Vattel 1863, p. 38

authoritative text on international law on the verge of the Opium wars. It is thus surprising to find that Yuan turned this into an argument where the establishment of prohibitions was described as hostile acts in the intercourse between nations, tentatively translated from the Chinese: "If there is no longer any reason for making such a prohibition, and the nation is not able to make clear the reason for it, the establishment of this kind of prohibition is difficult to apprehend. This may thus be considered a hostile act discontinuing the mutual intercourse between nations."[32] This is one of the cases where Yuan Dehui relied solely on his own interpretation of Vattel, as the texts in *Haiguo tuzhi* do not contain a Parker translation of this passage, and it may be assumed that Parker never did translate this section for the *Haiguo tuzhi* project. It would be tempting but inappropriate to accuse Yuan Dehui of wittingly misleading his master Lin Zexu in this case.[33] It is nevertheless clear that he did give Lin unnecessarily weak arguments for expelling the foreign opium merchants—obviously a remarkable position for an associate of opium commissioner Lin Zexu.

Yuan Dehui used various translational devices in order to make his text more comprehensible to the Chinese readership. We have seen that he reformulated and shortened passages and complex arguments to adapt international law to the China of 1839. He also omitted passages or concepts not applicable or appropriate to the Chinese situation in 1839, in particular passages touching upon the sovereign acting as the representative of the public will and considerations on "the will of the nation". In addition he reinterpreted the social and political message of Vattel. Where Vattel argues for legal entities as necessary elements in a society where the sovereign is acting on behalf of the common will and where the laws are seen as the highest expression of rules for a well ordered society securing the welfare of every citizen, Yuan turned these into arguments for human relations based on traditional Chinese ethics. Yuan translated international law by applying the language of Chinese ethics, bringing the matter from an international to an interpersonal level, and from a presumably objective matter of legal entities to subjective matters of feelings and sentiments. A few examples from his vocabulary of terms clearly with

[32] *Haiguo tuzhi* (1847), *juan* 52, pp. 19b-20a
[33] That would eventually have to be substantiated by other corresponding evidence.

traditional Chinese connotations and with no exact equivalents in Vattel's language would be: *jiangben qiuli* (將本求利) (take profit as one's basis); *beique benfen* (背卻本分) (turn against one's fate); *yi renyi zhi lüfa er jiezhi zhi* (以仁義之律法而節制之) (repress it by benevolent [*ren*] and upright [*yi*] laws); *duanjue wanglai* (斷絕往來) (discontinue mutual intercourse); *yuren gebie* (與人隔別) (keep a distance to others); *xinhuai yuanhen* (心懷怨恨) (harbour resentment); *han yuan* (含怨) (bear hatred); *suohuai zhi fen* (所懷之忿) (the infuriation one harbours).

It is surely an anachronism to observe that whereas Vattel seeks to establish an understanding of international law based on a normative legal and moral order of Christian ethics, Yuan Dehui translates and explains Vattel in a language and argumentation bringing Vattel to the core of what is frequently termed Confucian ethics. That does not, however, make Yuan Dehui, nor in comparative perspective also Parker's translations, uninteresting and irrelevant for the process of introducing international law in China. Quite on the contrary these two texts present us with a unique opportunity to study the problems facing the early translators of Western texts in general and international law texts in particular and the techniques and devices with which they sought to solve them.

These two translations may serve as an interesting illustration of the differences between how a Westerner and a native Chinese conducted this interpretative task at the time of the Opium war. Peter Parker kept strictly to the Chinese language current at the time and to the presumed original intention and language in Vattel's text. He struggles to convey the logic and semantic correlations of European legal philosophy in his Chinese language and subsequently is compelled to reformulate the original text, creating a "hybrid" language for international law barely comprehensible to a contemporary Chinese readership. Yuan Dehui found Parker's language inadequate for the purpose and, based on Parker's text, reformulated his passages into a Chinese more familiar to the Chinese readers. He applies a Chinese language much closer to the current literary standard but tends to twist the argumentation of Western international law. Yuan is also found to misinterpret the arguments from Vattel's text when he does not have a Parker translation at hand. Yuan created a small number of semantic neologisms for central concepts, and simplified and sinified the entire argumentation. In spite of the fact that Parker avoided creating a neologism for 'rights', he nevertheless attempted to convey the idea of nations having rights and duties when acting in international affairs. Yuan, on the other hand, stressed the ritually and traditionally Chinese ethical aspects of international relations, indicating that the primary question is a nation's conviction of what is reasonable rather than which rights and duties it presumably would have in international affairs. These two short translations may serve as an early example of the challenges and approaches to the task of translating and conveying Western political thought and international theory question into late Qing China. The consequences and ramifications of importing a comprehensive presentation of the Western legal and customary system of international relations into China were, however, only accentuated and made visible when Martin embarked on the grand task of translating Wheaton into Chinese in the 1860s. Only then did Chinese intellectuals get access to a tool for interpreting international law in the Chinese environment.

MARTIN, TONGWENGUAN AND THE FIRST SYSTEMATIC TRANSLATIONS OF INTERNATIONAL LAW

Many international issues became more overtly pressing to China in the 1860s compared to the situation in the early 1840s. The translations by Yuan and Parker were widely distributed but do not seem to have had any major influence on the dissemination and reception of international law as a discipline of Western learning in Qing China. China was not ready for a new interpretation of her international position based on an orientation towards international law as a framework during the first two decades after the Opium war and the Nanjing treaty. The national and international situation in the middle of the 1860s was, however, to compel the Chinese discursive orientation in a new direction. The new political situation opened up for an extensive body of translated texts on international law, a groundwork that was later to pave the way for a fully-fledged discourse on international questions and international law in China from the late 19th century. The translations of international law texts by W.A.P. Martin and the staff at the Tongwenguan may indeed represent the first systematic vehicle for a new Chinese international orientation based on the Western discipline of international law.

Below we shall take a closer look at the environment and subject matter of the translations and the language of Martin's international law translations.

Martin's translation of Henry Wheaton[34]

William A. P. Martin[35] (1827-1916) was born in Indiana in the United States April 10 1827. He arrived for the first time in China in 1850 as a missionary. After the 1858-60 conflicts between the Qing court and the British-French forces Martin left for Shanghai to pursue his missionary calling, and it was during his temporary stay in Shanghai in 1862 that Martin started to translate the text *Elements of International Law* by Henry Wheaton.[36] His interest in international law was kindled during his engagement as interpreter during the international conflicts in 1858-60. This activity had also convinced him that Chinese officials needed to learn more about the Western law of international relations.[37] Law had not been on his study curriculum in Indiana, but Martin's engagement in these conflicts of an international nature pertaining to China's role and response to foreign pressure had a lasting impact on Martin's personal as well as professional life. He had originally intended to translate the European Emmerich de Vattel's *The Law of Nations*, the text which had been the basis for the passages on international law in *Haiguo tuzhi* discussed above, but was advised by John E. Ward, United States Minister to

---

[34] This subchapter is partly based on the following sources: Angle 2002, pp. 107-110; Biggerstaff 1983; Covell 1978, pp. 145-150; Dudden 1999; Chiu 1967, pp. 486-491; *Chouban yiwu shimo;* Hsü 1960, pp. 125-138; Hughes 1968, pp. 104-109; Katô Shûichi & Maruyama Masao 1996; Farquhar 1971, p. 138; Li Guilian 1998a, p. 11; Li Zhaojie 1999, pp. 96-115; Liu 1999; Liu 2004, pp. 108-139; Martin 1900; Masini 1993, pp. 46-48; Pusey 1983, p. 140; Qi Qizhang 2001, pp. *qianyan* (前言) 1-7; Spence 1969, pp. 129-140; Teng & Fairbank 1981, pp. 97-99; Tian Tao & Li Zhuhuan 2000, pp. 356, 364; Tian Tao 2001, pp. 34-62; Tsiang 1931; Wang Jian 2001, pp. 138-186, 236-239; Wang Lixin 1997, pp. 261-265, 271-276, 365-377; Wang Tieya 1998, pp. 377-381; Wang Weijian 1987; Wu Xuanyi 1983; Zhang Haipeng 1998; Zhang 1992; *Zhongguo falü tushu zongmu* 1991, p. 738; Zou Zhenhuan 1989; Zou Zhenhuan 1996, pp. 55-58.

[35] In Chinese he is known under his Chinese name Ding Weiliang (丁韙良)

[36] Wheaton's *Elements of International Law* was first published in 1836. Martin's translation is based on the 1855 edition of Wheaton's work, which is the 6th edition of Wheaton's text and the first edition annotated by William Beach Lawrence.

[37] Covell 1978, p. 145

China during the 1860 crisis, to choose Wheaton's text. Martin had been working as Ward's interpreter during that time and took his advice as representing the American government's official view. A copy of Wheaton's book had been sent by the United States Department of State to the American commissioner in China in 1855 but the copy was lost in transit. The American minister Reed purchased another copy of the book in 1857 that most certainly was the basis for Martin's translation. Wheaton does not intend to hide national American interests in his work and was thus regarded as a better choice for American trade and diplomacy in China. Martin also found Wheaton more up to date and practical as a guide for a first introduction to the Western system of international law in China, as he relates in the preface to his translation:

> For the choice of my author, I offer no apology. My mind was first inclined to Vattel; but on reflection, it appeared to me, that the work of that excellent and lucid writer, might as a practical guide be somewhat out of date; and that to introduce it to the Chinese would not be unlike teaching the Ptolemaic system of the heavens.[38]

Robert Hart, at that time chief assistant to the inspector general of the Chinese Maritime Customs, had earlier translated 24 sections on the rights of legation, chapter 1 of part 3 in Wheaton's text, for the Zongli yamen (總理衙門). When Zongli yamen and its Grand Secretary Wenxiang (文祥) (1818-1876) in spring 1863 requested the American minister in Beijing, Anson Burlingame, for advice regarding a suitable text on international law for translation into Chinese, he also suggested Wheaton. It became at the same time known that Martin was already working on the translation in Shanghai. Martin's unfinished translation was consequently brought before Prince Gong, Wenxiang and the Zongli yamen.[39] Martin relates the occasion in *A Cycle of Cathay*:

> The Chinese ministers expressed much pleasure when I laid on the table my unfinished version of Wheaton, though they knew but little of its nature and content. "Does it contain the 'twenty-four sections'?" asked Wenhsiang, referring to a selection of important passages made for them by Mr. Hart. Being told something of the extent and scope of the work, he added: "This will be our guide when we send ministers to foreign countries." The translation, I explained, was not complete, but I

[38] Preface to the 1864 edition of *Wanguo gongfa*
[39] See Teng & Fairbank 1981, pp. 97-99

> intended to finish it without delay. All I asked of them was to appoint a competent official to assist me in a final revision, and then to print it at public expense.[40]

A special commission consisting of Chen Qin (陳欽), Li Changhua (李常華), Fang Junshi (方濬師), and Mao Hongtu (毛鴻圖) was assigned for the final revision and a sum of 500 taels was granted for printing and publication.

Yet there was still a certain hostility towards Martin's translation among Chinese officials and the final imperial sanction for publication was initially not granted. The imperial sanction was only given when a situation occurred where the text proved to be applicable to resolving a case pertaining to China. The situation was that Prussia has captured three Danish ships off Dagu port outside Tianjin in spring 1864 as prizes of war because of Bismarck's war with Denmark in Europe. Prince Gong maintained that Prussia had no right to capture Danish ships within Chinese maritime jurisdiction. His arguments were based on China's treaty with Prussia and Wheaton's arguments for territorial neutrality in time of war. In a memorial to the emperor from Prince Gong and the ministers if the Zongli Yamen on August 30th 1864 we read:

> We, your ministers, have compared this book on foreign laws and found that it does not completely correspond to the Chinese system. But in it there are occasional passages that are useful. For instance, in connection with the case where Danish ships were captured by Prussia in the waters outside of Tianjin, we, your ministers, used some parts from the book, without expressly saying so, in our argumentation. The Prussian minister acknowledged his mistake without saying a word. This is evidence [of its usefulness].

In the same memorial we find that Prince Gong and the other ministers argue together with Martin that a Chinese translation of Wheaton could be very useful to China without compelling China to follow the entire system on international law:

> We, your ministers, having guarded against making use of [such] books and following them, have told [Martin] that China has her own laws and institutions and that it would not be appropriate to refer to foreign books. Martin, however, has pointed out that although the *Collected Laws of the Qing dynasty* has been translated in foreign countries, China has never attempted to coerce these foreign counties to follow them. It

[40] Martin 1900, pp. 233-234

> cannot be that just because a foreign book [has been translated into Chinese] China will be forced to follow its customs.[41]

The case with the Danish ships was successfully resolved and Prince Gong won acceptance for the publication of Martin's translation that same year. Martin was also provided with an office near the Yamen to finish the translation, and the text was completed by mid-April 1864. Prince Gong was also asked by Martin to favour him with a preface to the publication. Prince Gong declined, aware of the potential hazard in being formally and perpetually associated with and supportive to foreign affairs and this branch of foreign learning. A minister of the Zongli yamen, Dong Xun (董恂) was entrusted with the task, writing a very low-key introduction to the translation of Wheaton's text and its relevance for China's international affairs. Zhang Sigui (張斯桂), a Chinese foreign affairs expert and later associate envoy to Japan was, however, in his preface to the text somewhat more courageous in his praise of international law as an instrument for China's international relations. The completed manuscript was published with the title *Wanguo gongfa* (萬國公法), *Public Law of Ten Thousand Nations*, at the Chongshiguan (崇實館) (Truth Hall Academy) in Beijing, which was a missionary school for poor Chinese children with an attached publishing house established by Martin himself in Beijing May 1864. Three hundred copies of the book were distributed to the provinces, and to the treaty ports in particular, for use by the local officials. The number of copies printed by Truth Hall Academy in 1864 must have been considerably higher than these 300.

Not only Chinese officials were initially hostile to the introduction of international law in China. The French chargé d'affaires M. Klecskowsky did not find it a good idea that China should be given an insight into European international legal practice: "Who is this man who is going to give the Chinese an insight into our European international law? Kill him–choke him off; he'll make us endless trouble."[42] We discern a European concern that China's role in the international community would be changing with the introduction of international law in China. This Martin's first translation of a text on international law became, however, the single most important text

[41] *Chouban yiwu shimo* vol. 5 (*Tong Zhi chao* 同治朝), *juan* 27, pp. 25a-26b; See also Covell 1978, p. 147 and Tsiang 1931.

[42] Martin 1900, p. 234

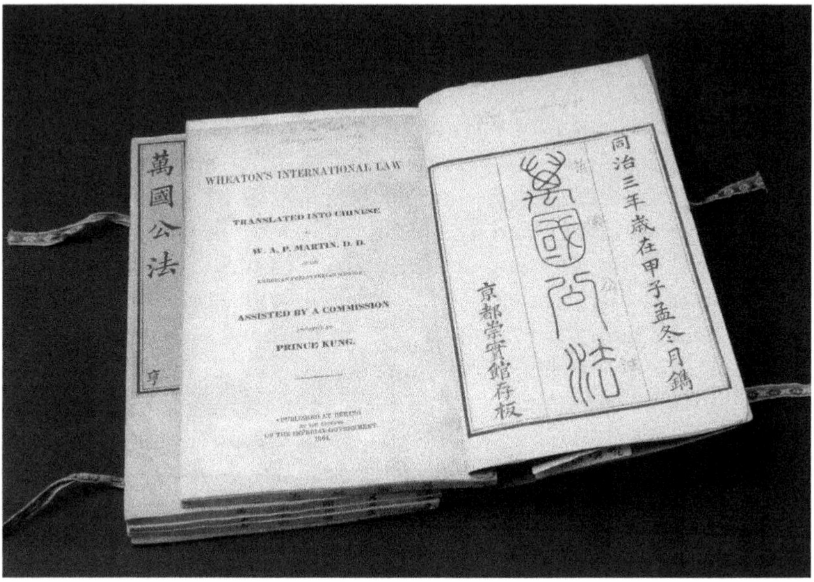

The 1864 edition of Wanguo gongfa *published by Chongshiguan.*

with regard to the introduction of international law in China as well as teaching material at the Tongwenguan (同文館) after Martin's first appointment as English teacher in 1865 and when he later was appointed professor of international law (*wanguo gongfa jiaoxi* 萬國公法教習) in 1867.[43] The translation was presented to Chinese officials both at central and provincial levels, and to officials in the five treaty ports to enable them to deal with the rights of foreign consular jurisdiction. Gradually also Chinese intellectuals and diplomats praised and recommended the *Wanguo gongfa* as a source for Chinese national strength and development. The diplomat and scholar Zeng Jize (曾紀澤) (1839-1890) is known to have often read and made frequent use of this text and other later Martin international law translations during his term as envoy to England, France and Russia 1878-1886.[44]

The *Wanguo gongfa* was republished in China both as a complete volume and in bits and pieces in other publications over the years. The first Japanese *kambun* edition of Martin's translation was published in

[43] Wang Weijian 1987, pp. 68-70

[44] Zou Zhenhuan 1996; Zou Zhenhuan 1989, p. 85; Tiao Tao 2001, pp. 125-126; Zeng Jize 1985

Kyoto in 1865, and the first partial Japanese translation was published in Tokyo in 1868. Partial and complete translations of Wheaton's text in Japan in the 1860s, 70s and 80s amount to more than a score, some based on the Chinese text and some later editions translated directly from the original. In 1872 Wheaton was also singled out as text for educational purposes in Japan. Wheaton became thus also in Japan the primary textual basis for the introduction of international law.[45] Through the Japanese edition Wheaton's text also found its way to Korea and thus secured the influence of Wheaton upon the development of international law in the Far East. Martin's translation was widely distributed in China and is the single most influential work with regard to the introduction of terminology as well as principles and practice in international law in late Qing times.

Tongwenguan and Martin translations in the 1870s and 1880s

Martin and the staff at the Tongwenguan started translating three Western texts on international law and diplomacy in the middle of the 1870s. The translation of the guide to diplomacy entitled *Manuel diplomatique*[46] by Charles de (Karl von) Martens (1790-1861) was the first of these texts to be completed, published in Chinese with the title *Xingyao zhizhang* (星軺指掌) in 1876.[47] A year later the translation of Woolsey's text was completed. Originally Bluntschli's *Das moderne Völkerrecht* was scheduled to be completed the year after, in 1878, but the work was delayed and the translation was published only in 1880.

The translation of Martens' text was done from the French text[48] at

[45] Wang Jian 2001, pp. 236-237

[46] Martens' work was first published in 1822 with the title *Manuel diplomatique*. Later editions carry the title *Guide diplomatique* or *Le guide diplomatique*. The Tongwenguan translation is based on the 5th edition of Martens' text annotated by M.F.H. Geffcken (Gefugen 葛福根) (1830-1896) and published in Leipzig and Paris in 1866.

[47] This text on the translation of Martens is primarily based on the following sources: Bennett 1967, p. 108; Chiu 1967, p. 488; Covell 1978, p. 194 n85; Farquhar 1971, p. 138; Hsü 1960, p. 138; Li Zhaojie 1999, p. 118; Liang Qichao 1896, p. 9a; Martin 1900, p. 235; Tian Tao & Li Zhuhuan 2000, pp. 356-357, 364; Tian Tao 2001, pp. 61, 65-67, 90-91; Wang Jian 2001, pp. 148-169, 237; Wang Lixin 1997, p. 367; Wang Tieya 1998, p. 381; Wang Yangzong 1995, p. 17; *Zhongguo falü tushu zongmu* 1991, p. 746; Zou Zhenhuan 1989, pp. 82-87

[48] Performed by Lian Fang (聯芳) and Qing Chang (慶常). Their manuscript was polished by Gui Rong (貴榮) and Du Fameng (杜法孟), while Martin subsequently

the French section of Tongwenguan.[49] Martens' original publication contains two parts, the first describing all practical and conventional aspects of diplomacy and diplomatic relations, the second being a collection of important documents on Western diplomatic relations. Only the first part of Martens' text was translated into Chinese. These Western documents were subsequently replaced by a few documents pertaining to Chinese diplomatic relations and attached to the text as a supplement.[50]

The original text is focussed on the functional and conventional aspects of diplomacy, being a practical guide to diplomacy, even including rules and conventions for the social life of diplomats. The only part of the French text where the more theoretical aspects of diplomatic relations between nations are brought up is in the introduction (*Considérations générales*) to Martens' work. Only the first part of this introduction is translated into Chinese, omitting the sections on positive vs. natural law of nations, the history and development of international law and treaties, and political economy, underscoring the pragmatic motivations behind this translation. Otherwise, the translation of the text proper is faithful to the original, also including most of the footnotes to the text.

The *Xingyao zhizhang* was published at a critical juncture in the history of the Chinese foreign service. China would be establishing diplomatic relations with Europe the coming year and a practical guide to diplomacy like this text came into immediate application.[51]

---

supervised the final proof-reading of the text.

[49] It appears that this same text by Martens was being translated into Chinese at the Jiangnan Arsenal in Shanghai simultaneously with the translation at the Tongwenguan. A list of texts being translated at the Jiangnan Arsenal and other Shanghai publishers but not yet published, printed in *Gezhi huibian* (格致彙編) August 1880 (p. 11b), refers to a title *Gongshi zhinan* (公使指南) translated by Carl T. Kreyer (Jin Kaili 金楷理) and Cai Xiling (蔡錫齡). One may find this title in a number of bibliographical lists of translations, including John Fryer's own lists referring to Martens and the *Guide diplomatique*, but never on the lists of already published books. Whether these references in fact are pointing to a separate Jiangnan translation of Martens' text or are erroneous references to the Tongwenguan edition cannot be determined. It may, however, be concluded that they all refer to the same original French text by Martens, and that the only published Chinese translation of this text is the Tongwenguan edition entitled *Xingyao zhizhang*.

[50] In a supplementary *juan* (*xujuan* 續卷) between the text proper and the Chinese diplomatic documents a translation of American consular regulations and treaties is inserted as a supplement to the otherwise French bias in the preceding text.

[51] A pocket edition of this text was even printed by private funding in Nanjing. (Zou Zhenhuan 1989, p. 85) Extensive portions of this book were also included in two

Wang Tao (王韜) (1828-1897) wrote a preface to a pocket edition printed as a practical handbook for Chinese diplomats, as the big character, large page Tongwenguan edition was not handy for the first generation of Chinese diplomats, where he emphasised the practicality of this text: "This book *Xingyao zhizhang* contains very detailed accounts of diplomatic relations between states. Anyone who is to serve Imperial China overseas may take this book as his guide."[52] Since the Tongwenguan, in addition to being a school of translation, also served as an educational institution for the first generation of Chinese diplomats to foreign countries, the *Xingyao zhizhang* became one of the most frequently used texts in these courses. From the very few extant exam papers left from the Tongwenguan exams we observe that most of the questions in the 1878 international law exam were related to diplomacy and the kind of diplomatic procedure introduced in the *Xingyao zhizhang* published only 2 years earlier. That was not so much the case in the later exams in the 1880s and 1890s, indicating that the content of Martens' text in the Tongwenguan exams gradually was replaced by the translations of Woolsey and Bluntschli after these texts had been published. We may conclude that the *Xingyao zhizhang* was the most important text in the education of China's first generation of diplomats in the 1870s. Equally, the *Xingyao zhizhang* was published in Japan already in 1879 and also served as a guide to the Japanese diplomatic service.[53]

In July 1868 Martin went back to America on furlough from his teaching duties at the Tongwenguan partly to pursue studies in international law for a period of one year. His sons Pascal and Winfred were students at Yale University at the time and Martin came into contact with the influential international law professor Theodore Dwight Woolsey (1801-1889) at Yale.[54] Martin had been appointed professor of international law and political economy at the College (Tongwenguan) in 1867, "committed the interests of the mission to other hands, and went home for special studies prior to entering the

---

editions of the state-craft texts, in the diplomacy section (*bangjiao* 邦交) of the *Huangchao jinshiwen xubian* (皇朝經世文續編) from 1888 (Ge Shijun 1964, *juan xia* 下, pp. 829-902) and the diplomacy section (*waijiao* 外交) of the *Huangchao jingshiwen tongbian* (皇朝經世文統編) from 1901 (Shao Zhitang 1972, pp. 1795-1799, 1923-1983; See also Tian Tao 2001, p. 67 n3).

[52] Wang Tao 1959, p. 246

[53] Wang Jian 2001, p. 237; Tian Tao 2001, p. 61

[54] Covell 1978, pp. 167-168 n169; See also Tian Tao 2001, p. 70

duties of my new chair".[55] Martin was inspired by the fact that Woolsey's book *Introduction to the study of international law: Designed as an aid in teaching, and in historical studies* was used for teaching purposes at Yale, and found it suitable also for training students at the Tongwenguan and for translation into Chinese. When Martin returned to the College in 1869 he took up his duties as professor of international law, and was also appointed president of the College. [56] Duly, the first text Martin worked on during his professorship at the College was Woolsey's influential work.[57] The translation was published with the title *Gongfa bianlan* (公法便覽) at the Tongwenguan in 1877.[58]

We may assume that the *Gongfa bianlan* was frequently used for teaching purposes at the Tongwenguan. Martin's translation of Woolsey was also used for the teaching of international law at other universities established after the Sino-Japanese war, such as the Hunanese Academy of Current Affairs (Shiwu xuetang 時務學堂) teaching international law from 1897. [59] In spite of the crucial importance the translation of Wheaton's text had in China, it has often been pointed out that Martin's translation of Woolsey was much more important in terms of giving imperial China a more scholarly, less nationally biased, more comprehensive, and a much more updated source to the current status of international law in the West.

Martin had translated two major American works on international law before 1880 and may have felt an urge to make up for the national bias by supplying the collection of international law texts in Chinese with a more recent and a non-English language text. His choice fell on the Swiss publicist Johann Caspar Bluntschli, whose text *Das*

---

[55] Martin 1900, p. 241

[56] Wang Weijian 1987, pp. 68-70

[57] In the translation Martin was assisted by Wang Fengzao (汪鳳藻), Feng Yi (鳳儀), Zuo Bing (左秉), Long Deming (隆德明), Gui Rong (貴榮) and Gui Lin (桂林).

[58] Woolsey's work was first published in 1860. Martin's translation is based on the 3rd edition of Woolsey's work published in 1871. A facsimile edition of the Chinese translation was printed in Japan in 1881. The text may never have had any influence in Korea since no edition of the text can be found in Korean libraries.

This text on the translation of Woolsey is primarily based on the following sources: Angle 2002, p. 110; Chiu 1967, p. 488; Covell 1978, pp. 156-158, 168, 194 n85; Farquhar 1971, p. 138; Hsü 1960, p. 138; Li Guilian 1998a, pp. 11, 39; Li Zhaojie 1999, pp. 115-118; Martin 1900, p. 235; Tian Tao & Li Zhuhuan 2000, pp. 357, 364; Tian Tao 2001, pp. 67-72; Wang Jian 2001, pp. 148-169; Wang Lixin 1997, p. 366; Wang Tieya 1998, p. 381; *Zhongguo falü tushu zongmu* 1991, p. 739

[59] Li Guilian 1998a, pp. 37-41

moderne Völkerrecht der civilisierten Staaten als Rechtsbuch dargestellt had been published in German in 1868.[60] Bluntschli's text could also to a greater extent than the former translations serve as a reference work on international law in Chinese, as the text is less theoretical and is organised in short instructive passages suitable as a reference guide.[61] The translated text was published at the Tongwenguan with the title *Gongfa huitong* (公法會通) in 1880.[62] Bluntschli became first and foremost known in China for his theories on political science, and his theories presented in the Chinese translation of his *Allgemeine Statslehre* are discussed in length by Liang Qichao (梁啟超) (1873-1929) in 1903.[63] Bluntschli was teaching law at Heidelberg University from 1861 and Martin went to visit him there in June 1881. Bluntschli expressed great enthusiasm for the fact that his book had been translated into Chinese.[64]

The French text on the rules of warfare on land entitled *Les Lois de la Guerre sur Terre* is based on a manuscript by the Swiss publicist

---

[60] Martin, however, did not work on the German edition but translated from the French edition entitled *Le Droit International Codifié* (1870) and subsequently revised the Chinese text against the German edition. The French department at the Tongwenguan had been established in 1866, while the German department was only to be established in 1888, which is why the text was not translated directly from its original publication in German.

[61] Bluntschli's *Geschichte des allgemeinen Statsrechts und der Politik* was translated into Japanese in 1881 with the title *Kokuhô hanron* (國法凡論). This book was not circulated in China as such but the introduction to the text (*xuyan* 緒言) was published in Chinese in the *Yishu huibian* (譯書彙編) vol. 1 and 2 (1900-01) in Tokyo. Bluntschli's work *Allgemeine Statslehre* was translated via Japanese into Chinese and published in Tokyo by Shanlin yishuguan (善鄰譯書館) in 1899 under the title *Guojiaxue* (國家學) ascribed to the authorship of *Bolunzhili* (伯倫智理 or 伯崙智理).

[62] This text on the translation of Bluntschli is primarily based on the following sources: Covell 1978, p. 194 n85; Farquhar 1971, p. 139; Harrell 1992, p. 92; Hsü 1960, p. 138; Huang, Yi 1995, pp. 85-88; Hughes 1968, pp. 116-118; Li Guilian 1998a, p. 11; Li Zhaojie 1999, pp. 118-119; Martin 1900, p. 235; Masini 1993, p. 74 n79; Pusey 1983, p. 140; Tian Tao & Li Zhuhuan 2000, pp. 356-357, 364; Tian Tao 2001, pp. 72-77; Wang Jian 2001, pp. 148-169, 237; Wang Lixin 1997, pp. 366-367; Wang Tieya 1998, p. 381; *Zhongguo falü tushu zongmu* 1991, p. 739; Zou Zhenhuan 1989, pp. 82-87.

[63] Liang Qichao 1996, *Wenji* (文集) *juan* 13, pp. 67-89. Through Liang's writings Bluntschli also became known in Korea. The *Gongfa huitong* was published in Japan already in 1881. (Wang Jian 2001, p. 237) The Chinese translation of Bluntschli's *Das moderne Völkerrecht der civilisierten Staaten als Rechtsbuch dargestellt* was in turn adopted and published in Korea with the title *Kongpop hoet'ong* in 1896. This edition was the first Korean text on international law and was already in 1897 applied as basis for the first Korean law based on Western legal theory and practice.

[64] Bluntschli 1884, vol. 3, p. 488

Gustave Moynier revised by Bluntschli and other English, French, Prussian, Russian, Austrian, and Italian members of Institut de Droit International.[65] The original text is formulated as a manual of rules for warfare on land and not as a theoretical text on international law. It was therefore taken up for translation at the Tongwenguan because of its applicative potential. Martin met Moynier in Europe in 1881 and was probably presented a copy of the *Les Lois de la Guerre sur Terre* by Moynier personally. This was also one of the important factors for including this short text into the library of Tongwenguan international law publications. The text was translated by Martin and the students at the French section of the Tongwenguan and published in 1883 with the title *Ludi zhanli xinxuan* (陸地戰例新選), *A New Collection of the Rules of Warfare on Land.*[66] The translated "original preface" in the Chinese text is in fact not a translation of the introduction to the text proper by Moynier but an abridged translation of the introduction to a supplement to the original text entitled *Notes Explicative du Manuel relatif aux Lois de la guerre*, also written by Moynier and dated 1880. Only minor changes have been made to the text for the translation.[67]

Martin's text on international law in ancient China

William A.P. Martin was already in 1864 determined to show that traces of an international code could be found in ancient China. In the English preface to his translation of Wheaton he draws up parallels between the ancient Greek and the Chinese political tradition:

> International law in its present form is the mature fruit of Christian civilization. It springs, however, spontaneously from the intercourse of

---

[65] The final text was discussed by the Institute and sanctioned at a general meeting of the Institute published in 1880.

[66] This text on the translation of the rules of warfare on land is primarily based on the following sources: Chiu 1967, p. 488, fn 37; Covell 1978, p. 194 n85; Hsü 1960, p. 138; Li Zhaojie 1999, p. 119; Martin 1900, p. 235; Tian Tao 2001, pp. 83-85; Wang Jian 2001, pp. 148, 150; Wang Lixin 1997, p. 367; Wang Tieya 1998, p. 381.

[67] The translation of 3 statutes for the Institute is also taken from the introduction to *Notes Explicatives*. The original text proper consists of 3 parts; *Principes Generaux*, *Application des Principes Generaux* and *Sanction Penale*, where the two last sections are divided into 90 enumerated regulations for the applications and sanctions of warfare on land. The Chinese translation has included all three sections among the enumerated passages without distinguishing between them, the entire text consisting of altogether 86 passages (*tiao* 條).

> nations; and a rudimentary code was even recognized by the states of Greece at an early date. About the same time, analogous rules were observed by the feudal kingdoms into which the Chinese empire then was divided. Acknowledging a nominal allegiance to the house of Chow, they were really independent, and the varying relations which they sustained to each other in the intercourse of peace and war through a succession of centuries gave rise to numerous usages, a collection of which would be at once curious and instructive.[68]

Martin indicates that China had a code of international intercourse during the Spring and Autumn period, which was shattered with the unification of the Central plains under the Qin. These deliberations regarding a rudimentary origin of international law in ancient China were not unfamiliar to contemporary Chinese intellectuals, as also expressed by Zhang Sigui in his preface to the same edition of *Wanguo gongfa*. This is also the point that Martin brings up in the conclusion of his publication on international law in ancient China:

> Chinese statesmen have pointed out the analogy of their own country at that epoch with the political division of modern Europe. In their own record they find usages, words, and ideas, corresponding to the terms of our modern international law; and they are by that fact the more disposed to accept the international code of Christendom, which it is no utopian vision to believe will one day become a bond of peace and justice between all the nations of the earth.[69]

From 1880 to 1882 Martin stayed in America, and during this time he was appointed by the Zongli yamen to collect information on education in different countries. Martin gathered information on different national educational systems in America, Europe and Japan and finally documented his findings in a book entitled *Xixue kaolüe* (西學考略) published in 1883. In this book Martin does not only discuss education but also emphasises the importance of international law in military education. During his travels in Europe he met with several specialists on international law and discussed with them his ideas about an ancient Chinese system of international law. One of the persons he met was Gustave Moynier, the main author of *Les Lois de la Guerre sur Terre*, who seems to have made a particularly good impression on Martin. When Martin was invited to give a talk at the Congress of Orientalists in Berlin September 13th 1881 he used this

[68] *Wanguo gongfa*, preface p. 1
[69] Martin 1894, p. 141

opportunity to elaborate his theories on a Chinese origin of international law in a presentation entitled "Traces of International Law in Ancient China".[70] Wang Fengzao (汪鳳藻) translated the text into Chinese and had it published at the Tongwenguan with the title *Zhongguo gushi gongfa lunlüe* (中國古世公法論略) in 1884.[71] Only two years after its Chinese publication the text was also published in Japan in 1886 with the title *Sina kodai bankoku kôhô* (支那古代万國公法).[72]

Martin argues, in his article, that the situation in ancient Greece and in China of the Spring and Autumn period was similar with regard to the existence of a rudimentary international legal code. When the Roman Empire disintegrated, that rudimentary code developed into a practice of international intercourse between independent and equal states in Europe. Since the history of the Chinese empire is fundamentally different with regard to the disintegration and subsequent re-establishment of a unified empire, a code of intercourse between equal, independent states based on a balance of power did not develop in China. In the East a tributary system of unequal and dependent states developed, and the Western model of international law was only introduced to China with the Opium wars and foreign trade on Chinese soil. Martin searches ancient Chinese literary and

[70] A condensed outline of his presentation was published in *Congrès des Orientalists* (no. 22, section 2, pp. 71-78) in Berlin 1882. A revised version of his paper was published in the *International Review* (no. 14, pp. 63-77) in New York January 1883 and reprinted in the *Chinese Recorder* (no. 14, pp. 380-393) in Shanghai September-October 1883. The paper was further revised and published with the title "International Law in Ancient China" in Martin's *Hanlin Papers* (second series, chapter 5) in Shanghai 1894 and in *Lore of Cathay* (chapter 22) in New York 1901. Martin's paper was also translated into French by Martin and Professor J. Hornung of the University of Geneva and published with the title "Les vestiges d'un droit international dans l'ancienne Chine" in *Revue de droit international* (no. 14, pp. 227-242) in 1882. For further references to non-Chinese editions of Martin's paper see Walker 1971, pp. 129-130. This text is primarily based on the following sources: Covell 1978, pp. 194 n. 85, 232; Farquhar 1971, pp. 128-141; Li Zhaojie 1999, pp. 54-76; Tan Ruqian 1981, p. 173; Tian Tao 2001, pp. 77-83; Walker 1971, pp. 129-132; Wang Jian 2001, pp. 148, 150; Wang Lixin 1997, p. 367; Zou Zhenhuan 1989, pp. 82-87.

[71] At the same time the introductory pages of this text were published in the Chinese language local Guangzhou daily newspaper *Shubao* (述報) (*Shubao* 1964, pp. 301-302, 361), one of the first of its kind in China.

[72] A study of the reception of Martin and the early reception of international law in Japan is found in Hirohiko Otsuka's article "Japan's Early Encounters with the Concept of the 'Law of Nations'" published in *The Japanese Annual of International Law* no. 13 1969. (Otsuka 1969)

historical sources to find traces of a system of international code and conduct in pre-Qin times. He draws up some of the main elements of such a system and claims that it is "quite possible that text-books on the subject of international relations may have existed in ancient China, without coming down to our times, just as the Greeks had books on that subject, of which nothing now survives but their titles".[73]

It may initially seem that Martin's deliberation on the Chinese origins of international law were better received by a Western audience than by the general Chinese. Liang Qichao comments negatively on the Chinese reception of Martin's analysis in 1896 but is apparently supportive of the idea of the existence of an ancient Chinese system of international laws himself:

> *Zhongguo gushi gongfa lunlüe* is a book of which W.A.P. Martin is very self-complacent. It is, however, not uncommon among Chinese scholars to ridicule a Westerner discussing ancient Chinese matters. [In fact,] in China's feudal era a number of states coexisted. International laws were held in high esteem, certainly not secondary to their position in ancient Greece. If the masters and scholars [of ancient China] had collected and compiled [these laws] they could have constituted stacks of books. There are many points where the principles of Western politics coincide with that of ancient China. Why should this be confined only to international law?[74]

The *Zhongguo gushi gongfa lunlüe* became a part of the Tongwenguan library of translated texts on international law. As we shall discuss in the following chapter, however, this text acquired a particular role in the subsequent discourse on international law in China. Martin's deliberations on a Chinese origin of an international legal code were forcefully advocated by Chinese intellectuals in the late 1890s, a discourse with extensions far into today's discourse on China in international affairs.

---

[73] Martin 1894, p. 141
[74] Liang Qichao 1896, p. 9a

"President W.A.P. Martin and the faculty of Chinese Imperial University". Photo in Martin's book The Lore of Cathay.

Texts on international law by Martin in the early 20th century

As we have seen above Martin had translated three major texts on international law during his presidency and time at the Tongwenguan between 1865 and 1894, two American and one Swiss-German texts. In order to make up for this national bias he was determined to translate an English text-book on international law and started working on the text *A Treatise on International Law* by William Edward Hall (1836-1894) when he was appointed president of the Imperial University (京師大學堂) in Beijing in 1898. His work was interrupted by the outbreak of the Boxer rebellion. He managed, however, to save the manuscripts and continued his work until the text was completed in December 1902. That same year Martin was released from his post at the Imperial University and went back to America.

The text is translated by Martin with the assistance of Qi Ce'ao (綦策鰲) formulating the Chinese text and published at the Society for the Diffusion of Christian and General Knowledge among the Chinese (Guangxuehui 廣學會) in Shanghai in 1903 with the title *Gongfa xinbian* (公法新編).[75] Martin's text is, however, strictly speaking not a translation of Hall's text. Martin has abridged and reformulated Hall's text and changed its form of presentation. The discursive text in Hall's book has been changed into a didactic form with simple questions and short answers. Martin states in the *Fanli* (凡例) that this was done in order to make the text more suitable for teaching purposes in China.[76]

Martin had left the Tongwenguan in 1894 and been appointed president of the Imperial University. The university was temporarily closed between 1900 and 1902, because of the Boxer rebellion, and Martin was officially dismissed from his post in 1902. Martin was on his way home to America when he received a telegram from governor general Zhang Zhidong (張之洞) (1837-1909) inviting him to take up a position as president of Wuchang University (武昌大學堂). He returned again to China and Wuchang in 1902 only to find that the university had not yet been established. Martin never became president of the Wuchang University but he enjoyed the remuneration and prestige as university president during his years in Hubei. In practice Martin's duties in Wuchang consisted of teaching international law, history and geography to Zhang Zhidong's officials at the Hubei Mandarin Institute, the Hubei Shixueyuan (湖北仕學院). Martin was serving as the president of this institution as well as of the Hubei Jimei xuetang (濟美學堂), positions he held until 1905. Martin went back to America in 1905 but returned to China already in 1906 and stayed there until his death in 1916.

In the preface to the publication of his lectures at the Mandarin

---

[75] Hall's first edition of *A Treatise on International Law* dated 1880 is partly based on an earlier publication by Hall, *The Rights and Duties of Neutrals* 1874. (Chapter IV of part 1 and chapters II-XI of part 4) *A Treatise on International Law* was re-published several times with certain additions and amendments every time. (For more biographical details on William Edward Hall see Holland 1898, pp. 302-305) The 4th edition was published in 1895 and is, most probably, the textual basis for the Chinese translation. *A Treatise on International Law* had been translated into Japanese with the title *Kokusai kôhô* (國際公法) already in 1899. Martin, however, does not make any reference to the Japanese text in his translation. This text on the translation of Hall is primarily based on the following sources: Farquhar 1971, p. 140; Li Zhaojie 1999, p. 119; Tian Tao 2001, pp. 97-98; Wang Jian 2001, p. 151; Wang Lixin 1997, pp. 367-368; Wang Tieya 1998, p. 381.

[76] Hall's basic division into 4 parts; general principles, laws in time of peace, laws in time of war and laws of neutrality, has been kept in Martin's translation. That is also generally the case with the division into chapters. But Hall's subdivision into sections under each chapter is replaced by Martin's topical questions. Occasionally the translators have also added their own comments and interpretations in smaller type at the end of the answer-text.

Institute Martin reflects on his students' lack of knowledge on history and how this inhibits their ability to comprehend the workings of international law:

> At the Mandarin Institute of this city, I have had for (sic!) hearer's, first and last, some hundreds of highly educated men, all in expectation of official appointments. But learned and gifted as they are, they know too little of history to understand the Nature of International Law. Hence I was led to insert among my other lectures an intercalary course on Political History.[77]

The lectures which comprise the basis for publication were given by Martin at the Hubei Shixueyuan, in addition to his regular courses on diplomacy and international law, in order to prepare his students for an understanding of international law. The Chinese publication of his lectures carries the title *Bangjiao tiyao* (邦交提要) with the English subtitle *Outlines of History with Special Reference to International Law*, and was published by the Society for the Diffusion of Christian and General Knowledge among the Chinese in Shanghai in 1904.[78] These lectures mainly focus on the history and geography of the European nations, including America, Thailand and Japan, with special emphasis on political history and diplomatic relations. Of a total of 24 lectures only the first two introduce some general aspects of international law and diplomacy.[79] Martin emphasises in the introductory explanations that this introduction in no respect may replace the four major Chinese texts on international law translated by himself, *Wanguo gongfa*, *Gongfa bianlan*, *Gongfa huitong* and *Gongfa xinbian*. This publication was only meant as a supplement to these major works on international law and as background reading for those not familiar with Western political history.

The lectures were orally performed by Martin and formulated in literary Chinese prose by Qi Ce'ao in much the same way as the two had worked on the translation of Hall's work on international law a few months earlier. The purpose of this publication is obviously also very much didactic as the text is formulated as short questions with

---

[77] *Bangjiao tiyao* English preface

[78] This text on Martin's lectures is primarily based on the following sources: Farquhar 1971, p. 140; Tian Tao 2001, pp. 97-98; Wang Lixin 1997, p. 368; Wang Weijian 1987, p. 71; Wang Tieya 381.

[79] The other 22 lectures all present the specific national political histories of these nations.

simple, instructive answers to students of international law and diplomacy. This publication was his last contribution to the introduction of international law into China. Chinese scholars trained in law in Japan were already very active both in the translation and introduction of terms for international relations in China. The Western period for the introduction of international law into China was coming to an end in the early years of the 20th century. Martin and Tongwenguan had, however, not been unaccompanied in the field of international law translations in late 19th century China. A parallel tradition of translations from Western texts on international law was taking shape in the Jiangnan area. Before we take a closer look at this contending tradition and the later influence from Japan, however, we shall engage in some considerations about the language and terminology established and practised by Martin and his Tongwenguan staff.

The terminological challenges facing Martin and the staff at Tongwenguan[80]

As we have seen above, William A. P. Martin was the first to be confronted with the task of systematically supplying the Chinese language with adequate and suitable modes for presenting the theories of international relations in a Chinese linguistic framework. When or if to accept the applicability of the Western system for international relations referred to as international law had important implications for China, which we will discuss in the following chapters. The discourse on China's role and position in the world community of states also took many twists and turns before the notions of sovereignty, balance of power, and national rights and obligations in the family of nations were accepted as a plausible way of identifying China as a state among states. The fact that Martin's "translingual practice" in the sensitive areas of international relations in fact primarily took place at the Tongwenguan under the auspices of the "foreign office", the Zongli yamen, is of course highly significant for the claims to power involved in the process of accessing the rules of

[80] Some of the material in this subchapter may also be found in Svarverud 2001 and Svarverud 2004

the game in international affairs as it was perceived by the Western nations. Had it not been for the special role of Martin and the Tongwenguan, Chinese access to international law would most probably have been postponed to a later phase of the modernisation of China. Martin coined the first lexicon of technical terms in international law in China under the scrutiny of Chinese authorities. The precipitation of the terms involved in international law into the Chinese intellectual discourse was, however, to a large extent not the result of Martin's endeavours. As we shall show later the high tide of the intellectual debate on international law and its application in China took place after the Sino-Japanese war and under strong influence from the Japanese experience.

Martin coined a relatively small number of neologisms for his international law translations from the 1860s onwards. In most cases of conveying new ideas within the theoretical discipline of international law he was drawing on the current Chinese lexicon of terms and phrases. The most prominent case of a term coined for his translations is his use of the binome *quanli* (權利) for 'rights', also encountered in early Chinese literature but adopted as a neologism and a technical term for 'rights' only by Martin in his 1864 translation of Wheaton. The term 'rights' in Wheaton is consequently translated into *quanli*, or short *quan* (權), throughout Martin's translation, for instance where Wheaton discusses "absolute international rights of states" (*zhuguo ziran zhi quan* 諸國自然之權): "The rights, which sovereign States enjoy with regard to one another, may be divided into rights of two sorts: *primitive*, or *absolute* rights; *conditional*, or *hypothetical* rights."[81] The challenges confronting the Tongwenguan translators when entering the task of translating Wheaton and later texts is not made explicit in the 1864 edition of Wheaton. We get, however, a glimpse of the considerations in the translators' introduction to the translation of Woolsey's *Introduction to the study of international law: Designed as an aid in teaching, and in historical studies* published in 1877:

> Public law is a separate field of study and there should thus be devised a specific vocabulary for this purpose. Therefore, when there occasionally are passages in the original text that are difficult to render

[81] Wheaton 1866 (1848), p. 75; 凡自主之國相待，操權有二，曰自有之原權，曰偶有之特權。(Martin 1864, *juan* 2, p. 1a)

> comprehensively in Chinese, then the text in Chinese may sometimes seem strained. Take for instance the character *quan* (權). In this book it carries not only the meaning of someone being in power but also the meaning of the share ordinary people ought to obtain ('rights'). Sometimes a character *li* (利) is added to this meaning, such as in the passage: 'the rights enjoyed by the common people' etc. Passages and terms like this may seem awkward at first sight but when one has encountered them several times one comes to realize that there is no way other than to use such an expression.[82]

Much can and has been written on the connotations of 'rights' in Chinese and its genetic relationship to the homonyme *quanli* (權力) meaning 'power' which will not be reiterated here. It suffices to conclude that Martin's translation of Wheaton was introduced into Japan in the 1860s[83] and gradually the *kanji* translation for rights (*kenri* 權利) imported from Martin became current in Japanese political discourse. It appears as if the later concurrence of these terms in Chinese and Japanese represents a return loan from Japanese.[84] But, in fact, the term *quanli* for 'rights' was current in China throughout the period. It was, however, with the intellectual currents from Japan influencing China in the early 20th century that the discourse on rights and popular power, and hence the use of the term *quanli*, gained momentum in China.

In other cases of neologisms coined for the translation of Wheaton, such as the term *wanguo gongfa* (萬國公法), or simply *gongfa* (公法), for 'international law' and the cluster of terms related to 'sovereignty' and 'independence' (*zhuquan* 主權, *zizhuquan* 自主權, *zili* 自立, *zizhu* 自主) Martin also contributed to the early formation of technical terms drawing on the current language. In the case of *wanguo gongfa*, this term strictly speaking only reflects the early notion of *jus gentium*, *law of nations*, discussed in chapter 1, and not the semantics of the

---

[82] *Gongfa bianlan*, *Fanli* pp. 2b-3a

[83] A copy reached Japan already in 1865 and, according to Alexis Dudden, a Japanese "translation" was published in 1869 (Dudden 1999, pp. 169, 171-172). Lydia Liu refers to a Japanese *kambun* edition published in 1865 and a new edition in 1876 (Liu 1999, p. 136). Wang Jian refers to the following years for editions of the text in Japan: 1865, 1868 (3 editions), 1870, 1871, 1875, 1876, 1881, 1886 (Wang Jian 2001, p. 236)

[84] Originally claimed by scholars such as Gao Minkai (高名凱) and Wang Lida (王立達) to be a return loan from Japanese. Recently, Masini has argued that *quanli*, and many other related terms, were in fact current in China throughout the period and are not return loans from the Japanese. (Masini 1993, pp. 47, 76, 87, 192; See also Liu 1995, pp. 18, 34, 279-280; Liu 1999, pp. 148-152; Svarverud 2001)

later term 'international law' coined by Jeremy Bentham (1748-1832) in the early 19th century. Martin's term did not outlive the later japanisation and the Japanese innovation *kokusai/guoji* (國際), which to a greater extent represents the notion of 'inter'- nationality. In addition, a number of words and phrases were applied systematically as technical terms for international legal concepts, such as *juwai* (局外) for 'neutrality', *gongyi* (公義) for 'justice', *dahai* (大海) for 'high seas', *dongwu* (動物) for 'movable property', *zhiwu* (植物) for 'real property', *junshi zhi fa* (均勢之法) for 'balance of power', *guofa* (國法) for 'constitution', *mingxu* (明許) and *moxu* (默許) for 'express consent' and 'tacit consent', *xingfa* (性法) for 'natural law', *guanxia* (管轄) for 'jurisdiction', *bu gui difang guanxia* (不歸地方管轄) for 'immunity'/'extraterritoriality', *minzhu zhi guo* (民主之國) for 'republic',[85] *junquan wuxian zhi guo* (君權無限之國) for 'absolute monarchy', *junquan youxian zhi guo* (君權有限之國) for 'limited (constitutional) monarchy', and a number of derived terms.[86] The most surprising gap in Martin's lexicon may be the absence of a technical term for the generic notion of 'duty'/'obligation', a gap that was only filled adequately by the 20th century importation of the Meiji Japanese *kanji*-term *yiwu* (義務).[87] In spite of Martin's efforts to make his language as lucid as possible by his choice of style and terminology, he was not entirely successful, if we are to judge from contemporary reactions. Lydia Liu ascribes this to Martin's use of neologisms, which certainly is a part of the problem: "Martin's translations often employed neologisms at the expense of intelligibility. Some of the vocabulary seems obscure at the time but has since grown self-evident. This is because the words have been gradually assimilated into the language as modern China itself

---

[85] Xiong Yuezhi argues that the term *minzhu* in *Wanguo gongfa* in fact already means 'democracy' (Xiong Yuezhi 2001, p. 74). That may be contested, and it seems that there are very few cases where the term *minzhu* in *Wanguo gongfa* may not equally be said to be referring to the political system of a republic rather than the principles of democracy as such. The differences between these two different semantic contents of the term *minzhu* are, however, not always very clear.

[86] See also Masini 1993, pp. 46-48, 189-190, 220-222; Liu 1995, pp. 267-268, 271, 279-281; Liu 1999; Wang Jian 2001, pp. 157-186

[87] Masini claims that the term *yiwu* appears in *Wanguo gongfa* in this meaning and was imported to Japan through that work. (Masini 1993, p. 213; see also Liu 1995, p. 268) I have not been able to identify any occurrences of *yiwu* in Martin's translation, even with the use of a computerised version of the text, and it appears as if Masini this time is mistaken.

underwent massive changes through increased exposure to translations of European texts in the past century."[88] Most probably, the subject matter itself and its alien theoretical substance have also contributed to the obscurity of his language in China in the 1860s.

Prince Gong also found Martin's language disorderly and difficult to grasp and complained that it would need to be explained in person.[89] Martin extends his own apologies in the preface for the sacrifice of literary style:

> In the choice of style, perspicuity has been my object rather than elegance, though both have been sacrificed when needful to the higher considerations of fidelity. To the native reader, it may therefore appear hampered by too close an adherence to the original; but this disadvantage is more than counterbalanced by the evidence which is thus afforded that the translator has not abandoned his text and undertaken to treat the subject in his own way.

Martin's semi-classical style is, however, simple and paraphrastic and will not have posed great linguistic problems for the contemporary literati, and will have given its contemporary Chinese readership a fairly accurate introduction to the laws and regulations of Western international law. Many contemporary Chinese historians have criticized Martin's language and international law lexicon for lacking accuracy and transparency. Such speculations lack historic socio-linguistic perspectives and evaluate the innovative language of an entirely new branch of learning by contemporary linguistic standards with all its later Japanese influence. One may assume that the topics of Martin's translations were unfamiliar and even obscure to its readers at first. That was, however, first and foremost due to unfamiliarity with the terms and conditions of Western international law. If Martin's language had to a larger extent survived the Japanese influence in the early 20th century Martin's translations may have seemed less obscure to contemporary Chinese historians.

The second translation of a text related to international law came with the publication of *Xingyao zhizhang* 1876 and made certain adjustments to the vocabulary established by Martin through the *Wanguo gongfa*. The two translators rely on Martin's vocabulary and formulations from *Wanguo gongfa* and seem to be quite comfortable

[88] Liu 1999, p. 148
[89] Teng & Fairbank 1981, p. 98

with the new language of international law and diplomacy in Chinese. They apply the terms for 'rights', 'neutrality', 'jurisdiction', 'extra-territoriality' etc. from Martin's vocabulary without hesitation. The only systematic difference from the translation of Wheaton is the introduction of the technical term *minzheng zhi guo* (民政之國) for 'republic', which is also explained in the *Fanli*. Otherwise one notices that the word *ziyou* (自由) as a translation of 'liberty'/'freedom' has been integrated into the current Chinese language, which may not, however, be attributed to the staff at the Tongwenguan.[90] The disinclination to establish a term for the generic notion of 'duty'/ 'obligation' from the translation of Wheaton is maintained in this text as well. Only the practical aspects of obligation in diplomacy are represented by the terms *zhishou* (職守) as appointments in office, and *ze* (責) or *zeren* (責任) as an area of responsibility.

With the 1877 translation of Woolsey the language and vocabulary follow the already well-established Tongwenguan lexicon in international law created by the translations of Wheaton and Martens. We may, however, see from this text that Martin is continuously working on the improvement of this lexicon. The term *minzheng* (民政) for 'republican' from the translation of Martens is maintained, while the earlier term *minzhu* (民主) for 'republican' seems to be taking on connotations of a democratic form of government, as in the term *minzhu zhengquan* (民主政權) as a translation of 'democracy' in the translation of Woolsey.[91] The inconveniences of the terms *dongwu* (動物) and *zhiwu* (植物) for 'movable property' and 'real property' are solved by replacing these with the two terms *xingchan* (行產) and *hengchan* (恆產). For the notion of 'duty'/'obligation' the term *zeshou* (責守), or short *ze* (責), is used relatively methodically without firmly establishing a generic technical term.

With the translations of Bluntschli and the rules for warfare on land in the 1880s the lexicon established by Martin at the Tongwenguan is continued. Only with Wang Fengzao's translation in 1884 of Martin's deliberation on international law in ancient China did an innovation in the Tongwenguan lexicon appear. Martin and the Tongwenguan staff never translated texts on private international law and did not establish

---

[90] cf. Masini 1993, pp. 221-222; See also Xiong Yuezhi 2001

[91] Again, the differences between references to 'republican' versus 'democratic' are often unclear. Se note on the term *minzhu* and Xiong Yuezhi's elaborations in note 85 above.

a technical term for 'private international law' or 'conflict of laws'. The terms *gongfa zhi sitiao* (公法之私條)[92] and *siquan zhi fa* (私權之法) used in *Wanguo gongfa* for the notion of 'private international law' does not reappear in later texts but has been replaced by the term *tongrong lüli* (通融律例) referring to the theoretical aspects of this part of international law usually designated 'conflict of laws'.

When Martin published his translation of Hall in Shanghai in 1903 he had already left the Tongwenguan and the Japanese Meiji vocabulary, which we will discuss later, was beginning to pour into the Chinese lexicon. *A Treatise on International Law* by Hall had been translated into Japanese already in 1899. There are, however, no indications that Martin made any use of the Japanese text in his work. Martin, on the contrary, maintains his own use of vocabulary on international law established through his earlier translations and makes no mention of any Japanese translation in his preface or in the *Fanli*. It is thus somewhat idiosyncratic to find that whereas Martin clings to his earlier translation of 'international law' as *gongfa* throughout his translated text, Duan Fang in his preface refers to the same term twice with the Japanese loan term *guojifa* (國際法). Again, when the translation of Martin's lectures at the Mandarin Institute appears in 1904 the text is formulated within the Martin and Tongwenguan tradition of international law vocabulary. No influence from the Japanese vocabulary, already gaining momentum in most other international law publications of this time, can be seen. The only exception may again be observed in Duan Fang's preface using the term *guoji* (國際) for 'international'.

Martin and the staff of translators at the Tongwenguan established the first systematic Chinese lexicon for international law. Through the translation of a number of such texts over a period of 40 years the vocabulary became fairly stable and well accepted in the circles of high-ranking officials, diplomats and politicians in China.[93] One would expect this lexicon to have gained prestige in the vocabulary of new learning through its semi-official status and its close relationship to the claims to power, thus securing its durability and stability

[92] See also Masini 1993, p. 173

[93] We also find that Martin's lexicon formed the basis for other translations and texts on international law in the early 20th century, such as Allen and Cai Erkang's translation of Lawrence's *A Handbook of Public International Law* published in Shanghai in 1903.

beyond the potential incursion from new and other sets of terms. That was, however, not the case. When John Fryer embarked on the project of translating a number of international law texts in the Shanghai area in the late 19th century, he established an entirely new set of technical terms in many respects competing with the Beijing Tongwenguan tradition. The claims to power vested in the Zongli yamen Tongwenguan tradition were manifest enough to withstand the relatively short-lived terminological influence from Fryer in Shanghai but not solid enough to ward off the later influx from Japan, which is the process to be discussed in the following. Let us first turn to the establishment of a "school" for the translation of texts on international law by John Fryer and then take a closer look at the language and terminology applied by the southern school.

FRYER, THE JIANGNAN ARSENAL AND AN ALTERNATIVE TRADITION FOR INTERNATIONAL LAW TRANSLATIONS

William A.P. Martin and the staff at the Tongwenguan left a deep imprint on the Chinese process of translating texts on Western law, and on international law in particular. From the 1860s they had the market, if we may even speak of a market for these texts, as their own. Their work was done in close affiliation with the Zongli yaman and Chinese central authorities and the market for their texts was primarily staff in the foreign service, diplomats and language students at the Tongwenguan. From the 1880s this situation was changing rapidly when the Jiangnan Arsenal (Jiangnan Zhizaoju 江南製造局) in Shanghai, renowned for their translations of texts on technology and in the natural sciences, also started translating texts in the social sciences. Some years later the impact from Japan was even more fundamental in terms of establishing alternative traditions both for the language and the choice of texts different from the semi-official tradition established by Martin at the Tongwenguan in Beijing. The topic of this subchapter is the tradition established by John Fryer (1839-1928)[94] at the Jiangnan Arsenal for translating international law texts from the 1880s onwards, and how this "school" of translation established itself as an alternative to the Tongwenguan tradition

[94] Known with his Chinese name Fulanya (傅蘭雅)

discussed above.

The young John Fryer, born in Hythe in England in 1839, was offered the position as head-master at St. Pauls College in Hongkong in 1861. Being employed by the Church of England he spent his first two years in China in Hongkong where he learned Cantonese as his first Chinese tongue. In 1863 he left for Beijing where he began studying the Northern Chinese dialect. His mentor in Beijing, John Shaw Burdon, was at that time teaching English at the newly established Tongwenguan. Fryer, with his outstanding language abilities, was soon also engaged by the Tongwenguan as their second English teacher. John Fryer wanted to bring his future wife, Anna Roleston, to China and formalize their relationship. Her trip and arrival in China turned out, however, to be a personal tragedy both for Anna and John Fryer[95] and they were compelled to leave Beijing and establish a life in Shanghai. John Fryer's relationship to his employer, the Church of England, was also very much strained after these events. When John Fryer took up his new career i Shanghai in 1865 he was very much dispirited by his failure as a missionary in Beijing. Little did he know that his career in Shanghai in fact was going to become the basis for his life-long engagement with the translation and dissemination of Western knowledge in China. He worked for some time as a teacher of English at the Anglo-Chinese School in Shanghai until he was formally employed by the translation bureau at the Jiangnan Arsenal May 31st 1868. He worked for the Arsenal until he was engaged as the first professor of Oriental Language and Literature in the US at the University of California in 1896. John Fryer played a crucial role in Chinese enlightenment, for the introduction of modern Western natural science and technology into China, and in establishing a lexicon for the natural sciences in Chinese during his years at the Arsenal. His role in introducing Western social sciences is, however, much more limited and less known. As we shall see, he did start working on some translations of international law already in the 1870s. These texts were, however, only published in the 1890s, in many respects too late to become influential for the establishment of a tradition of social science translations and a corresponding lexicon at the Arsenal.

John Fryer's translation entitled *Gongfa zonglun* (公法總論) is

[95] Wang Yangzong 2000, pp. 11-15

based on the article "International law" in the 9th edition of *Encyclopaedia Britannica* written by Edmund Robertson.[96] The Jiangnan edition does not reveal its date of publication, which may be deduced from Fryer's own bibliographical lists as some time between 1886 and 1894.[97] Fryer's major translation work on international law is the voluminous *Commentaries upon International Law* by Robert J. Phillimore. The Chinese translation of the first three volumes of Phillimore's text was nearly complete already in 1878 but only published in 1894.[98] That indicates that the much smaller text by Robertson was translated and published as Fryer was preparing to have his comprehensive translation of Phillimore published. The text from the *Encyclopaedia Britannica* is translated by Fryer in collaboration with Wang Zhensheng (汪振聲) (1883-1945).[99]

The Robertson text in *Encyclopaedia Britannica* is one continuous text of about 7 pages, while Fryer has divided his translation into 18 chapters according to the different matters of international law discussed by Robertson. The translation follows closely the original English text and is less paraphrastic than Martin's earlier translations. This text is relatively short and there are many aspects of international jurisprudence that are not touched upon. It spite of its limited scope, however, we may already in this text clearly discern Fryer's attempt to establish an alternative way for Chinese international law through this text. Fryer's main undertaking in terms of international law translations is, however, the voluminous work by Sir Robert Joseph Phillimore.

[96] The sources consulted for this text are primarily: Bennet 1967, p. 100; Pusey 1983, pp. 139-140; Spence 1969, pp. 140-160; Tian Tao & Li Zhuhuan 2000, p. 364; Tian Tao 2001, pp. 103-105; Wang Jian 2001, p. 150; Wang Yangzong 2000; Xiong Yuezhi 1994, p. 539; *Zhongguo falü tushu zongmu* 1991, p. 738.

[97] Wang Yangzong 1995, p. 6

[98] See the following subchapter for these texts

[99] Who also took part in the reading of the proofs for Fryer's translation of Phillimore. If indeed the official recognised birth-date of Wang is correct, it must be assumed that the work with this translation took place early 1890s rather than late 1880s. It seems that the young Wang found law and politics an interesting area and left for Japan in 1904 to study law at Waseda University (早稻田大學) in Tokyo. He also obtained a law degree at Waseda and later a degree in politics and law in China in 1909. (Zhou Mian 1999, p. 198; Li Shengping 1989, p. 329)

Fryer and his translation of Phillimore

John Fryer had to leave his duties at the Arsenal in the summer of 1878 to accompany his wife and two sons on their way back to England. Fryer's wife had caught a disease and was advised by her doctor to leave the climate of China in order to improve her health. Fryer had apparently been working on a translation of Sir Robert Joseph Phillimore's (1810-1885) *Commentaries upon International Law* before he left Shanghai and had brought his work with him to England.

The manuscript of the first 3 volumes on public international law, with the working-title *Wanguo jiaoshe gongfalun* (萬國交涉公法論), was presented to Guo Songtao (郭嵩燾) (1818-1891) at the Chinese legation in London in the autumn of 1878. Only 2 *juan* of the third volume were still not translated, in addition to the fourth volume on private international law which he had not yet worked on.[100] Shortly afterwards Fryer was asked to travel to Berlin to assist his old friend and colleague from the Arsenal Li Fengbao (李鳳苞) (1834-1887) to establish the first Chinese permanent legation in Berlin. The translation of the 3 volumes was completed after Fryer returned to Shanghai.[101] Fryer himself lists the title *Geguo jiaoshe gongfa* (各國交涉公法), which is the translation of these 3 volumes of Phillimore's work, among translated texts ready for publication in August 1880.[102] Yet the manuscript was delayed for another 14 years before publication, as this rather voluminous text was published by the Jiangnan Arsenal only in 1894. The reason for this long delay is not known.[103] Phillimore's text has a strong English bias and supplies thus, together with the translation from *Encyclopaedia Britannica*, a certain English counterweight to the American and continental

---

[100] Guo Songtao 1984, pp. 746-748

[101] This subchapter is primarily based on the following sources: Bennet 1967, pp. 99-100; Chiu 1967, p. 488; Li Zhaojie 1999, p. 119; Tian Tao & Li Zhuhuan 2000, p. 364; Tian Tao 2001, pp. 105-113; Wang Jian 2001, pp. 149, 150; Wang Yangzong 1995, pp. 6, 18; Wang Yangzong 2000, pp. 48, 64-65; Xiong Yuezhi 1994, p. 539; *Zhongguo falü tushu zongmu* 1991, p. 740.

[102] *Gezhi huibian* August 1880, p. 11b

[103] Based on Qian Guoxiang's notes on the proofs dated 1894, where Qian also confirms that the manuscript had been completed at least 10 years before publication, Tian Tao has concluded that deliberations on the technical vocabulary of international law to be used by the Jiangnan Arsenal were the main reason for the delay. (Tian Tao 2001, p. 108)

European bias in earlier Chinese international legal translations.

Phillimore's *Commentaries upon International Law* was first published in Philadelphia 1854-57 in three volumes containing the sections on public international law. The fourth volume on private international law was issued with a London edition in 1861. The second edition of Phillimore's entire work in four volumes was printed in London 1871-74 and is the textual basis for Fryer's translation.[104] Parallel to its English precedent the Chinese translation of Phillimore's work was also published as two separate editions, one part on public international law and one on private international law. The first Chinese edition discussed above contains the part on public international law in volume 1 to 3 and is entitled *Geguo jiaoshe gongfalun* (各國交涉公法論), *A Discussion on Public International Law*, when it was published by the Arsenal in 1894. The last volume four on private international law was published as a separate publication some time later also by the Jiangnan Arsenal with the title *Geguo jiaoshe bianfalun* (各國交涉便法論), *A Discussion of Private International Law*, as a translation of the fourth volume of Phillimore's *Commentaries upon International Law* entitled "Private International Law or Comity".[105] This translation by the Jiangnan staff represents the first translation of a text on private international law into Chinese. The Jiangnan Arsenal edition does not disclose the date of the Chinese publication but Wang Yangzong has drawn the conclusion that it was printed some time between 1898 and 1902.[106]

It was a daring move of Fryer to establish an entirely new tradition of international legal translations in Shanghai in the 1890s in spite of the massive body of earlier Martin translations and its reception in official Chinese circles. His courage to start this project may at least in part be ascribed to the growing importance of Shanghai and the Jiangnan region, not only economically but also intellectually and politically, towards late Qing times. He met anyway with certain scepticism among those already familiar with Martin's translations.

---

[104] For biographical details on Sir Robert Phillimore see Holland 1898, pp. 300-301

[105] The major part of the translation was performed by John Fryer, doing the oral translation, and Yu Shijue (俞世爵) formulating the written text. The proofs were first read by Wang Zhensheng and Qian Guoxiang (錢國祥). In addition Qing Chang and Liu Fuxu took part in the translation of certain parts of the text during Fryer's stay in Germany, as we have seen.

[106] Wang Yangzong 1995, pp. 6, 18

Liang Qichao makes an interesting comment on the two different traditions of Tongwenguan and the Jiangnan Arsenal in 1896:

> Professor W.A.P. Martin of the Tongwenguan is a specialist in international law. Therefore Tongwenguan has translated a number of books on international law. There are several tens of hundreds of Western international legal publicists, and Martin's translations of Wheaton's *Elements of International Law* is not the most extensive. The translation of Phillimore's *Commentaries upon International Law* by the Jiangnan Arsenal is divided into 3 sections and contains 16 volumes. I regard the Tongwenguan translations to be the better.[107]

Shortly after its publication the translation of Phillimore was included in the curriculum on international law at the Hunanese Academy of Current Affairs (Shiwu xuetang 時務學堂) from 1897.[108] Otherwise not much is known about the application and reception of this text after its publication, except for the fact that its reproduction already in the late 1890s speaks for a relatively good reception before the turn of the century. Fryer embarked upon one other major translation project in the field of international law during his time in Shanghai.

Fryer's translation of Ferguson

Jan Helenus Ferguson (1826-1908) served as Dutch ambassador to China from January 1872 until November 1894 when he returned to Holland due to health problems. Ferguson wrote works on Chinese international questions during his time in China, such as *Juridiction et exterritorialité en Chine* in French and after returning to Holland, such as *A Glossary of the Principal Chinese Expressions Occurring in Postal Documents* in English. None of these were ever translated into Chinese. His *Manual of International Law* in 2 volumes was, however, published during his time of service in China, translated by Fryer and published by the Gezhi shushi (格致書室) (Chinese Scientific Book Depot) in Shanghai in 1901 with the title *Bangjiao gongfa xinlun* (邦交公法新論).

During his time in Shanghai, in addition to his service for the Arsenal, John Fryer engaged in the spreading of "useful literature" among the Chinese and in 1885 he established the Chinese Scientific

[107] Liang Qichao 1896, p. 8b
[108] Li Guilian 1998a, p. 39

Book Depot. The Depot served as a library and bookstore for Western scientific literature, the only one of its kind in China of the time, and lists 372 items for sale already in 1886. Also Martin's four major translations of international law texts were found on the shelves and almost 900 titles on their list which appeared in 1888. The Depot expanded its influence and set up similar Depots in all major Chinese cities within a few years. Fryer also used the Depot as a publishing house for some of his own translations, such as the translation of Ferguson's text, which was published five years after Fryer himself had left China to take up a chair as professor of Oriental Language and Literature in 1896.

Ferguson's book was taken up for translation at the Arsenal because of the inconveniently extensive size of Phillimore's text. The translation of Ferguson was orally performed by Fryer and taken down in literary Chinese by Cheng Zhanluo (程瞻洛). The work was commenced while Fryer was still a Chinese employee at the Arsenal.[109] When Fryer left for California in 1896, leaving Cheng with an incomplete manuscript, Cheng continued working on the draft for a final publication. Fryer came back to China for a short period in 1901, as he did every summer between 1897 and 1903,[110] and the two discussed the publication and decided to have the text printed as soon as possible. In order to give the manuscript a final proof-reading Le Zhirang (樂志讓) at the Chinese Scientific Book Depot was asked to smooth out the language of the manuscript and ascertain a unified use of proper names and titles of books. He completed his task within a few months and the book was printed and published that same year at the Depot.[111]

Ferguson's work in two volumes is formulated as a manual of international law, for the use of navies, colonies and consulates as the title indicates, hence stressing the practical and applicative aspects of international law. His work draws up the origin of law in general and its presumed evolution from the universal and moral laws of nature. Ferguson furthermore briefly describes the history and development of international law before he proceeds to lay out the applications of

---

[109] Where Cheng officially was enlisted with the Shuileichang (水雷廠)

[110] Wang Yangzong 2000, p. 117

[111] This subchapter is primarily based on the following sources: Bennett 1967, pp. 63-66, 100; Tian Tao 2001, p. 112; Wang Jian 2001, p. 150; Wang Yangzong 1995, p. 17; Wang Yangzong 2000, p. 88.

international law in 5 parts; the individual rights of states, maritime and commercial international law, the rights and responsibilities of states in time of peace, war and its appurtenances, and the re-establishment of peace. The Chinese translation differs radically from Fryer's earlier translations in terms of faithfulness to the original text. Whereas Fryer in his earlier translations has rendered the original passage by passage without paraphrasing the text, he is in this instance heavily abridging and rewording Ferguson. The division into chapters and paragraphs in Ferguson's text is kept and no issue is left untranslated. The text is, however, largely rewritten and paraphrased to the extent that the translation appears in many parts as a mere summary of Ferguson's treatises.[112] The degree of condensation of the text is, however, not uniform throughout the translation. The part on maritime and commercial international law is treated to the fullest extent, while the part discussing rights and responsibilities of states in time of peace is severely abbreviated. The considerations underlying these variations of textual accuracy will inevitably reflect the presumed interest and market for these deliberations in China at the time. The Chinese state had already embarked on its active role as a member of the family of nations and established diplomatic relations with the West. The rights of a state to establish treatises and legations abroad were not the most urgent needs for the diplomatic corps and others concerned with China's international status. Rights and obligations of states in time of war must have seemed more of a pressing issue for China shortly after the Sino-Japanese war, while questions of how to conduct their overseas trade and how to adapt to rules for international commercial and maritime activity must have appeared most useful to Fryer and Cheng considering the potential demand of the market in the late 1890s.

The Jiangnan Arsenal and Fryer's terminological alternative to Martin

As we have seen, John Fryer translated a number of international law texts at the Jiangnan Arsenal in Shanghai in the 1880s. The Jiangnan

[112] Quotations from other writers on international law are never quoted in full and in most cases entirely omitted from the translation.

Arsenal tradition distinguishes itself from the Tongwenguan tradition in its choice of terminology and lexicon. In fact, Fryer's Jiangnan Arsenal translations hardly bear *any* resemblance to the Tongwenguan tradition in terms of technical vocabulary. Fryer did make use of Martin's terms for 'sovereignty' (*zhuquan* 主權) and 'independence' (*zizhu* ,自主 *zili* 自立), and his application of terms for 'neutral' (*juwai* 局外) and 'high seas' (*dahai* 大海) coincide with Martin's terms drawing on the current vocabulary. Otherwise Fryer established an altogether independent Jiangnan tradition for these translations.

In John Fryer's relatively short translation from *Encyclopaedia Britannica* we may already discern Fryer's zeal to establish a terminology different from the Tongwenguan "school" since he has chosen to supply an alternative set of terms where Martin's terms had not yet been established in the Chinese vocabulary. The most prominent of these are Fryer's use of the terms *fen suo dang de* (分所當得) for 'rights' and *fen suo dang xing* (分所當行) or *fen suo dang wei* (分所當為) for 'duty', avoiding Martin's *quanli* (權利). Also the introduction of the terms *jiaoshe gongfa* (交涉公法) as a technical term for 'international law' and *bianfa* (便法) or *wanguo bianfa* (萬國便法) for 'private international law' distinguishes Fryer's translations fundamentally from Martin's earlier translations. Tang Caichang in the Hunanese reform movement adopted Fryer's terms for public and private international law as well as for rights. In an article in *Xiangxue xinbao* issue no. 8 we find the following explication of these terms:

> In international law there are regular laws (*zhengfa* 正法) and customary laws (*bianfa* 便法). ... For all sovereign states with duties (*fen suo dang wei* 分所當為) we call these laws regular laws [of international relations]. There are customs in the intercourse between states gradually established after many years of contact. These are called international customs (*gongli* 公例) or customary law.[113]

Furthermore, Fryer has not adopted the term *ziyou* (自由) for 'liberty'/'freedom' but applies the term *zizhu* (自主) for this notion, a term which is also used for 'independence' and 'sovereignty' of states. Fryer has not applied Martin's term *zhuquan* (主權) for 'sovereignty' in this translation. Denominations for political systems, such as 'republic' and 'monarchy', are applied parallel to Martin's early translations, and he has thus not accepted Martin's later term

[113] *Xiangxue xinbao*, no. 8, p. 29b

minzheng (民政) for 'republic'. The term *guofa* (國法) applied by Martin for 'constitution' is only used for 'national laws' by Fryer, while 'constitution' is rendered *guozheng* (國政) by Fryer, regardless of whether he is referring to the political system or the legal constitution. Where Martin has systematically applied *tiaoyue* (條約) for 'treaty' in all his later translations Fryer has used *heyue* (和約) for all kinds of general treaties and not only 'peace treaty'. Martin has not devised a specific term for 'positive law'. Fryer has in this translation from *Encyclopaedia Britannica* applied the term *shizai* (實在)[114] with these connotations three times. This tendency to establish a technical term for 'positive law' is, however, not continued in Fryer's later translation of Phillimore.

The vocabulary in the extensive body of the text by Phillimore translated by Fryer, comprising all four volumes on public and private international law, concurs with the lexicon established in the translation from the *Encyclopaedia Britannica.* Because of the extensive size of this text, however, a few more details of Fryer's technical lexicon may be identified. Martin's term *xingfa* (性法) for 'natural law' is replaced by Fryer's *tianran (zhi) lüfa* (天然(之)律法) or *tianran zhi fa* (天然之法), while 'positive law' is left without a technical term translation parallel to the lexicon in Martin's texts. 'Revealed law' is by Fryer translated *yincheng zhi lüfa* (隱成之律法). The term 'right of self-protection' translated *zihu zhi quan* (自護之權) by Martin appears as *zixing baowei* (自行保衛) or short *zibao* (自保) in Fryer, as he was unable to construe sub-rights through his choice of terms for 'rights'. Martin's term *guanxia* (管轄) for 'jurisdiction' is replaced by Fryer's *guanli* (管理), Martin's *junshi zhi fa* (均勢之法) for 'balance of power' is replaced by Fryer's *pingquan zhi li* (平權之理), Martin's terms for 'movable property' and 'immovable property' is replaced by Fryer's *neng yidong zhi wuchan* (能移動之物產) and *buneng yidong zhi wuchan* (不能移動之物產). The term *guozheng* (國政) applied for 'constitution' is sometimes made to refer more explicitly to legal constitution by the term *guozheng zhangcheng* (國政章程). The term *guohui* (國會) applied by Martin as one of several terms for 'parliament'/'congress'/'diet' is in Fryer's text applied as a technical term for 'confederation', while 'parliament' in Fryer's text is systematically rendered *gonghui* (公會). The term *juwai* (局外) used

---

[114] Used in the compounds *shizai lüfa* (實在律法) and *shizai gongfa* (實在公法)

as the only term for 'neutrality' by Martin is accompanied by the term *zhongli* (中立) in Fryer's text. Fryer is using both these terms as technical terms for 'neutrality', also in composite terms such as a 'neutral state' (*juwaiguo* 局外國, *zhongliguo* 中立國) etc. When a definition of the notion of 'neutrality' of a state is translated, however, Fryer applies *juwai* as the technical term and *zhongli* as the descriptive term for a subject in a position between the parties involved (*in bello medius*). In Fryer's translation from the *Encyclopaedia Britannica* the term *jiaoshe gongfa* (交涉公法) appears together with *wanguo gongfa* (萬國公法) as terms for 'public international law'. In his translation of Phillimore the term *wanguo gongfa* appears only very few times, and Fryer's terms *geguo jiaoshe gongfa* (各國交涉公法), *jiaoshe gongfa* (交涉公法), or simply *gongfa* (公法) appear as technical translations for this term. Martin had never reached a satisfactory solution to the question of how to express the notion of 'private international law', or 'comity', in Chinese. Fryer has systematically applied his own neologism *geguo jiaoshe bianfa* (各國交涉便法), *jiaoshe bianfa* (交涉便法), or short *bianfa* (便法), throughout his texts. The term *bian* (便) in this context refers to the fact that the regulations of private international law are liable to social convenience and not legal necessity. We may perceive Fryer's motivations for this *bianfa* term when we study a passage in Phillimore: "The *obligationes juris privati inter gentes* are not—as the *obligationes juris publici inter gentes* are—the result of legal necessity, but of social convenience, and they are called by the name of Comity—*comitas gentium*."[115]

The most awkward feature of Fryer's language may seem to be his term for 'rights', which has also proven to be counterproductive for the formation of sub-related 'rights'. Fryer seems to have attempted to make up for this defect by adding the terms *yichu* (益處) or *liyi* (利益) to some of his existing terms but nevertheless reformulates passages when specific rights are discussed and never construes these terms as 'rights' in themselves.

The vocabulary of Fryer's translation discussed above refers to the main body of the text. One finds, however, by reading Fryer's

[115] Phillimore 1871-74, vol. 1, pp. 12-13. This passage is rendered as follows in Chinese by Fryer and his staff: 各國交涉之法有兩種務須分別。一為交涉約法所當為之事。一為交涉公法所當為之事。其約法非律法所必有之事。因交涉事中所便宜而行者，故亦謂之交涉便法。 (*Geguo jiaoshe gongfalun* 1894 vol. 1, p. 2b)

translation, that the language is not entirely consistent throughout the text. The language and vocabulary applied in *juan* 13 and 14 of the text on public international law differ from the main body of the text on a number of points. The most striking feature of the translation in these two *juan* is the term 'rights' translated systematically by the term *liquan* (利權), the two same characters as in Martin's translation but in opposite order. Through this manoeuvre the translator has also been able to coin a few related 'rights'-terms such as 'right of visit and search' (*chayan zhi liquan* 查驗之利權) and 'right of capture' (*nahuo zhi liquan* 拏獲之利權). This translator has also established the converse term of 'rights', namely the term *benfen* (本分) systematically applied for 'duty'. Otherwise one may notice that 'neutrality' is systematically translated *juwai* whereas the two terms *juwai* and *zhongli* both appear as stylistic variations in all other sections of the text. Also other terms are systematically applied differently in these two sections of the text. These two *juan* have evidently been composed and translated by a different author, possibly also at a different time, and it is tempting to conclude that these two *juan* are the two *juan* of the third volume of Phillimore's text not yet translated in 1878 when Guo Songtao was presented with a copy of the translation in London.[116]

Whereas the translation of Phillimore's three first *juan* on public international law compelled Fryer to construe an entirely new set of Chinese technical terms for notions in public international law, very few new terms had to be coined to complete the last volume of Phillimore's work on private international law. It appears that most of the operations of private international law, primarily pertaining to the relationship between individuals and states, were juridical constructs and relations already known to the Chinese and described in the

[116] Textual variations in *Geguo jiaoshe gongfalun* are not, however, only limited to these two *juan*. Also the last few pages of the final *juan* 16 contain a number of terminological variants. To one's surprise one may find on these pages Martin's *quanli* (權利) for 'rights' together with a number of terms related to specific rights, such as 'right of electing' (*zezhu zhi quan* 擇主之權), 'right of property' (*zhengye zhi quan* 掌業之權), and 'private rights' (*siquan* 私權). On these same pages the terms for 'movable' and 'immovable property' are also changed to *dongye* (動業) and *dingye* (定業). It is again evident that these few pages have been composed by someone not involved in the entire translational project from the beginning and who has supplied the last pages of the translation in accordance with Martin's set of terms, possibly shortly before publication, without consulting the lexical standard and vocabulary of the main text-body.

current language. The only notable difference from the sections of public international law is that whereas Fryer avoided a technical term for 'positive law' in the *Geguo jiaoshe gongfalun* translation, he has introduced the term *teshe zhi lü* (特設之律) for 'positive law' and used it systematically throughout this *Geguo jiaoshe bianfalun* translation. The establishment of a new term for 'positive law' different from the term *shizai lüfa* (實在律法) applied by Fryer in his translation of the text from *Encyclopaedia Britannica* is striking.

Fryer and Cheng Zhanluo as the translators of the work by Ferguson, possibly also in cooperation with Le Zhirang who worked on the final manuscript before publication, have made certain adjustments to Fryer's earlier Chinese language and vocabulary of international law. In general, Fryer's earlier terminological apparatus is put into operation and no traces of Martin's specific terminology may be discerned. 'Freedom' and 'independence' are both translated *zizhu* (自主), 'neutrality' is variously translated *juwai* (局外) and *zhongli* (中立), 'balance of power' is expressed through Fryer's term *pingquan* (平權), and Fryer's terms for 'jurisdiction' and for 'movable property' and 'immovable property' follow Fryer's earlier terms. For 'positive law' one finds both earlier forms; *teshe lüfa* (特設律法) and *shizai zhi fa* (實在之法), where the latter seems to be the technical term applied for 'positive law' whereas the former refers to specific laws. In treating 'rights' and 'duties' of states the terms *fen dang de zhi yi* (分當得之益) and *fen dang wei zhi shi* (分當為之事) are the most frequently used. As a development of the terms used in Fryer's translations of the last volume of Phillimore's text the term *yi* (益) has been applied also to denote specific rights, such as 'right of existence' translated *changcun zhi yi* (常存之益) and 'sovereignty rights' translated *zizhu zhi yi* (自主之益). The employment of this term *yi* for 'rights' is, however, very limited and not applied generatively, and no parallel term is established for 'duties' or 'obligations'. Fryer and his team have thus been faced with the same difficulties in referring to distinct aspects of the 'rights' and 'duties' of states in this text and have in most instances reformulated the passages, occasionally applying general terms involving the term *fen* (分) indicating one's 'lot', 'portion' or 'share' in life.

The most striking development from Fryer's earlier texts to the translation of Ferguson is his terminology for 'international law' and its sub-categories. Whereas the term *wanguo gongfa* (萬國公法)

appears a number of times referring to the former term *jus gentium* (*law of nations*), the general term used for 'international law' is *bangjiao gongfa* (邦交公法). Through the use of this technical term Fryer indicates that he aims at coining a Chinese term semantically more proximate to the English term 'international public law' and finds this term more suitable than his former terms *geguo jiaoshe gongfa* (各國交涉公法) or simply *jiaoshe gongfa* (交涉公法). He has, however, not attempted to apply the new term *bangjiao* generically for other terms including the notion of 'international', except for the term *bangjiao bianfa* (邦交便法), 'private international law'. As we have seen above, Phillimore focused on 'social convenience' in his definition of 'comity' for 'private international law' and Fryer used terms applying the notion of 'convenience' (*bian* 便) in his earlier translations. Ferguson has in his book, however, made a distinction between the terms 'comity', 'private international law' and 'conflict of laws':

> Private International Law (*jus gentium privatum*) is that part of the General International Law which regulates, not the mutual relations of the States, but the private relations which occasionally occur between individual members of one State and the laws of another State. ... Now, as an individual, thus situated, may often have recourse to the law-courts of one State to execute contracts or to secure or attest rights, entered into or acquired under the differing legislation of another State, his case must give occasion for conflict between his own rights, as the laws under which some of his rights are acquired and the laws which must secure the effect, are not always the same and may sometimes be contradictory. This is what is termed *Conflict of Laws*, ... Private International Law is the term under which are collectively comprehended those rules and principles through which the Conflict of Laws, arising out of certain juridical actions and transactions of aliens and non-domiciled subjects, is decided, and which, in general, solve the questions as to *which law* is to govern those cases of actions and transactions which come under the operations of more than one code of Municipal Legislations or Jurisdiction. ... Comity, in a stricter sense, is the reciprocal exercise of politeness between Governments of States, and has regard to cases of mere courtesy, based on the general principle of the Right of Respect, or it comprehends some special voluntary acts, not due by treaty, which may serve to facilitate the interests of internal policy of either party.[117]

[117] Ferguson 1884, vol. 1, pp. 142-146

These deliberations by Ferguson have the consequence that the term *bangjiao bianfa*, or simply *bianfa*, indicating the aspects of 'convenience' has been reserved for the notion of 'comity' in the translations of Ferguson's work. Fryer has therefore been compelled to coin a specific technical term for 'private international law', *minshi gongfa* (民事公法), which he uses throughout his discussions of topics on that subject.[118] In his abridged way of translation Fryer renders the deliberations on 'conflict of laws' in Chinese without coining a specific term for it.[119]

As we have seen above, the technical vocabulary established by Fryer and the Jiangnan Arsenal team of translators has only retained terms for 'sovereignty', 'independence', 'neutrality' and 'high seas' from Martin's Tongwenguan vocabulary. Otherwise Fryer has established a separate lexicon for these technical terms in Shanghai. The Fryer vocabulary was, like the Tongwenguan vocabulary, subject to certain adjustments over time. It is, however, clear that these two traditions in terms of applied vocabulary appear as two distinct and separate traditions for international law traditions in late 19th century China. The vocabulary of the voluminous Fryer translations on international law between 1886 and 1901 suggests that his translations met a fate similar to Martin's later translations, being without discernible practical application or otherwise important for the political developments in contemporary China. The only time Fryer's translations of international law texts are known to have exercised practical influence was when Guo Songtao acquired a copy of Fryer's unfinished Chinese translation of Phillimore's text in London in 1878, 16 years before its publication at the Arsenal.[120] At that time only Martin's translations of the theoretical works of two American publicists were available in China, but as the first Chinese envoy to Europe and as delegate to the Conference for the Reform and

---

[118] The first passage in Ferguson's text quoted above is thus translated: 民事公法與各國家交涉事無關，特為一國人民，與各國人民，所有交涉之事耳 (*Bangjiao gongfa xinlun* 1901, *juan* 2, pp. 1a-b)

[119] Ferguson's observations regarding 'comity' are translated as follows: 有一便法，原行於各國交涉事內，即本國情願不與他國為難，使他國事能取便，凡相往來之事，各示相讓，顯有相待以禮之意，此固各國推誠願為，並非因立和約而不能不為者 (ibid.)

[120] Fryer's manuscript was then referred to as *Wanguo jiaoshe gongfa lun* (萬國交涉公法論) and not with the title of the translation *Geguo jiaoshe gongfa lun* (各國交涉公法論) published later.

Codification of International Law that same year Guo presumably found it inappropriate to refer to these American philosophers of international law. In spite of his voluminous production, however, Fryer's terminological apparatus was not permanently taken up in the Chinese language and did not enter contemporary dictionaries. Neither did Fryer's translations and his technical vocabulary have any discernible influence on the developments in Japan, which in turn later had such a strong impact on China.

INDIGENOUS CHINESE INTRODUCTIONS OF INTERNATIONAL LAW

Simultaneous with the massive current of Chinese students leaving for Japan after 1895 in order to benefit from the modernised and westernised educational institutions and curricula, a current which soon was to strongly influence the flow of international law translations into China, a number of Chinese scholars sought to build a Chinese indigenous tradition for international law in China. As we shall see, these attempts were established upon the two main current traditions described above, the Martin and the Fryer traditions. Because of time limitations and the rapidly growing influence from Japan in the early 20th century, however, these attempts developed into little but an intermezzo between the two main periods for the introduction of international law in late imperial China. As two attempts, one in Jiangsu and one in Hunan, to establish traditions other than the translated Western tradition, however, this process may be observed as a very significant intermezzo.

The earliest attempt at establishing a Chinese textual tradition in international law was based on the earlier works of Martin. Ding Zuyin (丁祖蔭) from Jiangsu selected passages from Martin's translation of Wheaton's *Elements of International Law* and discussed these supported by passages from other early translations of international law texts and quotations from the Confucian classics. The text was published in Changshu in 1898 with the title *Wanguo gongfa shili* (萬國公法釋利).[121] Ding selected passages from all the major sections of Wheaton's text and divided them into two *juan*, the first discussing international law in time of peace, the second

[121] Wang Jian 2001, p. 150

international law in time of war. Ding's chapters are divided into a canonical (*li* 例) and expositional (*shi* 釋) text under each topical subheading. The canonical part consists of selected passages from different chapters in Martin's translation organised under individual subheadings. The expositional text discusses the topic touched upon in the Wheaton passages where Ding substantiates his own arguments with quotations from other translations of texts on international law. These translations include all the major Chinese translations on public international law available at that time, texts translated by Martin as well as texts from the Fryer Jiangnan Arsenal tradition. Inevitably, Ding falls into some of the pitfalls of confusing the difference in technical vocabulary applied by the two translators, and subsequently refers to different texts without recounting that different Chinese terms are used for one and the same concept in international theory. The result of this terminological confusion must have appeared somewhat bewildering to Ding's readership, unless they were already well versed in the two different traditions.

In addition to comparing and quoting the different Chinese translations of Western texts on international law Ding attempts to analyse aspects of international law in light of the Confucian classics. The Chinese relevance of each topic in Ding's expositions is substantiated by references to the Chinese Confucian canon, substantiating the basics of international law within the indigenous Chinese tradition. Ding's conclusion is that whereas international law may simply regulate and control the balance of power between nations by strict regulations, only the Way of Benevolence (*rendao* 仁道) can permanently establish harmony among the different peoples. Ding Zuyin is thus promoting international law as a means in China's struggle for existence with the presumption that China in fact has a comparable tradition in early Confucian thought underlying the adoption of Western principles for the intercourse of nations. It does not appear that Ding Zuyin's attempt to discuss international law on the basis of the Confucian classics left much of an impact on the development of this field of Western learning in China.[122]

Tang Caichang (唐才常) (1867-1900), an active student of Western learning and a New Text Confucian, was among the key members and

---

[122] When Cai E briefly sums up the history of the reception and recognition of the principles of international law in China in his preface to *Guoji gongfa zhi* (國際公法志) in 1902, he does not mention Ding's work.

an activist in the reform movements in Hunan of the late 1890s together with Tan Sitong (譚嗣同) (1865-1898), both as a writer and as an active organiser of armed revolts. From 1897 he acted as chief editor of the influential Hunan reform-periodical *Xiangxue xinbao* (湘學新報),[123] where he was also an active contributor. Tang Caichang may also be identified as one of the first advocates of Social Darwinian ideas in China. He wrote a number of articles discussing different theoretical and applicative aspects of Chinese international relations, all published in the Hunanese periodical *Xiangxue xinbao* and the daily newspaper *Xiangbao* (湘報)[124] in 1897-98. The text that was later published with the title *Gongfa tongyi* (公法通義) was first published as a serial in the volumes 8 to 15 of *Xiangxue xinbao* between June 30th and September 7th 1897. The text appended to the *Gongfa tongyi*, the *Geguo jiaoshe yuanliu kao* (各國交涉源流考), was published in the same periodical, volumes 5 to 7, between May 31 and June 20 the same year.[125]

In this publication Tang Caichang quotes passages from earlier Chinese translations of international law texts and adds his own interpretations and commentaries applying the principles and practice of international law to a Chinese context. Tang was a firm advocate of a strengthening of international law in China as a means of gaining what had been lost through the decline of the traditional Chinese

[123] *The Hunan study news*

[124] *Hunan news*

[125] Parts of the text were also reprinted in the *Jichengbao* (集成報) issues 11 and 12 published in Shanghai 1897. (*Jichengbao* vol. 1, pp. 597-600, 663-666)

A number of other articles by Tang Caichang on international relations published in these periodicals include: *Jiaoshe zhenwei* (交涉甄微) (*Xiangxuebao* volume 1 April 22nd 1897), *Gongfa xuehui xu* (公法學會敘) (*Xiangbao* volume 43 1898), *Tongsai saitong lun* (通塞塞通論) (*Xiangxu xinebao* volume 4 and 5 May 22nd to 31 1897), *Geguo caiji shiqing lunzheng* (各國猜忌實情論證) (*Xiangxue xinbao* volume 21 to 23 November 5th to 24th 1897), *Lun Zhong Ri tongshang tiaoyue* (論中日通商條約) (*Xiangxue xinbao* volume 24 and 25 December 4th to 14th 1897), *Lun Gaoli yu geguo jiaoshe qingxing* (論高麗與各國交涉情形) (*Xiangxue xinbao* volume 25 and 26 December 14th 1897 to February 1st 1898), *Lun Zhongguo yi yu Ying Ri lianmeng* (論中國宜與英日聯盟) (*Xiangbao* volume 23 1898), *Shixue yaoyan* (使學要言) (*Xiangxue xinbao* volume 16 to 21 September 17th to November 5th 1897), *Waijiao lun* (外交論) (*Xiangxu xinebao* volume 4 April 22nd 1897). All of these were included in the *Juedian mingzhai neiyan* (覺顛冥齋內言) (1898), in the *Xinxue da congshu* (新學大叢書) (1903), and in the *Tang Caichang ji* (唐才常集) (1980).

The text on Tang Caichang is primarily based on the following secondary sources: Ding Pingyi 2000; Harrel 1992, p. 95; Judge 1996; Pusey 1983, pp. 127-154; Wang Jian 2001, p. 150; Wang Lixin 1997, p. 369; Zou Zhenhuan 1989, p. 85.

political order. He claimed that what the West had gained through international equality and the establishment of a balance of power in Europe had been lost in China since the early Confucian tradition. Tang realised, however, also the narrow potentiality of promoting international law in China in order to turn China into an equal partner with the Western nations, and hence he approved of radical reforms, or even revolution, in China through a Darwinian national struggle for existence.

The *Gongfa tongyi* contains the main text entitled *Gongfa tongyi zonglun* (公法通義總論) and the appended text *Geguo jiaoshe yuanliu kao*. The text proper is formulated as questions and answers to topics in international law. The answers are all based on quotations from earlier texts, in some cases earlier translations of Western texts on international law, while in other cases on quotations from the Confucian classics in order to illustrate the existence of an international order based on Confucian ethical and political principles in China in pre-Qin and Han times. Similarly to Ding Zuyin, Tang was obviously familiar with both Tongwenguan and Jiangnan Arsenal translations of international law texts and also shows familiarity with all the current translations. It is, however, evident that his main source of knowledge about Western international law is Fryer's translation of Phillimore's volumes on public international law. He does not explicitly identify his sources but his main influence may be perceived through his use of vocabulary and general language. It is unavoidable that also Tang commits the same mistake as Ding in not identifying different word-translations from Martin and Fryer of the very same Western notion, or at least confuses his readership by not pointing out that these are different translations of one and the same notion. If Tang himself was aware of these terminological peculiarities, which he most probably was, he has certainly made the task difficult for his readership by failing to explain the differences between the two traditions in use of vocabulary.

The Potential Merging of Traditions into an Indigenous Chinese School of Translation

As I have attempted to show above, two independent schools of international law translations were established in China in the latter half of the 19th century. These schools were independent from each other both in terms of political affiliation, in terms of selection of texts, and most importantly in terms of their technical terminology for central terms of international law. Since no indigenous debate on the issues of China's international role and position based on the principles of international law surfaced in any substantial way in China before 1895, the two institutions representing these two independent traditions, Tongwenguan and Jiangnan Arsenal, were operating independently from each other and no urge was felt to establish a "national" common standard for these terms. When the first debates on theoretical issues pertaining to Western international law did surface shortly after the treaty of Shimonoseki, a temporary confusion of terms and ideas was caused by Martin's and Fryer's very different use of terminologies. The most apparent examples of such confusion of terminology are to found in the works by Ding Zuyin and Tang Caichang.

In the work by Ding Zuyin we find that a burgeoning native debate on the significance of international law in China is hampered by what most probably is a confusion of the two terminological traditions. Ding refers to and quotes texts from both camps without explicating the terminological differences between these texts. When Tang Caichang and the educational reforms in Hunan make use of texts from both traditions in their curriculum on international law, we see a similar effect. Tang Caichang himself was most likely well aware of these differences and the classes at the Academy of Current Affairs in Changsha may well have taken these differences into consideration when studying and discussing questions pertaining to the international situation, international law and international relations. For the readers of their periodicals and their written deliberations on international law intended for an external readership, however, the terminological differences must have caused confusion. That would surely have been solved over time. The strong terminological influence from Japan, however, put an end to the merging of the two and the potential establishment of an indigenous Chinese terminological apparatus in international law.

The Chinese students first publishing texts in the Chinese language in Japan and later returning from Japan after years of Western style university education, brought back the entire international legal vocabulary from the Japanese language. These students had very little or no experience of the two Chinese traditions and the early translations of international law, most of them being young and receptive to the modern Japanese educational system and Western scientific disciplines in Japanese interpretation, and brought an entirely new set of terms for this new reality back to China. The entire Chinese discourse on international questions was "japanised" in terms of vocabulary and the Tongwenguan and Jiangnan Arsenal traditions were rejected within a matter of months. The only remnants of the early Chinese terminological traditions in the modern Japanese and Chinese vocabularies may be found in the terms 'rights' and 'sovereignty', which were Martin innovations transferred to Japan as early as the 1860s.[126] Otherwise the Japanese Meiji influence on China was pervasive at a time when Chinese intellectuals were searching for ways of defining China's international role after the Sino-Japanese war. Before we turn to the period of Japanese influence on the field of international law in China in chapter 5, however, we shall take a brief glance at the scattered arguments in the Chinese discourse on international law before the turn of the century. That burgeoning debate on international law in China was based on the textual and terminological foundation discussed in this chapter.

---

[126] For a discussion of the introduction and early Chinese influence upon the introduction of international law in Japan see Dudden 1999.

CHAPTER FOUR

THE EARLY DISCOURSE ON INTERNATIONAL LAW IN CHINA

In the previous chapter we have seen that international law was introduced into China with a solid base in texts and in the written vocabulary and language during the period between the Opium war and the late 19th century. I have also claimed that one of the reasons why translations over a period of several decades could develop in two different and distinct directions without an urge either to merge the two traditions or to replace the one by the other was the lack of a wide-scale discourse among intellectuals and officials on the international position and role of China in this period. Historic events pushing these questions to the forefront and the reactions to these questions from the Chinese scholarly elite were yet to come. Those are the questions to be addressed in chapters 5 and 6. In spite of the lack of large-scale national concerns about China in international relations in the latter half of the 19th century, however, a burgeoning debate on questions relating to international law in China is noticeable. That debate is the topic of this chapter.

INTERNATIONAL LAW AS SELF-STRENGTHENING

The early reactions based on international law to the international challenges China was facing after the Opium war and to the first translations of international law texts may be observed in the writings of the gentry-literati and the first Chinese diplomats. Historically this coincides with the expansion of Chinese diplomacy to also include permanent missions abroad. Guo Songtao, China's first ambassador to London and Paris, had an affirmative view on international law. He saw the world of inter-state relations, in China and in the West, ruled by reason (*li* 理) rather than might (*shi* 势). In a situation of deficient might and power, as in the case of China in the 1870s, reason would be the only way to deal with the West, according to Guo. International law regulating the relations between states of different power in the West is based upon reason and principles. Hence, according to Guo, all nations in Asia and Africa would have to study and abide by international law in order to meet the challenges of political and military dominion from the West.[1] In a similar fashion, the reformist Chen Chi (陳熾) (1855-1900) was concerned that Chinese strength in international relations was not only a matter of military but also economic strength. In times of chaos the strong subdue the weak, the many abuse the few. The only measure to avoid this tendency in international relations is adherence to the common principles of international law. According to Chen Chi international law is based on principle and reason and not on might, it is based on the common benefit of all involved parties and not the benefit of one party, it is based on the regulated and not the unstable.[2] These considerations by Chen Chi were written in 1894, on the verge of war with Japan, in a world quite different from that of Guo Songtao and the 1870s. The general trend of thought is, however, the same, namely that China needs to get accustomed to international law in order to improve her position in international relations, be it in a European or an East Asian context, and must exhibit a relative trust in the law of nations. Such affirmative views on the application of international law in China are representative for a number of prominent members of the gentry-literati and the first Chinese diplomats in the late 19th century.

Zheng Guanying (鄭觀應) (1842-1921) is one of the early most fervent advocates of international law and its application in Chinese foreign policy in late Qing. Zheng was from his early years engaged in foreign trade in Shanghai, learned English and was a passionate spokesman for reform and international orientation. He was an early close associate of Sun Yatsen, actively involved in questions of national interest, and deeply concerned with the Chinese position in the 1894-95 Sino-Japanese war. In both of Zheng's two major works, the *Yiyan* (易言)[3] and the *Shengshi weiyan* (盛世危言)[4], there are chapters dedicated to international law and international relations.

[1] Tian Tao 2001, pp. 169-171
[2] Chen Chi 1997, pp. 1-146; Tian Tao 2001, pp. 171-172
[3] Published between 1871 and 1880, being a continuation of his first work the *Jiushi jieyao* (救時揭要) (Wang Yiliang (ed.) 1998, pp. 9-11)
[4] Published between 1884 and 1894 (Wang Yiliang (ed.) 1998, pp. 11-12)

From his perspective in international trade Zheng Guanying had a strong sense of China's weakness in international affairs, in diplomacy as well as in trade, and does not fall back on traditional Chinese conceptions of international relations in order to strengthen China's position. He argues that international law was established as a system of relations between nations of relatively equal strength in the West. When strong nations deal with weak nations, then the strong is inevitably the one to dominate the relationship. "When a nation is strong in power, then it is also strong in reason, and when a nation is weak in power, then it is also weak in reason. Only when the strength of the two parties is equal may one speak of reason and of international law."[5] Weak nations like China can enhance their strength and hence operate on an equal footing in international affairs only by applying the rules of European international law. Only through the use of international law can China obtain a position in international law. Once international law is applied and a nation is accepted into the international society, then that system of laws will secure the rights and benefits of that nation and secure a balance of power. International law is a system for the protection of all its members, and any state, regardless of domestic political structure, will find that it does not impose any limitations on the autonomy of a state.[6] Like many of his contemporaries Zheng Guanying argues favourably for the application of international law in spite of its apparent theoretical foundation in the Western international context, not necessarily because of his support for the universality of that system but rather for more pragmatic reasons. The key notion in Zheng's argumentation is strength and that international law may serve China in the enhancement of her strength in international affairs. We do not find arguments among these reform-minded officials that traditional tribute relations and the hierarchical world order of East Asia should be utilized for strengthening China in her foreign relations.

Xue Fucheng (薛福成) (1838-1894), diplomat and ambassador to England, France, Italy and Belgium 1890-94, takes a similar position in favour of international law as a means for the promotion of China's strength in the late 19th century. In the article "On the harms of China

[5] Tian Tao 2001, p. 176
[6] Wang Yiliang (ed.) 1998, pp. 29-30; Tian Tao 2001, pp. 172-176

being outside of international law"[7] published in 1892 Xue argues that the substance of international law appears different for strong and weak nations. There are, in Xue's view, however, also principles in international law that may serve as tools for securing equal rights and benefits for weak nations. In China's weak position in international relations in 1892 China has no other option other than to adapt to international law out of mere pragmatic reasons.[8] Li Hongzhang (李鴻章) (1823-1901) also saw the need for the adoption of international law in the aftermath of the devastating Boxer rebellion in 1900. In 1901 he acknowledged that international law was becoming a part of Chinese political reality in his preface to William A.P. Martin's translations of Hall's *A Treatise on International Law*:

> International Law belongs to all the nations of the globe. If they observe it, they may dwell in quiet; if they neglect it, they are sure to have trouble. A year ago, the Boxer bandits arose, murdered a Foreign Minister and laid siege to the Legations. This unheard-of proceeding was due to a clique of narrow-minded ministers who, not knowing the lessons of history, could not be expected to know International Law. ... As we in the first instance had failed to observe International Law, (the Allied Forces) set aside International Law in dealing with us—as a sort of retribution. Yet when the North was in commotion, the South-East remained quiet. That it remained undisturbed in such a crisis was due to the fact that we observed International Law, and the foreigners also observed it.[9]

Wang Tao is primarily known for his promulgation of Western studies, in politics and economy as well as in natural sciences and technology, for the education of the Chinese people. Wang Tao was active in the political debates in the late 19th century and was an ardent advocate of legal and political reforms. He was an active writer and may be reckoned among the most influential journalists and editors of the newly established periodicals in Hong Kong and Shanghai in the early years from the 1870s.[10] Wang was explicit in his view on international law: "This [international law] is something which a strong nation may dismiss or make use of at its own will. But

[7] "Lun Zhongguo zai gongfa wai zhi hai" (論中國在公法外之害)

[8] Tian Tao 2001, pp. 176-179; See also: Chien 1993

[9] *Gongfa xinbian* 1903, preface p. 1a. Li Hongzhang's text was first published in the 158th issue of Young Allen's Chinese language periodical *Wanguo gongbao* (萬國公報) (*A Review of the Times*) in March 1902 (Allen 1968, vol. 33, p. 20836).

[10] Chen & Fang (eds.) 1998, pp. 1-30; See also Britton 1966, pp. 41-47

when a weak nation wants to apply international law, then international law is not at its disposal."[11] He does not afford international law much esteem as a theoretical system also protecting the interests of weak nations. In his view international law does not constitute an actual limitation on the international conduct of strong states. On the other hand, the conclusion and recommendation for action are at any rate the same as we have seen above, namely that China has no other option than to adopt international law. In Wang Tao's political universe the motivation is that legal reforms strengthen China, and the adoption of international law is a part of the reforms necessary for China in order to strengthen and educate, modernize and Westernize the Chinese nation. A strong China is the best guarantee for a profitable Chinese foreign policy.[12] In the words of Paul A. Cohen: "Wang's underlying view of international law was one of extreme cynicism."[13] Wang Tao did not see much justice, in particular for weak nations, in international law, but he found international law an indispensable tool for China in the strengthening process.

A more explicit condemnation of international law as a tool for China may be observed in the chapter "Against disarmament"[14] of the *Quanxuepian* (勸學篇)[15] by Zhang Zhidong published in 1898. The *Quanxuepian* is formulated as a guide to reforms written by the reform minded official Zhang Zhidong to be used in the promulgation of new learning in the educational commissions of the provinces of China. The chapter on disarmament is written in opposition to the proposed meeting on international disarmament in Sweden. Zhang refers to "disarmament as an international joke and international law as a deception".[16] In the relations between strong and weak states, between the West and China, there is a fundamentally unequal balance of power and no law may substitute for this. International law is established and maintained only for the regulation of intercourse between states of equal strength. The foreign powers do not treat China as an equal partner in trade and in questions pertaining to penal and civil law in their operations in China and do not accept China into

---

[11] "Yangwu shang" (洋務上) in Chen & Fang (eds.) 1998, pp. 80-81
[12] Chen & Fang (eds.) 1998, pp. 26-28; Tian Tao 2001, pp. 179-180
[13] Cohen 1974, p. 94; See also Cohen 1967, pp. 138-145
[14] "Fei mibing" (非弭兵)
[15] *Exhortation to study*
[16] Li Zhongxing (ed.) 1998, p. 165

the international community. Why then should China adhere to international law, is Zhang's argumentation.[17]

In spite of Zhang Zhidong's frontal attack on the applicability and reliability of international law in China and the more general distrust in the reliability of the system as a protector of the rights of weak states, the general tendency among these scholars and diplomats engaged in the early debate on international questions is that international law must be applied in Chinese international relations. The arena of international relations appeared like a brutal battlefield where strong states had the upper hand. China's position in late Qing international relations was perceived as weak and frail, and international law was one of the most important tools with which China could acquire a stronger position in her relations with other states. But international law would not help China if China did not adhere to international law herself. Traditional world orientations from China's past are not called upon as frameworks for regaining China's strength. These deliberations and calls for an introduction of international law in Chinese foreign policy and a general international orientation are significant voices of support for the process that was to follow—the gradual identification of China's international role with the terms and conditions of the European system of international law. The more important process of intellectual adaptation to these terms and conditions, however, may not be observed in these supportive declarations of sponsorship for the application of international law by Guo, Chen, Zheng, Xue, Wang, Li etc. but rather in the extensive discourse on related questions taking place in the periodicals of late Qing times and involving people with political and social concerns from many walks of life in late imperial China. The major debate on these questions takes place after the Sino-Japanese war and the strong Japanese influence on these debates in China, subjects to be discussed in chapter 6 below. In this chapter we shall briefly take a look at a number of specific arguments in the Chinese discourse prior to the Japanese influence from the early 20th century.

[17] Ibid., pp. 164-166; Janku unpublished paper 2004, p. 3

STATECRAFT AND INTERNATIONAL LAW

The statecraft (*jingshi* 經世) tradition in China is closely affiliated with humanism in the Confucian tradition, stressing the importance of social participation, and can be interpreted as a reaction against the metaphysical accentuation of Confucian ideals of the human society in Neo-Confucian thought. This school, as a practical and this-worldly approach to the social and political challenges confronting China, re-emerged as an influential trend in Chinese intellectual circles in the 19th century. The early group of statecraft thinkers also included reformers who were concerned with Western elements in China's self-strengthening program, most notably the Canton opium commissioner and editor of the *Haiguo tuzhi*, Wei Yuan. One of the major efforts of this early group of statecraft advocates was the compilation of a collection of texts on practical measures in the solving of China's most pressing socio-political problems entitled *Qing jingshi wenbian* (清經世文編) or *Huangchao jingshi wenbian* (皇朝經世文編)[18] edited by Wei Yuan and He Changling (賀長齡) (1785-1848) and published in 1827. In this compilation, following in the tradition of a similar compilation of statecraft documents from the Ming dynasty, "Wei Yuan set forth two basic approaches of the statecraft school: emphasis on the present, and stress on the importance of practical application. What were the pressing problems of China during this time? In the first decades of the nineteenth century, a major concern of the *ching-shih* literati was the problem of domestic administration, resulting from the slow process of dynastic decline in general and the White Lotus Rebellion in particular."[19] Hence, international questions were not the major concern of this group. This *Qing jingshi wenbian* project was followed by a number of continuations, in addition to the many reprints of the original Wei/He compilation.[20] One of the later editions formally edited by Mai Zhonghua (麥仲華)[21] was sponsored by Liang Qichao. "In

[18] *Collection of Qing dynasty writings on statecraft*

[19] Hao & Wang 1980, pp. 145-146

[20] Three different *xubian* (續編) were published between 1882 and 1897. Three different editions of statecraft texts with the title *xinbian* (新編) appeared in the late 19th and early 20th centuries, and a number of other editions entitled *sanbian* (三編), *sibian* (四編) or *tongbian* (統編) appeared about the same time. (Hummel 1943, p. 282)

[21] The younger brother of Mai Menghua, a student of Kang Youwei and married to

sponsoring this new edition, Liang clearly placed himself in the tradition of Confucian concern with practical statesmanship, which was the mainstream of late Ch'ing thought."[22] As I shall return to later, Liang was an outspoken advocate of new learning and the application of Western ideas and theories in Chinese reforms. There is, however, no contradiction between this Confucian school of statecraft and liberal ideas on reform and change. On the contrary, we find in the compilations on statecraft from the early 20th century that the promotion of international law as an orientation for China's foreign policy is prominent within this tradition. The practical statesmanship goes very well with pragmatic ideas on how to introduce elements of Western international law in order to strengthen China. Tian Tao has shown the relatively affirmative tone towards international law in these statecraft texts[23] and the sheer number of translated texts and introductions to international questions in the light of international law, in particular in the diplomacy section of the *Qingchao jingshiwen tongbian* (清朝經世文統編) published in 1901, reinforces this impression.

The statecraft compilations confirm the impression that international law in many circles was taken as a means to strengthen China in late Qing. The theoretical implications and the historical context that comprise the foundation of international law were not of major concern. The applicability of international law in positioning China in world politics seemed more pressing and of greater concern for officials, diplomats and statecraft Confucians. In other circles, however, the historical and theoretical aspects involved in adopting international law became a part of the international discourse in China. The Shanghai newspaper *Shenbao* was an early vehicle for such debates.

SHENBAO AND AN EARLY DISCOURSE ON INTERNATIONAL LAW

The *Shenbao* (申報) office was established in Shanghai in May 1871 through investments by the British businessmen and brothers Ernest Major (1841-1908) and Frederick Major together with two of their

---

Kang's daughter Kang Tongwei (康同薇)

[22] Chang 1971, p. 62

[23] Tian Tao 2001, pp. 205-219

fellow countrymen. When the first issue of the *Shenbao* was published on the 30th of April 1872 a new page in the history of the Chinese press was opened. There were already Chinese language newspapers on the market in the treaty ports, such as the *Shanghai xinwen* (上海新聞) in Shanghai established a decade before the *Shenbao* and mainly run by missionaries. The *Shanghai xinwen*, however, was mainly an organ for foreign business and Chinese businessmen with little space for news (mostly translated) or debate, while *Shenbao* gradually directed its editorial policy towards a literary Chinese readership, providing space for journalistic creativity and debate on current issues. *Shenbao*'s success as a Chinese language newspaper, and its long history of publication until 1949, may to a large extent be ascribed to its successful address to a politically and socially engaged Chinese literati. *Shenbao* established an editorial column for debate on the first page of each issue, a policy which attracted many readers and which set the standard for later Chinese newspapers and periodicals.[24]

In the early history of the Chinese press *Shenbao* has commonly been categorised as a foreign newspaper (*waibao* 外報), in contrast to official gazettes (*guanbao* 官報) and private newspapers (*minbao* 民報) because of its foreign capital and ownership. It is also common to consider the modern indigenous history of the Chinese press and periodicals to have its origin in the Japanese influence after the Sino-Japanese war 1894-95. Surely, there is a fundamental difference between the debates conducted by the journalists and contributors of the *Shenbao* and the strongly politicised debate in the periodicals established after 1895. Andrea Janku has, however, pointed out that the political debates in the leading articles (*lun* 論) of the *Shenbao* dating back to its early years certainly have a resemblance to the later political and social debates in papers such as the *Shibao* (時報), and that there may not be such a sharp line of division between the political debates of early *Shenbao* and the post-1895 periodicals as commonly assumed.

> Sicher war die früe Shenbao kein Massenmedium im modernen Sinne, und das Wort shelun 社論, der moderne chinesische begriff für "Leitartikel", ist vor 1907 nich belegt. Sicher unterschied sich der politische Character der Shibao, die weithin die Position der Konstitutionalisten vertrat, wesentlich von dem der Shenbao der Literatenjournalisten. Und dennnoch hatte sich die Shenbao schon bald

---

[24] Ma Guangren 1996, pp. 57-64; Janku 2003, pp. 19-23, Mittler 2004

> nach ihrer Gründung 1872 in aktuellen politischen Debatt engagiert, und mit dem Abdruck politischer Artikel in Form des lunshuo 論說 auf ihrer Titelseite war dieser zu einem Äquivalent des Leitartikels der westlichen Presse geworden.[25]

The leading articles in the *Shenbao* were established on an ancient Han-dynasty tradition where a man of literary ability and ambition explains the difference between the correct and erroneous interpretation (*lun shifei* 論是非) of the ancient texts. "Der lun war eines etabliertes Genre politischer Kritik, das nicht in einen eng definierten Bereich der bürokratischen Öffentlichkeit gehörte."[26] In the early modern press the *lun* genre became a discursive space where the journalist and man of political and social commitment could vindicate his position and make public his sense of responsibility for social morality and order. It served as an organ for vertical communication of political opinion, in the early days of the *Shenbao* in its embryonic form. Yet, with the later development of greater space for political and social debate, the *Shenbao* leading article can be seen as the beginning of the liberation of the political discourse from the previously formal hierarchical structure.[27]

In 1875 the leading articles of the *Shenbao* started to engage in questions pertaining to international law. On the 14th of January 1875 *Shenbao* printed excerpts of an article in the Hong Kong newspaper *Xunhuan ribao* (循環日報) on the new international regulations regarding restrictions on warfare for reasons of humanity. These included prohibition on using poisonous weapons, prohibition on pursuing and killing fleeing enemies not carrying weapons, prohibition on using explosives against civilians etc. On the following day the leading article in *Shenbao* issued a reaction to its implications, arguing against the claim that the Western agreements in international law are expressions of a humane and just attitude towards humanity. The international community should primarily make agreements on how to solve international conflicts and focus on inhumane actions towards humanity in time of peace, not merely make regulations for wartime international relations, claims the author of this leading article. In other words, these agreements on humane warfare are not sufficient in order to secure peace and welfare for the common people,

[25] Janku 2003, p. 6
[26] Ibid., p. 26
[27] Ibid., pp. 23-33; See also Britton 1966, pp. 63-69

who have greater need for agreements on protecting humankind in time of peace. It appears that the author has a limited understanding of international law outside the facts presented in the report from the Hong Kong newspaper, which is hardly surprising in Shanghai in the middle of the 1870s.

The author claims further that the moral principles of wise rulers should guide all national and international conflicts and military actions should only be taken against those forces that threaten the security and prosperity of the common people, such as the actions of brutal and despotic rulers. China has been criticised in the Western press for its actions against rebellions threatening Qing authority. In the perspective of the *Shenbao* editorial these are justified because they otherwise would jeopardise the social and political order within the Chinese borders. The military actions of the Western powers in China, on the other hand, and military engagements outside the sphere of Chinese political power earlier in history are inhumane actions not to be permitted. China may very well be weak and a target for international ridicule in the 1870s, but China will one day train troops and produce weapons to become strong. Nonetheless, China will never abandon her civilised manners and become brutal (like the West).[28] The author of this article takes these new regulations on warfare as a starting point for a discussion in a rather traditional fashion on the relationship between civilised China and the brutal West. He does not make any other reference to international law or to the Tongwenguan translation of Wheaton, which had been published more than 10 years earlier, and he may not be familiar with the entire range of implications in international law. Yet this early contribution to the Chinese discourse on international law shows the traditional and Qing loyal perspective on the relationship between China and the West in terms of physical strength and level of civilisation in China of the mid-1870s, implicitly evoking the more traditional Chinese world-views discussed in chapter 1.

The viewpoints presented through the *Shenbao* leading articles show a different and more sophisticated attitude towards international law in the mid-1880s. Martin had published a number of translations of international law texts in Chinese, as we have discussed in the previous chapter. In addition, China, together with Japan, had been

[28] *Shenbao* 14th and 15th January 1875

"The French chieftain Courbet". Amédée Anatole Courbet (1827-1885) commanded the French marine forces in their attacks on Vietnam and Taiwan in 1883-84. This drawing of a battle with Chinese naval forces was printed in the Chinese newspaper Shubao (述報) *on 30 October 1884.*

invited to take part in the sixth meeting of the Association for the Reform and Codification of the Law of Nations in 1878. Guo Songtao, China's first minister to England, served as China's representative at this meeting and Guo was elected honorary vice-president of the association, a title later also conferred on Zeng Jize.[29] In an article published in November 1885 entitled "A discussion on why China ought to participate in international law"[30] an explanation as to why China should accept the conditions of international law is spelled out. International law is a commonly agreed system of international conduct and relations. It balances advantages and disadvantages of

[29] Hsü 1960, pp. 206-207
[30] "Lun Zhongguo yi yuyu wanguo gongfa" (論中國宜與於萬國公法)

participating states and takes into consideration the policy of states and the livelihood of its peoples. With such a system all the Western nations have ways to avoid conflict and instruction on how to deal with international conflicts and exchange, the article claims.

> When we observe matters of conflict in Asia, Europe, America and Africa in recent times, we find that there are always constraints on what actions are taken and some intentions which are not acted upon in these matters. The reason is the power of the writings on international law.[31]

The article further argues that the principles in international law may have been suggested by one single person or by one single country. But when they have been approved by the international community and proven to function as a guide to the international community in inter-state affairs, these principles are accepted as part of the international system of laws and practices. With the translations of Martin and the approval of the Zongli yamen China has in fact also recognised the importance of the principles laid down in international law. Opponents to the application of international law in China have claimed that China was not present when the practices in international law were agreed upon, and is hence not bound by the regulations in international law. China is, in this argumentation, outside the scope of international law. The *Shenbao* argument acknowledges the fact that China's position was not considered when these regulations were drawn up. On the other hand, *Shenbao* argues, all international affairs nowadays are conducted according to the commonly accepted practices of international law and China has had success in the negotiations with France through reference to international law. Since international law is used by foreign states in their conduct of relations with China, it means that China is regarded as a member of the community of states circumscribed by international law. When the international community places blame on China by referring to international law, the international community is also compelled to regard China as a member of the family of nations. China must in the future insist that she is a member of the international community and insist on being consulted when new regulations in international law are being drafted and discussed. China needs more translations on international law and needs to adhere to international law in her conduct of international affairs. "Then, if in the future there is an

[31] *Shenbao* 28th November 1885

incident in international relations where a Western nation puts blame on China by using international law, then China will have no difficulties in using international law to argue against such an accusation."[32] The leading articlc in *Shenbao* is arguing against Western papers claiming that China does not have a chair in the announced international convention on international affairs in Paris. There is an apparent lack of experience and knowledge in international law in China at this time. But there is also a growing realisation among intellectuals that China can only be recognised in international affairs if she adheres to and takes part in negotiations on international laws and regulations. The translations by Martin had by this time started to form an opinion on international affairs in the direction of accepting the entire Western system of international law as a sequel to the establishment of permanent foreign legations some years earlier.[33]

The article from November 1885 presents a pragmatic and rather down-to-earth attitude towards world politics. In quite a different fashion a utopian vision of an international community in peace and unity is drawn up in the leading article in *Shenbao* 26th February 1888. This is probably the first utopia of a peaceful world community based on the principles of equality in international law designed in China, years before Kang Youwei's (康有為) (1858-1927) utopian vision of the Datong world community, which we shall address later. The technical term for this utopia applied in *Shenbao* is *hetong* (和同), signifying 'peaceful coexistence'. The title of the article is "A discussion on the way of international law which is peaceful coexistence",[34] and the main argument is that the commonly acknowledged regulations in international law in fact represent a system of standards and principles with inherent prospects for a utopian world community. The crux of the matter is the principle of

[32] Ibid.

[33] *Shenbao* is not the only newspaper to engage in a debate on questions pertaining to international law in the 1880s. The daily newspaper *Shubao* (述報) published in Guangzhou from 18th April 1884 to 3rd April 1885 printed a number of articles discussing the French position in China and Vietnam in light of international law and regulations of international trade. The main argument in these articles is similarly that China must become familiar with and adhere to the principles of international law in order to be in a position to compel foreign nations to comply with international agreements and treaties. (*Shubao*, pp. 497, 657, 705, see also Fang Hanqi (ed.) 1997, vol. 1, pp. 480-484)

[34] "Lun wanguo gongfa dao zai hetong" (論萬國公法道在和同)

public standards (*gong* 公) in opposition to private standards (*si* 私). Public international law represents *par se* the public standards for the public good, and all international conduct must be performed in accordance with the system of commonly accepted standards, according to this leading article.

> In all matters under heaven there are private standards for what is right and what is wrong (*si shifei* 私是非), and there are public standards for what is right and what is wrong (*gong shifei* 公是非). The standard of one single person belongs to the category of private standards, while the standard of many people belongs to the category of public standards. The standard of one single family belongs to the category of private standards, while the standard of a state belongs to the category of public standards. The standard of one single state belongs to the category of private standards, while the standard of ten thousand states (e.g. the international community) belongs to the category of public standards. What is advantageous for one and not for the other does not belong to the category of public standards. What is suitable for A and not for B does not belong to the category of public standards. That which is the public standard has its basis in reason, and laws are established according to reason.[35]

In international affairs it is necessary to have a set of public standards for acceptable conduct in order to distinguish between what is accepted as a public and what is rejected as a private standard. It is not possible for a state to establish its own standards since no state can be without neighbours, friends or enemies. Even when individual persons have established the standards of international law, these publicists have had the public, common good in mind when working out the principles of international law, and hence there is no contradiction in this theory. Public standards in the relations between states may only be found in international law. "International law is the tool with which public standards correct private standards. Public [international] law is the tool with which the international community is united in peace."[36] In the opinion of the author international law is bestowed with near magical powers to unite what is separated, to make peaceful what is in dissent, to make submissive what is in opposition, and it will cause the strong not to subdue the weak, the many not to dishonour the few, and the big not to insult the small. How then, the author asks, is it possible that the international community at present is ruled by inequality and

---

[35] *Shenbao* 26th February 1888

[36] Ibid.

private standards? If international law is a standard which will obliterate all inequalities and international indignity, then how is it that only Europe and America are members of the community of international law? The high public standards of international law are in no way realised in the world today, the author claims. "A day of international unity in peace will one day arise. Today that day has not yet come."[37] The author ends his essay with a prophetic vision for the future: "I secretly hope that a grand man will appear on the five continents, a man who will advocate an end to all private wars, a man who will restrict all wanton and offensive acts of states." And if such states rise, then all other states will act unanimously according to the standards of international law to fight against all such intentions. The influence of international law will grow as a number of single international crises are solved, and gradually all states will be subject to one common system of public international law. The theories of international law will gradually be more sophisticated and complete, and its influence will subsequently be propagated to all corners of the five continents. The world will resemble a Buddhist paradise where all countries will prosper in peace and tranquillity and there will no longer be differences between large and small, strong and weak, many and few, and then "every one will enjoy peace in their own country, every one will protect their territory, every one will cherish their ruler and every one will venerate their people." The effects of adhering to the public standards of international law in this article apparently go far beyond the commonly acknowledged regulations of communication and cooperation between single states in a community of states. The utopian society of states envisioned by the *Shenbao* author appears to have Buddhist utopian overtones and is not representative of the general attitude towards international law in the late 1880s. This article is, however, an interesting early explication on how the future of the international community may have appeared through a first reading of international law texts in Chinese and an illustrative example of a contrast to the very pragmatic attitude of other contemporary journalists. This article is also a fascinating prelude to the utopian visions of the international community in the light of Kang Youwei's three stage theory and the utopian society in the Age of Great Peace to be discussed later, even if there is no apparent direct

[37] Ibid.

relationship between these two utopian illusions.

The leading article of the *Shenbao* was very much involved in all kinds of argumentation on the development and consequences of the Sino-Japanese war 1894-95. Hardly any of the articles, however, applied the principles of international law to their analysis of the war in the East. International law had until this time in the *Shenbao* articles served as a framework for visions and prospects for China's future in the international community. But none of the articles had discussed the implications of accepting international agreements on sovereignty, jurisdiction, rights and obligations. Such deliberations could have been appropriate and possibly profitable for China during the Sino-Japanese war. Only with the experiences and lessons from that war did the principles of international law and not only a vision of its framework start to enter the Chinese discourse. One of the examples of this development is also to be found in the leading article column of the *Shenbao*, as described in a paper by Andrea Janku entitled "Der Fall Kang Youwei (1898) und das völkerrechtliche Prinzip der Nichtauslieferung politischer Flüchtlinge in der Shaghaier kommerziellen Presse" where she discusses the application of international agreements on the extradition of political refugees in *Shenbao* and other papers in 1898.[38] Only by this time do the precise terms and conditions of international law enter the discourse in *Shenbao*.

As we have seen above, the arguments presented in the leading articles of the *Shenbao* do not constitute a politically or philosophically consistent and coherent contribution to the discourse on international law in late Qing China. Rather, this column in *Shenbao* gives us an impression of the wide array of interpretations and applications of international law in late imperial Chinese discourse. *Shenbao* with its editorial column is an early vehicle for public political debate in China. Soon, however, other periodicals were to take over as the most important media for the promotion of political and social discourse. The reformers, indebted to the political and social visions of Kang Youwei and Liang Qichao, and their periodicals are a starting point for a more diverse theoretical political and social discourse in late imperial China, which we shall take a closer look at in chapter 6 below. There is, however, one other early

---

[38] See also a discussion of the principles of extradition and the case of Sun Yatsen in the paper *Shixuebao* in 1897 in chapter 6.

debate on international law in 19th century China that is close linked with the introduction of international law in late Qing China, namely the question of international law in ancient China.

THE DISCOURSE ON INTERNATIONAL LAW IN ANCIENT CHINA

As we have seen in the preceding chapter, W.A.P. Martin promoted in the 1880s the idea that China had had a system of inter-state regulation resembling the regulations of inter-state relations in Western international law already in the Zhou era before the unification of the Chinese central plains in the 3rd century BC. The early Chinese discourse on international law did not only engage in a debate on the present with visions for the future. Predictably, when the question about the adaptability of the Western science of international law came up in late Qing China, someone also raised the question: Did China maybe also have a system of international law in her ancient past? Does international law in fact have an origin in China? Martin's publication of these ideas was followed by a discourse on the significance and implications of this presumption in late Qing China with resonances all the way into contemporary China as well as into the West, which is the topic of this sub-chapter.

States and relations in ancient China

In China of the pre-Qin period before 221 BC the idea of a former unified cultural and political entity on the Chinese plains, referred to as the Zhou (周), was very much alive among the scholars and literati. The Zhou was symbolically used in the political discourse of ancient China as a standard for a well administered, prosperous and thriving society to be emulated. The last period of the Zhou leading up to the unification of the central Chinese plains under the first emperor of Qin (秦) in 221 BC, referred to as the Eastern Zhou, is usually sub-divided into the Spring and Autumn period (Chunqiu or Ch'un-Ch'iu 春秋) (722-481 BC)[39] and the Warring States period (Zhanguo 戰國)

[39] The era in Chinese history referred to as the Spring and Autumn period (*Chunqiu*) has taken its name and dating from a text with the same title. The *Chunqiu* is a chronicle recording events taking place in the small state of Lu (魯), Confucius'

(403-221 BC).[40] Philosophers and scholars of the Eastern Zhou refer its political and cultural heritage to the idea of a magnificent and rich Zhou culture before it moved eastwards in 770 BC, usually referred to as Western Zhou. The brilliance and wealth of the ancient Western Zhou was, however, most probably not much more than an image in the minds of the people of the war-ridden states of the Warring States period. We find very little evidence to show that the political or cultural influence of the ancient state of Zhou on neighbouring areas was very great, or that the Eastern Zhou in fact was the political successor of an ancient influential state that had been split into a large number of smaller states by perpetual struggle and war. The philosophers of the pre-Qin times, and not least the philosophers and officials of the later unified Qin and its successor the Han dynasty, had an interest in creating an image of an ancient unified and stable political entity, an ancestor to the Chinese state. Hence an image of a prosperous early Zhou and a direct line of political and cultural inheritance between the Western Zhou and the Eastern Zhou was created. The more likely situation is that a number of smaller states grew up in what today is northern China, and that one of these was the state of Zhou. With only very simple means of communication and trade these states had relatively little contact. As trade, the material culture, and the political systems developed, however, these states came more and more often in contact with each other and conflicts arose. These conflicts became more severe towards the 4th and 3rd century BC, influencing the relative wealth and prosperity of these states and the livelihood of its peoples.

We are from chapter 2 familiar with the assumption that the multi-state system of ancient Greece is the earliest known system of

---

home state, between 722 and 481 BC. The actual authorship of the text is not known but traditionally its composition is ascribed to Confucius himself. Subtle phrasings in the texts are supposed to contain Confucius' praise and blame of historical events that can be read as a key to political morality which has the capacity of restoring the Golden Age of the Zhou. Several commentaries to the *Chunqiu*, explaining Confucius' interpretations of history (such as the *Gongyang* (公羊), the *Guliang* (穀梁) and the Zuo (左) commentaries), constitute the core of Confucian canonical texts. (Nylan 2001, pp. 253-306; Loewe (ed.) 1993, pp. 67-76) The term *chunqiu*, Spring and Autumn, refers in general to chronological events in history. It refers to the historical period between 722 and 481 BC, it refers to the historical annals of the state of Lu, and finally it carries the meaning of Confucian teaching in itself.

[40] This period has its name from a text with the title *Zhanguoce* (戰國策), *The strategies of the Warring States,* recording historical events of the period. The dating of this period varies in different sources.

inter-state relations in the West, a system that may have contained the earliest elements of what later became the inter-state system of Europe, and which subsequently is the predecessor of the later system of regulated international relations referred to as international law. The Western system of inter-state relations between states of equal status disintegrated with the establishment of Roman supremacy in 168 BC. A new international order in the West grew out of the Middle Ages. In China any ancient order of inter-state relations crumbled with the establishment of Qin supremacy in 221 BC, a situation very much parallel to that of ancient Europe. In China, however, the idea of the great empire continued to identify prosperity and wealth with a unified central Chinese area. The multi-state system of Europe of the Middle Ages was never a fact in China in later history, neither was it an ideal among the Chinese literati. The idea of an ancient prosperous state, be it the ancient Zhou or the Qin and Han dynasties, was always the lofty ideal in China in times of war and disintegration. Thus, both historic realities and political ideals in these two parallel universes developed quite differently, in spite of their similar early developments. Whereas the system of inter-state relations grew ever more sophisticated in Europe, there was no such system in operation within the Chinese cultural and political sphere.

We know that the states of the Spring and Autumn period developed a relatively sophisticated system of inter-state relations. We find that they waged war, they entered and changed alliances (even with non-Chinese tribes), and signed treaties for mutual benefit. We also know that they developed a system for the exchange of diplomatic missions, granted free passage for envoys through a third state upon permission, and had agreed upon a system for the extradition of criminals. Inter-state meetings or conventions were also held in order to settle agreements between several states on matters of common interest. A number of these measures and the respect shown for the independence of another state resemble the rights of a state later in international law referred to as sovereignty.[41] This resemblance is, however, weak since sovereignty in the sense of modern international law involves many aspects not present in the ancient Chinese system. The main tool for protecting one's state in ancient China was not that of being able to claim sovereignty and rights in

---

[41] Walker 1971, p. 24

international relations regardless of the size or power of one's state. Without the military strength to protect one's territory and wage war, possibly even expand one's territory, there would be no means of maintaining the influence of a state over time. "The final measurement, of course, was the actual power test—war."[42] "In general, the rules which governed the intercourse among the states of the Ch'un-Ch'iu period prevailed only where they were mutually beneficial."[43]

Martin on the ancient Chinese origin of international law

During the process of adaptation to Western learning in many new fields of study in the late 19th century we may also observe a tendency to look for ancient Chinese parallels or origins of the "modern" sciences being introduced from the West, often referred to as "Chinese origin of Western knowledge".[44] The same phenomenon may be found within the science of international law. Surprisingly, the quest for a Chinese origin of international law does not mainly have its source in the Chinese discourse on these questions but in the writings of a foreigner, William A.P. Martin, as we have seen above. Martin fully accepted the idea that the states of the Spring and Autumn period had inherited the political, legal and cultural legacy of the ancient state of Zhou:

> The Chinese States were not, like those of Greece, a cluster of detached tribes who had together emerged from barbarism, without any well-defined political connection; they were the fragments of a disintegrated empire, inheriting its laws and civilization, as the States of modern Europe inherited those of Rome.[45]

As these states of ancient China gained independence from the state of Zhou, "the feudal princes threw off the semblance of subjection, and pursued without restraint the objects of their own private ambitions".[46] "We find, as we have said, a family of States, many of them as

---

[42] Ibid., p. 41
[43] Ibid., p. 92
[44] *Xixue dongyuan* (西學東源). See entries on this term in Lackner, Amelung & Kurtz (eds.) 2001 and Lackner & Vittinghoff (eds.) 2004.
[45] Martin 1901, pp. 429-430
[46] Ibid., p. 430

extensive as the great States of western Europe, united by the ties of race, literature, and religion, carrying on an active intercourse, commercial and political, which, without some recognized *Jus gentium*, would have been impracticable."[47] Martin has found evidence that these states balanced each other by the principles of balance of power also securing the rights of the weak states. He finds a certain system of neutrality being practised and an elaborate system of diplomacy performed by men of diplomatic profession. He also describes the sophisticated system of treaties in the Spring and Autumn period. He recognises the lack of a text systematically laying out the rules of this intercourse and suggests that such a text *may* have existed but was lost during the destruction of "heterodox" texts under the first Qin emperor. Martin's main source are the ritual texts referring its ancestry to the ancient state of Zhou, the *Zhouli* (周禮), *The Rites of Zhou*. In Martin's mind all the main states on the Chinese central plains during the Spring and Autumn, except for the state of Qin, had inherited the rites and traditions of the Zhou to the effect that a written code of inter-state conduct was unnecessary. The code of conduct in these states, and in particular between these states, was identical to the extent that the system of conflict of laws, known from the West to solve matters of differences in national laws in matters involving more than one state, was superfluous:

> [T]he laws and usages of the several States were so uniform—all being copied from a common model—that there was little occasion for the cultivation of that branch of international jurisprudence, which in modern times has become so prominent under the title of the "conflict of laws".[48]

By acclaiming the notion that the states in ancient China all owed the legacy and their tradition to the ancient state of Zhou, Martin has created an allegiance between these states that accounts for more than the sources in fact tell us about the relationships and details of inter-state conduct in China at this time. Martin was aware of the discrepancies between the ancient Chinese system of inter-state conduct and the modern European system called international law, defined not only in custom and rituals but also in systematic and theoretical deliberations of the foundations for such an international

[47] Ibid., p. 431
[48] Ibid., pp. 434-435

system of conduct, as we have discussed in chapter 1. The lack of any systematic and theoretical description of the ancient Chinese system is accounted for through the common allegiance of states to the Zhou and by the idea that it is "quite possible that text-books on the subject of international relations may have existed in ancient China, without coming down to our times, just as the Greeks had books on that subject, of which nothing now survives but their titles".[49] Martin is cautious when he uses the term 'international law' for the ancient Chinese system, preferring to refer to it as an 'international code' or 'consuetudinary law' to indicate a principal difference from the modern system and theories of international law. His conclusion is, however, distinctly in favour of seeing the ancient system as parallel to the Western system with its antecedents in ancient Greece. China had an international code analogous to the Western system, is Martin's conclusion, bolstering the Chinese argumentation that the modern system of international law in the West has its antecedents in ancient China. And Martin is not alone in finding such parallels:

> Chinese statesmen have pointed out the analogy of their own country at that epoch with the political division of modern Europe. In their own records, they find usages, words, and ideas, corresponding to the terms of our modern international law.[50]

This sets off a lasting tradition in China, and in the West, for supporting the idea that China had an ancient system of international law in the Spring and Autumn period, the debate that Richard Louis Walker is referring to when he speaks of "students of interstate law of the Ch'un-Ch'iu" who fail to recognise that the *Zhouli* is a later fabrication and that the states of the Spring and Autumn period had much less allegiance to the state of Zhou than assumed earlier.[51] In the Chinese context the identification of the Spring and Autumn period with the *Spring and Autumn Annals*, allegedly edited by Confucius himself, also gives further prominence to these ideas. The very fact that an indigenous system of international law may be identified in these sacred writings, at the time of Confucius himself, and in the sacred tradition of the golden age of the ancient Zhou, has given these ideas high prestige in Confucian circles in China and in East Asia.

---

[49] Ibid., p. 448
[50] Ibid., p. 449
[51] Walker 1971, p. 74

The legacy of Martin's assumptions

The elaborations by Martin on the ancient Chinese system of international law have had a long-lasting effect on the interpretation of the ancient inter-state systems in China in Western literature until this day. Works with titles such as *Le droit des gens et la Chine antique,*[52] *Doctrines du droit public en Chine antique,*[53] *International law at the time of Chan-kuo,*[54] and *La doctrine du droit international chez Confucius*[55] have maintained this same tendency in their analyses of the ancient Chinese inter-state system. The idea promoted by Martin is still accepted in the world history of international law, as presented in the *Encyclopedia of Public International Law* published in 1984:

> It is nevertheless possible, even given the gaps in our knowledge, to accept as proven that there is, beyond the world of the Near East and Europe evidence of international law scattered over the earth in abundance. There are at least two cases, in the ancient Chinese system of States in the first half of the last pre-Christian millennium, and in the Central American society of States existing in the last pre-colonial phase, where international law existed and flourished over a long period of time.[56]

In Japan these ideas have also been able to withstand the test of time, even if they have taken on a slightly different shape. Keishiro Iriye, professor of international law and lecturer in diplomatic history at Waseda University in Tokyo, has written an article entitled "The Principles of International Law in the Light of Confucian Doctrine" published in 1967.[57] Iriye discusses a number of Japanese and Chinese contributions to the discourse on ancient Chinese international law, and agrees with the view of the sceptics, contending that: "I believe that there are a number of difficulties in seeing the Ch'un Ch'iu period as having established a pure system of international relations and a genuine order of international law."[58] Iriye's main argument is not that

---

[52] Hsü, Ch'uan-pao (Siu Tchoan-pao) 1926/1927

[53] Li, Sin-Yang 1928

[54] Yu, Mo-gung 1936

[55] Chan, Nay Chow 1940

[56] *Encyclopedia of Public International Law* 1984, vol. 7, p. 128

[57] Iriye has also published other works on China and questions pertaining to international law, such as; *Anglo-Russian Conflict in the Chinese Borderlands*, 1935; *Alien Status in China*, 1937; *The Sino-Indian Dispute and International Law*, 1964; *International Law in the Chinese Classics*, 1966.

[58] Iriye 1967, p. 7

a system of rudimentary modern international law is to be found in the ancient Chinese inter-state relations, even if he indicates that a system of quasi-equal relations existed between the states in late Zhou times. His principal argument is that the system of Confucian rites represents the order that maintained a system resembling modern international order. Iriye's project appears to be to identify a resemblance between the Confucian rites and political ethics practised in East Asia and the modern system of political science: "Inter-state relations at that time did not constitute, strictly speaking, international relations, but many principles which governed mutual relations are basically analogous to those of the present." [59] Iriye finds the embryonic forms of international relations not in the ancient Chinese inter-state relations but in Confucianism itself. He does not question the traditional viewpoint on the authorship of the *Spring and Autumn Annals* or the authenticity of the texts on rituals as genuine representations of the ancient Confucian ritual order. According to Iriye the Confucian classics contain the idealised form of government in a state and the governing of relations between states, regardless of the differences in status or rank between these states. The states of ancient China did not practise a system that may be said to resemble the modern order of international law among equal states. But the rites and principles of Confucianism contain the seeds of proper inter-state relations. Keishiro Iriye's reasoning seems to be a reasonable line of argumentation for a modern Japanese scholar of international law with an inclination towards Confucian thinking, though also very questionable in terms of scholarship on ancient texts and the early Chinese philosophical tradition. It is not very likely that Confucius did in fact harbour all the intentions that later Confucians and commentators have ascribed to him. It is unlikely that the texts Iriye is referring to contain any of these systematic prescriptions for inter-state relations. It is not very likely that the states of the Spring and Autumn period, or the Warring States period, practised anything resembling a Confucian inter-state system. Iriye has identified a resemblance between the ancient inter-state relations in ancient China, similar to those identified in the texts referred to above. His conclusion is, however, not that the system that developed between these states bears any resemblance to modern international law. He

[59] Ibid., p. 5

finds these resemblances in the Confucian texts and ascribes this resemblance to Confucius himself and Confucian teaching rather than to any parallels to the ancient Greek inter-state order.

Having said this much on the Western and Japanese reception of these ideas, what is in fact the Chinese legacy of Martin's assumptions after they were translated into Chinese and published in 1884? The participants in Chinese discourse on this topic generally maintain the same line of argument that we find in the Western discourse, namely that China had in fact a system of international law in ancient times built upon the allegiance of each state to the ancient culture in Zhou. Martin's text on the origin of international law in ancient China was received with enthusiasm and support in China. In general, we find that Martin's deliberations created an atmosphere of self-confidence in international affairs when the traces of an advanced system of inter-state relations had been detected in ancient China. Liang Qichao was supportive of the idea that China had had a tradition of international law in ancient times. The leading article in *Shenbao* on the 8th of September 1884, the same year that Martin's text was published in Chinese, refers to a Chinese tradition for handling inter-state affairs from ancient times until today: "Why should [we] have to be based upon a European book on international law for the principles of inter-state affairs?"[60] The observation of similarities between the ancient Chinese state system of the Spring and Autumn and the Warring States periods was maintained by many Chinese intellectuals and diplomats such as Zheng Guangying, Ma Jianzhong (馬建忠) (1845-1900), Zeng Jize, Zhang Zhidong and other in the late 19th century. "They maintained that during the periods of the Spring and Autumn Annals (772-481BC) and Warring States (403-221 BC), the Chinese world was made up of a conglomeration of separate states and principalities that resembled the multistate system of the late nineteenth century."[61]

In early 20th century a surge of Chinese literature on the Chinese inter-state system of the Spring and Autumn period surfaced, a debate continuing till this day mainly revolving around the topics already discussed and mainly reaching the same conclusions.[62] Wang Tieya

[60] *Shenbao* 8th September 1884
[61] Hao & Wang 1980, p. 189
[62] The debate was headed by publications by Xu Jiaju (徐家駒), Lan Guangce (藍光策), Liu Renxi (劉人熙), Zhang Xinzheng (張心澂), Xu Chuanbao (徐傳保), Chen

(王鐵崖), one of the most influential scholars on international law in China today, has also included the topic of traces of international law in ancient China in his research. His article "China and International Law—In History and Contemporary Times"[63] is critical to Martin's motivation for introducing international law into China. Martin had been explicit in his missionary zeal when hoping for China to accept the moral code of Western international law. By showing that international law as it had developed in the West was consistent with the ancient, Confucian tradition of China, Martin had hoped that Chinese politicians would be more receptive to accepting the Western standard for international intercourse: "The effect of his (Martin's) efforts is difficult to estimate. His major contribution is to be found in his scholarship", according to Wang.[64] He criticises Martin for his motivation but he does not necessarily question his conclusions. At the end of his deliberations on inter-state relations in ancient China he keeps open the possibility that the ancient Chinese inter-state was a system similar to international law, and hence parallel to the embryonic forms of international law in ancient Greece, and even with a certain resemblance to modern international law:

> May not these regulations and practices anyway be recognised as international law? That is to say, can they not be recognised to have certain points in common with modern international law? Or, maybe we can describe them as embryonic forms of international law, similar to the international law of the city-states in ancient Greece. This is a question worth pondering upon.[65]

Wang Tieya does not continue this line of argumentation but clearly wants to keep open the possible speculation that early Chinese inter-state relations were the early forms of the system that later developed into modern international law—in spite of his arguments which point in the diametrically opposite direction.

Guyuan (陳顧遠), Hong Junpei (洪鈞培), Chen Shicai (陳世材), and most recently Sun Yurong (孫玉榮) and Li Zhaojie.

[63] "Zhongguo yu guojifa—lishi yu dangdai" (中國與國際法—歷史與當代) (Wang Tieya 1991); Nearly identical with chapter 9, "Zhongguo yu guojifa—gudai yu jindai" (中國與國際法—古代與近代) ("China and International Law—In Ancient and Modern Times"), in Wang Tieya 1998.

[64] Wang Tieya 1991, p. 8

[65] Ibid., pp. 12-13

Martin's legacy permeating both time and place

As we have seen, Martin's initiative to find traces of international law in ancient China was well received in China, bolstering attempts by reform-minded scholars to introduce international law as the framework for China's international orientation. Martin's deliberations were also well received in the West. The potential effect of his conclusions did not have any negative implications on the way the West conducted its international relations with China, since these practices anyway belonged to the pre-Christian era. Even in Japan the idea that China had had a system of international law in ancient times based in the classical age of Confucianism was received with enthusiasm. Modern scholarship has rejected most of the fundamental assumptions leading to Martin's conclusions. His ideas about the inter-state system and the existence of rudiments of international law in ancient China have, however, until this day been maintained and elaborated in China, in Japan and in the West. It appears that the political and cultural potency of Martin's conclusions have had a strong capacity, in the socio-political discourse, to curb attempts to negate his conclusions by more scholarly means.

In this chapter we have discussed the main features of the early discourse on international law in China. What is most striking in these arguments is the relatively affirmative attitude towards international law as a field of Western learning and its potentiality for application in China. We are also struck by the comparatively uninformed contributions to this early discourse in terms of its procedural aspects, taking into consideration the amount of available texts on international law in Chinese translation at the time. Most of the contributions to the debate idealise the nature and origin of international law, and they are fragmented to the extent that they scarcely form contributions to one common discourse on these questions. We see a growing concern and interest in international law as a means of entering China into the world community of states but we do not yet find that this discourse in any substantial way creates one or more world-views on China's place in the international community. On the other hand, no arguments in favour of traditional East Asian world-views, such as the tribute system, are called upon as alternatives to international law. We have also seen in this chapter that the early affirmative perception of international law in China contributed to an interpretation of an ancient Chinese origin of an international order resembling international law. Those arguments have been exceptionally pervasive in Chinese intellectual history both in the West and in the East until this day.

We have so far only been concerned with the development of the translation, reception and discourse on international law until the Sino-Japanese war. In the following two chapters we shall see how these processes take significant turns after the war in 1894-95 and how international law indeed starts to take shape as a basis for new ways of understanding China in the world order of the 20th century.

CHAPTER FIVE

JAPAN AND CHINESE TRANSLATIONS OF INTERNATIONAL LAW

Above we have discussed the introduction and reception of international law, and also a burgeoning debate on China in the international community growing out of the early exposure to the theories of this discipline of Western studies prior to the Sino-Japanese war in the later 19th century. In spite of the voluminous corpus of translated texts, the early discourse on China's place in the international family of states was only taking international law as a set of structural principles, to use the terms introduced by Osiander, deliberating the possible effects on China's strength in international relations, but not addressing the implications for China of the procedural rules inherent in this system. In the period following the war the Chinese basis in and discourse on international law changed radically. The war in 1894-95 and the peace treaty of Shimonoseki forever changed China's interpretation of herself in inter-state relations. It is evident that the outcome of the war would have implications for the way China perceived her role in the East Asian society of states and henceforth in a larger international context. We shall, however, not primarily engage here in a debate on the political implications of that war but rather focus on the way that the discourse on international law took new directions after the war. The immediate cause of those changes was the intellectual influence from Japan rather than the political and military consequences of the war. We shall in this chapter first address the question of texts and language which constitute the basis for the discourse and subsequently engage in an analysis of that discourse in more detail in the following chapter.

After the war Chinese students started to leave for Japan to take part in modern style education in the Western sciences, first on state sponsored study programs and later on an individual basis. Thousands of young Chinese students left for Japan, many of whom completed their degrees in Japan and went back to China to take part in educational and political reforms in the early 20th century.[1] Many of these students were already politically active as contributors to student periodicals and as translators of scholarly texts during their period in Japan, and lots of texts which would otherwise have been difficult to publish for the Chinese readership in China were published for the same readership in Japan and subsequently distributed through the treaty ports and other open channels to their Chinese readership on the mainland. Many of the Chinese students of law in Japan took an active part in the debates on Chinese legal questions from their base in Japan, and from 1902 a number of these students also started to translate texts and lecture notes from Japanese into Chinese. From this time on the Chinese market was flooded with new texts on law in general and international law in particular. The texts were occasionally translations from Japanese published books on relevant topics. More often, however, these texts published by Chinese law students in Japan partly contained translated material from Japanese texts, partly extracts from lectures at Japanese universities, and partly deliberations and explanations by the students themselves. It is often not possible to distinguish between these different categories of texts and passages in these publications. The author may not be distinguishable from the editor or the translator of the texts.

These texts on international law were primarily concerned with the general structural principles and procedural rules of international law and seldom directly involved in questions pertaining to China and international law. The debates on China and her status in international law were mainly discussed in articles in the periodicals, which are the topic of the following chapter. These "translated" texts were less concerned with the theoretical or historical perspectives on European international law and more concerned with the practice and customs in international relations, thus giving Chinese intellectuals of the early 20th century a better basis for discussing the recent procedural rules in international relations. The theoretical and historical introductions in these texts are commonly very short and not of a very abstract kind.

The language of these publications was heavily influenced by the Japanese language, the Japanese technical vocabulary and its general lexicon, as I shall show below. Within months the entire lexical foundation for translating international law into Chinese built by the

[1] See Harrel 1992; Saneto Keishu 1982

two traditions in China, the Martin and Fryer traditions discussed in chapter 3, was completely abandoned and replaced by a technical lexicon in international law and diplomacy established upon the language of Meiji Japan. The year 1902 is a demarcation line in terms of the Japanese influence on this process in China.

1902—THE YEAR THAT CHANGED THE INFLUX OF INTERNATIONAL LAW TRANSLATIONS

Three texts published in the year 1902 may facilitate our appreciation of the significance of this particular year in terms of international law translations and texts on related issues in China. We clearly see from these texts that a new era was dawning on the introduction of international law in China where the Japanese experience was rapidly gaining momentum in this intellectual domain. The technical language was borrowing heavily from the Japanese. Simultaneously, we find that for the first time texts on international law are being written by Chinese intellectuals and scholars themselves, and we also observe that China is being written into the history and theories of international law and introduced as such in China.

The text *Guoji gongfa zhi* (國際公法志) ascribed to the editorial work by Cai E (蔡鍔)[2] (1882-1916) and published in Shanghai in 1902, as the first of this kind of texts, may serve as an illustrative example. Cai E was a native of Shaoyang (邵陽) in Hunan province. He received classical education under private tutors and obtained his *shengyuan* degree in 1895. Through one of his tutors he was then introduced to Tang Caichang, teaching at the newly established Academy of Current Affairs and to Tan Sitong. In 1897 Cai entered the academy and came under the strong influence of Liang Qichao, who was at that time lecturing at the academy. After the failure of the Hundred Days Reform in 1898 the academy was closed and Cai was refused admission to other academic institution because of his association with the Hunanese reformers, Tang Caichang and the Kang-Liang reformist group. At the invitation of Liang Qichao Cai went to Japan for the first time as a student from 1899 to 1900. He studied with Tang and Liang in Japan before he entered a school set

[2] Style: Songpo (松坡)

up by Liang and others for Chinese students whose studies had been interrupted by the abrupt political changes in China. In 1900 he returned to China to take part in the military uprising organised by Tang Caichang in Hankou. When the plot was discovered and 18 of his fellow conspirators were executed, Cai fled back to Japan to pursue military studies. Cai E began working on his own solutions to China's problems and started publishing articles on the backwardness of China and the need for development of her national power. He graduated from the Shikan gakkô (士官學校) in 1904 and returned to China. Upon his return he held many important local military positions in Jiangxi, Hunan, Guangxi and Yunnan during the last years of the empire until 1910. After the Wuchang incident in 1911 he took an active part in the anti-Manchu military campaigns. He served as governor in Yunnan until 1913 and from June 1916 Cai was appointed governor of Sichuan under the new republic.[3]

In the preface to the *Guoji gongfa zhi* Cai is depicted as a follower of the first Chinese tradition of international law studies established by Tang Caichang in Hunan. A number of other features of the text also connect Cai to the Tang-Liang Hunanese reform-group.[4] Hence, this first publication with a discernibly strong Japanese influence grows out of the Hunanese reform movement, which is not a very surprising combination of affiliations, considering Cai's political and personal associations. The main body of this publication is dedicated to the regulations of inter-state relations in time of peace, from sovereignty and the rights and obligations of states to regulations of international trade and diplomatic courtesy. The most interesting feature of Cai's publication is the fact that it appears to be the earliest individual general treatise on international law written by a Chinese national. The book does not discuss China's status in international relations but is entirely dedicated to a universal introduction of international law with most examples and illustrations taken from European history. Chinese cases in international relations are brought in as illustrations only on two occasions; once when discussing Western extraterritorial

---

[3] For more information on Cai E and his publications see: Boorman 1967-71, vol. 3, pp. 286-290; Ding Pingyi 2000, p. 91; Li Shengping 1989, p. 714; Tian Tao & Li Zhuhuan 2000, p. 364; Tian Tao 2001, p. 142; Wang Jian 2001, p. 150; *Zhongguo falü tushu zongmu* 1991, p. 742; Zhou Mian 1999, p. 429.

[4] Fairbank & Liu 1980, pp. 310, 546

rights in the East[5] and once when discussing the opening of China and Japan by Western traders.[6] We may, however, assume that large parts of Cai's material are taken from Japanese sources on international law, some of which may have been retrieved from originally Western texts. Cai does not disclose any familiarity with earlier Chinese translations of international law texts, even if we may assume that he must have known the writings of Tang Caichang. His Japanese experience gained through his studies in Japan and his admiration for the international strength and respect gained by Japan in the late 19th century turned his publication towards the Japanese environment. By relying on Japanese sources and experience he inevitably also started using the Japanese *kanji* vocabulary for the technical terms of international relations and international law, as we shall look more closely into below.

The second important contribution representing the Japanese influence on the introduction of international law in China in 1902 is ascribed to one of the constitutionalists of the early 20th century, Yang Tingdong (楊廷棟) (1861-1950). Yang was a native of Wuxian (吳縣) in Jiangsu born in 1861. He went to Japan as a foreign student at the Waseda University (早稻田大學) in Tokyo and became an active political figure in late imperial and early republican China after his return from Japan. Yang was a frequent visitor to the Xilou (息樓) "club" situated above the *Shibao* (時報) newspaper offices, a centre of political and cultural debate in early 20th century Shanghai.[7] He belonged to a group of Jiangnan constitutionalists and is the author of two works on constitutionalism and the provincial assemblies.[8] Yang Tingdong's name is attached to the publication *Gongfa lungang* (公法論綱), printed in Tokyo and distributed in Shanghai in 1902. Yang does not explicate the sources of his work but we may assume that his deliberations on international law are based on material gathered at university lectures at Waseda. In the preface he compares the experience of the Meiji restoration in Japan with the last 30 years

---

5 *Guoji gongfazhi*, pp. 32a-b, 46a
6 Ibid., p. 37b
7 Judge 1996
8 He organised a constitutional preparation society, Xianzheng yubeihui (憲政豫備會), and published the journal *Xianzheng zazhi* (憲政雜誌). (Svensson 1996, p. 89; Tian Tao & Li Zhuhuan 2000, pp. 359, 365; Tian Tao 2001, pp. 132-133, 161-163; Zhou Mian 1999, p. 134.) Yang also translated Rousseau's *Social Contract* (published in the *Yishu huibian* (譯書彙編) in 1901).

development in China, demonstrating that he is deeply troubled by China's position "outside the scope of international law", as he formulates it.

It would be an overestimation of Yang's and Cai's works to claim that they alone paved the way for the introduction of the Meiji Japanese influence of international law in China. They represent, however, two of a number of contemporary Chinese intellectuals and students in Japan contributing to the establishment of a new and "modern", Meiji Japanese influenced tradition of international law translations, and Yang was certainly one of the first and most influential of these early Chinese law students in Japan. Cai E and Yang Tingdong did not extensively discuss questions pertaining particularly to China and international law in their 1902 publications. China's status in international law in the early 20th century was, however, introduced to China via a French lawyer Desjardins and a Japanese translation of one of his works.

Arthur Desjardins (1835-1901) was a distinguished French lawyer and a specialist on international law, maritime law and trade laws. He was born in Beauvais in France, trained as lawyer and obtained his doctoral degrees in law and literature in 1858.[9] Desjardins was also engaged in international questions of the East, particularly Japan. He came to know Ariga Nagao when Ariga stayed in Paris working on a publication on the international situation in the East.[10] The last publication from Desjardins' hand was the article "La Chine et le Droit des Gens" published in December 1900. The article was translated into Japanese by the China Investigation Society (Shina chôsakai 支那調查會) with the title *Kokusai Shina* (國際支那) and published in Tokyo 1901. Shortly afterwards the text was taken up for Chinese translation from the Japanese by Wu Qisun (吳啟孫) because

[9] He held several prominent positions as judge and lawyer in France throughout the second half of the 19th century, and became a member of L'Institut de France, Académie des sciences morales et politiques, section des législation, in 1882. From 1891 he served as French representative to L'Institut de droit international (Institute of international law). Desjardins was consulted as adviser in several French disputes pertaining to international law, including serving as mediator in a conflict between England and Belgium in 1898. He died at the age of 67 in November 1901.

[10] Ariga and Desjardins co-authored an article discussing the Sino-Japanese war in an international legal perspective. The French lecture entitled "La guerre Sino-Japonaise au point de vue du droit international" presented by Desjardins at L'Institut de France was published in Japanese with the title *Nisshin Sen'eki kokusai hôron* (日清戰役國際法論) at Rikugun daigakkô (陸軍大學校) in Tokyo 1896.

of its relevance and current perspective on the Chinese situation in international legal terms. The translation was published with the title *Zhina guojilun* (支那國際論) in Shanghai in 1902, while the text was printed in Tokyo. Not much had so far been written and published in China on the Chinese international legal situation seen from a European perspective. The text is highly critical of China's role in international affairs and will have indicated to its readers that China was not highly regarded as a reliable partner in international affairs. Japan, on the other hand, is described by the author as a trustworthy member of the international society. Desjardins is particularly critical of and appalled by the cruelty of the Chinese penal practice and China's lack of an understanding for basic humanitarian principles in the legal system, topics we have already touched upon as parts of the Western discourse on China in international law in chapter 2 above. In spite of its potential importance as one of the very few early translations of a Western treatise on the Chinese current international position, this publication does not seem to have become very influential. Copies of this text are hard to come by and no reference to this text is to be found in contemporary bibliographies or debates on China's international position.[11] Deficient distribution and an insufficient network of key persons among the gentry-literati in China may partly account for this effect. For our purpose, however, this text is another strong indication of the changing climate for international law translations in China in 1902.

JAPANESE INTERNATIONAL LAW TRANSLATIONS IN CHINA

No Japanese influence can be observed prior to these 1902 publications. A number of texts translated in the earlier Tongwenguan and Jiangnan Arsenal traditions, such as Martin's translation of Hall (1903), Allen's translations of Lawrence (1903), and Martin's translation of the Mandarin Institute lectures (1904), were published after 1902. These traditions were, however, rapidly losing any market of readers and publishers in the shifting orientation in international

---

[11] The only exceptions are a number of references to the title without an analysis of its significance in the process of introducing and debating international law in China; Qi Qizhang 2001, *qianyan* (前言) p. 8; Tian Tao & Li Zhuhuan 2000, p. 364; Tian Tao 2001, p. 142; *Zhongguo falü tushu zongmu* 1991, p. 739.

law translations after 1902. Except for two publications of translations from European languages,[12] and Wu Qisun's 1902 translations of Desjardins work via Japanese, all other Chinese publications on international law between 1902 and 1911 were based on Japanese books, publications and lectures. The Chinese translations from Japan may be attached to a small number of Japanese international law publicists, both because of their status as such in Japan and because of their role as teachers and professors in institutions where Chinese students attended their law courses. The main influence may be discerned to originate from the four international law scholars Nakamura Shingo, Ariga Nagao, Takahashi Sakue and Yamada Saburô.

Nakamura Shingo (中村進午) (1870-1939) obtained his university degree from the Tôkyô teidai hôka daigaku (東京帝大法科大學) in 1894 and was appointed professor of law at the Gakushûin (學習院) in 1897. He also studied law abroad in France and England for 3 years. In 1901 he obtained his doctoral degree in law, specialising in international law. Because of his attitude and views on the Russo-Japanese war 1904-05 he was removed from his chair as professor of law. In 1906 he was again appointed professor of law, this time at the Tôkyô kôtô shôguô gakkô (東京高等商業學校). Nakamura retired in 1930 but continued his work as honorary professor of law until his death in 1939. Nakamura gave lectures on law in general and international law in particular at a number of Japanese universities, among them the Hôsei University (法政大學), where several Chinese law students became familiar with Nakamura and his presentations of international law. Lecture notes and various unidentified sources related to Nakamura's lectures are the main sources for a number of Chinese publications on international law in

[12] These are; the *Guoji gongfa dagang* (國際公法大綱) published in 1903 and the *Guoji gongfa tigang* (國際公法提綱) published in 1910. The *Guoji gongfa dagang*, which is a translation of *Das Völkerrecht: Systematisch Dargestellt* by Franz von Liszt (1851-1919), shows that the Japanese technical vocabulary in international law was established even in translations performed in Shanghai in 1903. The second text of this kind is the *Guoji gongfa tigang*, which is Dan Tao's (但燾) (1881-1970) Chinese translation of *The Principles of International Law* by Thomas Joseph Lawrence (1849-1919). Dan Tao was a law student of Nakamura Shingo in Japan, and translated the second of Lawrence's books into Chinese. While the first was performed by Allen in 1903 within the former Chinese tradition, Dan Tao made full use of the Japanese vocabulary in his translation and makes no reference whatsoever to Allen's publication.

the early 20th century. Ye Kaiqiong's (葉開瓊) *Pingshi guoji gongfa* (平時國際公法), a translation from Japanese of Ye's notes and material collected at Nakamura's university lectures, may serve as a typical example of the kind of texts edited and translated from lectures at Japanese universities. Another of Nakamura Shingo's Chinese students at the Hôsei University, Zhang Fuxian (張福先), has supplied the *Fazheng congbian* (法政叢編) with a volume on regulations for international intercourse after the peaceful coexistence between states has been interrupted, entitled *Zhanshi guoji gongfa* (戰時國際公法),[13] and also based on lecture notes and material supplied by law professors lecturing at Hôsei, among them Nakamura Shingo.[14] The *Fazheng congbian*, containing altogether 19 titles on law and politics, was printed in Tokyo and subsequently also reached the Chinese domestic market. The entire series became very popular and was reprinted already the first year after its initial publication, indicating the interest in and need for this kind of updated and comprehensive introduction to modern social sciences among the Chinese of the time. This series on law and politics is the first of its kind in terms of size and scope introducing modern Western-Japanese political and legal sciences to a Chinese readership. All the volumes in this series are based on notes and material gathered by Chinese students at the Hôsei University.

Nakamura's printed publications on public international law in Japanese had been published already in the early years of the 20th century. Two Chinese texts on public international law in time of peace and in time of war[15] are the first translations of Nakamura's own publications on public international law.[16] Compared to the earlier translations and editions of Nakamura's lectures, these two publications appear as much more systematic and comprehensive

[13] This text also has a parallel in a text with the same title translated by Chen Jiahui (陳嘉會) based on Nakamura's lectures and published in the series *Fazheng cuibian* (法政粹編). Jin Baokang (金保康) translated Nakamura's lectures in 1905-06 on international law in time of war and the principles of neutrality published in the series *Fazheng jiangyi* (法政講義) in 1907.

[14] Tan Ruqian 1980, pp. 376, 396; Tian Tao 2001, pp. 136-137; *Zhongguo falü tushu zongmu* 1991, pp. 745, 746; *Zhongguo jindai xiandai congshu mulu* 1979, p. 699.

[15] Translated into Chinese by Chen Shixia (陳時夏) and published by Shangwu yinshuguan (商務印書館) in Shanghai 1911

[16] Tan Ruqian 1980, pp. 377, 396; Tian Tao 2001, pp. 140-141; *Zhongguo falü tushu zongmu* 1991, pp. 740, 744.

treatments of international legal theory and practice, which also brought about their relative popularity in China. The re-publication of these works five times within four years from 1911 to 1915 indicates the continuous demand for systematic introductions to public international law in Chinese also in the early years of the Republic. At the same time this indicates the continued Japanese influence also on the introduction and implementation of international law in China after 1911. Nakamura Shingo is primarily known for his work on public international law. However, as the text *Xinyi guoji sifa* (新譯國際私法) translated by Yuan Xilian (袁希濂) and published in Shanghai 1907 shows, Nakamura also lectured on private international law in Japan. Yuan Xilian has based his text on Nakamura's lectures on private international law at the Chûô University (中央大學) in 1905 and some of his published material.[17]

Ariga Nagao (有賀長雄) (1860-1921) was born in Osaka in 1860 and studied at Tôkyô University, where he obtained his degree in literature and history in 1882. After graduation he started working on a systematic treatise on Japanese sociology, which was completed in 1883 and published with the title *Shakaigaku* (社會學) (*Sociology*) in 3 volumes. Ariga Nagao was heavily influenced by the Spencerian evolutionary theories introduced into Japan by Toyama Shôichi and others. Ariga, however, interpreted Spencerian evolutionary theories much further in terms of the necessity of a strong state than Toyama had done, and hence became one of the most influential proponents of statism in Japan. According to Ariga, state control will have to be maintained even at the later stages of social evolution, contrary to Spencer who had concluded that state control would be gradually minimised in the later stages of evolution.

Ariga Nagao was appointed assistant professor lecturing in history and government official, later secretary to the Japanese prime minister, before he went to Europe to study at Berlin University in 1886. He studied European cultural history and psychology before he went to Austria to study law under a Professor Stein. After his return to Japan he was appointed professor of international law at the Army College (Rikogun Daigakkô 陸軍大學校), and later summoned by Ito Hirobumi and appointed member of a government investigation

[17] Most likely Nakamura's *Kokusai shihô kôgi* (國際私法講義) published in Tokyo in 1898. See also: Tan Ruqian 1980, p. 393; Tian Tao 2001, p. 137; *Zhongguo falü tushu zongmu* 1991, p. 743.

committee for national relationships during the Sino-Japanese war 1894-95. This indicated Japan's endeavour to observe international law in her international relations and thus to explain and justify Japanese imperialist engagements in legal terms. It also shows the growing status Ariga was gradually attaining in Japan as premier scholar of international law. Ariga was later also directly involved in the war as legal adviser to the Second Army in Liaodong and Northeast Shandong. Immediately after the war he went to Paris where he published in French on the Sino-Japanese war and its implications for international law. This is also the time when he became acquainted with Arthur Desjardins, which we have discussed in chapter 2 above. In 1896 he returned to Japan where he was appointed professor of international law at Rikugun daigaku (陸軍大學). Ariga Nagao held several prominent international positions, such as delegate to International Red Cross conventions and to the Hague Conference 1899. He was also appointed professor at Waseda University (早稲田大學). He obtained his doctoral degree in law in 1897 and a doctoral degree in literature in 1911. During the Russo-Japanese war 1904-05 he was stationed at Lüshun as an international law adviser. He continued to travel to Europe also after the war and wrote extensively on the international legal questions relating to the war between Japan and Russia. In 1912 he was invited to serve as legal adviser to the newly appointed Chinese president Yuan Shikai, a post he retained also after Yuan Shikai's death in 1916. Ariga Nagao was also an active partner in discussions pertaining to the establishment and institution of Chinese constitutionalism, and was a fervent participant in the constitutional debates in the periodical *Xianfa xinwen* (憲法新聞) published and distributed in Beijing and Shanghai between April and December 1913.

The *Zhanshi guoji gongfa* (戰時國際公法) published in Changsha in 1908 is a translation of Ariga Nagao's book *Senji kokusai kôhô* (戰時國際公法) on public international law in time of war, and is one of the few Chinese translations entirely based on a Japanese publication on international law in late imperial times. The Chinese text is ascribed to a Chinese law student in Japan, Yan Xianzhang (嚴獻章), probably one of Ariga Nagao's students at Rikugun daigaku. Ariga Nagao's deliberations and analyses on international treaties and regulations for warfare were of course of particular interest to China because of Ariga's direct involvement in the Sino-Japanese war and the Russo-Japanese war. This and other publications on public international law in time of war and on neutrality[18] show his important position in the introduction of these topics within international law in China.[19]

Takahashi Sakue (高橋作衛) (1867-1920) received his university diploma in law at the Tôkyô teidai hôka daigaku (東京帝大法科大學) in 1891. He started working on international law and diplomacy and was appointed professor of international law at the Kaigun daigakkô (海軍大學校)[20] and later at the Tôkyô teidai hôka daigaku (東京帝大法科大學). During the Sino-Japanese war he was engaged as legal adviser to the Japanese fleet and served also as interpreter to the Japanese forces in Port Arthur. After the war he was sent to Europe by the Ministry of Culture to study European law. He spent time both in England, France and Germany, where he obtained a European doctoral degree and where he made acquaintance with prominent European scholars on international law, of which Professor Thomas Erskine Holland probably became the most important. After he had obtained his degree in 1900 he returned to Tokyo and took up his position as law-professor at the Tôkyô teidai hôka daigaku. After some years at the university he left academia and devoted all his time to politics. He was appointed vice-president of the International Law Association in London. He was selected as author of the legal section of the official Japanese history of the Sino-Japanese war. He was also a member of the legal committee in the Imperial Japanese Department for Foreign Affairs during the Russo-Japanese war. Takahashi has written a number of important works in Japanese on international law, Japanese diplomatic and jurisdictional questions, of which a few have been translated into Chinese.[21] Takahashi was one of the single most influential Japanese international law specialists for the modernisation of international law in China during his time at the Tôkyô teidai hôka

[18] Such as his involvement in the publications *Zhongliguo faze* (中立國法則) in 1904, *Zhanshi guoji gongfa* (戰時國際公法) in 1905 and *Juwai zhongli* (局外中立) in 1905

[19] Dudden 1999, pp. 184-186; Michio Nagai 1954, p. 62; Tan Ruqian 1980, p. 396; *Zhongguo falü tushu zongmu* 1991, p. 744.

[20] Variously translated Imperial Naval Staff College or Naval University

[21] His texts and lectures are the basis for the following titles in Chinese translation; *Zhanshi guoji gongfa* (戰時國際公法) 1905, *Wanguo gongfa tiyao* (萬國公法提要) 1905; *Pingshi guoji gongfa* (平時國際公法) 1907; *Zhanshi guojifa yaolun* (戰時國際法要論) 1908.

daigaku after the Sino-Japanese war. Through his English publication on the position and role of international law during the Sino-Japanese and the Russo-Japanese wars he was also instrumental in instituting imperial Japan as a reliable and sound member of the international family of nations under the common framework of international law on an equal footing with European states, as we have discussed above.

Yamada Saburô (山田三良) (1869-1965) graduated from Tôkyô University in 1896. He became professor there in 1900 and lectured on private international law until his retirement in 1930. Yamada served as chairman of the Faculty of Law at Tôkyô University, president of the Korean Keijô University in Seoul, president of the Japanese Academy, and as director-in-chief of the Japanese Association of International Law (Kokusai Hôgakukai). Yamada is the most influential Japanese scholar on private international law in terms of the introduction of this branch of legal science into China. Both notes and material from Yamada's university lectures and some of his publications were translated and published in Chinese.[22]

The Chinese publications on international law after 1902 were based on the works and lectures of a number of Japanese scholars, of which these four are the most prominent both in terms of Chinese influence and in terms of their position in Japan. Theoretical and historical deliberations on international law and international relations may have been a part of the law training for the Chinese students in Japan. Judging from the publications in Chinese, it is nevertheless obvious that the parts of international law with direct and practical implications for China and her international role and position were the central interest of these students, reflecting a major change from the earlier translations by Martin and Fryer. There are very few publications on the structural principles of public international law in general among these Japanese-inspired texts. The pragmatic application, the procedural rules, of international law in time of peace and

[22] Cao Lüzhen (曹履貞) has based his 1905 Chinese translation published with the title *Guoji sifa* (國際私法) on Yamada's lectures and possibly also on some of Yamada's Japanese publications on private international law. In 1907 Fu Qiang (傅彊) based his translation with the same title on Yamada's lectures and his teaching compendium printed at the Hôsei University from 1905. The Shangwu yinshuguan (商務印書館) in Shanghai published three volumes on international law in 1911, all translations from Japanese printed publications. The volume on private international law based on Yamada Saburô's published work(s) on private international law was carried out by Li Zhou (李倬).

time of war is the most common topic of these publications. Frequently the specific questions related to neutrality are the topic of publications from 1904 onwards. The reason for this is of course the questions related to China's neutrality in the Russo-Japanese war 1904-05. Otherwise we find a few publications on private international law, but then again on very pragmatic issues related to the conflict of law.

TWO CHINESE TRADITIONS REPLACED BY THE INFLUENCE FROM JAPAN

In the latter half of the 19th century texts on international law were translated into Chinese with the efforts of missionaries like W.A.P. Martin in Beijing and John Fryer in Shanghai, thus making the theories of international law available in China. As we have seen, the first indications of an indigenous Chinese debate and deliberations on inter-state relations in terms of international law commenced in China during this time. The massive influx of texts from Japan discussed above, however, established a new basis for China's orientation in international law. At that time Chinese students were going to Japan *en masse* to receive modern style education in Meiji Japan, including many students studying international law in Chinese universities and other institutions. They were exposed to international law as it was conceived and applied, with great success, in Japan and none of them had been trained in the 40 year old tradition in international law texts established by Martin. Very much similar to the situation in related areas of legal studies and legal codification, these young students embarked on the task of introducing the seemingly alien concepts of legal studies to the Chinese readership, as described by Jean Escarra in 1936:

> Modern codification had its beginning in China a little more than 30 years ago. It first endured a period of groping, characterized especially by a tendency to translate almost literally foreign codes. At that time, the members of the commissions on codification were often young men recently returned from Japan, Europe, or America, where they had studied law. Without experience, often ignorant of the history of

> legislative evolution of their own country, they elaborated codes almost entirely foreign to the mentality of the people.[23]

These young students were very receptive to the Japanese influence and embarked upon a project to intellectually imitate Japan in her efforts to adapt to international law in the name of modernisation. In this process they inevitably also came under strong influence from the Japanese technical vocabulary in law, political science and international law. Above I have argued that a Japanese influence on the orientation in international law in China took place with the first texts originating in Japan from 1902 onwards. I shall in the following argue that a study of the terminological changes that took place in these texts compared to the pre-war translations further verifies the assumption that the influx from Japan was very important in China's intellectual orientation in international law from this time on.

THE JAPANESE TERMINOLOGICAL INFLUX

Japan had been sending students to Europe to study international law as early as 1862 and already in the early 1880s a vocabulary of international law, based on *kanji*, was firmly established in Japan.[24] At the same time a number of Western texts on international law were translated and published in Japan. In 1902 the Japanese Association of International Law was established and in the same year the *Journal of International Law*[25] was published for the first time. It has earlier been suggested that the Japanese influence on the terminology in China took place during the early decades of the 20th century.[26] A study of the early translations and works on international law by Chinese students in Japan or returned from Japan indicates, however, that this transition to a vocabulary influenced by Japan in fact took place during a short period of time between 1902 and 1903 simultaneously with the first Chinese students returning from Japan. This terminological change may be discerned in the Chinese translations from Western languages as well as in the translations from Japanese

---

[23] Escarra 1961, p. 152
[24] As confirmed through the dictionary *Tetsugaku jii* (哲學字彙) published in Tokyo in 1881
[25] *Kokusaihô zasshi* (國際法雜誌)
[26] Chiu 1967, p. 489

texts on international law.

Wang Jian (王健) has studied the terminological influx from Japan in the general field of law and legal studies and has found that a number of Chinese works on Japan published in the 1880s, such as Huang Zunxian's (黄遵憲) *Riben guozhi* (日本國志), had initially a prominent role in the introduction of the legal system of Meiji Japan in China, including terms and terminology.[27] The Sino-Japanese war and the massive flow of Chinese students to Japan greatly increased this trend, and the modernisation of Chinese legal thinking and the terms on which it was based in late Qing were to a large extent a direct result of the influence from Japan: "There is no doubt that the reforms in the legal system in late Qing to a large extent were fashioned on the Japanese model. The contribution from Japanese legal advisers in China, and in particular from Chinese students of law in Japan, on the introduction and dissemination of Japanese legal terminology and concepts was great; The entire set of modern Chinese legal terminology is established specifically on this basis."[28]

Terminological shift in 1902

As discussed above there were three texts introducing international law in China in 1902 that have obvious Japanese links. Among these we find a surprisingly high degree of newly imported terms from the Japanese terminological inventory on international law. Among examples of Chinese terms which were open to the Japanese influx on Chinese international law texts and translations from 1902 we find indispensable international law terms such as: 'duty', '(public) international law', 'private international law', 'natural law', 'positive law', 'extraterritorial rights' and 'right of self-protection'. In fact, only faint traces of the two former Chinese terminological traditions are to be identified in these texts. Yang Tingdong has made use of some of the basic terms from the earlier Chinese translations, mainly those terms shared by both the Beijing and the Shanghai traditions. These terms include *quanli* (權利) for 'rights', *juwai* (局外) and *zhongli* (中立) for 'neutrality', *gongfa* (公法) for 'public international law', and

---

[27] Wang Jian 2001, pp. 240-243
[28] Ibid., p. 247

zizhu (自主) for 'sovereignty'. Where the notions of 'extradition' and 'extraterritoriality' are treated in his text, he does not introduce any technical term for these two notions, which he obviously easily could have borrowed from the Japanese vocabulary. Neither has he introduced to his readership the still unfamiliar terms in China *guoji* (國際) and *guojifa* (國際法) for 'international' and 'international law'. In most other cases of applying technical terms, however, he borrows extensively from the Japanese vocabulary, introducing terms such as *yiwu* (義務) for 'duty'/'obligation', *gongheguo* (共和國) for 'republic', *xingzheng* (行政) for 'administration', *xianfa* (憲法) for 'constitution', *minfa* (民法) for 'civil law',[29] *zhimindi* (殖民地) for 'colony' in addition to modern concepts such as *zhongzu* (種族) for 'race'[30] and *zongjiao* (宗教) for 'religion'. In Cai E's text we find none of the terms earlier coined in China and only applied in China and not in Japan. When terms originally coined in China are found in Cai's technical vocabulary, it is only because these terms have been taken up from the early Chinese Martin translations and used in Japan as a part of that lexicon on international law, such as the terms for 'rights' and 'sovereignty' (*zhuquan* 主權). Otherwise the new vocabulary imported from the Japanese technical lexicon dominates this text. In addition to the terms also applied by Yang Tingdong we find terms such as: 'public international law' (*guoji gongfa* 國際公法), 'private international law' (*guoji sifa* 國際私法), 'movable property' (*dongchan* 動產), 'immovable property' (*budongchan* 不動產), 'diplomacy' (*waijiao* 外交), 'suzerain' (*zongzhuguo* 宗主國), 'dependency' (*fuyongguo* 附庸國). 'Neutrality' is rendered either *juwai zhongli* (局外中立) or simply *zhongli* (中立) but never only *juwai* (局外), which again is a discontinuity with the early Chinese traditions. 'High seas' is either referred to as *yinghai* (瀛海) or *gonghai* (公海), and not with the earlier Chinese technical term *dahai* (大海). A number of other more general terms are also clearly of Japanese origin, such as: 'society' (*shehui* 社會),[31] and 'repre-

---

[29] See also Masini 1993, pp. 189, 206

[30] See also Masini 1993, p. 219

[31] In an article on new terms in the Chinese language in issue no. 2 of the *Zhejiangchao* (浙江潮) published in 1903 the term *shehui*, 'society', as a new term in Chinese borrowed from the Japanese lexicon, is defined as "A group of more than two people who live their lives in association. More specifically, it has three main elements; a) An associated group consisting of a number of people … b) There must be more than two people in order to form a society … c) The most important element

sentative' (*daibiao* 代表). Some of these terms are in fact return graphic loans from Chinese via Japanese but were in any case conceived as new terms for new ideas in Chinese when they were imported from the Japanese in the early 20th century.[32]

In Wu Qisun's translation of Desjardins we also find the same overwhelming influx of the new terminological apparatus, also applying the borrowed term *zhiwai faquan* (治外法權) for 'extraterritoriality'.[33] The most interesting feature of this publication in terms of terminology is its deliberations on the use of the term for 'international law' (*guojifa* 國際法)[34]:

> This [term] 'international law' (*guojifa*) corresponds to what we in our country have termed 'public law' (*gongfa* 公法). But since [the term] 'international law' also encompasses 'private law' (*sifa* 私法), the term 'public law' cannot be applied as the comprehensive term [for 'international law'].[35]

Wu thus introduced the Japanese terminological distinction between private and public international law and thereby solved the lexical problem that had vexed translators of international law ever since the early Tongwenguan translations. Since none of the terms introduced earlier either by Tongwenguan, Jiangnan Arsenal or other translators had been generally accepted in the technical lexicon, it was only by

---

in a society is the fact that it is an association of the lives [of its members]." (*Zhejiangchao*, no. 2, *fulu* 附錄 p. 2) In the same article a number of terms related to states and the composition of states are introduced, such as 'duty' (*benfen* 本分), 'obligation' (*yiwu* 義務), 'rights' (*quanli* 權利), 'simple state' (*danchunguo* 單純國), 'complex state' (*fuheguo* 複合國), 'independent state' (*duliguo* 獨立國), 'protectorate' (*baohuguo* 保護國), 'confederation' (*liangbangguo* 聯邦國), 'union' (*hezhongguo* 合眾國), 'colonial protectorate' (*zhimin baohuguo* 殖民保護國), 'dependency' (*shuguo* 屬國), etc. (ibid., pp. 1-10) Many of these are new borrowings from Japanese.

[32] See also Masini 1993, pp. 163, 195, 208, 222; Liu 1995, pp. 290, 301, 303, 310, 336; For a list of legal terms see Wang Jian 2001, pp. 218-220

[33] The term *zhiwai faquan* had in fact been introduced into China earlier. Huang Zunxian (黃遵憲) presented and explained the term in a chapter on the diplomacy of neighbouring states (*Linjiaozhi* 鄰交志) in *Ribenguo zhi* (日本國志) (*Treatises on Japan*) written between 1880 and 1887 and published around 1894 (1901 Shanghai shuju (上海書局) edition, *juan* 6, pp. 37b-38a). The term was, however, not immediately taken up in the Chinese discourse and only reappeared after the new translations from Japanese in the early 20th century. (See also Masini 1993, pp. 98-103)

[34] The term *kokusaihô* (國際法) was coined in Japan by Mitsukuri Rinsho (箕作麟祥) (1846-1897) in 1873. (Hsü 1960, p. 129; Li Guilian 1998a, pp. 27-37; Li Zhaojie 1999, pp. 103-104)

[35] *Zhina guojilun* 1902, *Yili* (譯例) p. 1

the introduction of these Japanese terms that this terminological problem was solved.[36]

The terms *guoji* and *guojifa* appeared unfamiliar in the Chinese technical language only for a short period before they were adopted without hesitation. In the 1903 publication of Lin Qi's (林棨) translation of a number of Japanese texts on international law the term appeared still in need of a certain introduction to its precise connotations and etymology:

> It is not fully known at what time and by whom the term 'public international law' (*Guoji gongfa*/*Kokusai kôhô* 國際公法) was created in Japan. It is, however, a fact that this term is already in current application in that country. Besides, the term is appropriate and there is a correspondence between the term and its reality. Therefore, it is still in use today. In our country we used to have the term 'public law of all nations' (*wanguo gongfa* 萬國公法) coming from the English 'Low (sic!) of nations', the French 'Droit des gens' and the German 'Völkerrecht', while the term 'public international law' has its origin in the English 'International law', the French 'Droit international' and the German 'International recht'. [...] Therefore, in light of this, the term 'public law of all nations' is conceived as largely inappropriate.[37]

The Japanese loan for 'international' readily within a year or so invaded the Chinese lexicon in international law in these translated texts. In other related areas it took some more time before the new terms seeped into the technical vocabulary.[38]

The rapidly expanding influence from the Japanese lexicon

Above, we have mentioned texts produced within the earlier Chinese tradition also after 1902, such as Martin's publication of his translation of Hall in 1903. Young J. Allen's publication of Lawrence's *A*

---

[36] Wu Qisun was, however, not the first to introduce the terms *guojifa* (國際法), *guoji gongfa* (國際公法) and *guoji sifa* (國際私法) in China. Kang Youwei (康有為) (1858-1927) in his list of Meiji-Japanese publications, *Riben shumu zhi* (日本書目志) published in 1898, introduced these terms in the titles of Japanese books. (*Kang Youwei quanji* 1992, vol. 3, p. 803) Yet Wu seems to be the first to introduce these terms into the Chinese discourse on international questions.

[37] *Guoji gongfa jingyi* 1903, p. 3

[38] For instance in the 1906 publication (introduction dated August 1905) on Chinese expressions in postal documents by J.W.H. Ferguson the term 'international' is rendered *waiyang geguo* (外洋各國) (Ferguson 1906, p. 25)

Handbook of Public International Law in Chinese in 1903 is also based on the Tongwenguan tradition with the intrusion of a very small number of terms from the expanding Japanese vocabulary, such as *zhiwai faquan* (治外法權) for 'extraterritoriality' and *zhimindi* (殖民地) for 'colony'. Except for these, the texts published on international law and international relations in China after 1902 are all heavily influenced by Japanese texts and the Japanese technical vocabulary. In addition to the vocabulary already introduced above we find also other Japanese borrowings in international legal terminology in use in Chinese publications from 1903, such as *yindu* (引渡) for 'extradition', *zhengyi* (正義) for 'justice', *ziranfa* (自然法) for 'natural law', *ziweiquan* (自衛權) for 'right of self-protection', *zhongjie* (中介) for 'mediation', and a number of terms such as *zhidingfa* (制定法), *shidingfa* (實定法) and *shitifa* (實體法) for 'positive law'.[39]

The extensive use of Japanese vocabulary in international law and the rapid shift from any Chinese tradition within this field of study may partly be explained by the experience of the Chinese students in Japan, or rather by their young age and thus relative lack of any training in the field of international law within the Chinese tradition prior to their Japanese experience. Partly, their rapid adoption of the Japanese vocabulary and the terms of the Japanese debates on international questions may also have been propelled by the need they saw for a debate on China's international role in the light of the Japanese experience, as will be scrutinized in more detail in the next

[39] In A.H. Mateer's 1915 publication entitled *New Terms for New Ideas: A Study of the Chinese Newspaper* we find further evidence that the Japanese technical lexicon generally had entered the more commonly used language of the periodicals in early 20th century China. Mateer's study of the use of relevant terms in international relations and government confirms that words like *juwai zhongli* (局外中立) or simply *zhongli* (中立) for 'neutral' (Mateer 1915, p. 22), *zhiwai faquan* (治外法權) for 'extraterritoriality' (ibid.), *yindu* (引渡) for 'extradition' (ibid. p. 135), *guoquan* (國權) or *zhuquan* (主權) for 'sovereignty' (ibid., p. 11) were in current usage in 1915. The only surprise in this respect in Matter's study is that the term 'international law' is once rendered *wanguo gongfa* (萬國公法) (ibid., p. 21) and once *guoji gongfa* (國際公法) (ibid., p. 55) in his lists of new terms. I take the continuous reference to Martin's term in addition to the Japanese term to be evidence for a more lasting effect of the earlier translations and terms in the general language, as used in the newspapers studied by Mateer, compared to the more specialised literature on international law and international relations studied above. This effect observed in the use of the term for 'international law' is most probably a result of the relative fame of Martin's first translation with this title.

chapter. Lastly, their readiness to accept the Japanese terms may also be an expression of their fear that the intent and implications of the Japanese original would be lost if the central vocabulary was changed into terms with potentially different connotation. The fact that these terms were easily adoptable to the Chinese lexicon was, of course, also an important factor. Ye Kaiqiong, making full use of the Japanese technical vocabulary in his publication in 1905, introduces his choice of terms, his motivations for doing so, and the history of this lexicon to his readers in the introduction:

> All the terms discussed in this book are creations from Western publicists translated by Japanese publicists. Anxious that the true meaning of these terms could be lost I have only explained their implications and not ventured recklessly to change these terms. Only where Chinese words may fully substitute for these terms have I made use of these Chinese terms. In these cases I have in addition also supplied the original term for the convenience of the reader.[40]

We sense a certain anxiousness not to lead astray his readership by changing what he perceives as the "true meaning" imbued in the Japanese terminology into a more obscure Chinese vocabulary. The same worry that the Chinese terminology is inadequate for conveying the true sense of international relations is found in the introduction to Guo Bin's (郭斌) text on private international law published the same year:

> It is very difficult to find appropriate Chinese translations of legal terminology. When the original Japanese terms occasionally are retained as additional explanations of terms in this book it is done so in order to avoid obscurities.[41]

This feeling of obscurity with the existing Chinese lexicon and certain unfamiliarity with the Japanese was rapidly exchanged for a familiarity with the Japanese after 1905. The kind of explanations and feelings of uneasiness revealed by Ye and Guo are not found again in texts published after 1905.

---

[40] *Pingshi guoji gongfa* 1905, *Liyan* (例言) p. 1
[41] *Guoji sifa* 1905, *Liyan* (例言) p. 2

CHINA'S THEORETICAL ORIENTATION IN INTERNATIONAL LAW AS A JAPANESE LOAN

Two separate traditions for translating texts on international law developed in China between 1864 and 1902, one of which, the Beijing Tongwenguan tradition, possessed close affiliations with official China in late imperial times. The alternative tradition established at the translations bureau of the Jiangnan Arsenal in Shanghai operated in the culturally flourishing Jiangnan area, where the market for international orientation in late Qing times had a greater potentiality. It was, however, none of the indigenous Chinese traditions for such translations that served as a basis for the growing debates on and concern for China's international position. It was the perceived strength of the Japanese "nation" adapted to international law and Western conditions for inter-state relations that convinced a band of young Chinese students in Japan in the early 20th century that the clue to an international strengthening of China was to be found in following Japan's path in these questions. China's membership in the international family of nations was in the early years of the 20th century defined on a basis of Japanese terms and terminologies.

How, then, is it possible that a nearly 40 year old indigenous tradition of translating international law texts in China to such an extent was open and subject to the rapid Japanese influx around 1902-03? My assumption is that this could take place because neither of the two contending traditions of translating international law texts from Western languages which had coexisted between 1864 and 1903, had managed to establish itself with a firm basis in the standard literary language and technical vocabulary of late imperial China. There was hardly any terminological interchange between the two, except for a tendency around the turn of the century to merge these two terminological traditions. This merging of terminology appeared, however, too late to contest the rapid Japanese influx. Japan had initially been influenced by the 1864 Martin translation but in the 1870s and 1880s established an indigenous Japanese lexicon of international law based on *kanji* terms. Only a very small part of that lexicon was originally Chinese. When Chinese students brought this lexicon back from Japan around 1902-03, it rapidly monopolized the Chinese vocabulary and dominated the later development of an understanding of international law in China at a period when China for the first time was embracing international law. As Wang Jian has concluded, these students were confronted with an international orientation involving China in ways fundamentally different from China's earlier relationship to foreign affairs and drawing their interest towards social, political and legal theories of the West:

> The situation [after the Sino-Japanese war] was fundamentally different from what it had been during the former *yangwu*-era, when only a small number [of scholars] had come into contact with international law. In the late 19th and early 20th century thousands of foreign students in Japan received training in Western politics, law and other social sciences, and their heads were filled with terms and ideas of Western liberalism, civil rights and the legal system. After they returned home they turned into the most ardent advocates and reformers of laws and the legal system.[42]

Precisely because the terminological influx coincided with a growing demand for knowledge on international law and debates on China's role in international law, the new terminological apparatus was readily accepted into the contemporary literary standard. Had the rights and duties of states been acknowledged as necessary instruments in China's international relations in the discourse prior to the Sino-Japanese war, the linguistic process would certainly have commenced earlier and with a basis in one of the earlier existing terminological traditions, as may be observed within most of the branches of the natural sciences. The terminological shift taking place within the language of international law in China 1902-03 is a firm confirmation of the gravity of the international crisis inflicted on China by Japan in 1894-95. The discourse on international law and China's changing role and orientation in international relations is the topic of the next chapter.

---

[42] Wang Jian 2001, p. 248

CHAPTER SIX

INTERNATIONAL LAW AS WORLD ORDER IN EARLY 20TH CENTURY CHINA

The title of this book indicates that I profess an interpretation of international law as constituting a new framework for Chinese world orientation in late imperial times. In the opening chapter I suggested that international law represents one of altogether four main different frameworks or modes of perceiving China in her inter-state relations during the Qing. Two of these are in this perspective "traditional" in that they are based upon international orientations conceived and practised prior to the intellectual impact on China from the West during the latter half of the 19th century. The tribute system is an age-old system of conducting diplomacy and trade within a suzerain-vassal outlook on China and her neighbours. An analogous system of private trade operated along other lines of international relations, although not excluding the tribute system operating on a more universal or national level, and secured trade on equal terms between trading partners. As the two main "modern" modes of conceptualising China internationally I have particularly mentioned Social Darwinism and international law, although not excluding other theoretical or philosophical, ancient or modern, elements contributing to the arguments. We shall see in this chapter that the intellectual discourse on China in the international community revolved to a large extent around these two latter modes of thinking, occasionally measuring these against traditional forms, and my main focal point will naturally be on international law. In chapter 4 we have looked into the discourse on China in international law in the late 19th century and found that the early translated texts only in a very limited and rather fragmented fashion initiated a discourse on the procedural aspects of China in international law. The early contributions to this discourse were generally affirmative to the prospects of applying the structural principles of international law to bolster a Chinese application for membership in the international family of nations. Considering the wealth of Chinese sources on international law available at the time, however, the discrepancy between the rich sources available and the limited range and implications of the arguments is striking. What I shall endeavour to show in this chapter is that the new sources available through the students and intellectuals in Japan, together with the Chinese experiences from and after the war with Japan and the texts and the language we have discussed in the preceding chapter changed that discourse in new directions. The Chinese intellectual orientation in international affairs was reformed for good at the beginning of the 20th century and international law became, I shall claim, the most important intellectual framework for exploring and engaging China in international relations towards the end of the Qing.

We should once again at this point remind ourselves that by intellectual orientation I intend to distinguish the focus of this topic from studies of treaties, diplomacy and trade. It may be argued that China *de facto* entered the procedures of international law with the early trade treaties or with the rejection of trade only to be conducted within the tribute system. It may equally and from another perspective be argued that international law was introduced into China by the 1842 and all subsequent "unequal" treaties following the Opium war. One may also claim that it was in fact the establishment of permanent foreign resident envoys in Beijing after June 1858 and the subsequent sending of permanent Chinese envoys abroad from 1876 that made China enter the framework of international law. It has been argued that the negotiations with the foreign powers from the middle of the 19th century to a greater degree involved Chinese interests, that these treaties may be interpreted as bilateral agreements securing the mutual interests of both parties, and hence mark a turning point in making China a member of the international family of nations in terms of international law. One could also argue that China is only to be recognized as a full member of the international community after the theoretical foundation in the political and legal theories of international law was known and applied by Chinese diplomats and politicians. One could claim that this happened with the 1847 translation of Emmerich de Vattel's work, with the 1864 translations of Wheaton's text or with the massive translation of Japanese international law texts from 1903.

Lydia Liu has convincingly argued that "the relationship between a translated text and its application in diplomatic practice is never self-evident. Instead of assuming a direct or indirect relationship between text and practice, we must first examine how a translated text produces meaning."[1] As I have discussed in chapter 2, the system that establishes the criteria for membership in the international family of nations at any given time in history is itself a product of theoretical deliberations, diplomatic practice and power relations between states at that particular time. The external recognition of the membership of a state is often based on deliberations of mutual benefit and profit in the international community. A new member is often adopted by the community after major restructuring events in international politics, and its membership becomes a *de facto* reality through conferences, treaties and diplomatic relations. The changing political realities are, however, also intrinsically related to a national discourse and to debates on the international position and relations of that state. So were also the changes taking place in China in the late 19th and early 20th centuries.

The focus of this chapter is, however, not the treaty system and the political processes that may define China as a member of the international community. My concern is to what extent and in what fashion the theoretical system of international relations was adopted and applied by the different groups taking part in the discourse in late imperial China, hence in what form the translated texts produced meaning in different discursive contexts and environments.

The general social and political discourse conducted through the various available media, such as periodicals, newspapers and other printed material in the late years of the 19th and at the beginning of the 20th centuries was soon to engage the participants in groups or circles of political or even ideological affiliations. These various groups were most often formed and maintained precisely through the media with which they formulated their opinions. This chapter will investigate how these various distinctive groups or camps formulated their arguments on international law in the discourse around the turn of the century so that we can perceive how international law was taken as a framework for a Chinese interpretation of the world order at this time. The first and most obvious point of departure for this study is within the group of reformers playing the politically most active role in these early years of forceful political debates.

[1] Liu 1999, p. 136

The Reformers on Darwin, Confucius and International Law

Kang, Liang and the reformist periodicals

Kang Youwei had a family background in Neo-Confucian teaching and was in his early years exposed to Buddhist writings that had a great influence on his life and intellectual horizon. In the 1880s he was introduced to Western learning, both secular and Christian, which also had a great impact on his later writings and ideas. Kang envisioned a new world where suffering and chaos would be replaced by a new morale and a political order, visions clearly influenced by the multi-facetted source of his world-view. Kang became engaged in political questions, in particular Western forms of government and in legal reforms, and advocated constitutional monarchy as the most viable form of government for China. Kang saw a crisis both in China's political and religious identity confronted with the challenge from the West. The core of Kang's reform program was the protection of the state (*baoguo* 保國) and the protection of the (Confucian) faith (*baojiao* 保教). To achieve these goals Kang advocated a number of radical reforms in the Chinese state, such as military reforms, educational reforms, and the establishment of a state religion based on Confucian teaching. Kang also presented the historical Confucius as an institutional reformer. His visions of the sacred master provoked his contemporary New Text Confucians. Kang was influenced by Western writings on history, whereas the epistemological foundation for his social and historical analysis was the Confucian tradition. He saw historical change as a linear process developing from an Age of Disorder (*juluanshi* 據亂世), through an Age of Increasing Peace (*shengpingshi* 升平世) to a final Age of Great Peace (*taipingshi* 太平世), ideas extracted and developed from early Confucian texts. In other writings the final and utopian age of human development was described as Great Unity, Datong (大同), and the way to this Great Unity goes through Small Unity (*xiaokang* 小康).[2] For each of the stages in development Kang envisioned an appropriate form of government. Hence, institutional change is inevitable in the process of historical development. The idea of development was a novel concept

---

[2] Which again has been introduced into the official socio-political discourse in China in early 21st century.

in Chinese perceptions of historical change.[3]

On the occasion of Kang Youwei's journey to Beijing in 1888 to take part in the metropolitan exams, he appealed to the emperor to change the established laws as a part of Kang's program for institutional reforms. The petition of 1888 did not draw much attention or have much effect on the institutional organisation in Beijing. He re-launched his venture in 1895 after the Chinese defeat in the war against Japan. The public image of China both domestically and internationally was fundamentally challenged in the eyes of Chinese intellectuals in 1895 and the Chinese were generally much more receptive to calls for change and reforms after the defeat at the hands of their Eastern neighbour. It was all of a sudden clear that China's self-strengthening program for decades had been a failure. Kang again went to Beijing in 1895 with his disciple Liang Qichao for the civil service exams when the humiliating results of the Shimonoseki peace treaty were announced. 1300 candidates for the exams signed a new petition for reforms and a new era for the reform movement was opened. The main difference from the 1888 campaign was Kang and Liang's attempts at winning support and momentum for change from below, not only as institutional reforms from above, as had been the strategy in 1888. Reforms and change became a heated topic for debate among all Chinese intellectuals engaged in the social and political discourse, and social organisations, such as study groups (*xuehui* 學會), and the many newly established periodicals developed into the most frequently used vehicles for this debate. The first study society to be set up was the Study Society for Self-Strengthening, the Qiangxuehui (強學會), established in Bejijing in August 1895. The society was run by Chen Chi, Liang Qichao and Kang Youwei, with the active participation of many Chinese intellectuals, high ranking officials and Westerners concerned with Chinese reforms and modernisation. The society founded a paper, *Zhongwai jiwen* (中外記文), where Liang and Mai Menghua (麥孟華) (1875-1915)[4] served as editors. In the autumn of 1895 a self-strengthening society was established in Shanghai, where the paper *Qiangxuebao* (強學報) was initiated. Both these two papers focussed on current affairs and reforms and were distributed free. The initial general cooperative

---

[3] Chang 1980, pp. 283-291, Chang 1971, pp. 50-51
[4] Judge 1996, p. 210

climate between officials and reform-minded intellectuals in these societies was soon replaced by a more hostile attitude from the government and officials. The efforts of these societies and the reform movement as such were soon considered a potential challenge to Qing imperial authority. The Qiangxuehui and the two papers were disbanded in 1896. Soon after, however, the resources of the Shanghai Qiangxuehui were used to set up a new reform paper, the *Shiwubao* (時務報)[5] in August 1896.[6] Liang Qichao was one of the main contributors to the *Shiwubao*, together with people like Mai Menghua, Huang Zunxian and Wang Kangnian (汪康年) (1860-1911), popularising and developing many of the ideas and perspectives introduced by Kang Youwei. "The *Shi-wu pao* had a tremendous influence in stimulating the intelligentsia into organizational and subsequent publishing activities."[7] One of Liang's central arguments in this period is that the former emphasis on self-strengthening had failed and that a simplistic import of Western technology is insufficient to change China. Political and social reforms modelled on the Japanese Meiji model are a more viable way of development for China, according to Liang. At the centre of this reform program we find a new agenda for modern education in China.

In addition to the influence from Kang's ideas on historical development, Liang was influenced by Social Darwinism which was introduced into China at this time by the translation of Huxley's *Evolution and Ethics* by Yan Fu (嚴復) (1853-1921). In fact, Liang was the single most influential advocate of Social Darwinian ideas in the Chinese discourse on social, political and historical issues. At the heart of Liang's Social Darwinian interpretations of society we find the concept of 'groups' (*qun* 群). A group could be any social formation taking part in the struggle for survival at local, national or international level. We may in these writings discern a growing opposition to the conservative ruling Manchu government and an inclination towards Han nationalism. Nationalism was, however, never the main element in Liang's political vision. His framework for a new political order was popular rulership built upon the common

---

[5] *Current Affairs, The Progress*, also referred to as *The Chinese Progress*

[6] Ma Guangren 1996, pp. 113-119, 168-180; Fang Hanqi (ed.) 1997, vol. 1, pp. 553-575; Levenson 1967, pp. 22-24

[7] Levenson 1967, p. 24

interest and benefit of all the members of society.[8]

After the 1898 debacle and the setback for the reforms in China, Liang Qichao and many other radical reformers left China and joined the band of increasingly more radical Chinese students in Japan. The first attempts at far-reaching reforms taking place in China between 1895 and 1898, being joint projects involving both reform-minded intellectuals and officials, ended with the Ci Xi coup and terminated a line of development that may have saved the monarchy. Yet the effect was the radicalisation of the Chinese reformers in Japan. Liang never became a revolutionary, but during his first years in Japan he was surely radical in his political and social outlook and started to use the word *geming* (革命), 'revolution', as a positive designation for socio-political change. Liang's Japanese periodicals were also outspokenly anti-Manchu and nourished a growing Han nationalism in China. Only after 1903, the radicalisation of *Subao* (蘇報), the establishment of radical periodicals in Japan, and in particular after the establishment of Sun Yatsen's *Minbao* (民報) in Japan, did Liang meet with competition as the most radical Chinese reformer. Liang's writings in his first journal published in Japan, the *Qingyibao* (清議 報),[9] and its successor the *Xinmin congbao* (新民叢報) were *the* most influential and widely read journals for reform and revolution in China. These journals were published and printed in Japan but their largest group of readers was inside China. The theoretical framework for Liang's universe of struggle and development continued to be his interpretation of Social Darwinism and "group-ism". China and its people would have to struggle for survival and change was necessary to make China apt for survival. The Chinese people would have to change, or even go through a revolution, in order to become a group, or nation, fit for existence. It was up to China herself to make sure she would survive the natural process of selection. The Chinese defeat in the Sino-Japanese war had also caused Liang to ponder these questions not only in a simplistic yellow-white racial dichotomy. International questions, also those involving the struggle between groups in East Asia, are much more prominent in the writings by Liang and his band of radical reformers writing in the Chinese reform press in Japan than what had been the case earlier.[10]

---

[8] Chang 1980, pp. 291-297
[9] *The Chinese Discussion*
[10] Pusey 1983, pp. 179-316

The *Qingyibao* was published in Yokohama every ten days from its start in 1898 and contained essays and translations on political, social, historical and other issues of current relevance. Liang was the editor in chief and Mai Menghua was second in line and responsible for the publication in Yokohama when Liang was absent. The proclaimed objective of the *Qingyibao* was to maintain a discussion on current issues and enlighten the people. The widespread distribution and influence of the paper in China caused Chinese authorities to issue an edict to stop the paper in February 1900. The publication of *Qingyibao* stopped in December 1901 not, however, because of the edict but because of a small fire in its offices in Yokohama. After only a couple of months Liang started up a new publication in Yokohama, the *Xinmin congbao*, with a new issue every 15 days. One of the main themes of this new publication was the idea of a 'new citizenship', or 'the renewal of the people' as the term *xinmin* (新民)[11] also may be understood. Liang wrote under the pseudonym The new citizen of China (*Zhongguo zhi xinmin* 中國之新民) advocating a thesis of traditional Chinese values and elements from Western political culture to raise the consciousness of a new type of citizenry. Besides articles written by Liang himself we find contributions from Kang Youwei, Mai Menghua, Zhang Binglin (章炳麟) (1869-1936) and others. The *Xinmin congbao* was also widely circulated in China and in Chinese communities abroad, and its distribution greatly outnumbered the former *Qingyibao*.[12]

The following sub-chapters will focus on the individual contributions to the discourse on international relations, international law and the struggle between nations as expressed in these reform periodicals. The relevant question is whether or not a specific interpretation of international relations may be identified among the reformers writing in these periodicals. Mai Menghua and his evolutionary interpretation of international relations may serve as a typical example of a reformist attitude to international law and international rights.

---

[11] Originally a Confucian term prominent in texts such as *The Great Learning* (*Daxue* 大學).

[12] Britton 1966, pp. 118-119, Fang Hanqi (ed.) 1997, vol. 1, pp. 643-660, Levenson 1967, pp. 62-69

Mai Menghua on evolution, national struggle and international rights

James Reeve Pusey has convincingly demonstrated the strength of Kang Youwei's vision of progress even before the introduction and publication of Yan Fu's Chinese translation of Thomas Huxley's work. Kang came to know the notion of progress from earlier translations of Western books published by the Jiangnan Arsenal, and concluded through studies of the Confucian tradition expressed through the *Chunqiu* (春秋) text and the "Liyun" (禮運) chapter of *Liji* (禮記) that China had in fact held a similar theory of progress already at the time of Confucius. "K'ang Yu-wei's conviction that Confucius himself was a prophet of progress was a true conviction."[13] Kang had in the Confucian *Chunqiu*-tradition identified the notion that man passes through three stages, or ages, on his way to happiness; The Age of Disorder, the Age of Increasing Peace and the Age of Great Peace.[14] He linked his theory of progress in three stages with the idea of Datong, Great Unity, from the "Liyun" chapter and hence formulated his universally influential Datong-theory of progress and a utopian society, embraced by revolutionaries, reformers and anarchists alike. In the *Liji*, probably written in the Han dynasty, the term Datong is used as a description of the golden age of the past (early Zhou times) and not a utopian vision or a promise for the future. The latter was, however, what it came to mean to many people in late Qing and Republican China through Kang's utopian ideas of progress. Kang became modern China's first determinist and claimed to have Confucius on his side when he described the coming of the age of Datong as a necessity of natural law.[15]

Mai Menghua employed this Kangian three-stage theory of progress for his own purpose in an attempt to redeem China's international position. In an article entitled "Zun xia pian" (尊俠篇) published in the *Shiwubao* he calls for a national spirit of chivalry, a fighting spirit similar to that of a knight-errant, in order to revive China's position in the family of nations. This knight-errant, this

[13] Pusey 1983, p. 27

[14] There was, however, a major problem with his Confucian theory of evolution. The three-stage theory of human progress could not be found in the *Chunqiu* itself but only in the commentaries to the commentaries from the late Han dynasty. Nor did these three stages really mean what Kang claimed they did. That did not seem to worry Kang Youwei, however.

[15] Pusey 1983, pp. 27-47

patriot, would willingly sacrifice his life to save the Chinese nation from the wrongs brought upon her by the Westerners. Mai anticipated equality and peaceful relations between states in the utopian age of Great Unity. In his own time, however, Mai Menghua recognised the need for national heroes to bring about fairness in a world of inequality. In Darwinian terms Mai appreciated the need for a struggle for survival in his own time. Quite un-Darwinian, however, was Mai Menghua's Kangian idea that states would obtain equal sovereign rights in the final stage of evolution. Mai saw the spirit of the knight-errant in striving for the equalisation of rights, just "what advocates of international law meant by equal rights". This interpretation was very typical for the Chinese explication of Darwinism, as James Reeve Pusey has shown. Evolution and progress were the laws of the natural process. But a strong national or individual spirit could, in a seemingly unnatural or even anti-natural way, influence and change the course of nature to accelerate the nation's way to a better future. Ahead one could discern the final stage in nature's progress, a utopian society of the Datong type, and an active struggle towards this goal would inevitably bring the group, such as the nation, closer to this goal. Both reformers and revolutionaries in China saw hope in the struggle for China's future, and they could see their own important role in the promotion of a national spirit of chivalry.[16] The framework for the relations between states in Mai's interpretation was thus the theory of evolutionary progress dependent on human endeavour, and the belief that China, in her conceived backward position in evolution, would need to strive for her own development. States have naturally-endowed rights in their relations with each other but these rights may only be applied in their full form when protected in an appropriate manner. Mai argued that China's long history as a great civilisation had left her incapable of struggle for own progress. In an article entitled "This is the time for the Chinese groups to develop"[17] he discusses the problem that China for too long has regarded herself as a superior civilisation and hence not submitted herself to the universal 'surge of struggle for existence'. China's development is not inevitable in Darwinian terms but is in

[16] Ibid., pp. 112-114

[17] "Lun Zhongguo jinri wei renqun fada zhi qi" (論中國今日為人群發達之期) in *Qingyibao* no. 45, vol. 3, pp. 2899-2904

fact in the hands of China's groups[18] in the same fashion that all progress is a result of struggle:

> Consider the development of all civilisations on earth. There is not one of these that is not based on struggle. China has never existed in a time of struggle and its people have never had a mind to struggle. Therefore, it is no wonder that China has not been able to develop. Today, however, [the Chinese people] are struggling with others. The 20th century is unquestionably the Chinese (group's) age of opportunity for development and the time when this ancient civilisation may be restored.[19]

According to Mai China's hope lies in fact in China's troublesome international relations. When China is forced to struggle she will progress.

International relations in the European interpretation involve rights for the protection of the interests of the weaker states. The idea of natural rights protecting the unfit in evolution appears, however, not consistent with ideas of Darwinian evolution. In an article in *Qingyibao* entitled "Explicating rights"[20] Mai Menghua elucidates his apparently anti-Darwinian synthesis of the role of human and national rights within the three-stage theory of evolution. He postulates that both individual and national rights are naturally given but may only be maintained through active protection. Individuals and nations are only able to survive as single and weak entities in a society of larger and stronger entities based on their protection through rights. If a person's rights are not protected in their full form, then that person may not be able to drink, eat, see or breathe by him or her self, is dependent on others in movements and activities, and may hence no longer be called a person. If a nation's rights are not protected in their full form, then its territory and people may not be governed by themselves and are subject to orders and administration by others, and even with a national territory it may no longer be called a nation. "That is why we may say that China today simply is not a nation, even if she has a territory of 20 million square *li*. And that is why we may say that China today simply has no people, even with a population of 400

[18] For a discussion of groups in Chinese Social Darwinism see Pusey 1983. pp. 60-67, 107-114, 244-251

[19] *Qingyibao* no. 45, vol. 3, p. 2899

[20] "Shuoquan" (說權) in *Qingyibao* no. 44, vol. 3, pp. 2833-2840

million."[21]

Mai has thus indicated that rights are not simply a matter of natural endowment but also a matter of human and political protection. This point is more explicitly formulated in his theoretical explication of the foundation of rights and how rights may be both natural and unnatural:

> What is the beginning of rights? They are naturally (heavenly) given and protected by human activity. Man is born by heaven and endowed with a mental spirit by heaven. Hence man is given the right to think and the right to speak. Man is endowed with intelligence and abilities by heaven and hence given the right to act. These rights are given man by birth. The strong may not take these away from the weaker, and the clever may not seize them from the stupid. The assiduous may not annex them from the indolent. That is why we may call them full and complete sovereign rights. But heaven, when endowing humans with rights, also empowers them each to serve their own cause. Humans have that which they should obtain (ie. rights) and that which they ought to perform (ie. duties).[22] If they serve their own cause, then their rights may be protected. But if they do not serve their own cause, then their rights will be sacrificed. These rights are retained when they are maintained but lost when they are neglected. Rights are therefore not something one obtains by passivity and protects by empty talk. This [resembles] the law of obtaining territory in international law.[23]

Mai has by these theoretical measures defended his theory that at his own time in history all men have rights and that these rights may temporarily be undermined by the stronger in the course of history. In an Age of Great Peace man will fully be able to protect his or her rights. Until that time arrives, on the lower stages of evolution, man will have to struggle actively in order to survive. International law, as it is practised in international relations, for Mai Menghua is a system describing the rules of the game, the workings of the international struggle for survival parallel to the spirit of chivalry described in the "Zun xia pian". It is built upon a set of naturally-endowed rights but is in practice a system advising nations on how to protect these rights in a time of struggle. The procedural rules of contemporary international law for Mai are thus not an expression of natural law as a final and complete system of international order but rather an expression of the

---

[21] Ibid., p. 2833

[22] The terms applied for 'rights' and 'duties' correspond to the technical terms applied in the Jiangnan Arsenal translations by John Fryer.

[23] *Qingyibao* no. 44, vol. 3, p. 2833

order of the natural struggle for survival.

According to Mai rights are heavenly endowed but protected and maintained in different fashions in different stages of evolution. Parallel to the Kangian three stages of socio-political order, there are also three stages of protection and maintenance of rights. In the Age of Disorder rights are protected by representation, hence called the Age of Representative Rights (*dai quan zhi shi* 代權之世). In the Age of Increasing Peace rights are fought for, hence called the Age of Contending Rights (*zheng quan zhi shi* 爭權之世). In the final Age of Great Peace rights are equal, and hence this age is called the Age of Equal Rights (*ping quan zhi shi* 平權之世). In the first Age of Representative Rights the struggle for survival is fierce and man in general does not have the means or ability to protect him or her self. That is why man organises in groups such as families and clans in order to seek protection by one person of greater ability. That person of great ability takes on the task of protecting and representing the rights of the entire group. In the Age of Contending Rights man has developed his abilities and means to protect his or her own rights, and each and every individual and nation will now seek to extend their own rights. The importance of active protection of these rights is realised. This perpetual struggle for rights secures a certain balance between states of equal status and between individuals of even strength. It is not the size of a nation that is important but its national rights. Nations and individuals are all players on the 'stage of struggle for rights', and no one has the means to avoid these forces of history. Through Mai's observation of the international order and China's role in international relations he has no hesitation in placing the present time in this category, at least in the relations between China and the West. But also this time will come to an end. The utopian Age of Great Peace will arise and bring about a society of Equal Rights. In that age the negative effects of struggle will be replaced by the civilised apprehension, both on a personal and on a national level, that both national and individual rights are best protected when maintained by each and every entity on its own. Rights will be maintained in their natural form and there will be no need, nor any desire, to encroach on the rights of others. In this age international law will reflect this natural form and strictly define the limitations of rights. Both weak and strong nations will adhere to a set of common principles and all nations will enjoy equal rights. In a fashion resembling a Daoist utopian society Mai describes the effects of both human and national rights being equalised:

> Then all men will perform the tasks and all will pursue their own lives. On the outside there will be no concern about violence, and on the inside one will enjoy the fortunes of a harmonious family life. By this time the period of struggle may be replaced by peace. And when the age has reached equal rights, then the order of Datong is not far away.[24]

For Mai Menghua nature has endowed man with two sets of principles for human and social development. The pre-eminent system is the three stage evolutionary process leading to the Kangian vision of a Datong utopia. International law in an ideal form will, in that age, serve as a system for describing the ideal international order within the overall order of human societies. The other natural system in Mai's theoretical universe is the Darwinian order of struggle for survival. Had Mai read his Darwin carefully, he would not have found that the rules for survival of the fittest describe only one particular stage in evolution. For Mai, however, the struggle for existence describes the rules for survival and protection of rights in the present age of development, a middle stage on man's evolutionary ladder towards the Great Peace and Datong utopia. Mai Menghua, like many of his contemporaries, was apparently not concerned about this apparent theoretical contradiction. International law works as a system for the protection of rights, as a means of protecting the rights of those weak enough to need it and still strong enough to utilise it at this present stage in evolution. There is yet another form of international law for the utopian stage in human development. The precise relationship between these two different forms of international law is not made explicit in Mai Menghua's writings.

Mai Menghua's interpretation of international relations in the framework of Darwinian struggle and protection of rights may serve as a typical example of a reformist attitude towards international law. His blend of evolutionary and social theory with a personal engagement in the international position of China has contributed to the formation of Mai's particular international analyses. Below a few other examples of reformist interpretations of the international situation and China's position will be discussed.

---

[24] Ibid. p. 2837

Ou Jujia and a Confucian international order

The Cantonese Ou Jujia (歐矩甲)[25] (1858/1868-1910/1912)[26] was a disciple of Kang Youwei, and when the Academy of Current Affairs was established in Hunan in 1897 Ou was, on the recommendation of Huang Zunxian, invited to be one of the assistants of the chief lecturer Liang Qichao.[27] At the same time Ou was an active pen in both periodicals *Zhixinbao* (知新報) and *Shiwubao*. After the 1898 debacle he linked up with Liang in Japan and assisted him in editing the *Qingyibao*. Politically Ou shared views with Kang, Liang, Mai and other reformists. He had, however, an inclination towards a revolutionary political agenda and took part in the attempts to unite the reformists with Sun Yatsen's revolutionaries in Japan. He later left for the US to edit Chinese reform periodicals in San Francisco.[28] Ou Jujia established a more explicit connection between the Kangian three-stage theory and international law itself, or rather between the sacred teaching of Confucius and international order on earth, than what we have seen in the writings of Mai Menghua. In his qualified determinist interpretation of evolution in international relations he holds that as long as a society adheres to the teaching of the Spring and Autumn [Annals], meaning Confucian teachings, certain events, or stages, in the development of the international order will inevitably follow. In the introduction to his book *Spring and Autumn International Law*[29] he elevates Confucius to an international law publicist by claiming that his teaching was meant not for single states but for the 'multitude of states', apparently not confined to the Chinese universe but also including all states who subjected themselves to the Confucian teaching.

By expounding on Confucius' teaching Ou elucidates his interpretation of the meaning of the three stages in Darwinian terms. "In far ancient times wild birds and beasts struggled with humans. In near ancient times man struggled with his kind. This struggle was sometimes fought between states, sometimes between races,

---

[25] The character *ju* 矩 often written with a 木 below

[26] Information on these dates varies in different sources

[27] Chang 1980, p. 305

[28] Li Shengping et.al. (eds.) 1989, p. 440

[29] *Chunqiu gongfa* (春秋公法). The introduction was published in *Zhixinbao* 24th November 1897

sometimes between clans, and sometimes between different religions." Even today this struggle is continuing to haunt human societies, in particular in the national struggles in the Far East. In Ou's view the only proper way to redeem this is to activate Confucian principles. Confucianism takes care of the people and hates war and violence, protects the small and detests the extermination of states, supports the integration of groups in society and rejects disintegration, abhors injustice and promotes benefits. Confucian teaching benefits all without exception and human societies will, given this foundation, inevitably develop from stage to stage.

> And then, when the great earth revolves, [society] will go from barbarity to enlightenment, and from enlightenment to civilisation. Those who in former times shut their door and [merely] protected themselves will at that day break open their door. And those who in former times gazed at others with enmity and hatred will at that day shake hands and co-operate with deference.

In a society guided by these Confucian principles evolution will go through the three Kangian stages described above.

> In the Age of Disorder strength will lead to victory. In the Age of Increasing Peace wisdom will lead to victory. In the Age of Great Peace benevolence will lead to victory. When strength is victorious, one will regard one's own state as internal and nearby foreign peoples as external. When wisdom is victorious, one will regard nearby foreign peoples as internal and distant foreign peoples as external. When benevolence is victorious, one will regard all under Heaven, large and small, distant and near, as one and the same. Trust and harmony will prevail and fighting and murder will cease. And all states on earth that are able to practise the intention of the Confucian teaching will come under the great order of Great Unity (Datong) and Great Submission [promoted] by our Confucius. That is why we say: The [teaching of] Spring and Autumn is the common political order of the multitude of states, which in fact is nothing but the common law of the multitude of states (eg. international law).[30]

These are the same principles that we find set forth in the writings of Grotius and Wheaton and in the forces of societies which protect the small entities and maintain peace in Ou's interpretation of international law and Confucian teaching.[31] Compared to Mai Menghua, Ou Jujia is more of a determinist, an idealist and a

[30] *Zhixinbao* no. 38, pp. 444-445
[31] Ibid.

Confucian in his promotion of international law. Ou puts less emphasis on the struggle for development and more emphasis on the inherent benevolent qualities in Confucian teaching. Whereas Ou Jujia places his full confidence in the teachings of the Spring and Autumn for an ordered and peaceful international community and for China's improved position, Mai Menghua believes in evolution and the improvement of China's international position but only when this is fought for through the protection of rights.

Liang Qichao on freedom, might and the extinction of states

Liang Qichao, on the other hand, is initially more of a Darwinian purist than Mai Menghua. Rights are clearly not meant to maintain the existence of the weak and unfit in Liang's Social Darwinian interpretation of human society. In his work *On freedom*[32] he treats in detail the concept of liberty and the right to liberty. In the chapter "The misdeed of neglecting rights"[33] he is explicit about the offence involved in failing to maintain one's own right of freedom. He cites a Western philosopher[34] as saying that the evil of neglecting one's own freedom is as great as that of encroaching on the freedom of others and adds that in his own mind the former is an even greater misdeed than the latter. To neglect one's own freedom goes in fact contrary to the principles of evolution itself and is accordingly not a sustainable way of conducting human life in society.[35] In the chapter "National rights and peoples' rights"[36] Liang takes this argument from the level of the individual to the level of international politics. He criticises those who blame the foreign powers and their encroachment on Chinese sovereign rights and claims that the blame is to be directed at the Chinese people itself. No one would be able to encroach on Chinese national rights if China had not neglected her own:

> If our country had not neglected her own right of freedom, then which of the predatory nations would have encroached [on her]? By the fact

[32] *Ziyoushu* (自由書)
[33] "Fangqi ziyou zhi zui" (放棄自由之罪)
[34] Most probably referring to Immanuel Kant
[35] *Qingyibao* no. 30, vol. 2, pp. 1929-1939
[36] "Guoquan yu minquan" (國權與民權)

"The extinction of states". The skinny face of this Russian represents the poverty of Russia and his stomach full of small people represents the domestic disorder in Russia. In spite of her poverty and internal chaos, however, Russia is still able to suppress the two figures lying on the ground, one of them being China and the other Korea.

(E'shi jingwen 俄事警聞 *19 December 1903*)

that others are able to encroach on us we may realise that the Chinese people are guilty of willingly sacrificing [their own freedom].[37]

Only by waking up and realising that they had in fact neglected their own cause did the peoples of France and Japan rise up and reform their states. From that day on no one would be able to encroach on the freedom of the peoples of France and Japan. "When the people have no rights and the country has no rights, then the guilt is entirely on the neglect of its citizens."[38] Only by turning the criticism against themselves will the Chinese be able to throw off the yoke of foreign

[37] *Qingyibao* no. 30, vol. 2, pp. 1930-1931
[38] Ibid.

influence in China, is Liang's Darwinian interpretation of China's international position.

In his explication of the forces in international relations "A treatise on the new ways of state extinction"[39] Liang further explains how the extinction of states is a part of the order of the day in evolution:

> The extinction of states is a principle in evolution. Every person in the world will have to fight for survival. In the struggle for existence[40] there are those more fit and those less fit. When there are those more and those less fit there will be victories and defeats.[41] The rights of those less fit who are doomed will be annihilated by those more fit who are victorious. This is the principle of the extinction of states.[42]

In former times the extinction of states was related to the extinction of individuals and families, as the states were based on these entities. In this modern age, however, Liang sees a much more intricate and sophisticated pattern of state extinction, what he terms the 'new ways of state extinction'. In former times the people of states were able to take precautions against this process. Nowadays, however, Liang warns that the methods used have the appearance of assistance to a state, such as trade, reduction of state loans, sending of support-troops, aid through national advisers, help in building means of communication and assistance in internal conflicts and revolutions. In fact, these are the new ways in which the Western nations subdue weak states.[43] Ways of countering the measures of Western countries attempting to encroach on Chinese freedom and extinguishing the state were for Liang a necessary element in the Chinese struggle for existence. The struggle against the foreign powers in China demanded not only the strength of the Chinese citizen but also a keen perception and a set of advanced international countermeasures.

"What about civilisation, what about international law, what about those who love others as they love themselves, who treat their enemies like their own friends?" Liang asks. The answer is as simple as it is illuminating: "When two equal states meet, there is nothing called might, reason is their might. When two unequal states meet, there is

---

[39] "Mieguo xinfa lun" (滅國新法論)

[40] A term introduced into Chinese by Yan Fu. See Pusey 1983, p. 136

[41] A Japanese/Chinese translation referring to the famous Spencerian slogan "the survival of the fittest". See Pusey 1983, p. 4

[42] *Qingyibao* no. 85, vol. 5, p. 5325

[43] Ibid., pp. 5325-5326

nothing called reason. Might is their reason."[44] When European states meet, reason guides their relations. When a European state meets a non-European state, might rules their relations. "This is the result of evolution and the necessity of struggle, and nothing to be surprised about."[45] Liang is at this time explicitly delineating international law as a system of rules for conduct between states of equal power. The law of nature is the struggle for existence, and only when entities of equal power meet, does a system of rules for inter-state relations become relevant and desirable. China has hence no need for international law in her relations with the European powers.

> There has never been such a thing as neutrality (*zhong*li 中立)[46] under heaven. If one is not being extinguished then one flourishes, and if one does not flourish then one is being extinguished.[47]

These deliberations on the harsh conditions of international relations and every group's or nation's responsibility to protect itself from extinction represent Liang Qichao's theoretical perspectives on international law in the late 19th century. Events in the early 20th century, however, brought about a change in Liang's attitude towards China's role and position in international relations.

Liang Qichao turns to international rights

In the prelude to the Russo-Japanese war in 1905 Chinese intellectuals were increasingly concerned that China no longer was in control of her own international role and position. The events in the latter half of the 19th century indicated an internal weakness in China, and the Sino-Japanese war in 1894-95 revealed China's relative weakness confronted with the rising military and political power of Japan. The early 20th century made it clear that China also was unable to secure her own position in the international affairs developing along her borders. Japan was entering into an alliance with Britain, supported by

---

[44] *Qingyibao* no. 86, vol. 5, p. 5387
[45] Ibid.
[46] Meaning 'a middle position'—here apparently playing on the term 'neutrality' in international relations
[47] *Qingyibao* no. 86, vol. 5, p. 5387

Russian and Japanese troops have invaded Manchuria and China is seeking neutrality. The Chinese citizen (guomin 國民) *is asleep while officials are pleading with the foreign powers for Chinese neutrality.*
(Jingzhong ribao 警鐘日報 *19 March 1904*)

America, in order to curb Russian expansion in East Asia, including Russian control in Manchuria.

> China reacted with a mixture of relief, shame and fear. Initially, there was a feeling of relief because the alliance was directed against Russia in favour of the preservation of China and Korea. A sense of shame followed because the foreign pledge for China's independence and territorial integrity put her into the same category as Korea and emphasised the fact that China's fate was not in her own hands but in those of her would-be protectors. Finally, there was fear that Japan would ultimately replace Russia as the chief imperialist in Manchuria.[48]

Indeed not a groundless fear. Russia did not give up her position in Manchuria and China depended on the alliance to put pressure on Russia. In 1903 Japan and Russia entered into negotiations where Japan demanded rights equal to those of Russia in Manchuria and Korea. Although Russia was not willing to cede any rights to Japan in Manchuria, Japan did get a certain control of Korea. War over

[48] Hsu 1980, p. 135

Manchuria was no longer avoidable.

In February 1904 negotiations between Russia and Japan ended and hostilities began immediately. The war was fought in Manchuria, on Chinese territory, which put China in an even more difficult position internationally. It would potentially be hazardous to join cause with any of the involved parties in case that party should be defeated. Yuan Shikai advised the Qing court to declare neutrality. International law had, for the first time on a larger scale, potentially become a means to secure China's international position. Japan also expressed a wish that China remained neutral in the war. It was clear to all that China did not have the military strength to defend Manchuria. Upon declaring neutrality China had one condition, however. The territorial rights of Manchuria should remain Chinese and none of the belligerent parties should occupy the territory. Japan accepted China's position but Russia refused to discuss the question regarding Manchuria's neutrality with China. In early February Washington urged the parties to respect China's position. Several of the Western powers with interests in China wished to maintain China's neutrality and keep her outside the scope of the coming hostilities. Japan and Russia agreed finally to accept China's neutral position but this agreement did not include Manchuria. Needless to reiterate, Japan defeated Russia and the peace negotiation opened in Portsmouth, New Hampshire in the summer of 1905. China relied on Japan to secure her rights in Manchuria. It was realised that Japan would not return to China all her privileges in Manchuria. In order to balance the Japanese influence Manchuria was opened to foreign commerce and residence. Both Japanese and Russian troops were withdrawn from Manchuria.[49] Chinese administration was re-established in Manchuria, although limited by both Japanese and other foreign concessions. China had, for a period, turned from the anti-Japanese policy following the Sino-Japanese war to a policy of co-operation with this growing imperialist in the East against the threat from Western powers.[50]

In an article entitled "The international law position of China in the Russo-Japanese war and some related questions"[51] published in the *Xinmin congbao* in March 1904 Liang Qichao argues for the

[49] Except for a small number protecting their railways
[50] Hsu 1980, pp. 130-141
[51] "Ri-E zhanyi guanyu guojifa shang Zhongguo zhi diwei ji gezhong wenti" (日俄戰役關於國際法上中國之地位及各種問題) in *Xinmin congbao* no. 50, pp. 29-40

protection of Chinese rights through international law. He places the responsibility for the poor protection of Chinese sovereign rights during the preceding decades specifically on the lack of competence in international law among the Chinese ruling elite. He forecasts that the voice of the Chinese students having studied subjects like international law abroad (Europe, America and Japan) in recent years will be heard on the international arena in the years to come. In the meantime Liang sees his own task as one of contributing with his own analysis of the present conflict in the light of international law. He is concerned that China is being misled by the foreign powers, including Japan, because of ignorance of the principles and practice of international law. He argues that by accepting the fact that China is allowed to remain neutral in the conflict and at the same time approving that Manchuria is kept outside this agreement on neutrality, China is in fact undermining her sovereign rights in Manchuria and possibly her sovereign rights as such. Both China and Japan have agreed that Manchuria is under Chinese sovereignty. Liang claims that this arrangement may not seem like a contradiction in terms with regard to political arrangements. But in international law, Liang argues, this arrangement is self-contradictory. He suspects the intentions of the foreign powers, well versed in modern international law, who have suggested, agreed on and worked out this arrangement.

> Scholars in international law have earlier argued that there is a difference between what is called complete neutrality and that which is called non-complete neutrality. Until recent times scholars agreed on this. But [lately] this dictum has been discredited. What may not be regarded as complete neutrality is in fact not neutrality. Then what is the definition of neutrality? A neutral state with regard to the two belligerent parties may not in any way contribute in favour of any of them in military affairs.[52] This means that the belligerents' obligation towards a neutral state is that they are not allowed to carry out military operations on the territory of that state. The neutral state's obligation towards the belligerents is that it may not give any of the parties involved in the hostilities access to the use of its territory for military operations. In terms of legal theory, if China claims that Manchuria in fact is China's territorial sovereignty then Manchuria may not be excluded from China's neutrality. And if Japan and other states recognise China's territorial sovereignty over Manchuria, then

[52] Note by Liang Qichao: "There are many definitions of neutrality. Today scholars disagree and are not able to come to a common agreement. The definition used here is limited to the use of the term in this particular case."

> Manchuria cannot be regarded as outside China's neutrality. By this declaration China has in fact sacrificed her sovereignty in relation to the other involved states. And through the tacit accord to this arrangement from the two belligerents and other neutral powers China's sacrifice of sovereignty is *de facto* accepted.[53]

Liang continues his arguments by addressing Japan and her role. The self-contradictory agreement regarding China's sandwiched role between the two belligerents, Japan and Russia, is not only threatening China's sovereignty over Manchuria but in fact potentially China's position in the war as such. Japan has recognised China's sovereignty in Manchuria. By fighting a war against Russia in Manchuria, Japan is treating China as an ally of Russia, he claims. If Japan does not see China as an ally of Russia then she cannot continue regarding Manchuria as a part of China's territory. By *de facto* treating Manchuria as enemy territory and obtaining recognition as such from other states, China may not have a saying with regard to Manchuria's fate after the war. According to international law territories may only be transferred by mutual agreement and the signing of a treaty between the involved states. Manchuria has not been transferred to Russia by any such agreement. But the declaration of Manchuria as outside the scope of Chinese neutrality is to be regarded as China's consent to such a transfer of sovereign rights to Russia, supported by Japan's concession to this arrangement. "Therefore, to say that the day neutrality was proclaimed was the day China sacrificed sovereignty over Manchuria is not an exaggeration."[54]

Liang Qichao has turned from faith only in one's own strength and in the struggle for existence in the late 19th century to the application of rights and duties in international law in the difficult position that China finds herself in the early 20th century, parallel to the general development in the Chinese discourse on international law and China's international position.

Darwin and Confucius in international relations

In the late 19th century the main reformist source of inspiration for the interpretation of inter-state relations was Darwin. The evolutionary

[53] *Xinmin congbao* no. 50, pp. 31-32
[54] Ibid., pp. 32-33

theories of Kang Youwei, Liang Qichao and Mai Menghua, also strongly inspired by an interpretation of Confucianism, constitute the core of any reformist interpretations of the struggle between states and the deplorable status of China in international relations at the dawn of the 20th century. At the same time the rights of nations as defined in international law, in the form that these were known in China through the works of Wheaton and others, were interpreted as potentially necessary tools for China's role in the international family of nations in the coming century. Different reformist attempts to theoretically reconcile the harsh laws of nature and evolution with the protective laws on the side of the weak and suppressed nations in international law were not all exceedingly convincing as theory.

The early 20th century is marked by a greater faith in international law and in the protection by rights and regulations stipulated and adhered to by China's adversaries. China was drawn into disputes and questions pertaining to China's sovereignty, national jurisdiction, rights and duties in international law, and very soon these questions also overshadowed the theoretical deliberations of natural law and the principles of evolutionary development, also among the reformers. The strong focus on Darwin and on the principles behind evolution is, however, not the theoretical framework for interpretations of the international situation applied by all participants in the late imperial discourse on international law. Positive international law and its procedural rules in Chinese translations were applied more often than in the early history of international law in China as a pragmatic tool for securing Chinese rights without any theoretical deliberations on its structural principles, the nature and rationale for the notion of nations having rights. Wang Renjun with his conservative interpretation of the applicability of international law in China is a good example of such a pragmatic approach to international law in late Qing China.

THE CONSERVATIVES AND A CONFUCIAN INTERNATIONAL ORDER

The *Shixuebao* (實學報) represents one of the more conservative periodicals of the late 1890s, published in Shanghai from August 1897 to January 1898. Wang Renjun (王仁俊) served as director of *Shixuebao* and wrote several of the periodical's most influential articles. Its main political line was one of conservative reformism. It promoted 'substantial learning' (*shixue* 實學), usually equated with 'new learning', and change within the traditional political framework, and served as a mouthpiece for conservative intellectual elements. It was conceived as a political opponent of the Kang-Liang group and the *Shiwubao* and is commonly considered an organ for opponents to all political and legal reforms. Its language was also more conservative and archaic than that of *Shiwubao*.[55]

In the series of articles entitled "A critique of democracy"[56] published in *Shixuebao* from September 17th 1897, Wang Renjun refutes the applicability of a republican and democratic system in China. Approving Mai Menghua's view that only monarchy is a viable form of government for China, although deploring the feebleness of Mai's arguments, he reminds his readers of the dismay Sun Yatsen is spreading through his advocacy of radical reforms in the name of democracy. China had a similar detrimental tradition in the past in the pacifist and equitable philosophy of Mo Di (墨翟),[57] Wang claims. This had already in the pre-Qin period been replaced by the rightful Confucian tradition, in Wang's view, thereby confirming his determinist view on Chinese tradition and historical necessity. Wang claims that in a democratic system any opportunist may rise and challenge the rightfully ruling monarch by maintaining his rights as a member of a democracy. Wang apparently also apprehends international law as an element of Western democracies when he calls for vigilance against political activists claiming sovereignty: "They will act and claim that: 'My power is sufficient to be sovereign. That is [a principle] not prohibited in international law'."[58] By refuting the applicability of any democratic principles in the governance of China and by approving the complete and indisputable sovereignty of the Qing monarchy, Wang Renjun, and with him the political line of the *Shixuebao*, disclaims the principles of international law. Wang has apparently not contemplated the principles of sovereignty and sovereign rulership described in the Chinese translations of international law protecting Chinese rights of sovereignty. Wang refutes

[55] *Shixuebao* introduction pp. 1-2; Fang Hanqi (ed.) 1997, vol. 1, pp. 621-622; Britton 1966, p. 95

[56] "Minzhu boyi" (民主駁義)

[57] Most often referred to as Mozi (墨子) (c. 470-391 BC), the founder of the mohist school of thought in pre-Qin China.

[58] *Shixuebao*, p. 146

the ideas of a legal code of sovereignty and international mutual recognition of rulership on a principal basis. Wang may agree with Mai Menghua on the question of which is the best system of government for China but they clearly disagree on the principles this government should adhere to in international affairs.

Wang Renjun may not be well versed in William A.P. Martin's translations of international law into Chinese. But he is clearly familiar with Martin's article and arguments on the Chinese origin of international law in the Spring and Autumn period. Sun Yatsen had the year before been detained by the Chinese legation in London but released after pressure from British authorities. Wang could not see how the foreigners could claim to be adhering to international law when they did not agree to extradite Sun in response to Chinese demands:

> During the Spring and Autumn Period the father of Sun Lin from the state of Wei fled to the state of Jin. Jin accepted him. This affair was ridiculed by men of learning. This is the international law of the Spring and Autumn Period.[59] Martin takes the practices of inter-state relations in the Spring and Autumn Period as the international law of ancient times. Why do not those diplomats struggle for these principles?[60]

Wang poses the question whether or not this only applies to internal Chinese affairs, since the story of Sun Lin's father in fact was a matter between two Chinese states.[61] No, is his answer, because there are also examples of similar matters in Chinese history where the same principles were applied to non-Chinese peoples. "China maintains the principle of not holding back [foreign felons]. But with Chinese criminals[62] foreign countries firmly adhere to the principle of not returning [them to their home country]. Is this reasonable?"[63] Wang

---

[59] Since the escape of Sun Lin's father to the state of Jin was regarded as an act of cowardice Wang concludes that the principle that a fugitive could seek refuge in a foreign state from prosecution in his own state was not acceptable in ancient China. Hence, Wang is in fact arguing in favour of the principle of extradition. Maria Khayutina has studied cases of extradition referred in the *Zuozhuan* and concluded, in an unpublished paper presented at the 15th EACS conference in Heidelberg September 2004, that there seems to have existed an unwritten convention for the extradition of refugees upon request in Spring and Autumn times.

[60] *Shixuebao*, p. 281

[61] In itself a historically peculiar way of seeing the relationship between native and foreign states in ancient China.

[62] Pointing to Sun Yatsen

[63] *Shixuebao*, pp. 281-282; Britton 1966, pp. 112-113

Renjun does not sanction the foreign claims for rights in international affairs:

> This is the sovereign right of my country. But when we are not even allowed to manage our own affairs, what avail is it to talk about rights? I do not understand what is meant by applying rights, I do not understand what is meant by international law.[64]

Wang Renjun argues in favour of the Chinese tradition, finding in it customs for the conduct of international affairs and apparently also sovereign rights. Where the reformers, such as Mai Menghua, seek protection for Chinese sovereign rights in adherence to international law, Wang Renjun has no confidence in the Western powers and their acceptance of China as a member of the family of nations in international law. The Sun Yatsen affair is the point where Wang evidently sees the plain face of the foreign lack of respect for Chinese sovereignty. If only China will keep to her own tradition, one day her ancient tradition will subjugate the West and replace the European hegemony, is Wang Renjun's utopian vision:

> Under a Confucian order disorderly ministers and villains have no place between heaven and earth to escape to. Even if Europe is far away, is it not also to be found between heaven and earth? Today the sacred [Confucian] learning is spreading to the West. It is still only in its early phase. But one day a great personage shall come forth and will establish an international law based on the [Confucian] Chunqiu-tradition. Then all criminals will get [as they deserve]. And if not, then [they] will seek refuge and cause rebellion.[65] The [Confucian] human order will be abandoned, and then also the [civilisation of the] West will crumble.[66]

The future for a Confucian order of international relations is at the core of Wang's international vision, and the fact that the rudiments of an international order may be identified in the Spring and Autumn period further consolidates Wang's faith in a traditional East Asian order of inter-state relations. Sovereignty, in Wang's interpretation, is not a matter of international recognition but of national tradition and history. The Confucian tradition and the principles of ancient Chinese inter-state relations are also at the core of the reformist interpretations of international law in Hunan. The Chinese tradition, together with the principles of Darwinian evolution, are, however, in Hunan taken as

[64] *Shixuebao*, p. 281
[65] Again pointing to Sun Yatsen
[66] *Shixuebao*, p. 763

the theoretical basis for arguments in favour of the application of international law in China, as we shall see below.

INTERNATIONAL LAW, DARWIN AND CHINESE TRADITION IN HUNAN

Education and publication for reform in Changsha

Hunan played a remarkably important role in the late 19th century reform movement in China. The newly appointed governor Chen Baozhen (陳寶箴) attracted a number of reform-minded officials and scholars to the capital of Hunan, Changsha after 1895. Among these Tang Caichang and Tan Sitong were themselves Hunanese. The most prominent reformist official taking part in these experimental reforms was Salt Commissioner Huang Zunxian. Their reform plans were strengthened when Liang Qichao decided to embrace their efforts and take an active part in their activities.[67] The combination of reform minded officials and a band of assiduous reform theorists and activists made Changsha a breeding ground for new ideas and reforms. "Their efforts, as Liang Ch'i-ch'ao later pointed out, did much to help create the climate that made the resulting "Hundred Days Reform" possible; they also did much to inspire the opposition that doomed the Hundred Days to failure."[68] In other words, the reforms in Hunan served as a spearhead in the accelerating reform efforts among groups of scholars in the late 19th century. But their activities were also the momentum that made their cries for change particularly provocative to the increasingly conservative political elite.

As James Reeve Pusey has shown, Darwin, evolution and the struggle for survival played important roles in the theoretical framework also for the Hunanese reforms.[69] These theories were debated and proliferated through the two main Hunanese reform publications, the journal *Xiangxue xinbao*, published every 10 days from April 1897, and the daily paper *Xiangbao* published for only 3 months in early 1898. In addition, a major element in the reform efforts was the establishment of an academy of new learning, the Academy of Current Affairs, the Shiwu xuetang, in October 1897.

[67] Levenson 1967, pp. 24-26
[68] Pusey 1983, p. 127
[69] Ibid., pp 127-154

Liang Qichao was invited to serve as Chinese head professor[70] of the Shiwu xuetang. The academy was based on what was perceived as modern, mainly Western, principles for education and had legal reforms and the strengthening of civil rights[71] as its main political agenda. The Shiwu xuetang became an important breeding ground for a new generation of reform-minded young intellectuals and officials nationally. The curriculum of the Shiwu xuetang was more innovative in terms of introducing modern education in China than the Tongwenguan.[72] A study society called Nanxuehui (南學會) was established by Tan Sitong and others in Changsha in February 1898, soon becoming the main organ advocating political and educational reforms in Hunan and holding weekly joint meetings for officials and scholars discussing topics of reform.[73]

The periodical *Xiangxue xinbao* was published by Tang Caichang, Chen Weiyi (陳為鎰) and others under the auspices of officials like Chen Baozhen and Jiang Biao (江標) (1860-1899), the first issue being published on the 22nd of April 1897. Publication ended with the 45th issue on the 28th of August 1898.[74] The main purpose of the periodical was to educate and enlighten the people of Hunan, to promote new learning and to save and strengthen the Chinese nation. Every issue has a number of thematically organised columns, such as history (*shixue* 史學) and international relations (*jiaoshexue* 交涉學).[75] Tang Caichang was, in addition to Tan Sitong, the main contributor to the *Xiangxue xinbao* and was responsible for the columns in history, politics and international relations. He was appointed associate professor[76] when the Shiwu xuetang was established in February 1898 and has been characterised as the most dedicated pen of all the writers of the Hunanese periodicals. After Zhang Zhidong turned against the Hunan reforms and had their publications closed, and after the failure of the Hundred Days Reform

[70] *Zhongwen zongjiaoxi* (中文總教習)
[71] *Minquan* (民權) is an ambivalent term also comprising the notion of popular power.
[72] Li Guilian 1998a, p. 40
[73] Shin 1976
[74] From issue no. 21 its name was changed to *Xiangxue bao* (湘學報).
[75] In the issues from 1 to 20 lists of suggested reading for each of the columns were also supplied, mainly listing translated works from foreign languages with short summaries of their contents.
[76] *Fen jiaoxi* (分教習)

in 1898, Tang fled to Japan and Hong Kong. In 1900 Tang initiated the Independent Army[77] uprising, proclaiming the establishment of an independent state, but was executed after its failure in August of that year.[78]

The daily newspaper *Xiangbao* was established in order to serve the demand for a faster responding organ, compared to the periodical *Xiangxue xinbao*, as a result of the rapid developments in the reform movement taking place in Hunan. It was published from March 7th 1898 until October 15th 1898, when it was closed down after a prolonged controversy with conservative officials and in connection with the Empress Dowager's crackdown on reform efforts after the failure of the Hundred Days Reform. Liang Qichao was initially connected to the paper but left its staff not long after its first publication and went to Japan after the reform failure. The main radical writers and activists on its editorial staff were Tan Sitong, Tang Caichang, Fan Zhui (樊錐) and He Laibao (何來保).[79]

Tang Caichang on evolution and international law

Tang Caichang was widely read and well schooled in international law through the Tongwenguan and the Jiangnan Arsenal translations. He himself wrote extensively on theoretical aspects of international law, as we have discussed in chapter 3 above. What Liang Qichao did for the introduction of evolutionary theories and Darwinism in China,[80] Tang did for the introduction of international law in general. Based on translated works on the principles of international law in Chinese from foreign languages, Tang Caichang used the international relations column of the *Xiangxue xinbao* to discuss the implications of international law in general, and in particular those cases involving China, often writing under the pseudonym Pingpizi (洴澼子).[81] The column

[77] *Zilijun* (自立軍)

[78] Fang Hanqi (ed.) 1997, vol. 1, pp. 586-593; Judge 1996, p. 211; Britton 1966, pp. 96-97

[79] Fang Hanqi (ed.) 1997, vol. 1, pp. 593-598; See also Ding Pingyi 2000

[80] See Pusey 1983

[81] Tang's name is not explicitly stated as the editor and author of this column but we may assume that he was the main figure behind these articles, as also concluded by Fang Hanqi. (Fang Hanqi (ed.) 1997, vol. 1, p. 590).

Each column had a responsible editor but it is not stated in the early issues who the

was formulated in a didactic way, using the *wenda* (問答) form of asking and answering relevant questions, and was evidently written to educate and enlighten the Chinese educated elite in a broad sense.[82] He introduced the principal notions of international relations in a way that made them relevant to the Chinese situation. In particular, he explained the international situation that China found herself in by seeing international relations in the framework of sovereignty, balance of power, national rights and duties, natural law vs. customary law and international treaties, right of self-defence, neutrality in time of war, the particulars of private international law, etc. Hugo Grotius had unexpectedly become one of the masters, sages, of the past, in addition to Confucius and Mengzi, quoted in order to substantiate arguments in the Chinese discourse on international relations. Rather than introducing international law as an alien system Tang Caichang included Grotius in the Chinese pantheon of ancient sages. There is, however, a major difference between the ancient Chinese Confucian sages and Western publicists such as Grotius, as we shall see below.

Pusey has argued that Tang Caichang, writing under the pseudonym Pingpizi, was an ardent advocate of Darwinian imperative action for survival, and hence not an exponent of the principles of rights and equality expressed in international law:

> "P'ing-p'i-tzu's" announced espousal of the naturalist Darwin did not lead him to believe that human affairs were all naturally determined. The "struggle for existence" was not a process to be watched with noble resignation, content in the conviction that the best man (or race) would win, but a call to action, an exhortation to struggle.[83]

Darwin obviously did not call the species into action when he applied the word "struggle" to the forces of evolution. Tang, however, like many of his contemporaries, called for action and did not believe in passively waiting for the justice of evolution to bring to China what

individual editor was, except for Tang's responsibility for the history column. From a list in issue no. 27 we understand that Yang Gai (揚概) had the editorial responsibility for the later issues of the International relations column.

[82] The *Jichengbao* (集成報) has made an excerpt of the main questions and answers in this *wenda* section of the *Xiangxue xinbao* published in the issues 17 through 22 in 1897-98. The column in the *Jichengbao* is entitled "*Xiangbao* shi gongfa" (湘報釋公法) (The *Xiangbao* explains international law). The texts are, however, not taken from the *Xiangbao* but in fact from the *Xiangxue xinbao*. (*Jichengbao*, vol. 1, pp. 953-956; vol. 2, pp. 1017-1022, 1069-74, 1123-1128, 1183-1188, 1237-1243.)

[83] Pusey 1983, p. 136

China deserved. He called his Hunanese and Chinese compatriots into action for survival. That does not, however, necessarily imply that Tang Caichang rejected the ideas of laws regulating a peaceful coexistence between groups, races or nations. Pusey has construed this apparent divergence in arguments as a contradiction in comprehension between some of the Hunanese reformers. Pusey refers to the "starry-eyed advocates of international law ... who really did want to 'repudiate the gladiatory theory of existence,' and said that such a thing was possible thanks to progress, had no fear, for example, that, by artificially preventing the struggle for existence, they might effectively legislate an end to progress."[84] These advocates of international law are depicted by Pusey in opposition to the advocates of Darwinian principles of struggle for survival such as Tang Caichang.[85] I wish to challenge this conclusion and suggest that all these arguments are based on the assumption that the means and principles for survival differ at the various stages in history. Let us suggest that the three-stage theory of evolution towards the utopian vision of Datong is applied, and that the principles of international law are the principles of natural law representing the peaceful coexistence of races and nation in the Age of Great Peace.[86] Then the optimistic view of Tantanzi (譚譚子), that international law would rule the races and nations after the twentieth century, the somewhat less optimistic view of Pi Jiayou (皮嘉祐) that such a time will only appear after a few hundred years, or the apparently pessimistic view of Tang Caichang that the survival of the races is in fact up to their own struggle, may not be contradictory in terms. Does this assumption have any bearing on the writings in the Hunanese periodicals?

Yes, we find a clue to this view also in the writings of Tang Caichang himself. In a dedication that he wrote for the opening of the Study Society of International Law[87] established by Bi Yongnian (畢永年) in Hunan, he refers to the Darwinian struggle for survival as the basic rule of all human affairs:

> The Western scholar Darwin has said that [all] is a struggle for survival. Spencer has expounded this meaning and said that groups compete with groups. Huxley has further explicated this assertion by saying that

[84] Ibid., p. 139
[85] Ibid., pp. 136-144
[86] Discussed in detail under the reformers earlier in this chapter
[87] Gongfaxue xuehui (公法學學會)

> heaven and man compete. Hence there are the studies of society, race, biology and evolution. There is no one among those who arduously seek survival in the war between man and things who does not take struggle as their main task.[88]

Men seek together in groups in order to unite their efforts in this struggle for survival, just as the study society was established to join forces to have China accepted in the international family of nations.

> By struggling for rights one can struggle for the race. And by struggling for the race one can struggle for the nation. And by struggling for the nation one can struggle for heaven. But when one is skilled at struggling where there is no struggle and when one is skilled at not struggling when there is a struggle, in order to depart from the way towards the Great Unity (Datong), then the words of the international law publicists are born.[89]

Tang, in this article, is explicitly claiming that the standards of international law represented in the works of international law specialists are only temporary theories promoted by ordinary men and simple scholars of the West.[90] In the age of Great Peace there are no borders and no struggle. In the present age, however, China should follow the words of Bi Yongnian, saying that the starting point towards no struggle is the struggle for survival.[91] When one develops from the Small Unity (*xiaokang*)[92] towards Great Unity (Datong) one moves from the principle of struggle towards the principle of no struggle.[93] Hence, in Tang Caichang's evolutionary vision, in advanced stages of evolution there is no longer need for a struggle for survival. For China in this time, however, there is a need for struggle and for a united effort in the international struggle for existence—hence the establishment of the study society.

What then are the principles guiding the society of the time of Great Unity if those principles are not found in the natural law explicated in international law? To the Hunanese reformers all utopian principles were to be found in the Confucian Chunqiu tradition

[88] *Xiangbao*, p. 343
[89] Ibid., p. 343
[90] Ibid., p. 343
[91] Ibid., p. 344; Pusey 1983, p. 143
[92] The notion of Small Unity, x*iaokang*, also refers to the stages of progression presented in the Confucian *Liyun* tradition. In the late Qing discourse it often refers to all the advanced stages in evolution prior to the Datong utopia. See Pusey 1983, pp. 40, 42.
[93] *Xiangbao*, p. 344

advanced by the former "uncrowned king",[94] referring to Confucius. In Tang's exegesis it is necessary to conform to the Western principles of international law in this age in order to be fit for survival, since the principles of international law apparently are based on the same natural principles as in Darwinism, conceivably all parts of the Western "sciences". In the age of Great Unity to come, however, there is no longer any struggle for survival and the Chunqiu standards will guide humankind in peaceful coexistence. In this perspective, there is no inherent contradiction between Tang Caichang's ardent argumentation in favour of struggle and those seeking temporary refuge in positive international law. There is only a difference in perspective. We find also other more explicit expositions of the relationship between law and struggle, and the fundamental position of the Chunqiu tradition, in the periodicals and the Shiwu xuetang curriculum, as we shall see below.

Education in Hunan between tradition and modernisation

We may assume that the model of training in international law at the Tongwenguan, [95] and Tang Caichang's personal concern with questions of international law brought about the relative emphasis on the teaching of international law in the Shiwu xuetang. The curriculum of the school[96] is divided into two parts, one general part consisting of common knowledge[97] and one part where the student specialises in one particular field of science[98]. Among the particular sciences the student may choose between public law (*gongfaxue* 公法學), political history (*zhangguxue* 掌故學),[99] and mathematics and the

[94] *Suwang* (素王)

[95] Su Jing 1978, pp. 42-53; Li Guilian 1998a, pp. 37-38; See also excerpts from Martin's *Tongwenguan timinglu* (同文館題名錄) published in *Wanguo gongbao* (萬國公報).

[96] In issue no. 102 of the *Xiangbao* we find a detailed description of the curriculum of the Shiwu xuetang (*Xiangbao*, pp. 940-948; Also included in *juan* 19 of the *Huangchao Jingshiwen xinbian* (皇朝經世文新編); See also Li Guilian 1998a, pp. 38-40)

[97] Common knowledge to be studied by every student (浦通學凡學生人人皆當通習)

[98] One particular field of science to be chosen by each student (專門學每人各占一門)

[99] Including political, administrative and legal systems, important historical figures, geography etc.

natural sciences (*gesuanxue* 格算學). Public law is again divided into internal public law (*neigongfa* 內公法) and external public law (*waigongfa* 外公法). Constitutional law, civil law and penal law constitute internal public law, while external public law includes international law (*jiaoshe gongfa* 交涉公法) and treaties (*yuezhang* 約章).[100] The timetable of the Shiwu xuetang indicates that most of the major translations on international law by the Tongwenguan and the Jiangnan arsenal were applied in their training. This fact is also confirmed by reading the introduction to Chinese translations on international law and diplomacy in the different issues of *Xiangxue xinbao*. It is also evident from the comments on the obligatory reading for the different courses that students of public law studied not only foreign law. These students were also expected to compare the translations of foreign law systems with the Chinese tradition, the tradition of Chunqiu and Confucius.

This combination of foreign sciences and the Chinese tradition is a salient feature of the Shiwu xuetang educational system and also the theoretical foundation of the reform movement in Hunan in the late 19th century, being an important element in the interpretation of international law within the Shiwu xuetang. The commentary to the Chinese translation of Theodore Dwight Woolsey's *Introduction to the study of international law* in the timetable reads: "All those who study public law must at all times search for evidence in the Chunqiu tradition."[101] This is further explained by Zhou Huichang (周會昌) in his introduction to the public law courses of the school: "With regard to the study of international relations, in China nothing is more splendid than the Chunqiu tradition, in the West nothing is more refined than the Roman tradition." Zhou claims that public law has developed in accordance with heavenly principles and follows the way of kings and rulers. There are, however, differences in the practice of international law due to the different stages in development. He again applies the theory dividing human progress on its way to a utopian society into three stages; The Age of Disorder, the Age of Increasing Peace, and the Age of Great Peace, a deterministic view on evolution which is familiar to us by now. When there are no rights or wrongs

---

[100] As observed by Li Guilian this division into internal and external public law should not be confused with the common division into private and public law. (Li Guilian 1998a, p. 40)

[101] *Xiangbao*, p. 943

and no equality, when the only principle is that the strong subdue the weak and the many defeat the few, then that particular society is in the Age of Disorder. When two equal forces do not resort to military power but employ the rights and wrongs established by publicists, then that is a sign of the Age of Increasing Peace. When those near and those far away, small and large all are like one, when all differences between men and women, between high and low, and all social and political relations are governed by one common law, then one will be experiencing the Age of Great Peace. The West, in Zhou's interpretation, is close to fulfilling the requirements of the Age of Increasing Peace but is evidently far from reaching the utopian stage of Great Peace. Development through these stages depends on the efforts by specialists in the required fields. Therefore, by training students in public law, including both inter-national and inter-personal relations, Zhou, the other teachers at the Shiwu xuetang, and finally the students after graduation, will be able to aid China on its way through the stages in evolution.[102] This three-stage theory of evolution is evidently the major theoretical framework for the Shiwu xuetang education, in addition to Darwinian evolutionary theories as shown above.

This utilitarian attitude towards international law is even more explicitly declared in the first international relations column in the *Xiangxue xinbao*, most probably composed by Tang Caichang. In the *wenda* fashion the author asks how it can be that in the West international law is seen as representing natural principles (*xingfa* 性理) while might (*quanshi* 權勢) apparently is the principle ruling international relations. "The weak are meat for the strong to eat. That is the same today as it was in ancient times.... Can international law serve as a foundation [in international relations]?"[103] Tang Caichang reiterates his arguments from the dedication to the study society, saying that Western publicists like Grotius, Bynkershoek, Leibniz, Kant, Wheaton, Phillimore and others are all ordinary men basing themselves on empty arguments, but nevertheless laying out the political workings of international relations in this age. Since these publicists represent the principles of the order of the day, it is necessary to adhere to these in order to save the weak for the next

[102] Ibid., p. 983
[103] *Xiangxue xinbao*, vol. 1, pp. 33b-34a

century. "This is the reason why experts on the Chunqiu tradition need to understand international law",[104] Tang claims. The way to apply international law on the basis of the Chunqiu tradition is more explicitly formulated in the next *wenda* section:

> I ask you: Would it not be hypocritical to explain the Chunqiu tradition by the use of international law? The answer is: *Chunqiu* is a book [explaining] the institutional reforms [promoted by] the uncrowned king (i.e. Confucius). Above it is based on the way of heaven, in the middle it applies the ways of the kings, and below it regulates human relations.... International law publicists sustain each other with empty principles, attempt to claim [basis] in heaven in order to explicate its significance. In former times, however, one referred to the *Chunqiu* as the sacred model book, and further referred to it as the book of correct names[105]... I will claim that if one is based on the Chunqiu when one is being trained in international law, then one will be able to understand the [writings of] people like Wheaton in a much more precise manner.[106]

In issue 4 of the *Xiangxue xinbao* Tang Caichang is even more explicit as to the significance of the Chunqiu tradition: "To proclaim the ways of Confucian learning is to [fashion ways] to rule for ten thousand generations and to rule the world after what people in the West refer to as the 20th century. That time is only in its germination today."[107] Thus we understand that the Chunqiu tradition is meant for better times to come, not only in China but for the entire world, as the fundamental principles fashioned in heaven, in accordance with Confucian teaching, and innately in accordance with human emotions and relations. These arguments resemble the arguments claimed by Wang Renjun, with the major difference that Wang, not seeing the world in evolutionary terms, disclaims the value of international law also in his own time.

Then, one could ask, what about Martin who in fact has written on the basis of international relations in the Chunqiu tradition? Tang Caichang has also asked that question in the international relations column in another issue of the *Xiangxue xinbao*. Martin has got things right, according to Tang, since Martin has lived in China for so long, namely that there is a basis for a particular form of international law in

---

[104] Ibid.
[105] *Zhengming* (正名)
[106] *Xiangxue xinbao*, vol. 1, p. 34b
[107] Ibid., vol. 4, p. 25a

the Chunqiu tradition. Martin's analysis is relatively superficial, according to Tang, but he has correctly observed that international law was present in ancient China both in terms of natural law and in terms of international customary law. The Chunqiu tradition was lost in China after the interruption of the Gongyang tradition from Mengzi. A re-establishment of international law within the Chunqiu tradition is the way to re-establish China's rightful glory and position in international relations.[108]

The common way to seek in the Chinese tradition for a theoretical framework in order to understand international law, as we have seen above and will discuss further below, was to examine the Gongyang tradition of the Chunqiu. Yi Nai (易鼐) (1875-?), however, takes a different and much more radical, Daoist inspired position regarding how to apply the Chinese tradition in order to strengthen China and make her a member of the world community of nations. In his article "An explication on how China should take weakness as a strength"[109] in the *Xiangbao* he suggests applying a strategy outlined by Laozi in order to make China strong, finding support for this in a passage in Yan Fu's "Whence Strength?".[110] He does not endorse the scheme of making China powerful by strengthening her cultural, economical, political and social position by traditional means. He quotes chapter 76 of the *Laozi* (*Daodejing*) claiming that by birth all things, including humans, are weak and by death all things are strong.[111] Hence, weakness is the companion of life and strength is the companion of death. He suggests four strategies for making China strong by weakening China:

> Firstly, change the laws in order to unify the laws. Secondly, standardise teaching in order to reduce [the importance of traditional] teaching. Thirdly, humiliate the elders in order to protect the elders. Fourthly, unite the races in order to secure the races.

He explains further in more detail what these four strategies imply. Changing the laws indicates changing Chinese laws so that they correspond to the legal systems of the West. By standardising teaching he suggests that China should apply both Chinese and Western systems of teaching in the education system. By humiliating the elders

---

[108] Ibid., vol. 8, pp. 29b-30a
[109] "Zhongguo yi yi ruo wei qiang shuo" (中國宜以弱為強說)
[110] "Yuanqiang" (原強). Pusey 1983, pp. 141-142
[111] *Laozi zhu* 1990, vol. 3, p. 45

he implies that all seniors should have their power reduced, and popular power should be given an equal importance in political matters. By uniting the races he suggests that the white and the yellow races should intermarry. If China does not apply these measures but only adheres to the traditional ways of strengthening China, it will be like sitting down waiting for death. In order to have the international community accept China on an equal footing, to treat China as a member of the international family of nations, and to see China as a friendly nation, she will have to use this strategy of weakness and consequently transform the strong elements in her tradition. China must enter the world community by adhering to international law on Western terms. By adhering to international law by weakening China, all claims towards China from the Western powers may be resisted by referring to commonly accepted principles in international law. And when China has claims against other nations, she may enforce these by adhering to international law. This is how the principle of weakness may be used to strengthen China.[112] Tradition may apparently be applied in many different ways when arguing for the adaptation to Western international law in Hunan.

The restoration of China's sovereignty is one of Tang Caichang's main arguments for the adaptation of international law in this age in China, and in particular an argument for the study of law to be included among the special subjects of modern style education in China. The Chinese legal system must be strengthened in order to strengthen the Chinese position in cases between China and foreign countries or nationals. This must be done through modern education. In Meiji-reformed Japan legal studies are an intrinsic part of their educational system and hence Japan was able to restore her sovereignty in the treaty with America. China has long lost her sovereignty in the treaties with foreign countries.[113] Both Switzerland and Morocco have been able to preserve their international position and their sovereignty in spite of their small size. This is only due to their acceptance of international legal principles. China, on the other hand, in spite of her size, is being humiliated in international relations, even when she adheres to international treaties. She needs more strength in terms of modern education in order to obtain a position in

---

[112] *Xiangbao*, pp. 153-155

[113] *Xiangxue xinbao*, vol. 1, p. 35b

the international family of nations. Sheer size and the adherence to a number of international treaties are not sufficient as measures to maintain Chinese sovereignty. Japan is a model for achieving such a goal, to re-establish Chinese sovereignty, and education is the means.[114] Sovereignty based on the acceptance of and adherence to international law, not only as an innate consequence of a number of international treaties, is for the first time in the Chinese discourse on international questions perceived as an imperative quality of the Chinese state. The later discourse on Chinese sovereignty may have its earliest foundations in the Hunanese interpretation and educational system.

Shiwu xuetang students on attraction, forces, evolution and international relations

One of the most interesting Hunanese contributions to the discourse on international law in late imperial China lies in the pedagogical effects of the Shiwu xuetang training in international law. In a number of articles in the *Xiangbao* based on student papers we may discern the effects of the theoretical training in international law on the young students. Their explications lack somewhat in theoretical depth but are altogether interesting examples of how the theories of Chunqiu, Darwinism and the three stage evolutionary theory are interpreted and construed in the heads of ambitious young modern Chinese students in late Qing. In a *Xiangbao* article by the 15 year old Shiwu xuetang student Zheng Baokun (鄭寶坤) the author presents the theoretical legal and evolutionary framework for international law and sovereignty based on the three-stage theory of evolution and the relative importance of the integration of Western and Chinese learning. In Zheng's presentation all motions in the world are ruled by the force of attraction (*aili* 愛力). Attraction in the sky is the ruling principle of the stellar bodies, attraction in physical objects is the law guiding the collision of particles and the attraction between humans is the principle behind the law. Internally laws cause interaction between those high and low in society and protect the right of independence, while externally international law is observed in order to maintain a

[114] Ibid., vol. 2, pp. 27b-28a

balance of power and to secure equal benefits for all. Zheng refers to international publicists and postulates that sovereignty is internally expressed in internal public law, namely the legal system of a country, and externally in international law. The reason for China not being respected in international affairs is, according to Zheng (and probably also his teachers at the Shiwu xuetang), that China does not transparently and firmly apply the law. China needs to establish its sovereignty in terms of international law, which is the only way to secure China's position in the world community. The West classifies China as a semi-civilised country and hence not subject to international law with the status of a sovereign state. Attraction is the force behind all evolution. China needs to develop from the Age of Disorder to the Age of Increasing Peace. The Chinese people are not attracted towards one single unity. Attraction is lost, leading to separation, and the 400 million Chinese people appear like 400 million individual countries rather than as one sovereign, national unit. That is the reason why the West does not respect China's position in international law. The starting point for an evolution towards the utopian Great Unity (Datong) society is attraction. The solution is in the hands of the 400 million Chinese people:

> If [we] want to save China, then [we] need to enter international law. If [we] want to enter international law, then we need to extend [our] sovereignty. And if [we] want to extend [our] sovereignty, [we] will have to start by changing the law.[115]

Another young student of the Shiwu xuetang, Gu Tianyou (辜天祐) is more specific with regard to the necessity of a system of international acceptance of sovereignty. He indicates that sovereignty in fact is an *a priori* quality of all living organisms in the world. All countries in the world have their sovereign rights and all animals and plants find their protection in their sovereignty. This is to be compared to the Roman state in ancient times. Rome had its internal laws that could not be applied in other states and its neighbour states had their internal laws that did not have effect in the Roman Empire. Hence, a system of international laws was established in order to regulate the relationship between these states. The sovereignty and rights of states with regard to each other in times of occupation and war were formulated in documents of international law. This is how the natural principle of

[115] *Xiangbao*, p. 1069

sovereignty is protected and defined in international relations.[116]

Gu Tianyou has also written an essay on the topic of international relations in the light of the traditional Mencian theory of "taking small matters as large and large matters as small".[117] Gu quotes Mengzi's passage from the "Liang Hui wang" chapter:

> The one who takes large matters as small is one who takes pleasure in heaven. The one who takes small matters as large is one who fears heaven. The one who takes pleasure in heaven protects all under heaven, [while] the one who fears heaven protects his own country.[118]

This, Gu claims, is the principle of all human relations: "All those who wish to protect a peaceful order under heaven must make sure that every man under heaven understands the natural principles of international law. He must make sure that the strong observe international law and do not dare to maltreat the weak, make sure that they respect international law and do not violate it." Gu Tianyou interprets the Mencian theory of small and large matters again in view of the three-stage theory of evolution, claiming that all matters will be one, the difference between small and large matters, between those close and those distant, will eventually all become one and all balance out each other in the last stage of evolution, in the Age of Great Peace. The principles set forth by Mengzi are thus representative of a utopian vision of human relations in the evolutionary theory applied by Kang Youwei and others. Gu claims that by taking pleasure in heaven and fearing heaven Mengzi was in fact referring to notions of taking pleasure and fearing heavenly, or rather, natural principles (*tianli* 天理), presumably since natural principles may be conceived as the principles guiding the final stage in evolution. In Mengzi's time there was no international law. But Grotius has explained that international law is nothing but natural law. Gu explains that Grotius has set forth international law based on natural principles as a branch of natural law. Hence, what is meant by the Mencian principle is in fact that one should take pleasure in and fear international law:

> Mengzi explains that the way of intercourse between neighbours has its basis in taking pleasure in and fearing heaven. To take pleasure in

---

[116] Ibid., p. 1517

[117] *Yi xiao shi da, yi da shi xiao* (以小事大以大事小)

[118] *Mengzi zhushu* 1982, vol. 2, p. 2675; See also *Mengzi zhengyi*, vol. 1, pp. 112-113. To 'fear heaven' in this passage is a description of one who has awe and respect for the greatness of heaven.

> heaven is to take pleasure in heavenly principles, and to fear heaven is to fear heavenly principles. This is nothing other than taking pleasure in and fearing international law. In ancient times there was no international law, so one referred to heaven in order to establish principles. Today international law also refers to heaven (nature) as its principles. These principles are one and the same. International law is these principles. When it comes to the precise significance of international relations, it is [also] necessary to apprehend the situation of the day in order to seek suitable ways of response and change.[119]

However, what Gu has explained is clearly not the reality of international relations of his own time. What Mengzi was referring to, and presumably what Grotius was referring to by natural law, is a utopia, the Age of Great Peace, quite different from the realities of late Qing China. The reality of the international situation, as Gu Tianyou sees it, is that in the name of protecting world peace international law is being misused by the strong powers as a tool for subduing the weak. International practice has become nothing but a law for the strong. When two strong forces meet, there is international law. When one strong and one weak force meet, then the law of the jungle rules. "Therefore, what Mengzi was talking about are human relations in the Age of Great Peace. Today is not that age."[120]

The reformers in Hunan display an array of different theoretical interpretations of international law in the framework of Chinese tradition. Darwin and evolution are important elements in their approach to the future of China's sovereignty and international position. International law is a tool for improving China's international position. According to these reformers none of these "modern" theoretical elements imported from the West may be applied without one or another foundation in the Chinese tradition itself, be it Daoist or Confucian. International law becomes an essential tool for securing China's international position among reform-minded Chinese students in Japan, as we shall see below. The adherence to Chinese tradition that we have seen taking place in Hunan as an important feature of the modernisation of China's international outlook was, however, among the students in Japan exchanged for a starry-eyed admiration for modernisation in the Japanese fashion.

---

[119] *Xiangbao*, p. 1553
[120] Ibid., p. 1553

INTERNATIONAL LAW AND CHINESE STUDENTS IN JAPAN

Chinese students and Meiji modernised Japan

There is no doubt that Japan in many respects played a crucial role in the events that finally led to the demise of Chinese imperial rule in 1911-12. It is beyond the scope of the present study to engage in any analysis of the Japanese force of impact on the Chinese court, on Chinese politics and society in the years after the Sino-Japanese war 1894-95.[121] It suffices in this context to remind ourselves of some of the main features of the government study program that started in the spring of 1896 with a group of 13 young Chinese students going to Tokyo Higher Normal School for a three year program and ended with large numbers of migrating Chinese students engaging in anti-Qing, anti-traditional activities in Japan ten years later.

> By the time these first overseas students, or liu hsueh-sheng (ryû-gakusei in Japanese), had completed their course in 1899, another 100 Chinese students were enrolled in Japanese schools. The figure for 1902 stood at 400-500; for 1903 it was 1,000. By 1905-06, a year after the Russo-Japanese war, between 8,000 and 9,000 were studying in Tokyo; in fact, some estimates suggest as many as 20,000. Over five years, what had started as a government-sanctioned overseas study program, modest in size, had mushroomed into a large-scale and largely unregulated migration of students abroad, the first such phenomenon anywhere in the world. Nor only was this a large group; it was an increasingly rebellious group, prone to the anti-dynastic dissidence that eventually led to revolution in 1911.[122]

The exposure to the advances of Meiji-reformed Japan, both materially and intellectually, had a great impact on these young Chinese students. This was a part of the general alienation of Chinese society from the central authorities in late Qing, particularly acute among young students, and even more so for students going abroad to study "modern", Western natural and social sciences. The decision taken by central authorities to send students to Japan after defeat in the Sino-Japanese war was part of small-scale attempts at reforms through the more open door policy of the late 1890s. The sense of a national crisis that the Shimonoseki treaty had produced in China fuelled the

---

[121] For more general studies of this period see for instance Harrel 1992

[122] Harrel 1992, p. 2

notion that the former policy of self-reliance in order to strengthen China had to be changed into some means of learning from the experiences of the West and Japan in order to strengthen China politically, economically and militarily. In many respects the study program in Japan became a great success. Many young Chinese students did get a modern style education and were trained in the modern sciences, contributing to the speed of modernisation in China. In particular, the experiences in Japan led to rapid changes in the Chinese educational system and finally to the abolishment of the traditional Confucian examination system in 1905. On the other hand, from the perspective of those who initiated the study program, the program turned into a catastrophe. Without the position of Japan as a breeding ground for young, revolutionary Chinese student movements and later also for Sun Yatsen's Tongmenghui (同盟會), the political events of the decade in China leading up to the 1911 uprising may have looked entirely different.

> As 1905 drew to a close, it became clear that, in terms of the political goals set out by the original planners, the study-in-Japan program was a dismal failure. The Ch'ing structure, far from being revitalised by the program, was weakening under pressures exerted in part by its products. And Sino-Japanese bonds, far from being strengthened were rapidly deteriorating. The overseas study experience had produced thousands of disaffected youth, core members of China's first truly national revolutionary organisation, the T'ung-meng Hui (Alliance Society), which was founded in August, and instigators of an anti-Japanese protest of unprecedented size and scope in December. From this point on, China's domestic politics entered a more turbulent period.[123]

We have no exact figures of how many of the Chinese students in Japan were engaged in law and political studies but the numbers were certainly not insignificant. The large number of works on international law produced by the students in Japan, which we have discussed in the previous chapter, is an indication of the impact and size of this group of students. The direct link between the dismay at China's political role in international affairs and Japan's position and the potential salvation inherent in the study of Western political and legal science was of course the main reason for many Chinese students engaging in these fields of study in Japanese institutions. "A mere ten years after

[123] Ibid., p. 7

its triumph over China in 1895, Japan ranked as an ally of Britain, victor over Russia, and defender of its own sphere of influence on the China mainland."[124] Japan served as a model for many of the students' attempts at modernising and strengthening China. Japan's position towards China and Chinese students in Japan, in particular with regard to the tension over the Japanese role in Korea and in Manchuria, was at the same time an element that the Chinese students in Japan disapproved of.

> The majority of students came away from their Japan experience with a strongly anti-Japanese and, more generally, anti-imperialist bias, and this was an important ingredient of modern Chinese nationalism. But even here there was a paradox: for a generation trying to establish China's place in the world, imperialism, defined in Social Darwinian terms as the ultimate in national power, was not only something to resist but something to strive for.[125]

Nationalism and Social Darwinian theories on national power were central in the intellectual environment that the Chinese students met in Japan. This was not altogether different from the theoretical framework that students and intellectuals in China were exposed to. The experience that distinguished these students in Japan from their fellow students and intellectuals in China was that the level of theoretical competence in other fields of Western sciences was much higher in Japan. Students were not merely exposed to a simplistic Darwinian model for evolution and natural selection applied on almost any sphere of human activity, as was very much the case in China. In Japan the theoretical fundamentals in all the social sciences were taught as separate fields of study. This gave the students in Japan potentially a better theoretical training in the different sciences. On the other hand, their training may not have been particularly apt in relation to political activism since it was less suitable for political slogans and organisational programs.

[124] Ibid., p. 9
[125] Ibid.

Students of politics and law on positive law in international relations

This latter situation is particularly the case for the discourse on questions related to international law among these students. A number of student periodicals serving students from particular regions in China, such as *Hubei xueshengjie* (湖北學生界)[126] for students from Hubei, *Zhejiangchao* (浙江潮)[127] for students from Zhejiang, and *Jiangsu* (江蘇)[128] for students from Jiangsu, were the main organs for political and social debate among the Chinese students in Japan. These magazines were published, and contributions to them were written by the student societies, the different Tongxianghui (同鄉會), in Japan from early 1903 and distributed through a wide network of distributors in Japan, on the Chinese mainland and abroad. Chinese authorities were not pleased with this development. Students were not expected to take part in these kinds of activities. They were ordered back to their studies under the threat that their scholarships would be withdrawn.

> The government's crackdown, combined with escalating costs of publication, helped bring the magazines to an abrupt halt after a year or so of publication. *Hupei Student Circle*, the first to appear, was the first to leave; its final issue was dated September-October 1903. *Tide of Chechiang* held on another month, putting out its tenth issue in November-December. *Kiangsu* maintained operation until June 1904.

It was not until 1905-06 that the number of Chinese periodicals in Japan, such as the *Minbao* (民報) again started blossoming.[129]

The student magazines had separate columns for articles on politics and law (*zhengfa* 政法) where mainly students of these fields engaged in writing on questions pertaining to public law and politics. In these columns Social Darwinian ideas were manifestly less prominent than what we have seen in the periodicals in China when discussing political, legal and international questions. In an article in *Jiangsu* one of the students, under the pseudonym Meigen (昧根),[130] explicates the origins of the law. He explains that the entire universe is ruled by laws. Most of these rules are very complex and far-reaching, operating

[126] *Hupei Student Circle*
[127] *Tide of Chechiang*
[128] *Kiangsu*
[129] Harrel 1992, pp. 105-106; See also Yu, Li & Chang 1970, pp. 25-54
[130] Translates 'root of ignorance'

beyond the realm of the human senses and intellect. The laws may be divided into two main categories. The first encompasses the world of natural forces and elements and has its origin in nature. The second comprises the laws of human activities in society and is fashioned by humans. The author does not expound the principles of natural law and is clearly more interested in the principles of positive law as it is formulated by humans: "What is that phenomenon that is the expression of laws fashioned by humans? It is nothing but legal regulations."[131] The basic human principles expressed through human laws are not ascribed to natural law but to the human realm. That human realm is universal in nature and is what Confucius called Benevolence,[132] Mozi called Concern for everyone,[133] Buddha called Passion and Jesus called Salvation. When the qualities of human nature are unevenly distributed and groups of individual humans come into contact with each other, then the forces of evolution begin to operate; Struggle is born and only the most fit and strong will survive in a ferocious battle for survival. Only the positive laws created by humans will be able to regulate these conditions and reduce the cruelty of the forces of evolution.[134] Laws, both domestic and international, are perceived to be positive laws created by humans, notably good in nature because humans are innately good. These positive laws are not directly derived from natural law. The violent forces of evolution may, on the other hand, be perceived as linked to nature. Positive laws work against the forces of evolution in order to better conditions for those doomed by selection.

The difference from the native Chinese discourse on the mainland is that the students in Japan were less concerned with the theories of natural versus positive laws, as we perceive from the rest of the writings on law in the student periodicals in Japan. They appear more as specialists in positive law and less as legal and political philosophers in the periodicals. They observe the harsh laws of nature but choose to ignore them in their deliberations on legal theory, quite contrary to their brothers and sisters in China. They are concerned with the operation of international law and the way it may be applied in cases pertaining to China for the recognition of Chinese sovereignty

[131] *Jiangsu*, issue no. 2, p. 241
[132] *Ren* (仁)
[133] *Jian'ai* (兼愛)
[134] *Jiangsu*, issue no. 2, pp. 242-243

and independence. The realisation and acceptance that international law is in fact nothing but a system of mutually acknowledged sets of international customs, based on European history and international custom, is an apparent consequence of the pragmatic attitude of these Chinese students. China may like it or not but it is the established forms of European international customs that have set the standards, seems to be the general attitude. An anonymous author in the *Jiangsu* explains these relations in an article entitled "Public international law and the international realities".[135] International law follows international custom. By adhering to the customary law established in European international relations, China will be able to resolve the questions originating in the treaties, in the system of extraterritoriality and in the establishment of international settlements in Chinese cities. The author does not raise any questions regarding the justice, the fairness or the justifications for China being coerced to adhere to sets of European international customs,[136] most typically for the attitude of these students in Japan. They kept their focus on the key issues in China's international relations in the early 20th century, being sovereignty, extraterritoriality, jurisdiction and neutrality.

Sovereignty, extraterritoriality and jurisdiction

One of the students, writing under the pseudonym Nazi (那子),[137] draws a direct link between the establishment of a modern legal system and national sovereignty, and argues for the pivotal importance of the existence of a civilised legal system for national stability and international recognition. The existence of a state, the lives and property of its citizens, are all dependent on laws. In fact, laws in a state regulate all relations between authority and its subjects, and all other communication between its citizens. "When the laws are established, then responsibilities and rights may be put into practice. Everyone will maintain their responsibilities and protect their rights, nobody will infringe on others and the state will enjoy the pleasures of peace."[138] Sovereignty, both in domestic and international matters, is

[135] "Guoji gongfa yu guoji shishi" (國際公法與國際事實)
[136] *Jiangsu*, issue 9/10, pp. 1577-1584
[137] Probably short for Zhinazi (支那子) meaning 'son of China'
[138] *Zhejiangchao*, issue no. 3, *Zhengfa* p. 1

built upon a civilised legal system. China's lack of a complete legal system is the main reason for her misery both domestically and internationally, in Nazi's view. He directs his artillery against the Manchu court, claiming that the uncivilised legal system of China undermines her sovereignty. Foreigners in China are unwilling to submit to its laws, thus establishing the system of extraterritoriality. The system of extraterritoriality has the consequence that different laws are applied for the same offence dependent on the nationality of the offender, which is severely unjust and undermines Chinese sovereignty. "This is where national sovereignty is completely lost. Alas, when it has come to this, is the nation still a nation?",[139] he asks. If China does not change her political system, if she does not make the laws express the will and understanding of its citizens, then China will remain a barbarian nation. And if she remains a barbarian, then foreign nationals and nations will not respect her laws and hence her sovereignty is at stake.[140] China needs to advance from a state of barbarism in legal and political terms. Then, and only then, according to Nazi, will her sovereignty be established and recognised internationally. There are no "sophisticated" theories of social evolution in a Darwinian framework in Nazi's thesis. His main interest and subject matter is the legal system and its implications for matters of international concern and sovereignty. The position of China as an equal and civilised partner in international affairs was to be built on a comprehensive system of domestic laws and adherence to international law and conventions.

A contemporary issue related to the question of extraterritoriality is the legal status of the foreign treaty ports and jurisdiction in these cities. The question of foreign rights in the treaty ports and the leased territories had been an issue in China for a long time. But these questions had only marginally been raised to the more theoretical distinction between right of administration, right of judicature, right of legislation and sovereignty in itself. The students in Japan, however, were theoretically better trained in legal and political issues and did raise this issue in their student periodicals. The most prominent example of such a line of argumentation is found in an article by Fufeng (芙峰) published in *Zhejiangchao*. He directs his anti-Manchu

---

[139] Ibid., pp. 2-3
[140] Ibid., p. 3

criticism against the authoritarian government for not involving the citizens of China in the policy of committing the entire nation to international treaties. Any treaty under international law is an agreement binding the citizens of the contracting nation to a number of duties. Hence, any government entering such agreements must obtain the consent of its people and must make sure that its people are aware the consequences and ramifications of that treaty. The Chinese government has failed both to involve the Chinese people in the political process and to make public the content and wording of the different treaties with foreign countries. Fufeng claims that the terms 'rights of jurisdiction'[141] and 'supreme rights'[142] conferred upon the foreign states in a number of treaties are applied in a sense equal to 'sovereign rights'. By using these two terms the foreign powers are concealing the fact that what their rights in the concessions encompass is in fact nothing less than sovereign rights in these areas. China has for all practical purposes abandoned her sovereignty.[143]

> If we continue claiming that this is the sovereign right of our country, who are we fooling? Are we fooling heaven? Alas! The existence of a state lies in its sovereignty. The existence of its sovereignty lies in its ability [to maintain its] sovereignty and the nature of that sovereignty. The most important [requirement] for the ability [to maintain its] sovereignty is the function of its legislation, judicature and administration. Today, none of these [abilities] belong [to China]. The most important [aspect] of the nature of sovereignty is its supreme and unlimited dimension. Today, this is constrained by a number of agreements. Its nature is lost and its ability is abolished, hence [China's sovereignty] has vanished. In the West this would be termed 'vanished sovereignty' or 'stripped sovereignty'. Alas! When it has vanished or when it is stripped, may it still be called sovereignty? No! ... When its right of legislation, right of judicature and right of administration are all gone, where then may sovereignty be found? There is no need to wait for [international law] experts to find an answer to these questions.[144]

But there is an apparent contradiction in terms in the treaty texts. In addition to specifying the rights of the foreign powers, these treaties also maintain and emphasise the sovereignty of China.

---

[141] *Guanxiaquan* (管轄權)
[142] *Gaoquan* (高權)
[143] *Zhejiangchao*, issue no. 3, *Zhengfa* pp. 4-5
[144] Ibid., p. 5

> Some may ask: Have you not read the unambiguous text of the treaties? There is not one that does not specify that the sovereignty of the Qing state is maintained. Then I ask in return: Have you not read the unambiguous text of the treaties? There is not one that does not specify the supreme rights of the allied powers and their liberty of jurisdiction?[145]

These rights vested in different authorities regarding the same territory cannot exist simultaneously. From the treaties it is evident that the supreme rights and jurisdiction of the foreign powers undermine the sovereignty of China. Hence, China cannot be said to have maintained sovereignty, even if the wording of the treaty texts signifies the opposite. Only by retrieving the rights of judicature, legislation, and administration through the treaties can China re-establish her position as a sovereign nation among equal nations, in line with Japan.[146] The hope for the Chinese people lies in a struggle for sovereignty. The European and the Japanese have won their sovereignty through struggle. Now it is up to the Chinese people. We can vaguely discern an influence from Darwin in these arguments when questions on progress and the differences between nations and races are concerned:

> Among people there is no one who does not have a mind to struggle. That which is most worth struggling for under heaven are rights. For the people of Europe rights were obtained already in the 18th century. For the people of Japan rights were obtained in the beginning of the Meiji restoration. Only for our people on the central plains of this continent are rights still concealed and have not yet been employed. If they from this day on continue to be concealed by a foreign European race, then I am afraid it will be like a plow sunk deep in mud with no hope of recovery. Alas, fellow countrymen!!! Rise in time!!! Rise in time!!! There will be hundreds and thousands of advantages for the government and not one disadvantage. For allegiance and loyalty nothing will be better than this.[147]

---

[145] Ibid., p. 7

[146] Ibid., pp. 7-13; Fufeng's elaboration follow the same line of argumentation also on pages 13-16 of this article and in its continuation in issue no. 7; *Zhejiangchao*, issue no. 7, *Zhengfa*, pp. 17-33

[147] *Zhejiangchao*, issue no. 7, *Zhengfa*, p. 23

Neutrality

As discussed above, the hostilities between Japan and Russia on Chinese territory in Manchuria 1903-05 were the single most important event distressing Chinese intellectuals on the question of China's international role and position in late imperial years. Liang Qichao claimed that the arrangements allowing Manchuria to be outside the scope of Chinese neutrality in the war undermined China's sovereign rights in Manchuria and in fact China's sovereignty as such. China, in international affairs, was by a number of Chinese intellectuals now understood and evaluated in terms of the principles of international law. The immediate significance of this is that China was slowly becoming an actor on the international arena governed by the principles and practices of the system referred to as international law. The effect of this shift in perspective was, however, that the weakness of the Chinese government became even more transparent. The students in Japan were more attuned to the workings of international law and practice, and possibly also more outspoken in their critique of the Manchu government in Beijing, and were consequently also distressed by the events of the Russo-Japanese hostilities. The opening of Mingxin's (明心)[148] article "The Russo-Japanese war and the position of China"[149] published in *Zhejiangchao* may well represent the level of frustration over the incapability of the Manchu government and the weakness of China's position:

> Listen carefully, compatriots? How is the position of China in the war between Japan and Russia! How is the position of China in the war between Japan and Russia!! When I speak of the position of China I cannot but curse the Beijing government for not realising its own uselessness. Its misdeeds are grave and serious. Even if it would wish to save [China] it is not able to.[150]

Mingxin's arguments resemble Liang's, only that Mingxin is more explicit in blaming the Manchu government for its incapability. The declaration of neutrality, according is a sign that China is unable to control the situation in Manchuria. Hence, neutrality is not a principal declaration of neutrality but only a practical measure to defend the position and actions of the impotent government.

---

[148] Probably a pseudonym, and translates 'enlightened mind'
[149] "Ri-E kaizhan yu Zhongguo diwei" (日俄開戰與中國地位)
[150] *Zhejiangchao*, issue no. 10, p. 25

The inhabitants of Manchuria suffer during the Russo-Japanese war. Russian soldiers are said to skewer Chinese children in Manchuria and play with them on their sticks until they die. Even in time of war such brutal acts against civilians are not permissible, is the commentary to this drawing by the editors.
(E'shi jingwen 俄事警聞 *17 January 1904*)

> What then is this neutrality based upon? This neutrality is not neutrality. The name of neutrality is quickly losing its meaning. And regardless of who wins and who loses in the war between Japan and Russia, Manchuria is no longer ours. And later Manchuria will either be enslaved by Russia or controlled by Japan.[151]

And the inhabitants of Manchuria will be those to suffer, according to Mingxin. The declaration of neutrality has, by the rules of international law, excluded China from taking any active measures on behalf of the people residing in Manchuria, since Manchuria is outside of Chinese territory, and the people in Manchuria are therefore left entirely on their own in the war between Japan and Russia.[152]

An anonymous student has similarly published an article on

---

[151] Ibid., p. 26
[152] Ibid.

neutrality in *Jiangsu* entitled "The question of neutrality".[153] His main concern is also the weakness of the Beijing government and the fact that China's neutrality in reality is dictated by Japan. China has been placed in an impossible situation by her own weakness:

> Today, in principle China cannot be neutral. If we discuss the reality of the situation, however, China cannot but be neutral. Manchuria is clearly a part of Chinese territory. Japan has declared war against Russia on this basis. How could China accept only to observe this from outside? If Japan and Russia fight a war in Manchuria without China protesting, then regardless of the outcome of the war Manchuria will no longer be ours. If we want to protect Manchuria, then we will have to enter into an alliance with Japan in order to resist Russia. This is the principle for not being neutral.

The frustration with the incapable Manchu government is evident in these articles, a frustration that is motivated by the international position and role of China—a role and position that can only be redeemed through the modernisation of China's interpretation of international law. The Chinese must adhere to international law on "modern" terms, is the main line of argumentation. Shousu goes even further arguing that China is already a member of the international community and must take an active part in defining her own terms in the international law of the future.

China to take an active part in international law

The Chinese students in Japan did not only engage in political discourse in the different regional student magazines. A group of students in Japan established a periodical for the introduction of political and legal theories and systems from the West. The periodical *Yishu huibian* (譯書彙編) started out as a vehicle for the publication of translated texts in political and legal theory, because, as expressed in its editorial policy, to import Western civilisation and learn from the Meiji Japanese experience is the only way that the reforms in China can be carried further. Political theory is the means by which all strong states have become strong, according to the editors of *Yishu huibian*.[154] During the first year of publication from 6th December

[153] "Zhongli wenti" (中立問題) in *Jiangsu*, issue 9/10, pp. 1731-1752

[154] Many important texts within this field, later published in full version, were first

1900 the magazine consisted merely of translated texts. However, from the 9th issue of the second year a column for debate was added and this monthly magazine was gradually turned into a vehicle for political debate among the Chinese students in Japan. The expressed reason for this change was that translated texts could only serve as a way to understand the ideas of others, while by publishing the ideas and opinions of fellow countrymen the magazine could contribute to the Chinese discourse on political, legal and economic questions. The political agenda of the *Yishu huibian* became more verbalised through these changes, and the final manoeuvre towards a magazine for political debate was made when the title of the periodical from its third year, 1903, was changed to *Zhengfa xuebao* (政法學報).[155] This periodical can be regarded as among the radical periodicals in the late Qing Chinese context. Its main political agenda was, however, not supportive of violent and abrupt political reforms or revolution. Its agenda was reformist with a strong inclination towards the introduction of theories and experiences from Japan and the West.

The authors of the leading articles of the *Zhengfa xuebao* as well as external contributors to the magazine demonstrate acquaintance with international law and a parallel theoretical perspective on China's role in international affairs. In 1903 Shousu (守肅) discusses China's role in international affairs in an article entitled "A discussion of China's future in the perspective of international law".[156] Shousu draws up the principle features and the history of international law and argues that China in fact has a history in international relations related to international law prior to the 1870s. Already in 1689 China signed treaties with Russia (the treaty of Nerchinsk), later followed by the treaty of Kiakhta, and thus entered the sphere of European international law. With the treaties following the Opium war in the early 1840s China is usually recognised to have entered the international community. It may be argued that China was forced into the international community for the benefit of others, while most other states have entered the international community for their own benefit

---

published in bits and pieces in the *Yishu huibian*. These include texts by Rousseau (*Du contrat social*), Montesquieu (*De l'esprit des lois*), Bluntschli (*Geschichte des allgemeinen Statsrechts und der Politik*) and the writings of a number of political and legal activists in Meiji Japan.

[155] *The Tsen fah shui pao, A monthly magazine of political and law works*

[156] "Lun guoji gongfa guanxi Zhongguo zhi qiantu" (論國際公法關繫中國之前途)

and of their own free will. On the other hand, Shousu argues, the fact that these states have entered on different conditions does not mean that their position with regard to degree of civilisation is different or that their position within that community is different. If China's position in the international community is equal to other states, then what is the reason for China to be ignored and discriminated against in international affairs, Shousu asks.

> The last 60 years of China's diplomatic history may be summed up in one term: a history of failure. Sovereignty is lost and the state system has been disrupted. All the phenomena that may not be allowed in international law can be found in China. And in search for the reason why this is so, [one can say that] it may not be ascribed to one reason alone. I dare say, however, that the main reason for this is the lack of understanding for international law.[157]

The author lists 3 areas of particular importance for China's international future. Firstly, every Chinese citizen must be educated in the principles of international law. These principles do not only have significance for diplomats and politicians. Every citizen of a state must recognise the rights and duties of the state and must understand the consequences of actions related to international affairs. Secondly, the failures of China's past are bygones, and the task now is to grasp the opportunity that China is facing. After the Boxer rebellion of 1900 China has to build new international relations, and international law is the factor that will decide China's fate in the years to come. International law as an international system is still developing and China today has an opportunity to take part in this development and ensure that China's position and particular terms and conditions are embodied in international law in the future. In Shousu's mind it is a mistake to see international law as a system only for and by the so-called civilised Christian states of the West. China's hope and future lie in grasping this historical opportunity. And thirdly, China must strictly adhere to all treaties of the future. Because China is regarded as an untrustworthy partner in international relations, every treaty with Western states is forced upon China, sacrificing China's rights. China must re-negotiate all treaties on the principle of equal status and power, and then make sure that these treaties are complied with and observed at every juncture.

---

[157] *Zhengfa xuebao* issue no. 3 1903, *Falü* p. 7

> To sum it up, no state today may close its doors, stubbornly protect itself, and practise a policy of locking its gates [to the outside world]. One must take one's position in the small universe as a condition. In our intercourse with other people we cannot at times avoid risking our own benefits and we must be willing to place ourselves in a losing position. This is one of the main principles in international law. Alas, the past is behind us but the days to come are many. All fellow citizens! I implore you![158]

Shousu argues that China must dare to take the risk of submitting to certain duties in order to obtain international rights and the status of an equal. He also argues that international law indeed is not a legal system only for the so-called civilised Christian Western nations. In Shousu's view international law is open to influence from the non-Western cultural sphere. His article demonstrates an infallible trust in the international community if only China would be willing to make the necessary sacrifices.[159] Shousu's article signifies the new era in the Chinese intellectual attitude towards international law. China's near past and her hopes for the future all lie in the international society of states and in the system referred to as international law. In Shousu's mind China's equal status, adherence to treaties and the benefits of joining the band of states defining the workings of international law is the framework that will secure China's status and position in the future.

"Professionalism" in international law

As anticipated by Liang Qichao the Chinese students of law in foreign countries had started to take China's international position seriously in terms of international law itself. The students in Japan were more inclined to see the advantages of the changes that had taken place in Japan, and they were in a better position to challenge the Manchu government in Beijing. The fact that neutrality itself was the topic of discourse on China's position in 1903-05 signifies that the terms of international law were becoming a part of the political polity in China and in the discourse among Chinese intellectuals in the early 20th century. It did not help China in its internationally sandwiched

---

[158] Ibid., p. 10

[159] Ibid., pp. 1-10; See also Fang Hanqi (ed.) 1997, vol. 1, p. 943

position at that time. But it is most distinctly a sign of a new time where international law is no longer only considered to represent a set of idealised principles for international intercourse at advanced stages in human development. China was for the first time educating a group of students with a professional and legally analytic attitude towards international law. International law is gradually for China and this new band of legally trained specialists becoming the set of rules and practices that China will need to adhere to in order to become a member of the international family of nations, and in order to secure China's sovereignty, national rights and an equal position in international relations. Not surprisingly, this "professionalism" and awareness is more acute among the foreign students abroad. The Chinese students in Japan were, however, not the only group of Chinese with an anti-Manchu radical political agenda in late Qing times. A number of Chinese revolutionaries in Japan also expressed high expectations for China's future as a nation in international affairs protected through adherence to international law, as we shall see below.

INTERNATIONAL LAW AND REVOLUTIONARIES IN JAPAN: XENOPHOBIA, ANTI-MANCHUISM AND THE PROTECTION OF HAN CHINESE NATIONAL RIGHTS

The question of international law and Chinese foreign relations addressed by the revolutionaries in Japan is primarily attached to the question of relations between the Han, the Manchus and foreigners in China. Hu Hanmin (胡漢民) (1879-1936) discussed the question of anti-foreign sentiments in China in a series of articles entitled "Xenophobia and international law" in *Minbao* in 1906.[160] The *Minbao* started its publications as a monthly magazine in Tokyo in October 1905 as a vehicle for the policy and ideological framework of

---

[160] "Paiwai yu guojifa" (排外與國際法). The articles published in issue no. 4 to 13 of the *Minbao* contain 6 chapters entitled; "Sovereignty of land" ("Lingtu zhuquan" 領土主權), "Equal rights of states" ("Guojia pingdengquan" 國家平等權), "The right of independence for states" ("Guojia duliquan" 國家獨立權), "The rights of self defence of states" ("Guojia ziweiquan" 國家自衛權), "Intervention" ("Ganshe" 干涉), "Treaties" ("Tiaoyue" 條約). The last part of the articles ends in issue no. 13 with the remark "to be continued". But there does not appear to be a continuation of the text in any part of the *Minbao*. See also Tian Tao 2001, p. 147.

the Sun Yatsen revolutionary agenda. Among the most ardent contributors we find Hu Hanmin and Wang Jingwei (汪精衛) (1882-1944).[161]

In Hu Hanmin's view xenophobia is a natural self-preserving attitude inherent in any people as part of a nation's quest for protection of its rights, and will inevitably involve even undue hostility and discrimination towards strangers, as had been the case in China in the early 20th century. Excessive anti-foreign sentiments are inappropriate in a nation's quest for national rights. In China these popular sentiments may, however, be explained, and to a certain degree also excused, by the unjust Manchu rulership of the Han people. The Manchu court has forsaken the national rights of China in a series of humiliating international events. Foreign nations have obtained privileges in China that they are not ready to relinquish, while the Han people are burdened with national obligations and left without political support.[162] "If [we] want to achieve the ambition of promoting the rights of our people, then nothing is better than to throw ourselves into the [anti]-Manchu revolution",[163] is a familiar argument in these circles. In Hu Hanmin's political agenda international law and the rightful allocation of national rights are basic justifications for a national revolution against the Manchu government. International law is the means with which Han national rights are to be revived. Hanmin argues for the application of international law for three reasons; Firstly, one must understand international law in order to understand the rights the Han people are entitled to and which have been abandoned by the Manchu government. Secondly, one must become aware of what international rights to uphold and what rights may be neglected. And thirdly, one has to know which acts are admissible under international law and which are not.[164] Han Chinese ignorance with regard to the principles of international law must be remedied:

> Rights are special acts defined and protected through the law. International rights are special acts defined and protected in international law. Hence, those who advocate national rights must know national laws. And those who advocate international rights must know

[161] Britton 1966, p. 113; Yu, Li & Chang 1970, pp. 71-82
[162] *Minbao*, no. 4, p. 59
[163] Ibid., p. 62
[164] Ibid., p. 66

> international law. Antiforeignism[165] in a narrow sense is not compatible with international law. In international law rights of equality and of communication are recognised, and antiforeignism represents a violation of these. When a state seeks the recognition of its rights and meets antiforeignism, then its interpretation of rights should follow that of international law. And if a state finds itself in a state of crisis and extends its acts [beyond ordinary measures], it will also have to do so fully in accordance with international law. Now, the anti-foreign perceptions of our people have their premise in international defeats, often related to rights defined and protected by international law. These perceptions do not rest in and cannot be extended from the principle of equality [among states]. Those who seek recognition of these rights will in some cases go beyond [what is admissible] and in other cases not employ that which is necessary [to reach their objective]. In these cases, because their intellectual capacity is insufficient, they will, in the pursuit of their ideas, act contrary to what is admissible in international law.[166]

Not surprisingly, in the tradition of the *Minbao* policy and the revolutionaries in Japan, Hu Hanmin sees the Manchu government at the core of China's international problems and the solution to these problems in the removal of the Manchu court through revolution. A certain degree of xenophobia and antiforeignism is explainable in any national struggle for rights and sovereignty, which is also the case for China. International law, however, representing the regulations protecting China's sovereign rights, must be observed. The Han people need to be instructed in the principles of international law, presumably as a means to prepare the Han nation for the proper governing of China's international affairs after a national revolution. The future China must, in international affairs, be fashioned on the principles of equality and mutual respect among sovereign states. Much in the same fashion as the students in Japan, the *Minbao* attitude towards international law is that of obtaining international recognition of China's national rights. Hu Hanmin does not touch upon the more delicate problems of history and the theoretical foundations of international relations or the relationship between Western international custom and the Chinese intellectual tradition, questions addressed by their main political protagonists in Japan at this time, the *Xinmin congbao* clique. While the *Xinmin congbao* authors discuss the

---

[165] *Paiwaizhuyi* (排外主義)
[166] *Minbao*, no. 4, pp. 65-66

theories of struggle and evolution in international affairs, Hu Hanmin seems only concerned with the position of the Han people and the international situation between China and its geographical neighbours and national enemies. His arguments are plainly nationalist and revolutionary, without any particular reference to Chinese tradition. Whereas the reformers look diachronically to all sides and synchronically both to the past, the present and the future in their national analyses, the revolutionaries, here represented by Hu Hanmin, are primarily concerned with the future prospects for the Han nation in their deliberations on China's international role and relations.

With its revolutionary agenda the *Minbao* also engaged in a debate with Liang Qichao and the *Xinmin congbao* editors on the potential dangers of carrying out a militant revolution against the Manchu government. It is significant of the positivist attitude towards international law that the right of self-defence represents one of the main controversies between these two groups in early 20th century Japan. In an article entitled "The revolutionary army and international law in time of war"[167] signed by Mengsheng (夢生)[168] and published as an incoming contribution to the *Minbao*, the author argues against the warnings issued by the reformers of the *Xinmin congbao* clique that a military intervention against the Manchu court could be seen as a destabilising action provoking other nations into defensive warfare to protect their privileges and positions. The *Xinmin congbao* argument claims that there is a latent danger that foreign nations will refer to the right of self-defence defined in international law when their interests, their lives and property, are threatened, and maintains that they may intervene in Chinese civil hostilities on these grounds. The result may be open hostilities with the Western allied forces. If this should happen the revolutionary army will have to take full responsibility for the consequences, argues the *Xinmin congbao*. Mengsheng defends a militant revolution against the Manchu court and refutes the dangers of a military conflict with the foreign powers by referring to the German publicist Liszt[169] who defined self-defensive actions to be permissible only in critical situations. In Mengsheng's interpretation of Liszt there would have to be a direct

[167] "Gemingjun yu zhanshi guojifa" (革命軍與戰時國際法)
[168] Possibly a pseudonym for Ye Xiasheng (葉夏生) (1883-?)
[169] Most probably referring to Franz von Liszt (1851-1919).

relationship between the actions taken and the harm to a third party's interests in order to justify intervention in terms of international law. And if indeed such a direct relationship exists, these foreign troops would only have the right to intervene to protect their own interests and not the right to establish military or civil governments. And further, according to international law in time of war, when a territory has been occupied by one party, this group has the right to establish a government, while any other belligerent party does not have that right.[170] Hence, international law will work for the protection of a rightful Han Chinese government in China and against foreign hostilities. According to Mengsheng, Liang Qichao has not understood the principles by which the Western allied nations conduct their affairs. In former conflicts such as the Boxer rebellion and the Russo-Japanese war foreign interests were directly threatened and hence they took action. A revolutionary uprising against the Manchu government will not directly involve foreign interests, and therefore there is no danger of foreign intervention.

> Is Liang Qichao able to claim that our revolutionary army will directly endanger other nations? Will the actions of our revolutionary army resemble those of the Boxers? If he maintains that the interests of the foreign nations will be directly endangered, then the revolutionary army will in fact have disturbed the order and impaired the sovereignty of foreign nations. If Liang is able to prove these points it will be acceptable [to make these claims]. If not, then stop making this hubbub![171]

Judging from the writings of Hu Hanmin and Mengsheng, the Chinese revolutionaries in Japan had staunch faith in international law even in times of conflicts of interest with the West. Domestic change in China was to be achieved by terminating Manchu rule and through a radical revolutionary agenda based upon Western political theories of republican rulership and sovereignty. International law was a part of that agenda protecting China's rights and sovereignty as a future republic and securing the recognition of China as an independent nation among nations. Rather than fearing the means by which the West were conducting their international relations, China should adhere to the same principles, play the game according to the same rules so to speak, in order to secure Chinese rights in times of conflict

[170] *Minbao*, no. 8, pp. 120-122
[171] Ibid., p. 123

or tension. Revolutionary faith in international law was, however, put to the test during the hostilities in Manchuria in 1903-05. The status of Chinese sovereignty, national rights, territorial rights and right of intervention are at the core of the international outlook of the revolutionaries in Shanghai in the early 20th century.

INTERNATIONAL LAW AND THE SHANGHAI REVOLUTIONARIES: NEUTRALITY AND NATIONAL RIGHTS IN MANCHURIA

Cai Yuanpei (蔡元培) (1868-1940) had been involved in the *Subao* affair (*Subao an* 蘇報案)[172] as an active member of the Zhongguo jiaoyuhui (中國教育會) in Shanghai in the summer of 1903 and had fled to Qingdao. Upon his return to Shanghai in late 1903 he, together with Liu Shipei (劉師培) (1884-1919) and others, became involved in the opposition against Russian advances in Manchuria in the northeast and organised The Fellowship Society against Russia.[173] The daily paper *E'shi jingwen* (俄事警聞)[174] became the mouthpiece of this group of anti-Russian activists in Shanghai, following in the footsteps of its predecessors, the revolutionary papers *Subao* and the *Guomin riribao* (國民日日報).[175] The *E'shi jingwen* published from December 15th 1903 to March 1904 had Russian imperialism as its main focus and appealed to different groups of people to engage in saving China from the Russian predator.

> The editors linked nationalism to opposition to the dynasty by pointing out the failures of Ch'ing foreign policy. Antidynastic sentiments were more subtlely presented than they had been in *Su-pao*, however.[176]

The paper *Jingzhong ribao* (警鐘日報)[177] was a direct continuation of the *E'shi jingwen* from March 1904.[178] The change of name was a

---

[172] Lust 1964; Rankin 1971, pp. 69-95
[173] Dui E tongzhihui (對俄同志會)
[174] *Warnings on Russian Affairs*
[175] Britton 1966, pp. 113-114
[176] Rankin 1971, p. 99
[177] *Alarming Bell Daily News*
[178] The *Jingzhong ribao* printed a translation of a Japanese article on purported German plans for advancing into Shandong. The German ambassador protested, had the Shanghai police raid their offices and brought the case to the Mixed Court in March 1905. Liu Shipei fled, 5 minor functionaries were arrested and the paper was subsequently closed.

*"Hear! Hear! The alarming bell (*jingzhong*)!" The people of China are sleeping, reading and smoking opium while the Japanese and Russian troops are invading Chinese territory.*

(Jingzhong ribao 警鐘日報 *26 February 1904)*

result of the commencement of war and the declaration of Chinese neutrality in Manchuria, when Cai and other members of the editorial board felt that the notion of alarming news about Russian affairs no longer adequately reflected the graveness of the situation. Both papers represented stark opposition towards the Qing Manchu government and worked for the restoration of Chinese national pride and the resurrection of Han Chinese national rights. They openly criticised the Manchu government for its diplomatic failures and promoted ideas of staging a national revolution against the imperial government. These papers had close political connections with the revolutionary movement led by Sun Yatsen in Japan. These papers helped bolster revolutionary sentiments, in particular among returning students from

Japan, in the time between the *Subao* affair and the active years of the Restoration society[179] from 1905 to 1907.[180]

The early Shanghai revolutionary papers such as *Subao* and *Guomin riribao* did not involve themselves in debates on international issues. Their main concerns were questions related to the racial relationship between the Han and the Manchu peoples, national issues of education and forms of government etc., and not to any extent international questions beyond immediate national concerns. This changed with the Chinese declaration of neutrality during the Russo-Japanese war. As with many other groups of intellectuals in 1904, debates on the issue of neutrality filled much space in the columns of the periodicals and newspapers. This was also the case with regard to the anti-Russian revolutionary papers *E'shi jingwen* and *Jingzhong ribao*. In a leading article entitled "A discussion of the unavoidable neutrality"[181] in the *E'shi jingwen* on 22nd February 1904, the author is primarily concerned with the negative effects of the declaration of neutrality on the lives of the common Han people caused by the Manchu government. In a familiar radicalist arguments the dichotomy of conflicting interests is to be found in the national opposition between the Manchus and the Han. In the author's view the declaration of neutrality is the Manchu way of protecting and safeguarding their own power. None of the measures taken give consideration to the lives and property of the common Han people. The daily lives of the people are subject to a number of harsh restrictions, while in international terms the declaration only imposes restriction on the foreign countries in order to maintain central Manchu control over the entire Chinese territory. The war has nothing to do with the Chinese, meaning the Han, people.

> The people and the territory of our country will remain as before. This is a war between two other parties on the border [of our country] and has nothing to do with us. We could avoid being looted and we could avoid loss of lives. But our government is only concerned with how to protect its own advantages.[182]

---

[179] Guangfuhui (光復會)

[180] Ma Guangren 1996, pp. 241-246; Fang Hanqi (ed.) 1997, vol. 1, pp. 740-741, Britton 1966, p. 114, Rankin 1971, pp. 99-112

[181] "Lun zhongli zhi bu mian" (論中立之不免)

[182] *E'shi jingwen* 22nd February 1904

"The declaration of neutrality should have been avoided." It is of no good for the (Han) people of China, concludes the author.[183] The question of neutrality in the Shanghai revolutionary press does not take into consideration the international ramifications of declaring neutrality, questions of concern for Liang Qichao. Liang is concerned that the declaration of neutrality jeopardises Chinese sovereign rights, an effect of the arrangement of keeping Manchuria outside of Chinese neutrality being a *de facto* sacrifice of Chinese control in Manchuria. In line with the Chinese students in Japan engaging in the debates on Chinese neutrality, the revolutionary papers in Shanghai were mainly concerned about the relationship between the ruling Manchu people and their Han subjects. They were apparently not concerned about the potential loss of Manchuria, nor disturbed by the ramifications on Chinese sovereignty by the declaration of neutrality. Rather, they interpreted the declaration of neutrality as a sign of weakness in the ruling Manchu elite, an auspicious sign of weakness and a latent opportunity for the Han to stand up against their oppressors. Rather than discussing neutrality in terms of international law, the revolutionaries exploited this international issue to promote their anti-Manchu agenda.

The right of intervention was another key issue in the Manchurian question and discussed in the Shanghai revolutionary press in 1904. In the *Jingzhong ribao* a leading article entitled "A discussion of the right of intervention in international law"[184] debates the right to intervention in light of the Russian advances. "Since the beginning of imperialism", the author declares, "all strong states have exploited the idea of suppressing the power of the strong and strengthening the weak in order to practise their own policy of territorial expansion. They have expanded their own rights in order to encroach on the sovereignty of other states. This is precisely what strong Russia has done in the Eastern provinces."[185] These strong states have applied their right to intervention as a means to justify actions beyond their own territory. It has been claimed that they have the right to do so according to international law. The way Russia has utilised the notion of intervention in Manchuria is, however, beyond the scope of just intervention as stipulated in international law:

---

[183] Ibid.
[184] "Lun guojifa ganshequan" (論國際法干涉權)
[185] *Jingzhong ribao* 5th April 1904, p. 2

Russia is attempting to confine China by tossing a ring over the Chinese government. France on China's right side is doing her utmost to support Russia, while Japan on her left is trying to pull China's sleeve and persuade her not to accept the Russian moves. This drawing illustrates the diplomatic situation in which China finds herself at the eve of the Russo-Japanese war in Manchuria.
(E'shi jingwen 俄事警聞 *1 January 1904*)

> International law is applied [in the relationship between] equal states. In the relationship of a strong state towards a weak state international law is not in operation. Therefore, it is clear that the right of intervention is not in accordance with just principles. ... In terms of the Russo-Japanese war, the actions of Japan are in accordance with the wording of international law. ... The actions of strong Russia, on the other hand, are not only contrary to just principles, they are also in contradiction of international law. When they claim to be acting on the principles of intervention, who in fact believes this?[186]

International law and its procedures have now permanently entered the Chinese discourse on political matters of national and international concern. The situation in Manchuria in 1903-05 is discussed by the revolutionaries in Shanghai in the context of the central terms in international law such as sovereignty, national rights, territorial rights

[186] Ibid.

and right of intervention. The terms of international law are potentially not very favourable to China facing a strong foreign power such as Russia, and the observation that right of intervention is in fact based on conditions defined by the strong powers and not by later members of the international family of nations such as China, is of course manifest and highly relevant. What the Sino-Japanese war did to open up a field for the introduction of international law terms and conditions into the Chinese discourse, the Russo-Japanese war has done to consolidate these in the debate and make it clear to all those concerned with China's international position that China cannot be without the recognition and application of these conditions in her international relations. Compared to the debate on international relations and international law among Chinese students and revolutionaries in Japan, however, we find that the revolutionary press in Shanghai expresses a weaker faith in international law as the protector of Chinese interests in international conflicts. The Han people were suffering under the yoke of the Manchus and only through struggle could they again redeem their rightful position in China. International law represents the condition for international relations but will not save China as such. The position of Darwin and the apparent need for struggle are stronger as ideological frameworks among revolutionaries in China than among their compatriots in Japan.

THE UNIVERSALIST APPROACH TO INTERNATIONAL LAW TOWARDS 1911

The demise of traditional approaches to China's international position

The last years of Qing rulership in China are a period of volatile and rapidly changing conditions. In spite of the failure of the 1898 reforms the early years of the 20th century are characterised by reforms both in the political, social and economic sphere, particularly after Empress Dowager Ci Xi's death in 1908. Most prominent for the period are the reforms towards constitutionalism and in education. The reforms drafted in 1898 as well as earlier attempts at reform and modernisation had been motivated by a resolve to strengthen China, including the Manchu government, in its battle against the foreign powers and foreign influence in China. In the early 20th century the tendency was, however, towards reforms aimed at strengthening the Manchu government against assaults from Han Chinese and foreigners. The internal opposition against the government was growing, both in China and among the groups of dissidents in exile, as we have also seen above. China's international policy was not a major focus for these reforms. In terms of military threat the challenge from Chinese revolutionary armies was greater than any international conflict at this time. Nevertheless, the general atmosphere of reform and change "ushered in a new phase in Chinese culture—the era of ideologies. … [T]he reform era witnessed an intellectual ferment brought about by a large scale influx of Western thought into the world of the Chinese gentry-literati. Thus started the disintegration of established world views and institutionalised values that raised the curtain on the cultural crisis of the twentieth century."[187] This large scale influx of Western ideologies in most domains was strongly influenced by the Meiji Japanese experience and theoretical framework. That is also the case with the influx of theories of international relations, as we have discussed above. The discourse on international issues, international relations and China's position in the international family of nations after 1905 clearly reflects the tendency for ideologies to be lifted out of the traditional framework, subjected to the Western influx via Japan and interpreted in a theoretical framework of international theory, international law, sovereignty and national rights.

International law and sovereignty as the platform for Chinese foreign policy

One of the most prominent examples of this era of ideologies in the sphere of international relations is the discourse on related issues in the *Waijiaobao* (外交報). This paper was run by Zhang Yuanji (張元濟) (1867-1959), who had a *jinshi* degree and initially a position in the central administration. He was reform-minded, though not an associate of the Kang-Liang groups, and was therefore expelled from his duties after the 1898 debacle. He took up a new career in Shanghai and started the *Waijiaobao* in late 1901. The paper was published

[187] Chang 1980, p. 329

from 4th January 1902 until 1911 and is the first Chinese periodical dedicated to international relations and foreign policy. The political position of Zhang and the *Waijiaobao* was that of constitutional monarchism.

The educational policy of the paper is clearly visible in its columns. Large portions of its content consist of translations of texts, mainly from Japanese. The Japanese success in establishing a firmer foreign policy is also expressed in the introduction to the paper's political line. Any nation must be based on two principles in its foreign policy, as claimed in the introduction to the first issue of *Waijiaobao*. The first is the external part of this policy, being diplomacy. The second part is the internal part of such a policy, being a cultivated antiforeignism. A nation, like any individual, will have own benefit as a main principle for its existence. This is a measure necessary to prevent insults and attacks on national sovereign rights. Hence, the aim of the paper is to promote the use of civilised manners to resist foreign nations in their attacks on Chinese national territory and pride.[188] By introducing international law and the principles in international relations mainly from Japanese sources, the paper seeks to educate and thus influence China's position in international affairs.

Waijiaobao is not particularly concerned with Chinese questions and challenges in international relations. It appears that the introduction of the principles of international law, the changes in Japan's international role and position, and the international situation for states in Europe and the Americas have a more prominent place in the paper than issues on China's foreign policy. On the other hand, in order to educate people in the civilised manners of international conduct, certain particular areas of international law are emphasised. These areas or topics include the role of treaties, the authority and privileges of embassies and diplomatic missions, extraterritoriality, the right to intervention in internal affairs, regulations on neutrality, the rights on occupied territory, the relationship between suzerains and protectorates, extradition of political refugees, sovereign rights over sea and waterways; all questions pertaining to the international situation that China has found herself in during the preceding decade. Hence *Waijiaobao* does not come across as a forum for a debate on China's international role and position. Rather, the paper serves an

---

[188] *Waijiaobao huibian*, no. 1, pp. 2a-3a

educational purpose to prepare China in dealing with expected difficulties in international affairs. International law in *Waijiaobao* is presented as an international system of relations completely bereft of deliberations on its essentially non-Chinese origin or its inapplicability in the Chinese context. The relationship between the principles of international law of the 20th century and any ancient Chinese system of inter-state relations, Chinese philosophy, or even the Chinese interpretation of the Darwinian struggles between races and nations, is entirely absent in *Waijiaobao*. The discourse on international relations and China's role is detached from a culturalist framework and turned into a topic of legal interest. International law also in China is being accepted as a legal system of relations between states similar to a domestic legal system of relations between its citizens. International law is construed as a legal system, quite different from the situation in the late 19th century when international law primarily was conceived as a system of conduct between the strong and wealthy states of the West.

China enters the international discourse on China's position

As part of her new policy in foreign relations China sent a diplomatic delegation to Japan in November 1877 in order to establish the first Chinese permanent legation in Tokyo. Japan had already in the 1870s started adopting the principles of international law in her diplomatic relations, and the Chinese delegation was met with official attitudes to Sino-Japanese ties quite different from what they knew as the traditional order in East Asia:

> The Japanese officials not only dressed like Westerners; they justified Japan's actions with Western logic. The Japanese intentionally ignored China's traditional ties with her tributaries, maintaining that only modern international law was a valid standard.[189]

By the time of the Sino-Japanese war in 1894-95 the principles of international law were well known in diplomatic and legal circles in Japan. Takahashi Sakue had already from 1898 started working in Europe on issues in international law pertaining to the Sino-Japanese war, as we have also touched upon earlier. Japan had been quite

---

[189] Kamachi 1981, p. 101

successful in adapting to international law and, not least through Takahashi's efforts, been able to induce the Western world to accept Japan into the international family of nations. Takahashi's strategy of writing on international issues in East Asia from a Japanese perspective, applying the terms and considerations of international law and writing in a European language proved to be a beneficial manner to influence the West into accepting Japan as an equal member in international affairs. China's efforts in this respect had not been paved with success in the early 20th century. It was not until 1907 that a similar process of introducing Chinese perspectives on China's international role and position in Europe in a European language was launched. It is true that Ma Jianzhong studied international law in France from 1876 to 1879 and after returning to China provided advice to Li Hongzhang and the Zongli yamen on international questions.[190] There are no indications, however, that Ma Jianzhong engaged actively in the debate on international relations on the whole and the role of international law in China. In spite of his theoretical studies of the subject he did not express any confidence in international law as a comprehensive system for securing China's interests. His understanding of international law was that the many diverging opinions in the theoretical field of international relations had caused the system to be nothing but a tool to argue for the rightful position of any involved party in an international dispute.[191] Ma Derun (馬德潤), on the other hand, studied law in Berlin for four years, took a doctoral degree, and wrote an exposition on China's position in international law that was published in German and in Chinese in 1907. The Chinese version is entitled *A treatise on China in public international law*.[192] The Chinese ambassador to Germany, Sun Baoqi (孫寶琦) (1867-1931), wrote a preface to the publication expressing his concern that in spite of China's efforts to enter the family of nations she was still by many regarded as an outsider in international society:

> The race of Europe is one, the history and the religion of Europe is also the same. That is why [the nations in Europe] are all equal with regard to diplomacy and trade. Our country is situated in East Asia and we have merely a history of treaties with the European nations of a few

---

[190] Li Zhaojie 1999, p. 116; Takeshi Hamashita 2006
[191] Tian Tao 2001, pp. 180-181
[192] *Zhongguo heyu guoji gongfa lun* (中國合於國際公法論)

> decades. Recently we have gradually opened the door [to our country] and we have made great efforts to adapt to what the Europeans call public international law. Those publicists of different countries who estimate these [performances] in light of international law also recognise China as a part of the community of international law. Still, there are those who see China as a semi-civilised state and hence not worthy of acceptance into [the community] of international law. International law … in recent history is not limited to certain races, [national] histories or religions. It has its foundation in the rights and obligations of international communication. Turkey has entered the European stage and Japan is an equal partner in international law. These conditions are all recognised by the international society and this is sufficient to attest that China in the future will be on equal terms [with the European nations] with regard to its independence and sovereignty.[193]

Ma Derun expressed the main purpose behind his book as: "to refute the fallacy claimed by Western publicists that our country cannot be recognised among equal states in international law and that China is nothing but a semi-civilised state[194]. I wish to influence legal scholars in Europe to change the image of China. That is the intent of this work."[195] Ma Derun has done a thorough job in arguing for the civilised status of China and the applicability of international law in China.

> There are none of these basic principles in international law that may not be observed in practice in China. The fact alone that China adheres to all the rights recognised by the international community suffices for China to be accepted as an integral part of the community of international law. Furthermore, all the rights promoted in China are also those that are suitable for all states in the international community.[196]

Ma Derun draws up the main features of China's international relations from Marco Polo through to the Jesuit missionaries, the early Portuguese trade in Macao, the Opium war and the Nanjing treaty to show that China has a long history of contact and relations with the outside world. Chinese history is not merely a history of closed doors.[197] He concludes:

---

[193] Sun Baoqi in Ma Derun 1907, *Xu* (序), p. 1
[194] *Ban kaihua guojia* (半開化國家)
[195] Ma Derun 1907, *Lieyan* (列言), p. 1
[196] Ibid., p. 16
[197] Ibid., pp. 21-31

> There is, however, one fact that cannot be misapprehended. The Nanjing treaty and the additional treaties signed with other countries in the wake of that treaty were based on the principles of international law. But the relations between China and countries of the West were not at that time without deficiencies. When related to the above-mentioned terms [in international law we will find that] the regulations in these treaties were very limited. The most obvious limitation was the regulation on the sending of diplomatic missions. These are measures that must be present in international law. Therefore, when addressing the question about China and the international community of states, in spite of the fact that China had entered the various treaties and gradually entered regular international relations [with these states], we still cannot claim that China had fully entered the international community.[198]

What caused China to fully enter the international family of nations, according to Ma, were the treaties beginning with the 1858 Tianjin treaty. The post-1858 history of Chinese foreign relations is characterised by extended diplomacy and the opening of large parts of China as a market for foreign trade, and all these measures were accepted by China through peaceful means and with China's consent. Thus, the basic requirements for recognising China as an equal member in international law are fulfilled.[199]

The fact that China is regarded as a member of the international community is also attested to by the tacit consent of other states, according to Ma Derun's conclusion:

> The conclusion of this exposition is that China must be seen as a full member of the community of states in international law, and is in practice and through tacit consent accepted as such. This means that all nations conduct relations [with China] according to international law and recognise her as party to international law. I am confident that no one will be able to deny this and keep her outside [this community].[200]

It is highly significant for our appreciation of the development of the Chinese perception of international law to observe how Ma Derun in this exposition makes use of the treaties to claim that China not only would benefit from entering the society of nations in international law but in fact that China was already a full member after the 1858 Tianjin treaty. Ma's argumentation is novel in China and with important

---

[198] Ibid., pp. 30-31
[199] Ibid., pp. 31-40
[200] Ibid., p. 56

implications. China's role was no longer to be negotiated nationally or internationally. China was already a full member of the international society and the task, in Ma's view, was to cause the world to apprehend the fact that China already *had* entered the international society of states united in international law as a civilised state on an equal footing with the Western nations.

China is *a member of the international family of nations*

In the last years of Qing rulership in China we find that the perspectives on China and international law that had developed among groups of Chinese abroad, mainly in Japan, where international law was gradually detached from considerations on the history and theories of evolution and traditional international relations in the East, are also becoming the main theoretical framework for interpretations of international law in China. Intellectuals concerned with China's role in international relations and the status of her sovereignty have recognised that all attempts at arguing for China's international position without basing these in positive international law are futile. China must base her status on the conditions drawn up by international law as it is described and practised in the West. Forget all the whys and concentrate on the hows, seems to be the general attitude in the early 20th century China after 1905. Ma Derun has argued that China will have to convince the West that China not only is willing to enter the community of nations but in fact *is* already a *de facto* fully civilised member of that community. This intellectual perspective on China is the historical perception that accompanies China when she enters an entirely new phase in her history as a nation in 1911-12.

INTERNATIONAL LAW FROM STRUCTURE TO PROCEDURE IN THE CHINESE DISCOURSE

An impassioned debate on China and her role in the family of nations may be observed in the periodicals and newspapers during the last 15 years of the Qing dynasty. At the beginning of that period China was not regarded as among the civilised nations or integrated into the theoretical framework of international law, her international orientation being mainly East Asian, while towards the end of the Qing dynasty China was gradually entering into international law, both in her international relations and in her intellectual orientation.

International law had grown out of the international relations in Europe and between the European states and in their relations to their colonies. Questions of jurisdiction over land and sea, the principles for conducting war, right to intervention, balance of power, national rights and obligations, national sovereignty and perspectives on natural law and Christian morality constituted a Eurocentric system with implications first for colonies on the American continent and later in Africa. East Asia was never colonised in the same manner and China was from the start only included in international law in a very piecemeal fashion at the favour and will of the European powers. Most of the theoretical deliberations on the foundation of international law had no direct relevance for China when the theories of international law were introduced from the 1860s. The early Chinese debate on international law considered these structural principles only in a superficial manner as affirmative ways that China could and should utilize to strengthen her position vis-à-vis the West. When intellectuals in China became acutely aware of the necessity for China also to define her international relations in a more universal context after the Sino-Japanese war, the long history and philosophical construction that international law is built upon did not initially make that much sense as a theoretical framework for Chinese international relations. Rather, the newly introduced theories of a Darwinian survival of the fittest and the evolutionary struggle towards a utopian peaceful society, built upon a particular interpretation of Confucian texts, seemed more apt and relevant as epistemological frameworks in China for understanding relations between states. International law as theory and practice was also integrated into this framework to form a particularly Chinese interpretation of the international arena of relations. Still, however, the structural principles rather than the procedural rules constituted the main focus of the arguments.

These debates on China's role and her status as a sovereign nation after the war represented deliberations on the values of these systems for the past, the present and the future of China's international relations and did not seriously touch upon questions of the procedural rules of international law. But gradually China was drawn into international circumstances, which occasioned Chinese scholars to consider China's international relations in more practical, procedural terms. The international position and policy of China was interpreted differently by different groups of Chinese intellectuals and scholars, notably different between conservatives, reformers and revolutionaries, between Chinese at home and Chinese abroad, between conservative elder scholars and open-minded young students. The main tendency is that over time towards the end of the imperial period Chinese scholars engaging in the debates on China's sovereignty departed from theoretical deliberations on evolution, the struggle between groups, and Confucian standards, and concentrated on the procedural application of international law in order to enter into stable relations recognising China and her sovereign rights. In political terms this for the most part took place after the establishment of the Republic in 1912. But the theoretical foundation for that development manifested itself in the minds and hearts of Chinese intellectuals, expressed through the media that the newly established periodical press constituted, during the 15 years between 1897 and 1911.

In this last chapter I have endeavoured to show how the intellectual debates on China in international relations during these last 15 years of the Qing revolved around terms and conditions supplied by international law as a field of Western learning in China. Traditional frameworks for identifying China in the world of inter-state relations, such as the tribute system or traditional trade relations, are not explored in late imperial China to renegotiate a Chinese world order. Social Darwinism and Confucianism are, as we have seen, much more important in this respect. Confucianism could have been explored as a means to maintain or revive the age-old world order of East Asia in this discourse, since the Confucian philosophical framework of relations was one of the cornerstones of the traditional East Asian community of states. That was, however, not the way Confucianism was utilized and interpreted in this discourse. It seems that the East Asian world order had become too narrow also for a Chinese world orientation. Chinese intellectuals were looking beyond East Asia towards the larger international community for a new Chinese world order, also when exploring new areas of Confucian influence. The intellectual orientation of Chinese inter-state relations was indisputably changed in the early 20th century, and international law is to be found at the core of that orientation.

APPENDIX

INTERNATIONAL LAW TEXTS IN CHINESE: A CHRONOLOGICAL BIBLIOGRAPHY 1847 - 1911

The following list of titles is a chronological bibliography of texts on international law in Chinese from the first translation of such a text in 1847 to the end of the imperial era in 1911-12. Primarily, this list contains texts translated from foreign languages into Chinese during this period. Texts on these topics written by Chinese in the Chinese language during this period which tend to discuss China's role and position in international relations are most often written as contributions in periodicals and very seldom as full titles published as books. Contributions to that debate are discussed in chapter 5 of this book and are not included in this bibliography. This list of works is provided as a supplement to chapter 2 on the process of translation and introduction of the general principles in international law into China. It is not to be avoided that there are common points of reference between these two processes of introducing and adopting international law in China. In these cases texts may be mentioned in two or more different contexts in this book. Translated texts in this list also refer to works consisting of translated and edited material from non-Chinese sources, most often lecture notes gathered by Chinese students in Japanese universities. There are also texts included in this list where the role of the person involved in the publication may be unclear, and the process may also be uncertain by which a text is created, either as a translation, as a text edited from various sources, or as a text entirely written anew by a Chinese author. In general, however, texts specifically treating China's position in international relations are not included. Books on specific international relations, on its history and on diplomacy are also omitted from this bibliography.

Most of the titles included in this list have been identified and accessed in libraries, and the library holdings are given in the list for easy accessibility for anyone who should be interested in consulting these works. When no specific edition is mentioned in the information on library holdings, the copy referred to is the earliest Chinese edition. For titles listed without information on library holdings the work has been identified only indirectly and described only through secondary sources. Notes on the content and composition of the text are added to this bibliography when such information is regarded as important and is not otherwise included and treated in the chapters above.

Articles and contributions to periodicals are not included in this list unless they are later republished in the form of a book. Titles are only included when they may be regarded as separate publications and not merely contributions to a larger compilation, an encyclopaedia or a periodical. The most prominent exception from this general principle is the first translation of a short text on international law into Chinese in the encyclopaedic work *Haiguo tuzhi* (海國圖志) in 1847, which could not be omitted from this list because of its significance as the first text of its kind in China. Examples of titles not included are for instance the text *Gongfa tanyuan* (公法探源) published in the periodical *Lingxuebao* (嶺學報) (*Chinese Students Review*, Canton) from issue no. 5 March 1898. The text is a translation from a German text by a certain Weilian Xifute (威廉奚夫特)[1] with a preface by Yang Wenbing (楊文炳).[2] In the early 20th century we also find a number of Chinese periodicals, published both in China and in Japan, with separate columns for law and politics (*Fazheng* 法政 or *Zhengfa* 政法) where shorter texts on international law, mostly Japanese texts, are translated and introduced. Examples are the early issues of *Yishu huibian* (譯書彙編) and the *Xin yijie* (新譯界) (*The New World of Translation*) published in Tokyo from 1906. The Chinese periodical *Fazheng xuebao* (法政學報) published in Tokyo with only five issues in 1907 had even a separate column for international law.[3] These texts are not included in this bibliography unless they were republished later as separate publications.

For the period 1902 to 1911 one will notice that the number of publications based on Japanese material, often printed and published in Japan by Chinese students of law, is very extensive. This list purports by no means to be complete. It does, however, contain most of the titles published during that period and certainly all important and influential works. All major secondary works and relevant

[1] Possibly William Schifter
[2] See also Xu Weize p. 25a
[3] Except for issue no. 4

bibliographies have been consulted for this purpose. Hence, the main tendency of the publishing policy and the inclinations in choice of material are certain to be found in this bibliography.

LIST OF MAJOR LIBRARIES CONSULTED

Beijing

Beijing tushuguan 北京圖書館 (Guojia tushuguan 國家圖書館)
Old Beijing tushuguan 老北京圖書館
Shoudu tushuguan 首都圖書館

Shanghai

Shanghai tushuguan 上海圖書館
gujibu 古籍部
jindai wenxianbu 近代文獻部
Shanghai Cishu chubanshe 上海辭書出版社
Shanghai shekeyuan 上海社科院 (Shanghai shehui kexueyuan 上海社會科學院)

Guangzhou

Zhongshan tushuguan 中山圖書館
tecangbu 特藏部

Hong Kong

Chinese University

Taiwan

Zhongyang tushuguan 中央圖書館

Europe/USA

Berlin Stabi (Staatsbibliothek zu Berlin)
University of Washington Law Library
Cornell University
University of Chicago
Harvard University Yenching library

Geguo lüli 各國律例

Date of first Chinese edition: 1847
Author: Emmerich de Vattel (1714-1767)
Author's Chinese name: Huada'er (滑達爾)
Translator: Peter Parker (伯駕) and Yuan Dehui (袁德輝)
Original text: *Law of Nations; or Principles of the Law of Nature, applied to the Conduct and Affairs of Nations and Sovereigns*. Philadelphia: T. & J.W. Johnson & Co, 1863.
Imprint Chinese text: 8 pages (in *juan* 52 of the 1847 60 *juan* edition of *Haiguo tuzhi* 海國圖志)
Prefaces etc.: No separate preface for this text
Place of publication: Yangzhou (揚州)
Publisher: Guweitang (古微堂)
Later editions and reprints: The first 1844 50 *juan* edition of *Haihuo tuzhi* did not include the translations of Vattel's text. The second 1847 60 *juan* edition contains the two Vattel translations, and so do all later editions of the *Haiguo tuzhi*. A recent three volume edition published by Yuelu shushe (岳麓書社) also contains this text. (Changsha, 1998: pp. 1992-1996).
Library holdings: 1847 edition: Shanghai tushuguan, gujibu (538864-79). Later editions are available in many libraries.
Note: This first and relatively short translation of an international law text is included in the 1847 edition of *Haiguo tuzhi* (海國圖志) edited by Wei Yuan (魏源).

Wanguo gongfa 萬國公法

Date of first Chinese edition: 1864[4]
Author: Henry Wheaton (1785-1848)
Author's Chinese name: Huidun (惠頓)
Translator: William Alexander Parsons Martin (Ding Weiliang 丁韙良) (1827-1916), assisted by He Shimeng (何師孟), Li Dawen (李大文), Zhang Wei (張煒), and Cao Jingrong (曹景榮). The final manuscript was proofread by Chen Qin (陳欽), Li Changhua (李常華), Fang Junshi (方濬師) and Mao Hongtu (毛鴻圖) appointed by the Zongli Yamen.
Original text: *Elements of International Law*. 6th edition annotated by William Beach Lawrence (Luoensi 羅恩斯) (1800-1881). Boston: Little, Brown, 1855.
Imprint Chinese text: 454 pages in 4 *juan*
Prefaces etc.: English preface by Martin dated 1864, 3 pages. Chinese preface by Dong Xun (董恂) dated 1865, 3 pages. Chinese preface by Zhang Sigui (張斯桂) dated 1863, 13 pages. Technical information on the translation in Chinese (*Fanli* 凡例), 3 pages. Maps and descriptions of the Eastern and Western hemispheres, 2 pages.
Place of publication: Beijing
Publisher: Chongshiguan (崇實館)

---

[4] The official year of publication is the third year of the Tongzhi reign (同治三年歲在甲子) according to the Chinese lunar calendar, roughly corresponding to the Gregorian year 1864. On the English title-page the year 1864 is given. However, the year of printing and publication must have been early 1865 since Dong Xun's preface is dated in the 12th month of the third year of the Tongzhi reign (同治三年歲次甲子冬十有二月). The printing of the book can only have taken place later than this date. (Zhang Haipeng 1998, p. 201, n3; Tian Tao 2001, p. 42 n1) Since the date on the English title-page gives the date 1864, however, this date is retained by most scholars as the official year of publication.

Later editions and reprints: The entire *Wanguo gongfa* text with the *Fanli* was reprinted as a serial in *Shanghai xinbao* (上海新報) New series no. 362 to no. 647 from June 7th 1870 to April 16th 1872. It was included in the series *Xixue dacheng* (西學大成) in 1888 and 1895. It was also reprinted by Shanghai Xinxue shuhui (新學書會) in 1898 with two supplementary texts; *Gushi gongfa lunlüe* (古世公法論略) by Martin and *Gongfa zonglun* (公法總論) translated by John Fryer (for these separate texts see below). An edition of the text was published by Zhuji shuzhuang (鑄記書莊) in 1901. In addition there are a number of unauthorised reprints and editions from late Qing times. The 1864 edition was reprinted in the Korean Series of Modern Law Texts *Han'guk kundae popche saryo ch'ongso* (韓國近代法制史料叢書) vol. 1 in 1981. There is also a recent Taiwan edition edited by the Zhongguo guojifa xuehui (中國國際法學會) (Taibei: Lianjing chuban gongsi 聯經出版公司, 1998).

Library holdings: 1864 edition: Shanghai tushuguan, gujibu (345376-79), Shanghai Cishu chubanshe (579 1263), Shoudu tushuguan (甲二 246), Chinese University of HK (JX2495 .E33), Zhongshan tushuguan, tecangbu (13173). *Xixue dacheng* 1888 edition: Arbeitsstelle für Geschichte und Philosophie der chinesischen Naturwissenschaft und Technik, Technische Universität Berlin. *Xixue dacheng* 1895: Beijing tushuguan (科 10.5/894). 1898 edition: Shoudu tushuguan (丙二 3435). 1901 edition: Shanghai Cishu chubanshe (579 1263). Un-authorized reprints: Shanghai tushuguan gujibu (長 264239-42; 長 418471-73). Korean reprint: Berlin Stabi, University of Washington Law Library.

Xingyao zhizhang 星軺指掌

Date of first Chinese edition: 1876

Author: Charles de (Karl von) Martens (1790-1861)

Author's Chinese name: Maerdun (馬爾頓)

Translator: Lian Fang (聯芳) and Qing Chang (慶常) under the supervision of W.A.P. Martin.

Original text: *Le guide diplomatique: Precis des droits et des fonctions des agents diplomatiques et consulaires: suivi d'un traite des actes et offices divers qui sont du ressort de la diplomatie, accompagne de piece et documents proposes comme exemples*. 5th edition annotated by M.F.H. Geffcken (葛福根) (1830-1896). Leipzig and Paris: 1866.

Imprint Chinese text: 321 pages in 3 *juan*, with an additional *Xujuan* (續卷) 181 pages.

Prefaces etc.: Preface by Dong Xun (董恂) dated 1876, 3 pages. *Fanli* (凡例), 8 pages.

Place of publication: Beijing

Publisher: Tongwenguan (同文館)

Later editions and reprints: The text was republished in unauthorised prints without time and place of publication. It was also included in the series *Xixue dacheng* (西學大成) in 1888 and 1895, and in *Zhong Xi xinxue daquan* (中西新學大全) in 1897.

Library holdings: 1876 edition: Shanghai tushuguan, gujibu (長 270625-28; 長 665340-43), Shoudu tushuguan (丙二 2474), Zhongshan tushuguan, tecangbu (0024212, 0024213), Taiwan Zhongyang tushuguan (A 578.8 7115), Cornell University, University of Chicago, Harvard University Yenching library. Unauthorised publications: Shanghai tushuguan, gujibu (366869-72 and 長 619256-59). *Zhong Xi xinxue daquan* 1897: Beijing tushuguan (科 10.5/893).

Gongfa bianlan 公法便覽

Date of first Chinese edition: 1877[5]

Author: Theodore Dwight Woolsey (1801-1889)

Author's Chinese name: Wuerxi (吳爾璽)

Translator: William Alexander Parsons Martin (Ding Weiliang 丁韙良) (1827-1916), assisted by Wang Fengzao (汪鳳藻), who did more than half of the work, Feng Yi (鳳儀), Zuo Bing (左秉), and Long Deming (隆德明). The proofs were read by Gui Rong (貴榮) and Gui Lin (桂林). Gui Rong had the final responsibility for polishing the entire text.

Original text: *Introduction to the study of international law: Designed as an aid in teaching, and in historical studies*. 3rd edition. New York: C. Screibner & co., 1871.

Imprint Chinese text: 634 in 4 *juan* + 40 (introduction 總論) + 182 (appendix 續卷)

Prefaces etc.: Preface by Xia Jiagao (夏家鎬) dated 1877, 2 pages. Preface by Chen Lanbin (陳蘭彬) dated 1877, 3 pages. A letter addressed to T.D. Woolsey translated from English into Chinese dated 1878, 3 pages. Preface by Martin translated from English into Chinese dated 1877, 5 pages. *Fanli* (凡例), 10 pages. Maps and descriptions of the world, 4 pages.

Place of publication: Beijing

Publisher: Tongwenguan (同文館)

Later editions and reprints: Reprinted in the series Wushi wenku (烏石文庫) in Guangzhou in 1879. Several unauthorised reprints without date of publication and publisher. The 1877 edition was reprinted in the Korean Series of Modern Law Texts *Han'guk kundae popche saryo ch'ongso* (韓國近代法制史料叢書) vol. 2 in 1981.

Library holdings: 1877 edition: Shoudu tushuguan (丙二 4790), Shanghai Cishu chubanshe (579 1263), Zhongshan tushuguan, tecangbu (14785, 19156), Harvard University Yenching Library, Cornell University. 1879 edition: Cornell University. Unauthorised reprints: Shanghai tushuguan, gujibu (長 55973-78; 長 66117-22; 長 106665-70). Korean reprint: Berlin Stabi, University of Washington Law Library.

---

[5] The title-page of this book gives the year of publication to be early autumn of the third year of Guangxu's reign (光緒三年孟秋). That would correspond to the autumn of the year 1877, which is also the year of publication commonly supplied for *Gongfa bianlan*. Three of the introductory texts are, however, dated in the 11th and 12th month of that Chinese lunar year, which would correspond to the first months of the year 1878. The completion of this publication could therefore not have taken place until early 1878 in spite of the official 1877 year of publication.

Gongfa huitong 公法會通 [6]

Date of first Chinese edition: 1880

Author: Johann Caspar (Johann Kaspar) Bluntschli (1808-1881)

Author's Chinese name: Bulun (步倫)

Translator: William Alexander Parsons Martin (Ding Weiliang 丁韙良) (1827-1916) supervising a group of translators of the Tongwenguan. The first half of the text is translated at the French language section at the Tongwenguan, performed by Lian Fang (聯芳), Qing Chang (慶常), and Lian Xing (聯興). The latter half of the text was orally translated by Martin and written down by Gui Rong (貴榮) and Gui Lin (桂林). Finally, the entire text is proof-read by Gui Rong and Bake Tane (巴克他訥).

Original text: *Das moderne Völkerrecht der civilisierten Staaten als Rechtsbuch dargestellt.* Nördlingen: C.H. Beck'schen Buchhandlung, 1868. Martin, however, did not work on the German edition but translated from the French edition entitled *Le Droit International Codifié* (1870) and subsequently revised the Chinese text against the German edition.

Imprint Chinese text: 640 in 10 *juan*

Prefaces etc.: Preface by Wang Wenshao (王文韶) dated 1880, 3 pages. Chinese preface by Martin, 3 pages. *Fanli* (凡例), 9 pages. *Nianbiao* (年表), 2 pages. (In some later editions a copy of an English letter written to the author Bluntschli may also be found.)

Place of publication: Beijing

Publisher: Tongwenguan (同文館)

Later editions and reprints: A later Tongwenguan edition was published in 1884. A new edition entitled *Wanguo gongfa huitong* (萬國公法會通) was set and printed by Feihongge (飛鴻閣) in Shanghai in 1896. That same year an edition entitled *Wang shi Gongfa huitong* (汪釋公法會通) was published by Mingda xueshe (明達學社). A new edition was published by Hunan shixue shuju (湖南實學書局) in 1898. In that same year a number of other editions were also published, such as those by Beiyang shuju (北洋書局) and by Changsha nanxuehui (長沙南學會). In 1899 a foreign publishing house in Shanghai with the name K. Wellington Koo published this title. Meihua shuguan (美華書館) in Shanghai published a reprinted edition from Yizhi shuhui (益智書會, Educational Association of China), probably from 1902. A Japanese edition was published by Rakuzendô (樂善堂) Tokyo in 1881. A Korean edition *Kongpop hoet'ong* was published in 1896 (Chaeju chongnija p'an). The Korean edition was reprinted in the Korean Series of Modern Law Texts *Han'guk kundae popche saryo ch'ongso* (韓國近代法制史料叢書) vol. 3 in 1981.

Library holdings: 1880 edition: Beijing tushuguan (社 192 95; 192 997); Shanghai tushuguan, gujibu (長 270713-17; 長 259084-88). 1884 edition: Harvard

---

[6] The text was first being translated under the working title *Gongfa qianzhang* (公法千章) and only later changed to *Gongfa huitong* for publication. There are a few secondary references to the title *Gongfa qianzhang* claiming that this should be the title of Martin, Lian Fang and Qing Chang's translation of William Edward Hall *A Treatise on International Law* (see below) (Wang Lixin 1996, pp. 367-368; Tian Tao 2001, p. 98). This is clearly a mistake since no primary bibliographic evidence supports this conclusion. Hall's text was translated by Martin and Qi Ce'ao and published with the title *Gongfa xinbian* in 1903. There can no doubt that the title *Gongfa qianzhang* was the working title of Martin, Lian Fang, Qing Chang and others at the Tongwenguan before publication (see *Gongfa huitong*, *Fanli* (凡例) 4b; Liang Qichao 1896b *fu* (附) p. 30b).

University Yenching library; Cornell University. 1896 Feihongge edition: Shanghai tushuguan, gujibu (長 418598-601; 長 65503-06); Old Beijing tushuguan (社 192.997), Zhongshan tushuguan, tecangbu (30251). 1896 Minda xueshe edition: Zhongshan tushuguan, tecangbu (14790). 1898 Changsha nanxuehui edition: Zhongshan tushuguan, tecangbu (14794). Meihua shuguan edition: Shanghai tushuguan, gujibu (長 18814); Cornell University. 1881 Japanese edition: Shoudu tushuguan (丙二 2320). 1896 Korean edition: Shanghai tushuguan, gujibu (389671-73), Harvard University Yenching library, Columbia University. 1981 Korean edition: Stabi Berlin (449 721-3), SOAS, Library of Congress, Harvard University Yenching library, Princeton University, University of Washington.

Ludi zhanli xinxuan 陸地戰例新選

Date of first Chinese edition: 1883

Author: Manuscript by Gustave Moynier later revised by Johann Kaspar Bluntschli and 12 other members of the Institut de Droit International (Gongfahui 公法會)

Author's Chinese name: Muniye (穆尼耶)

Translator: William Alexander Parsons Martin (Ding Weiliang 丁韙良) (1827-1916) and the students at the French section of Tongwenguan

Original text: *Les Lois de la Guerre sur Terre. Manuel Publié par L'institut de Droit International*. Genève: Imprimerie Charles Schuchardt, 1880.

Imprint Chinese text: 31 pages in 1 *juan*

Prefaces etc.: Preface by Chen Lanbin (陳蘭彬) dated 1883, 2 pages. Chinese preface by Martin dated 1883, 3 pages. Abridged translation of original preface, 2 pages. Translation of statutes of Institut de Droit International, 1 page.

Place of publication: Beijing

Publisher: Tongwenguan (同文館)

Later editions and reprints: Reprinted in the series *Xizheng congshu* (西政叢書) 1897.

Library holdings: 1883 edition: Shanghai Cishu chubanshe (579.42 1263).

Zhongguo gushi gongfa lunlüe 中國古世公法論略[7]

Date of first Chinese edition: 1884

Author: William A.P. Martin (1827-1916)

Author's Chinese name: Ding Weiliang (丁韙良)

Translator: Wang Fengzao (汪鳳藻)

Original text: "Traces of International Law in Ancient China" published in several different versions

Imprint Chinese text: 31 pages

Prefaces etc.: Martin's preface dated 1884: 5 pages.

Place of publication: Beijing

Publisher: Tongwenguan (同文館)

Later editions and reprints: Reprinted in the series *Xizheng congshu* (西政叢書) in Shanghai 1897 and by Shanghai Xinxue shuhui (新學書會) in 1898 as a supplement to Martin's translation of *Wheaton's Elements of International Law*.

Library holdings: 1884 edition: Shanghai tushuguan, gujibu (549482; 520496). 1898 *Xinxue shuhui* edition: Shoudu tushuguan (丙二 3435)

---

[7] The text is also referred to as *Gushi gongfa lunlüe* (古世公法論略) or *Zhongguo gushi gongfa* (中國古世公法).

Gongfa zonglun 公法總論[8]

Date of first Chinese edition: Between 1886 and 1894
Author: Edmund Robertson
Author's Chinese name: Luobocun (羅柏村)
Translator: John Fryer (Fulanya 傅蘭雅) (1839-1928) and Wang Zhensheng (汪振聲)
Original text: "International law" in *Encyclopaedia Britannica.* 9th edition. Edinburgh: Adam and Charles Black, 1875-89.
Imprint Chinese text: 50 pages in 1 *juan*
Prefaces etc.: None
Place of publication: Shanghai
Publisher: Jiangnan zhizaoju (江南製造局)
Later editions and reprints: Reprinted in the series *Fuqiang congshu* (富強叢書) Shanghai 1896, and *Xizheng congshu* (西政叢書) Shanghai 1897. In 1898 the text was reprinted in Shanghai (Xinxue shuhui 新學書會) as a supplement to Martin's translation of Wheaton's *Elements of International Law.* Text was also included in *Junzheng quanshu* (軍政全書).
Library holdings: The Jiangnan arsenal edition is available in Shanghai tushuguan, gujibu (長 270712; 長 66131), Shanghai Cishu chubanshe (579.07 6944), Zhongshan tushuguan, tecangbu (14791). The Martin translation of Wheaton with the Robertson translation included as a supplement is available in Shoudu tushuguan (丙二 3435).

Geguo jiaoshe gongfalun 各國交涉公法論

Date of first Chinese edition: 1894
Author: Sir Robert Joseph Phillimore (1810-1885)
Author's Chinese name: Feilimo Luobade (費利摩羅巴德)
Translator: John Fryer (Fulanya 傅蘭雅) (1839-1928), Yu Shijue (俞世爵), Wang Zhensheng (汪振聲), Qian Guoxiang (錢國祥).
Original text: *Commentaries upon International Law.* Volume 1-3. 2nd edition. London: Butterworth, 1871-74.
Imprint Chinese text: 2396 pages in 16 *juan*
Prefaces etc.: Two prefaces introducing the first volume (*Chuji* 初集); one preface to the first 1854 edition, and one preface to the second 1871 edition of volume 1: 66 pages. One preface to the second edition of volume 2 (*Erji* 二集): 8 pages. One preface to the second edition of volume 3 (*Sanji* 三集), 6 pages. Notes on the proofs (by Qian Guoxiang) dated 1894: 36 pages. Conversion tables for Western/Chinese dates: 9 pages.
Place of publication: Shanghai
Publisher: Jiangnan zhizaoju (江南製造局)
Later editions and reprints: The text was republished in the series *Fuqiang congshu* (富強叢書) in Shanghai 1896, and again by Jiangnan zhizaoju in 1898.
Library holdings: 1894 edition: Shanghai tushuguan, gujibu (長 270748-63), Shoudu tushuguan (甲二 549), Zhongshan tushuguan, tecangbu (17341), Taiwan Zhongyang tushuguan (A 579 6072). 1898 Jiangnan zhizaoju edition: Shanghai tushuguan, gujibu (311388-403).

---

[8] Later also entitled *Wanguo gongfa zonglun* (萬國公法總論).

Geguo jiaoshe bianfalun 各國交涉便法論[9]
Date of first Chinese edition: Between 1898 and 1902
Author: Sir Robert Joseph Phillimore (1810-1885)
Author's Chinese name: Feilimo Luobade (費利摩羅巴德)
Translator: John Fryer (Fulanya 傅蘭雅) (1839-1928) (translation) and Qian Guoxiang (錢國祥) (proofs).
Original text: *Commentaries upon International Law*. Volume 4: *Private International Law or Comity*, London: William Benning & Son, 1861.
Imprint Chinese text: 777 pages in 6 *juan*
Prefaces etc.: None
Place of publication: Shanghai
Publisher: Jiangnan zhizaoju (江南製造局)
Later editions and reprints: Not known
Library holdings: Shanghai tushuguan, gujibu (長 64872-77)

Wanguo gongfa shili 萬國公法釋利
Date of first Chinese edition: 1898
Author: Ding Zuyin (丁祖蔭)
Author's Chinese name:
Translator: The text is edited by Ding Zuyin
Original text: Edited text based on a selection of passages from Wheaton's *Elements of International Law.*
Imprint Chinese text: 133 pages in 2 *juan*
Prefaces etc.: Preface by Ding Zuyin dated 1898, 4 pages. *Gongfa mingjia biao* (公法名家表, list of Chinese name translations for Western international law publicists), 13 pages.
Place of publication: Changshu (常熟)
Publisher: Changshu Dingshi congshu (常熟丁氏叢書)
Later editions and reprints: Not known
Library holdings: Shanghai tushuguan, gujibu (562624-25)

Gongfa tongyi 公法通義
Date of first Chinese edition: Between 1898 and 1902[10]
Author: Tang Caichang (唐才常) (1867-1900)
Author's Chinese name:
Translator: None
Original text: The text is written by Tang Caichang himself
Imprint Chinese text: 79 pages in 1 *juan*
Prefaces etc.: Preface by Yu Sunxie (榆孫謝), 2 pages.
Place of publication: Not known
Publisher: Not known
Later editions and reprints: *Juedian mingzhai neiyan* (覺顛冥齋內言) (1898). *Xinxue da congshu* (新學大叢書) (Shanghai: Jishan qiaoji shuju 積山喬記書局, 1903. *Tang Caichang ji* 1980)
Library holdings: Shanghai tushuguan, gujibu (435823)

---

[9] Also referred to as *Jiaoshe bianfalun* (交涉便法論).
[10] The text was first published in volumes 8 to 15 of the Hunanese *Xiangbao* (湘報) 1897, and later, some time between 1898 and 1902, printed as a separate publication.

Bangjiao gongfa xinlun 邦交公法新論
Date of first Chinese edition: 1901
Author: Jan Helenus Ferguson (1826-1908)
Author's Chinese name: Fokaisun (佛揩孫)[11]
Translator: John Fryer (Fulanya 傅蘭雅) (1839-1928), Cheng Zhanluo (程瞻洛), Le Zhirang (樂志讓)
Original text: *Manual of International Law: For the use of Navies, Colonies and Consulates*. The Hague: M. Nyhoff, and London: W.B. Whittingham and Co., 1884 (in 2 volumes)
Imprint Chinese text: 406 pages in 5 *juan*
Prefaces etc.: Preface by Le Zhirang dated 1901, 2 pages. Preface by Cheng Zhanluo dated 1901, 2 pages.
Place of publication: Shanghai
Publisher: Gezhi shushi (格致書室, Chinese Scientific Book Depot)
Later editions and reprints: Not known
Library holdings: Shanghai tushuguan, gujibu (長 50938-42)

Guoji gongfa zhi 國際公法志
Date of first Chinese edition: 1902
Author: Cai E (蔡鍔) (1882-1916)
Author's Chinese name:
Translator: None
Original text: The text is written by Cai E himself
Imprint Chinese text: 98 pages in 1 *juan*
Prefaces etc.: Preface by Zhao Bizhen (趙必振) dated 1902, 1 page.
Place of publication: Shanghai
Publisher: Guangzhi shuju (廣智書局)
Later editions and reprints: Reprint of the same edition at Guangzhi shuju in 1903 only half a year after its first publication. Also partly reprinted in the *Xinxue da congshu* (新學大叢書) in 1903.[12]
Library holdings: Shoudu tushuguan (丙二 5183), Shanghai Cishu chubanshe (579 4981), Zhongshan tushuguan, tecangbu (0025231).

Gongfa lungang 公法論綱
Date of first Chinese edition: 1902
Author: Yang Tingdong (楊廷棟) (1861-1950)
Author's Chinese name:
Translator: None
Original text: The text is written by Yang Tongdong himself
Imprint Chinese text: 91 pages in 5 *juan*
Prefaces etc.: Preface by Yang Tingdong dated 1902, 4 pages
Place of publication: Shanghai (printed in Japan)
Publisher: Putong xueshushi (普通學書室) and Kaimingshe (開明社)
Later editions and reprints: Not known
Library holdings: Shanghai Cishu chubanshe (579.02 4914)

---

[11] Elsewhere referred to as Feiguosun (費果蓀).

[12] The title *Gongfa suyuan* (公法溯源) is a reprint of *Zonglun* (總論) chapter, and otherwise all the chapters *Lun waijiao shang zhi liyi* (論外交上之禮儀), *Lun shichen zhi quanli yiwu* (論使臣之權利義務), *Lun lingshi zhi quanli yiwu* (論領事之權利義務), *Lun bangguo zizhuquan* (論邦國自主權), *Lun bangguo ziweiquan* (論邦國自衛權), *Lun ganshequan* (論干涉權) from *Guoji gongfa zhi* are reprinted in this *congshu*.

Zhina guojilun 支那國際論

Date of first Chinese edition: 1902
Author: (Achille-)Arthur Desjardins (1835-1901)
Author's Chinese name: A'erqiu Tiezhuidun (阿爾邱鐵隹敦)[13]
Translator: Wu Qisun (吳啟孫)
Original text: "La Chine et le Droit des Gens". In *Revue des Deux Mondes*. December 1st and 15th 1900 (Paris: Bureau de la Revue des Deux Mondes), pp. 522-549, 815-844.
Imprint Chinese text: 87 pages in 4 chapters
Prefaces etc.: Explanations (*Yili* 譯例), 2 pages. Translator's preface (*Yixu* 譯序) dated 1902, 2 pages. Short biography of Desjardins (*Tiezhuidunshi lüezhuan* 鐵隹敦氏略傳), 2 pages.
Place of publication: Shanghai (printed in Tokyo)
Publisher: Putong xueshushi (普通學書室) and Kaimingshe (開明社)
Later editions and reprints: Not known
Library holdings: Shanghai shekeyuan, lishi yanjiusuo tushuguan

Guoji gongfa zonggang 國際公法總綱

Date of first Chinese edition: 1902
Author: Various Japanese authors
Author's Chinese name:
Translator: Wang Hongnian (汪鴻年)
Original text: Different Japanese texts
Imprint Chinese text: Not known
Prefaces etc.: Not known
Place of publication: Tokyo
Publisher: *Zhengtie congshu* (政鐵叢書) no. 4.
Later editions and reprints:
Library holdings: Not known
Note: This publication is strictly speaking not a translation from Japanese into Chinese but in fact a compilation of different material in Japanese from Wang's time as a student at Tôkyô teikoku daigaku (東京帝國大學). In the series *Zhengtie congshu*, edited by Wang himself, a number of other titles on international law were planned for publication; *Pingshi guoji gongfa yaoyi* 平時國際公法要義 (no. 5), *Guoji quanxian zhengyi yaoyi* (國際權限爭議要義) (no. 6), *Haishang guoji gongfa yaoyi* (海上國際公法要義) (no. 7). It is not known if these latter three ever were published. (Sources: *Zhongguo falü tushu zongmu* 1991, p. 746; Tian Tao 2001, pp. 133-134)

Wanguo gongfa yaolüe 萬國公法要略

Date of first Chinese edition: 1903
Author: Thomas Joseph Lawrence (1849-1919)
Author's Chinese name: Laolinci (勞麟賜)[14]
Translator: Young J. Allen (Lin Lezhi 林樂知) (1836-1907) and Cai Erkang (蔡爾康) (1852-1920)
Original text: *A Handbook of Public International Law*. London: Macmillian & Co., 1898.
Imprint Chinese text: 140 pages in 4 *juan*
Prefaces etc.: Preface by Allen dated 1902, 3 pages. Two translated prefaces by

---

[13] Occasionally also transcribed Tiezhuideng (鐵隹登).
[14] Also referred to as Lulinsi (盧麟斯).

Lawrence dated 1885 and 1897, 4 pages. "Hints as to Reading-books of Reference, &c", 1 page.
Place of publication: Shanghai
Publisher: Society for the Diffusion of Christian and General Knowledge among the Chinese (Guangxuehui 廣學會)
Later editions and reprints: Retranslated by Zhong Jianhong (鐘建閎) and published with the new title *Guoji gongfa yaolüe* (國際公法要略) by Shanghai Shangwu yinshuguan (商務印書館) in 1924 based on the 7th 1910 edition of the original Lawrence text.
Library holdings: Shanghai tushuguan, gujibu (長 73183), Shanghai Cishu chubanshe (579 9446). The 1924 retranslation: Shanghai tushuguan, jindai wenxianbu (367346).

Gongfa xinbian 公法新編

Date of first Chinese edition: 1903
Author: William Edward Hall (1836-1894)
Author's Chinese name: Huo'er (霍珥)[15]
Translator: William Alexander Parsons Martin and Qi Ce'ao (綦策鰲)
Original text: *A Treatise on International Law*. Oxford: The Clarendon Press, 1895.
Imprint Chinese text: 230 pages in 4 *juan*
Prefaces etc.: Chinese preface by Li Hongzhang (李鴻章), 2 pages. Chinese preface by Duan Fang (端方), 2 pages. Chinese preface by Martin, 2 pages. Chinese preface by Qi Ce'ao, 1 page. *Fanli* (凡例), 3 pages. Chinese historical table, 2 pages. English preface by Li Hongzhang, 2 pages. English preface by Martin, 2 pages. "Terms and Phrases", 22 pages. Map of the two hemispheres,[16] 2 pages.
Place of publication: Shanghai
Publisher: Society for the Diffusion of Christian and General Knowledge among the Chinese (Guangxuehui 廣學會)
Later editions and reprints: Not known
Library holdings: Shanghai tushuguan, gujibu (525242-43), Shoudu tushuguan (丙二 2452)

Guoji gongfa 國際公法

Date of first Chinese edition: 1903
Author: Hôjô Motoatsu (北條元篤) and Kumagai Naota (熊谷直太)
Author's Chinese name:
Translator: Donghua yishushe (東華譯書社)
Original text: A non-identified Japanese textbook on international law
Imprint Chinese text: 27 pages in 1 *juan*
Prefaces etc.: None
Place of publication: Shanghai
Publisher: Huiwen xueshe (會文學社)
Later editions and reprints: Not known
Library holdings: Shanghai tushuguan, gujibu (504388-487, 436494-592), Shanghai Cishu chubanshe (082 4114)
Note: The text is included as volume 48 of the encyclopaedia *Putong baike quanshu* (普通百科全書) edited by Fan Diji (范迪吉) et. al. The Japanese texts included in this encyclopaedia were all textbooks for an intermediate level Japanese education.

---

15 Occasionally also referred to with the semantic translation *tang* (堂) meaning 'a hall'.
16 Similar to the maps in Martin's translation of Wheaton but more detailed.

The didactic design of these texts has made them specifically suitable for Fan Diji's project, and the encyclopaedia was very well received in China. Many of the texts were also taken up as textbooks in Chinese schools. This text on public international law is divided into 5 chapters and discusses the history, the significance, the origin, the publicists of public international law, and finally the principles of international law in time of peace. The text docs not treat the questions of international law in time of war, presumably because that was not relevant in a textbook for young Japanese students.

This Chinese translation appears strikingly modern in its vocabulary and language, indicating that the language introduced through the first translations of Japanese texts did readily gain acceptance and became the later standard vehicle for the translations and discourse on international law as well as other branches of the social sciences in China. The new terminological apparatus of technical terms for political and social sciences in general, and for international law in particular, imported from the modern Meiji-Japanese lexicon is evident. (Sources: Wang Jian 2001, p. 151; Xiong Yuezhi 1994, pp. 646-651; Tan Ruqian 1980, p. 389; *Zhongguo falü tushu zongmu* 1991, p. 742.)

Guoji sifa 國際私法

Date of first Chinese edition: 1903
Author: Nakamura Tarô (中村太郎)
Author's Chinese name:
Translator: Donghua yishushe (東華譯書社)
Original text: A non-identified Japanese textbook on international law
Imprint Chinese text: 35 pages in 1 *juan*
Prefaces etc.: None
Place of publication: Shanghai
Publisher: Huiwen xueshe (會文學社)
Date of publication: 1903
Later editions and reprints: Not known
Library holdings: Shanghai tushuguan, gujibu (504388-487, 436494-592), Shanghai Cishu chubanshe (082 4114)
Note: The text is included as volume 49 of the encyclopaedia *Putong baike quanshu* (普通百科全書) edited by Fan Diji (范迪吉) et. al. Whereas the Japanese text on public international law included in Fan Diji's encyclopaedic project is in part a translation of Western text-passages on the origins and history of public international law and in part the Japanese author's own deliberations on the subject in a Japanese context (see the text *Guoji gongfa* above), this text on private international law is entirely composed by its Japanese author. The text discusses the origin and development of private international law but focuses mainly on the practical aspects and implications of the 'conflict of laws'. The vocabulary, and in particular the technical terminology, applied by the translator(s) of this text clearly reflects the Japanese Meiji-influence. (Sources: Wang Jian 2001, p. 151; Xiong Yuezhi 1994, pp. 646-651; Tan Ruqian 1980, p. 390.)

Guoji gongfa jingyi 國際公法精義

Date of first Chinese edition: 1903
Author: Various
Author's Chinese name:
Translator: Lin Qi (林棨) (editor and translator)
Original text: Various Japanese texts
Imprint Chinese text: 79 pages in 2 pian (篇)

Prefaces etc.: None
Place of publication: Tokyo
Publisher: Minxuehui (閩學會)
Later editions and reprints: Not known
Library holdings: Shanghai tushuguan, jindai wenxianbu (111570)
Note: This text is published in the series entitled *Minxuehui congshu* (閩學會叢書) including a number of texts on modern social sciences and the humanities translated and edited mainly from Japanese sources by Chinese nationals living and studying in Japan. The texts were translated and edited in Japan, printed and published in Japan and then distributed among the Chinese through the Fujianese study-society Minxuehui in Tokyo. Many of the copies also found their way to the Chinese mainland. This particular text on public international law is translated and edited from a number of unknown sources, presumably mainly Japanese sources or other texts translated into Japanese. The only reference to a particular source in addition to the common quotations from European and American international law publicists is a reference to the definition of 'law' on page 1 where Lin Qi quotes a 'prominent' Japanese specialist on public law Nakamura Seigo (中村正午).[17]

Lin Qi was himself a Fujianese who went to study law at Waseda University (早稲田大學) in Tokyo. He held a number of prominent posts in law educational institutions upon his return to China. After the establishment of the republic in 1912 he was appointed to high ranking jurisdictional positions. The announcement for this publication recognises the long tradition of international law texts in Chinese translation but finds them outdated and dysfunctional in form and content for the contemporary international state of affairs. In addition to a general introduction to the basic terms and conditions for public international law, the text is divided into two sections. The first section discusses the subjects of international law, the second elaborates on the rights and obligations of states in international affairs. The notion of private international law is only mentioned briefly in the introductory essay. International law in time of war is not discussed. The technical vocabulary of international law applied by Lin Qi is identical with the Meiji-Japanese vocabulary. (Sources: Li Shengping 1989, p. 430; Tan Ruqian 1980, p. 390; Tian Tao & Li Zhuhuan 2000, p. 364; *Zhongguo falü tushu zongmu* 1991, p. 742.)

Wanguo gongfa yaoling 萬國公法要領

Date of first Chinese edition: 1903
Author: Numazaki Jinzô[18] (沼崎甚三)
Author's Chinese name:
Translator: Yuan Fei (袁飛) (editor and translator)
Original text: Not known
Imprint Chinese text: 65 pages
Prefaces etc.: None
Place of publication: Tokyo
Publisher: Yishu huibian she (譯書彙編社)

---

[17] There does not seem to be any prominent public law specialist in Japan with the name Nakamura Seigo (中村正午). There is a slight possibility that this name is an erroneous reference to the well-known Japanese international law specialist Nakamura Shingo (中村進午).

[18] Since the Japanese author of this title is not identified as the author of other titles with his name transcription, it is also possible that his family name may be Numasaki. The correct pronunciation of his given name is also uncertain.

Later editions and reprints: Not known
Library holdings: Shanghai tushuguan, jindai wenxianbu (024710)
Note: The text is included as no. 7 of the *Zhengfa congshu* (政法叢書), including titles on politics and law published between March 1902 and June 1903, and is in fact the only title on international law in this congshu. The Japanese author is not known as author of other titles and no other biographical facts are known. The Chinese translator of the text is equally uncertain. There is no preface introducing the text, which leaves us relatively uninformed about the origin and transmission of this text from its Japanese origin to its Chinese translation.

The text is divided into two sections, one on international law in time of peace and one on international law in time of war. After a very brief introduction to the universality of international law the text proceeds to discuss the different aspects of public international law in time of peace and war subsequently in a very concise and unpretentious manner. The text discusses the practice of international law with a few examples from European and American history, only occasionally involving Japan and never China. The Chinese language and technical vocabulary applied in this publication is largely borrowed from the Japanese lexicon. (Sources: Tan Ruqian 1980, p. 393; Tian Tao & Li Zhuhuan 2000, p. 365; Xiong Yuezhi 1994, p. 643; *Zhongguo jindai xiandai congshu mulu* 1979, p. 734.)

Guoji gongfa dagang 國際公法大綱

Date of first Chinese edition: 1903
Author: Franz von Liszt (1851-1919)
Author's Chinese name: Leishite (雷士特)
Translator: Shangwu yinshuguan (商務印書館)
Original text: *Das Völkerrecht: Systematisch Dargestellt*. Berlin: O. Häring, 1898.
Imprint Chinese text: 61 pages in 1 *juan*
Prefaces etc.: None
Place of publication: Shanghai
Publisher: Shangwu yinshuguan (商務印書館)
Later editions and reprints: Not known
Library holdings: Shanghai tushuguan, gujibu (480810)
Note: The Chinese translation is included as vol. 8, series 2 of the *Zhengxue congshu* (政學叢書). The original 4 parts (*Buch*) and 43 chapters in Franz von Liszt's *Das Völkerrecht* have been reduced to 34 chapters in one single section in the abridged Chinese translation. The Chinese text paraphrases the original German text and leaves out major parts of the text that are not strictly essential for the meaning. Many illustrative examples from European history of international law are left out. Furthermore, larger chunks of text on the administration of international law have been omitted, and the last part (*Buch*) in Liszt's text on the rules and rights of war is reduced from 47 German pages to 4 Chinese pages.

The text is directly translated from German and is strongly influenced by the newly imported Japanese vocabulary on international law, indicating that a number of Japanese terms were becoming current as technical terms for certain notions within international law not only in translations from the Japanese. In a few cases the Chinese text gives the English terminological equivalents in parenthesis, indicating that the English terminology was regarded as a standard set of terms even after the Japanese influence caused radical changes in the set of Chinese terms for concepts of international law. This is particularly striking as the text is in fact translated from German. There are, however, a large number of spelling mistakes in these few terminological references, presumably making them more confusing than enlightening to their readership. (Source: Wang Jian 2001, p. 151)

Guoji sifa 國際私法

Date of first Chinese edition: 1903
Author: Ôta Masahiro (太田政弘), Katô Masao (加藤正雄) and Ishii Kingo (石井謹吾)
Author's Chinese name:
Translator: Li Guangping (李廣平)
Original text:
Imprint Chinese text: Not known
Prefaces etc.: Not known
Place of publication: Tokyo
Publisher: *Fazheng congshu* (法政叢書) no. 6. Yishu huibian she (譯書彙編社)
Later editions and reprints:
Library holdings: Not known
Note: Li Guangping (also: Li Shutong 李叔同) was later to study in Japan. At the time he published this book, however, he was still studying in Shanghai. The original Japanese text was being used in Japanese universities teaching private international law. (Sources: *Zhongguo falü tushu zongmu* 1991, pp. 742, 746; Tian Tao 2001, pp. 134, 164)

Guojifaxue 國際法學

Date of first Chinese edition: 1903
Author: Imanishi Kôtaro[19] (今西恆太郎)
Author's Chinese name:
Translator: Wang Yunian (汪郁年)
Original text:
Imprint Chinese text: Not known
Prefaces etc.: Not known
Place of publication: Shanghai
Publisher: Mengxuebaoguan (蒙學報館)
Later editions and reprints:
Library holdings: Not known
Note: Wang was a student at Waseda University (早稻田大學) when he translated this comprehensive introduction to international law by Imanishi Kôtaro. (Sources: *Zhongguo falü tushu zongmu* 1991, p. 743; Tian Tao 2001, 134-135, 161)

Bangjiao tiyao 邦交提要

Date of first Chinese edition: 1904
Author: William A.P. Martin and Ch'i Ts'ne-ao
Author's Chinese name: Ding Weiliang (丁韙良) and Qi Ce'ao (綦策鰲)
Translator: Text originally in Chinese
Original text: Revised edition of a series of lectures Martin gave at the Mandarin Institute, Hubei shixueyuan (湖北仕學院), in Wuchang.
Imprint Chinese text: 240 pages in 2 *juan*
Prefaces etc.: Preface by Duan Fang (端方) dated 1904, 2 pages. Preface by Li Jia (李佳) dated 1904, 2 pages. Explanations, 2 pages. Historical tables, 3 pages. Errata, 2 pages. Maps of the two hemispheres, 2 pages.
Place of publication: Shanghai
Publisher: Society for the Diffusion of Christian and General Knowledge among the Chinese (Guangxuehui 廣學會). Printed by Shanghai Shangwu yinshuguan (商務印書館).

---

[19] His name may also be Imanishi Tsunetarô.

Later editions and reprints: Not known
Library holdings: Shanghai Cishu chubanshe (710.7 1221)

Guoji zhongli faze tigang 國際中立法則提綱

Date of first Chinese edition: 1904
Author: Various
Author's Chinese name:
Translator: Wang Hongnian (王鴻年) (editor and translator)
Original text: Various texts on neutrality
Imprint Chinese text: 44 pages
Prefaces etc.: Preface by Wang Hongnian, 1 page. Preface by Fang Yannian (方燕年) dated 1904, 1 page.
Place of publication: Tokyo
Publisher: Shûeisho (秀英舍)
Later editions and reprints: Not known
Library holdings: Shoudu tushuguan (341.5 112.3)
Note: Wang Hongnian received his education in international law at the Nihon hôka daigaku (日本法科大學). After graduation he entered Tôkyô teikoku daigaku (東京帝國大學) where he continued working with law, in particular questions relating to international disputes. During the Russo-Japanese war 1904-05 he started compiling material on the neutrality of states in time of conflict. He edited a collection of regulations for the neutrality of states based on notes from his own time as a student of law in Japan and on quotations from prominent publicists. The result, which is the present publication, was intended to serve as reference regarding rights and obligations of states declaring neutrality in time of war. It may easily be perceived that Qing officials and the Chinese minister to Japan were particularly interested in these questions pertaining to the Chinese role in the ongoing conflict between Russia and Japan on Chinese territory. When Wang Hongnian continued to work on the current international regulations in time of war following this publication, he was also supported by the Chinese minister to Japan, Yang Shu (楊樞). Wang also served the Chinese government after the establishment of the Republic, and in the 1920 he headed a delegation investigating border incidents in Manchuria.

Wang's compilation is divided into 7 parts all discussing different aspects of neutrality, the regulations, history, kinds of neutrality, and rights and obligations of neutral states. The technical vocabulary corresponds to the Meiji-Japanese vocabulary of international law. The text is edited, printed and published in Tokyo and distributed among its Chinese readership both in Japan and on the Chinese mainland. (Source: Tian Tao & Li Zhuhuan 2000, p. 365.)

Zhanshi xianxing guoji fagui 戰時現行國際法規

Date of first Chinese edition: 1904
Author: Various
Author's Chinese name:
Translator: Wang Hongnian (王鴻年) (editor and translator)
Original text: Various international rules and regulations for warfare
Imprint Chinese text: 102 pages
Prefaces etc.: Preface by Wang Hongnian dated 1904, 3 pages. Preface by Yang Shu (楊樞) dated 1904, 2 pages.
Place of publication: Tokyo
Publisher: Shûeisho (秀英舍)
Later editions and reprints: Not known

Library holdings: Shoudu tushuguan (341.4 112.4)

Note: Similar to his work on regulations for the neutrality of states (see the text *Guoji zhongli faze tigang* above) Wang Hongnian has collected and translated a number of important current international documents regulating the relations between states in time of war. This text consists of 6 sections, each containing a translation of one of these documents; 1) The Declaration of Paris of 1856, 2) Regulations for Land Warfare 1899, 3) Regulations for Maritime Warfare 1900, 4) The Japanese Declaration of Neutrality 1896, 5) The Russian Regulations of War 1904, 6) Japanese Contraband Goods in Time of War 1904. The book was published only one month later than Wang's work on regulations for neutrality. Also these documents and regulations were of crucial importance for official China during the Russo-Japanese war 1904-05. The Chinese minister to Japan, Yang Shu, officially supported Wang's publication by dedicating a preface to it, thus giving the publication a semi-official status as Chinese translations of important international law documents pertaining to the current situation in the eastern region.

Zhongliguo faze 中立國法則[20]

Date of first Chinese edition: 1904

Author: Various

Author's Chinese name:

Translator: Wu Zhenlin (吳振麟) (editor and translator).

Original text: A number of Japanese publications by international law scholars, such as Takahashi Sakue (高橋作衛), Ariga Nagao (有賀長雄) and Nakamura Shingo (中村進午), on periodicals, on English, French and Russian works and lectures on international law.

Imprint Chinese text: 170 pages in 2 volumes (vol. 1: 77 pages, vol. 2: 93 pages)

Prefaces etc.: Vol. 1: Preface by Wu dated 1904, 3 pages; *Fanli* (凡例), 2 pages. Vol. 2: Preface by the author, 2 pages. In addition vol. 2 contains an appendix consisting of the regulations of the War-time International Law Investigation Bureau (戰時國際法調查局簡章) and the Japanese rules for seizure (日本捕獲章程), altogether 21 pages.

Place of publication: Tokyo

Publisher: Senji kokusaihô chôsakyoku (戰時國際法調查局)

Later editions and reprints: Not known

Library holdings: Zhongshan tushuguan, tecangbu (143921)

Note: The War-time International Law Investigation Bureau (戰時國際法調查局簡章) was set up in Japan as an advisory organ for Chinese provincial authorities and business societies in questions pertaining to neutrality and war-time international law. In lack of a strong central Chinese authority in the ongoing conflict with Russia this organ formulated its functions as a national body protecting Chinese national sovereign interests. A number of Chinese experts on international law in time of warfare were engaged in the bureau. Japanese legal experts could also, according to the regulations of the bureau, be consulted when necessary and the bureau would pay for their services dependent on the magnitude of the task. The bureau was established for the first time in a Chinese context, modelled on similar organs in foreign countries. (*Regulations of the War-time International Law Investigation Bureau* p. 1) Since the bureau apparently had funding to pay for external services, it may be assumed that it obtained financial support through official Chinese channels. Wu Zhenlin served as head of this bureau (*juzhang* 局

[20] The book also carries the Chinese title *Juwai zhongliguo faze* (局外中立國法則) and the English title *Law of Neutrality* on the cover page.

長) with its base in Tokyo, Japan.

Wu is concerned about the lack of knowledge and official application of international law in China compared to America, France, Germany and Japan. In the preface to this book he praises Japan for having made use of international law in the ongoing war with Russia by investigating the international situation in order to protect Japanese sovereign rights. He also compliments Japan for having sent scholars to Europe to study international law at an early stage of the Japanese reforms. This, he emphasises, has not only made Japanese scholars able to deal with the international situation in favour of Japan but has also contributed to the patriotic spirit of every school-boy and school-girl throughout Japan. China, on the other hand, has proclaimed neutrality in the ongoing war. But China has not been effectively able to avoid the calamities of the war. China has translated works on international war since the first Tongwenguan translations, but those books are of no avail in the present situation. Recently a few new works on international law in time of peace have been translated into Chinese. But also these are of no application in the present time of war. Wu Zhenlin has, as a result of these considerations, compiled the present book on neutrality.[21] Wu also makes it clear that his aim has been to make the principles of neutrality easily accessible to his reader and has not endeavoured to make the language refined and eloquent in his publication. There was probably a strong feeling at this time that extensive use of Japanese terms, which must have appeared as colloquialisms in the written Chinese language, made the language appear rather unrefined and less eloquent than what could be expected from an educated Chinese scholar. (Sources: Tian Tao & Li Zhuhuan 2000, pp. 364-365; Tian Tao 2001, p. 144; *Zhongguo falü tushu zongmu* 1991, pp. 745-746.)

Zuijin gongfa tiyao 最近公法提要

Date of first Chinese publication: 1904
Author: Not known
Author's Chinese name:
Translator: He You (何祐)
Original text: Not known
Imprint Chinese text: Not known
Prefaces etc.: Not known
Place of publication: Not known
Publisher: Not known
Later editions and reprints:
Library holdings: Not known
Note: (Source: Tiao Tao & Li Zhuhuan 2000, p. 364)

Pingshi guoji gongfa 平時國際公法

Date of first Chinese edition: 1905
Author: Nakamura Shingo (中村進午) (1870-1939)
Author's Chinese name:
Translator: Ye Kaiqiong (葉開瓊) (editor and translator)
Original text: Lecture notes from Nakamura Shingo's lectures at the Hôsei University (法政大學), edited and translated by Ye Kaiqiong.
Imprint Chinese text: 159 pages
Prefaces etc.: *Liyan* (例言), 2 pages.
Place of publication: Tokyo

---

[21] Vol. 1, *Xu* (序), pp. 1a-2a

Publisher: Hubei fazheng bianjishe (湖北法政編輯社)
Later editions and reprints: The *Fazheng congbian* was reprinted in 1906
Library holdings: Shanghai Cishu chubanshe (580.81 3131). 1906 reprint: Shanghai tushuguan, jindai wenxianbu (050244)
Note: The text is included as volume 11-1 of the *Fazheng congbian* (法政叢編)

Zhanshi guoji gongfa 戰時國際公法

Date of first Chinese edition: 1905
Author: Nakamura Shingo (中村進午) (1870-1939), also containing material from other prominent Japanese law professors such as Matsubara Kazuo (松原一雄), Takahashi Sakue (高橋作衛), Ariga Nagao (有賀長雄) and Akiyama Masanosuke (秋山雅之介).
Author's Chinese name:
Translator: Zhang Fuxian (張福先) (editor and translator)
Original text: Lecture notes etc. from the Hôsei University (法政大學)
Imprint Chinese text: 159 pages
Prefaces etc.: *Liyan* (例言), 2 pages.
Place of publication: Tokyo
Publisher: Hubei fazheng bianjishe (湖北法政編輯社)
Later editions and reprints: The *Fazheng congbian* was reprinted in 1906
Library holdings: Shanghai Cishu chubanshe (580.81 3131). 1906 reprint: Shanghai tushuguan, jindai wenxianbu (050245)
Note: The text is included as volume 11-2 of the *Fazheng congbian* (法政叢編).

Guoji sifa 國際私法

Date of first Chinese edition: 1905
Author: Mita Hiroshi (三田博士)
Author's Chinese name:
Translator: Guo Bin (郭斌) (editor and translator)
Original text: Lecture notes from lectures by Mita Hiroshi and others
Imprint Chinese text: 152 pages
Prefaces etc.: *Liyan* (例言), 2 pages.
Place of publication: Tokyo
Publisher: Hubei fazheng bianjishe (湖北法政編輯社)
Later editions and reprints: The *Fazheng congbian* was reprinted in 1906
Library holdings: 1906 reprint: Shanghai tushuguan, jindai wenxianbu (050250)
Note: Guo Bin has supplied the *Fazheng congbian* (法政叢編) with the third volume on international law as volume 12 in this series.. This text on private international law is mainly based on Mita Hiroshi's lectures supported by a number of other Japanese non-attributed theorems and theses. Guo Bin claims in his introduction that China never before has had private international law (吾國尚無國際私法), which of course is historically correct. Private international law had never been introduced as practice into China. Guo seems, however, unaware of the fact that Phillimore's extensive text on private international law had been translated by Fryer and published in China about 5 years earlier. Guo Bin has not applied English terminology in his text but supplies the Japanese equivalents in a few cases where there is a terminological difference between his Chinese technical terms and the Japanese: "It is very difficult to find appropriate Chinese translations of legal terminology. When the original Japanese terms occasionally are retained as additional explanations of terms in this book it is done so in order to avoid obscurities." (*Liyan* 例言 p. 2) Otherwise the text generally applies the Meiji-Japanese technical vocabulary. (Sources: Tan Ruqian 1980, p. 390; Tian Tao

2001, pp. 136-137; *Zhongguo falü tushu zongmu* 1991, pp. 742, 746; *Zhongguo jindai xiandai congshu mulu* 1979, p. 699.)

Pingshi guoji gongfa 平時國際公法

Date of first Chinese edition: 1905
Author: Nakamura Shingo (中村進午) (1870-1939)
Author's Chinese name:
Translator: Liao Weixun (廖維勳) (editor and translator)
Original text: Lecture notes from Nakamura's lectures at Hôsei University (法政大學)
Imprint Chinese text: 110 pages
Prefaces etc.: *Liyan* (例言), 1 page
Place of publication: Tokyo
Publisher: Tokyo namiki kappanjo (東京並木活版所)
Later editions and reprints: The *Fazheng cuibian* was republished in Tokyo by the Zhongguo shulin (中國書林) and distributed in China (Hunan and Hubei) through the Qunzhi shushe (群治書社) in 1906.
Library holdings: 1905 edition: Shanghai tushuguan, jindai wenxianbu (289210); 1906 edition; Zhongshan tushuguan, tecangbu (0028854).
Note: The text is included as volume 10-1 of the *Fazheng cuibian* (法政粹編). Simultaneously with the compilation of the *Fazheng congbian* another parallel project was in progress among the Chinese law students in Japan based on much of the same material. This *Fazheng cuibian* also grew out of lectures in law at the Hôsei University (法政大學) in Tokyo. The series contains 23 titles covering a range of subjects very much parallel to the *Fazheng congbian*. It may be assumed that the titles of volumes in these two series roughly correspond to the curriculum at the Hôsei University. (Sources: Tian Tao 2001, p. 143; *Zhongguo falü tushu zongmu* 1991, p. 745.)

Zhanshi guoji gongfa 戰時國際公法

Date of first Chinese edition: 1905
Author: Nakamura Shingo (中村進午) (1870-1939)
Author's Chinese name:
Translator: Chen Jiahui (陳嘉會) (editor and translator)
Original text: Lecture notes from from Nakamura's lectures at Hôsei University (法政大學)
Imprint Chinese text: 141 pages
Prefaces etc.: *Fanli* (凡例), 2 pages
Place of publication: Tokyo
Publisher: Tokyo namiki kappanjo (東京並木活版所)
Later editions and reprints: The *Fazheng cuibian* was republished in Tokyo by the Zhongguo shulin (中國書林) and distributed in China (Hunan and Hubei) through the Qunzhi shushe (群治書社) in 1906.
Library holdings: 1906 edition: Zhongshan tushuguan, tecangbu (0028854)
Note: The text is included as volume 10-2 of the *Fazheng cuibian* (法政粹編). Chen Jiahui's text is primarily based on Nakamura Shingo's lectures on international law in time of war at the Hôsei University. He has consulted other works on international law and added passages from these when he has found Nakamura's lectures to be insufficient for his use. He has also added his own explanations and examples in brackets in the text. Because Chen recognises the Chinese lack of knowledge on foreign history and geography, he has also added some notes on such relevant issues when necessary. The result is hence partly a translation and

partly Chen's own work as compiler and author of this book. Proper names in Japanese are also added in brackets, since so many contemporary Chinese scholars were familiar with Western names in Japanese, as was Chen himself. (Sources: Tian Tao 2001, p. 144; *Zhongguo falü tushu zongmu* 1991, p. 746.)

Guoji sifa 國際私法

Date of first Chinese edition: 1905
Author: Yamada Saburô (山田三良) (1869-1965)
Author's Chinese name:
Translator: Cao Lüzhen (曹履貞) (editor and translator)
Original text: Lectures and possibly publications by Yamada Saburô
Imprint Chinese text: 169 pages
Prefaces etc.: Cao Lüzhen's preface dated 1905, 4 pages. *Liyan* (例言), 2 pages.
Place of publication: Tokyo
Publisher: Tokyo namiki kappanjo (東京並木活版所)
Later editions and reprints: The *Fazheng cuibian* was republished in Tokyo by the Zhongguo shulin (中國書林) and distributed in China (Hunan and Hubei) through the Qunzhi shushe (群治書社) in 1906.
Library holdings: 1905 edition: Shanghai tushuguan, jindai wenxianbu (289216); 1906 edition: Zhongshan tushuguan, tecangbu (0028854).
Note: The text is included as volume 11 of the *Fazheng cuibian* (法政粹編).

Zhanshi guoji tiaogui jilan 戰時國際條規輯覽

Date of first Chinese edition: 1905
Author: Various
Author's Chinese name:
Translator: Jiang Yong (江庸) (1877-1960) (editor and translator)
Original text: 23 international documents and treaties pertaining to rules and regulations in time of war.
Imprint Chinese text: 106 pages
Prefaces etc.: None
Place of publication: Tokyo
Publisher: Minxuehui (閩學會)
Later editions and reprints: Not known
Library holdings: Shanghai tushuguan, jindai wenxianbu (111573)
Note: The text is included in the series *Minxuehui congshu* (閩學會叢書).

Jiang Yong was a native of Changting (長汀) in Fujian province. He went to Chengdu in 1897 to study English. Upon graduation in 1901 he left for Japan to continue his studies at the Tôkyô seijô gakkô (東京成城學校) where he graduated in 1903. He was then accepted at the law and economy department of the teachers college at Waseda University (早稻田大學師範部法制經濟科) where he studied until 1906. During his time at the Waseda University Jiang Yong was at the same time responsible for the Chinese foreign students of law and politics taking the intensive courses at Hôsei University (法政大學). Jiang Yong also engaged in translation as well as teaching activities during his years in Japan. The present translation of 23 international documents and treaties pertaining to rules and regulations in time of war is one of the outcomes of his undertakings during his time at Waseda University.

Jiang Yong became a very influential politician and jurist after his return from Japan. He was appointed president of the Tianjin beiyang fazheng xuetang (天津北洋法政學堂) and Jingshi fazheng xuetang (京師法政學堂) in late imperial years. After the establishment of the republic he was appointed supreme court presiding judge in 1912, vice-minister of justice in 1913 and minister of justice in 1917. He also held positions as president of Beijing fazheng daxue (北京法政大學) and Chaoyang daxue (朝陽大學) under the republican government. In the 1920's he served as chairman of the Law Codification Commission. He withdrew from his positions in 1948 and served in several important positions also for the new government after 1949. He became a member of the Committee for politics and law of the new state council (政務院政治法律委員會委員) and was also appointed member of the two first periods of the National political consultative congress (全國政協委員).

For this publication Jiang Yong has collected a number of important regulations and international treaties for the regulation of interaction in time of war. He has translated these regulations, presumably from English and Japanese, and annotated them with his own comments and illustrations from European and Asian history. The technical vocabulary of his translations and annotations is borrowed from and identical to the Japanese vocabulary. (Sources: Li Shengping 1989, p. 187; Zhou Mian 1999, p. 112.)

Wanguo gongfa tiyao 萬國公法提要

Date of first Chinese publication: 1905
Author: Takahashi Sakue[22] (高橋作衛)
Author's Chinese name:
Translator: Not known
Original text: A text by Takahashi
Imprint Chinese text: Not known
Prefaces etc.: Not known
Place of publication: Tokyo
Publisher: Taitô dôbun kyoku (太東同文局)
Later editions and reprints: Not known
Library holdings: Not known
Note: According to Tan Ruqian this title is a Chinese translation of one of Takahashi's works (Source: Tan Ruqian 1980, p. 393.). The text has not been identified and the title does not correspond to any of Takahashi's Japanese publications.

For a further analysis of Takahashi's role in the discourse on China's role in international law see chapters above.

Juwai zhongli 局外中立

Date of first Chinese publication: 1905
Author: Ariga Nagao (有賀長雄)
Author's Chinese name:
Translator: Zhang Zhiben (張知本) (1881-1976)
Original text: Lectures
Imprint Chinese text: Not known
Prefaces etc.: Not known
Place of publication: Hubei
Publisher: Zhengzhi julebu (政治俱樂部)
Later editions and reprints:
Library holdings: Not known
Note: Zhang Zhiben studied at the Hôsei University (法政大學) in Japan from 1904

[22] His name is also transcribed Takahashi Sakuyé in some of his English language publications.

and became a member of the revolutionary organisation Tongmenghui (同盟會) in 1905. After 1912 he held several high political, administrative and scholarly positions. He accompanied the republican government when it withdrew to Taiwan in 1949. In this 1905 publication he translated lectures by Ariga Nagao (有賀長雄). (Sources: *Zhongguo falü tushu zongmu* 1991, p. 741; Tian Tao 2001, p. 142; Li Shengping 1989, p. 366)

Guoji sifa 國際私法

Date of first Chinese publication: 1905
Author: Xia Tonghe (夏同和)
Author's Chinese name:
Translator:
Original text:
Imprint Chinese text: Not known
Prefaces etc.: Not known
Place of publication: Nor known
Publisher: Not known
Later editions and reprints:
Library holdings: Not known
Note: This appears to be a text written by Xia and is not a translation. (Sources: *Zhongguo falü tushu zongmu* 1991, p. 742; Tian Tao 2001, p. 143)

Guojifa 國際法

Date of first Chinese publication: 1905
Author: Not known
Author's Chinese name:
Translator: Not known
Original text:
Imprint Chinese text: Not known
Prefaces etc.: Not known
Place of publication: Shanghai
Publisher: Zuoxinshe (作新社)
Later editions and reprints:
Library holdings: Not known
Note: No information is available on the author and translator of this text. (Sources: *Zhongguo falü tushu zongmu* 191, p. 742; Tian Tao 2001, p. 143)

Pingshi guoji gongfa 平時國際公法

Date of first Chinese edition: 1906
Author: Ogata Iichi (緒方維一)
Author's Chinese name:
Translator: Xiong Kaixian (熊開先) (editor and translator)
Original text: Lectures by Ogata Iichi
Imprint Chinese text: 112 pages
Prefaces etc.: None
Place of publication: Shanghai
Publisher: Shangwu yinshuguan (商務印書館)
Later editions and reprints: Reprinted in 1911
Library holdings: 1911 edition: Shanghai tushuguan, jindai wenxianbu (334620)
Note: The text is included as volume 13 of the *Jingcha jiangyilu* (警察講義錄)[23]

[23] Ogata was a jurist employed at the county level police administration Keishichô

edited by Zhao Xiangqian (趙象謙). The two volumes on international law in time of peace and in time of war in this series are based on Ogata Iichi's lectures on these topics in Japan. Xiong Kaixian, a Chinese law student from Hanyang (漢陽) in Hubei province, has attended his lectures on public law in time of peace and subsequently edited his own notes and had them published in Chinese. The series is edited by another Hubei student in Japan, Zhao Xiangqian, and printed and published by the Shangwu yinshuguan in Shanghai. The series was distributed through their offices and branches in all major Chinese cities. The reprinting of this series 5 years later indicates a large market for these texts on international law in the early 20th century and in particular during the years after the Russo-Japanese war. However, none of these texts discusses the situation in the Far East in particular. The topics of Ogata's lectures are international law, in time of peace and war, in general. (Sources: Tian Tao 2001, p. 142; *Zhongguo falü tushu zongmu* 1991, p. 739.)

Zhanshi guoji gongfa 戰時國際公法

Date of first Chinese edition: 1906
Author: Ogata Iichi (緒方維一)
Author's Chinese name:
Translator: Zhao Xiangqian (趙象謙) (editor and translator)
Original text: Lectures by Ogata Iichi
Imprint Chinese text: 113 pages
Prefaces etc.: None
Place of publication: Shanghai
Publisher: Shangwu yinshuguan (商務印書館)
Later editions and reprints: Reprinted in 1911
Library holdings: 1911 edition: Shanghai tushuguan, jindai wenxianbu (334621)
Note: The text is included as volume 14 of the *Jingcha jiangyilu* (警察講義錄) edited by Zhao Xiangqian (趙象謙) himself. Zhao Xiangqian is both the editor of the series Jingcha jiangyilu and the editor and translator of this particular volume on international law in time of war. Zhao is a native of Zhijiang (枝江) in Hubei province, a fellow provincial and probably an associate of Xiong Kaixian. Also this text primarily discusses the principles and regulations of hostility and warfare between states. However, whereas history and inter-state relations in the Far East did not make any contributions to the principles and practice of international law in time of peace, the recent war between Russia and Japan, and China's position in and handling of the situation, is of a certain significance in Ogata's lectures. Ogata depicts China as a passive partaker in the world community of states whilst Japan is numbered and discussed among the active and important authorities in world politics. This significant shift in the Japanese international role and attitude is first of all occasioned by the Sino-Japanese war and further manifested through the recent Russo-Japanese hostilities. (Sources: Tian Tao 2001, p. 143; *Zhongguo falü tushu zongmu* 1991, p. 744.)

Guoji sifa tujie 國際私法圖解

Date of first Chinese edition: 1906
Author: Ishimitsu Saburô (石光三郎) and Mori Sônosuke (森惣之祐)
Author's Chinese name:
Translator: Feng Yinmo (馮闇模)
Original text: Not known

(警視廳), hence the title of the series, *Records of police lectures* (*Jingcha jiangyilu*).

Imprint Chinese text: 260 pages
Prefaces etc.: None
Place of publication: Not known
Publisher: Jiaoyu shijieshe (教育世界社)
Later editions and reprints: Not known
Library holdings: Shanghai Cishu chubanshe (579.9024 3174), Shoudu tushuguan (341.9 350; 丙二 4803; 丙二 4804), Shanghai shekeyuan (P96 S472)
Note: The text does not disclose much of its origin. It is based on the writings of Ishimitsu Saburô and Mori Sônosuke, possibly a Japanese text with an identical title, and translated by Feng Yinmo from Chongming (崇明) just north of Shanghai. The translation may have been performed in Japan but the market for distribution was the Chinese mainland. The peculiar title indicates that the system of private international law is explained in tables and diagrams. The text discusses private international law in general with a few examples and references to the laws and traditions in East Asia. The technical vocabulary is identical with the current Meiji-Japanese lexicon. (Sources: Tian Tao 2001, p. 143; *Zhongguo falü tushu zongmu* 1991, p. 742.)

Guoji gongfa xuanyao 國際公法選要

Date of first Chinese publication: 1906
Author: Not known
Author's Chinese name:
Translator: Shi Shu (史書)
Original text:
Imprint Chinese text: Not known
Prefaces etc.: Not known
Place of publication: Tokyo
Publisher: Qingguo liuxuesheng huiguan (清國留學生會館)
Later editions and reprints:
Library holdings: Not known
Note: (Sources: *Zhongguo falü tushu zongmu* 1991, p. 742, Tian Tao 2001, p. 143)

Pingshi guoji gongfa 平時國際公法

Date of first Chinese publication: 1906
Author: Cheng Shude (程樹德) (editor)
Author's Chinese name:
Translator:
Original text:
Imprint Chinese text: Not known
Prefaces etc.: Not known
Place of publication: Shanghai
Publisher: Puji shuju (普及書局)
Later editions and reprints:
Library holdings: Not known
Note: Cheng Shude (1876-?) studied law at the Hôsei University (法政大學) in Japan. He held a number of political positions upon his return to China. He served also several years as lecturer and professor of law and politics at Peking University and Qinghua University. His main scholarly contribution lies within the field of the history of China's legal system. Cheng's precise role in the making of this book from 1906 is not known. (Sources: *Zhongguo falü tushu zongmu* 1991, p. 745; Tian Tao 2001, p. 143; Li Shengping 1989, p. 677)

Guoji gongyue guanxi zhu tiaoyue ji fagui 國際公約關係諸條約及法規

Date of first Chinese publication: 1906
Author: Not known
Author's Chinese name:
Translator: Ye Liang (葉良)
Original text:
Imprint Chinese text: Not known
Prefaces etc.: Not known
Place of publication: Tokyo
Publisher: Kagaku henyakusha (科學編譯社)
Later editions and reprints:
Library holdings: Not known
Note: (Sources: *Zhongguo falü tushu zongmu* 1991, p. 742; Tian Tao 2001, p. 142; Tian Tao & Li Zhuhuan 2000, p. 365)

Pingshi guoji gongfa 平時國際公法

Date of first Chinese edition: 1907
Author: Nakamura Shingo (中村進午) (1870-1939)
Author's Chinese name:
Translator: Jin Baokang (金保康) (editor and translator)
Original text: Nakamura Shingo's lectures at Chûô University (中央大學) and Nihon University (日本大學) in 1905-06, also supplied with quotations from other texts.
Imprint Chinese text: 234 pages
Prefaces etc.: *Fanli* (凡例), 3 pages
Place of publication: Tianjin (printed in Tokyo)
Publisher: Bingwushe (丙午社)
Later editions and reprints: The Fazheng jiangyi series was reprinted in 1913
Library holdings: Shanghai Cishu chubanshe (579 8120), Shanghai shekeyuan (P9 J476). 1913 reprint: Shanghai tushuguan, jindai wenxianbu (367330)
Note: The text is included as volume 17, series 1 of the *Fazheng jiangyi* (法政講義). Jin Baokang was a Chinese student of law at the Hôsei University (法政大學) in Japan. The two volumes on public international law in time of peace and in time of war included in the series *Fazheng jiangyi* (*Lectures on law and politics*) are both edited and translated by Jin Baokang. The two texts are based on Nakamura Shingo's lectures on public international law. Occasionally the text is also supported by quotations from other international law texts, invariably introduced by the commentary marker *an* (案).

The *Fazheng jiangyi* consists of 23 titles on political and legal subjects ranging from finance, economy, political science and administration to civil law, penal law, administrative law and international law. The first 1907 edition of the *Fazheng jiangyi* was printed in Tokyo, published by the Bingwushe in Tianjin and sold through bookstores in both China and Japan. When the series was reprinted in 1913 it was published by the same Bingwushe but this time printed and distributed by the Qunyi shushe (群益書社) in Shanghai. (Sources: Tan Ruqian 1980, p. 390; Tian Tao 2001, pp. 138-139, 167; *Zhongguo falü tushu zongmu* 1991, pp. 745-746.)

Zhanshi guoji gongfa 戰時國際公法

Date of first Chinese edition: 1907
Author: Nakamura Shingo (中村進午) (1870-1939)
Author's Chinese name:

Translator: Jin Baokang (金保康) (editor and translator)
Original text: Nakamura Shingo's lectures at Chûô University (中央大學) and Nihon University (日本大學) in 1905-06, also supplied with quotations from other texts.
Imprint Chinese text: 149 pages
Prefaces etc.: None
Place of publication: Tianjin (printed in Tokyo)
Publisher: Bingwushe (丙午社)
Later editions and reprints: The *Fazheng jiangyi* series was reprinted in 1913
Library holdings: Shanghai Cishu chubanshe (579 8120), Shanghai shekeyuan (P9 J476).
Note: The text is included as volume 18, series 1 of the *Fazheng jiangyi* (法政講義). See note on the translation of Nakamura Shingo for the title *Pingshi guoji gongfa* in this same series above.

Guoji sifa 國際私法

Date of first Chinese edition: 1907
Author: Yamada Saburô (山田三良) (1869-1965)
Author's Chinese name:
Translator: Fu Qiang (傅彊) (editor and translator)
Original text: Yamada's lectures and his teaching compendium printed at the Hôsei University (法政大學) in 1905.
Imprint Chinese text: 297 pages
Prefaces etc.: *Fanli* (凡例), 1 page.
Place of publication: Tianjin
Publisher: Bingwushe (丙午社)
Later editions and reprints: The *Fazheng jiangyi* series was reprinted in 1913
Library holdings: Shanghai Cishu chubanshe (579.9 2212), Shanghai shekeyuan (P9 J476). 1913 reprint: Shanghai tushuguan, jindai wenxianbu (366930)
Note: The text is included as volume 19, series 1 of the *Fazheng jiangyi* (法政講義). See note on the translation of the title *Pingshi guoji gongfa* in this same series above.

Xinyi guoji sifa 新譯國際私法

Date of first Chinese edition: 1907
Author: Nakamura Shingo (中村進午) (1870-1939)
Author's Chinese name:
Translator: Yuan Xilian (袁希濂), proof-read by Pan Cheng'e (潘承鍔)
Original text: Nakamura's lectures on private international law at the Chûô University (中央大學) in 1905 and his published lectures, most likely Nakamura's *Kokusai shihô kôgi* (國際私法講義) published in Tokyo in 1898.
Imprint Chinese text: 292 pages
Prefaces etc.: *Liyan* (例言), 2 pages
Place of publication: Shanghai
Publisher: Zhongguo tushu gongsi (中國圖書公司)
Later editions and reprints: Not known
Library holdings: Shanghai Cishu chubanshe (579.9 4743), Shoudu tushuguan (341.9 454.3), Shanghai shekeyuan (P96 Z643).
Note: Nakamura Shingo is first and foremost well known for his work on public international law. His works and lectures on public international law have been edited and translated into Chinese by a number of Chinese foreign law students in Japan. However, as this work shows, Nakamura also lectured on private international law in Japan. Tian Tao and Li Zhuhuan refers to a title *Xinyi guoji*

gongfa (新譯國際公法), thus on public and not on private international law, written by Nakamura Shingo and translated by the same Yuan Xilian and published the same year 1907 by the same Shanghai publisher. It is possible that these are two separate texts. It appears, however, more probable that there is a printing mistake in Tian and Li's list of translations. (Tiao Tao & Li Zhuhuan 2000, p. 365) (Sources: Tan Ruqian 1980, p. 393; Tian Tao 2001, p. 137; *Zhongguo falü tushu zongmu* 1991, p. 743.)

Pingshi guoji gongfa 平時國際公法

Date of first Chinese edition: 1907
Author: Takahashi Sakue (高橋作衛) (1867-1920)
Author's Chinese name:
Translator: Lu Bi (盧弼) and Huang Bingyan (黄炳言)
Original text: *Heiji kokusai kôhô* (平時國際公法)
Imprint Chinese text: Not known
Prefaces etc.: Not known
Place of publication: Tokyo
Publisher: Rijing Qingguo liuxuesheng huiguan (日京清國留學生會館),[24] distributed through the Changming gongsi (昌明公司) in Shanghai
Later editions and reprints: Not known
Library holdings: Not known
Note: In the *Fanli* (凡例 p. 2) of the *Pingshi guoji gongfa* in the *Fazheng jiangyi* series vol. 17 dated 1907 (see above) two Chinese translations of Takahashi's texts are mentioned; *Zhanshi guoji gongfa* (戰時國際公法) and *Pingshi guoji gongfa* (平時國際公法). These titles correspond to two of Takahashi's three general works on public international law; *Senji kokusai kôhô* (戰時國際公法) and *Heiji kokusai kôhô* (平時國際公法) For a Chinese translation of the third of Takahashi's major works, *Senji kokusaihô yôron* (戰時國際法要論), see below for the *Zhanshi guojifa yaolun* (戰時國際法要論) published in Chinese in 1908. There is no other information on the Chinese publication of the *Zhanshi guoji gongfa* (戰時國際公法) by Takahashi in Chinese. (Sources: A notice in the 1905 edition of *Fazheng cuibian* (see above) announcing a forthcoming publication; *Zhongguo falü tushu zongmu* 1991, p. 740; Tian Tao 2001, p. 142.)

Guoji sifa 國際私法

Date of first Chinese publication: 1907
Author: Yamawaki Sadao (山脅貞夫)
Author's Chinese name:
Translator: Zhang Renjing (張仁靜)
Original text: Lectures
Imprint Chinese text: Not known
Prefaces etc.: Not known
Place of publication: Not known
Publisher: Not known
Later editions and reprints:
Library holdings: Not known
Note: This book is compiled and translated from notes based on lectures by the Japanese judge and jurist Yamawaki Sadao (山脅貞夫). (Source: Tian Tao 2001, pp. 137-138, 165)

[24] The *Zhongguo falü tushu zongmu* 1991 and Tian Tao 2001 claim the *Fazheng xinshuju* (法政新書局) to be the publisher.

Zhanshi guoji gongyue 戰時國際公約
Date of first Chinese publication: 1907
Author: Minobe Tatsukichi (美濃部達吉) (1873-1948)
Author's Chinese name:
Translator: Xiong Fanyu (熊范輿) and Jin Baokang (金保康)
Original text: Not known
Imprint Chinese text: Not known
Prefaces etc.: Not known
Place of publication: Tianjin
Publisher: Bingwushe (丙午社)
Later editions and reprints:
Library holdings: Not known
Note: (Sources: *Zhongguo falü tushu zongmu* 1991, p. 744; Tian Tao 2001, p. 143)

Pingshi guoji gongfa 平時國際公法
Date of first Chinese publication: 1907
Author: Tan Chuankai (譚傳愷) (editor)
Author's Chinese name:
Translator:
Original text:
Imprint Chinese text: Not known
Prefaces etc.: Not known
Place of publication: Shanghai
Publisher: Zhengfa xueshe (政法學社)
Later editions and reprints:
Library holdings: Not known
Note: Tan's precise role in the making of this book and the identity of the author(s) are not known. (Sources: *Zhongguo falü tushu zongmu* 1991, p. 745; Tian Tao 2001, p. 143)

Pingshi guoji gongfa 平時國際公法
Date of first Chinese publication: 1907
Author: Chen Hongci (陳鴻慈) (editor)
Author's Chinese name:
Translator:
Original text:
Imprint Chinese text: Not known
Prefaces etc.: Not known
Place of publication: Tianjin
Publisher: Bingwushe (丙午社)
Later editions and reprints:
Library holdings: Not known
Note: Chen's precise role in the making of this book and the identity of the author (s) are not known. (Sources: *Zhongguo falü tushu zongmu* 1991, pp. 745-746; Tian Tao 2001, p. 143)

Guoji sifa 國際私法
Date of first Chinese publication: 1907
Author: Liu Gengguang (劉庚光) and Xiao Hongjun (肖鴻鈞) (editors)
Author's Chinese name:
Translator:
Original text:

Imprint Chinese text: Not known
Prefaces etc.: Not known
Place of publication: Shanghai
Publisher: Zhengfa shuyi (政法述義) no. 22. Zhengfa xueshe (政法學社)
Later editions and reprints:
Library holdings: Not known
Note: Liu and Xiao's precise roles in the making of this book and the identity of the author(s) are not known. (*Zhongguo falü tushu zongmu* 1991, p. 746; Tian Tao 2001, p. 144)

Zhanshi guoji gongfa 戰時國際公法

Date of first Chinese edition: 1908
Author: Ariga Nagao (有賀長雄) (1860-1921)
Author's Chinese name:
Translator: Yan Xianzhang (嚴獻章)
Original text: *Senji kokusai kôhô* (戰時國際公法). Tokyo: Waseda University publishing house (早稻田大學出版部), 1904.
Imprint Chinese text: 106 pages
Prefaces etc.: Preface by Yan Xianzhang dated 1908, 3 pages. *Liyan* (例言), 12 pages.
Place of publication: Changsha (長沙)
Publisher: Hongwen tushushe (宏文圖書社)
Later editions and reprints: Reprinted in 1915
Library holdings: 1915 reprint: Shanghai tushuguan, gujibu (520224-30).
Note: The text is included in the series *Hanxian congshu* (漢峴叢書).

Zhanshi guojifa yaolun 戰時國際法要論

Date of first Chinese edition: 1908
Author: Takahashi Sakue (高橋作衛) (1867-1920)
Author's Chinese name:
Translator: Xu E 徐鍔 and Guo Enze (郭恩澤)
Original text: *Senji kokusaihô yôron* (戰時國際法要論), *Nichiro sensô kokusai jiken yôron* (日露戰爭國際事件要論), and *Senji kokusai hôki têyô* (戰時國際法規提要)
Imprint Chinese text: 716 pages (*Zhanshi guojifa yaolun* (戰時國際法要論), 335 pages; *Ri-E zhanzheng guoji shijian yaolun* (日俄戰爭國際事件要論), 133 pages; appendix entitled *Zhanshi guoji fagui tiyao* (戰時國際法規提要), 248 pages)
Prefaces etc.: Author's original preface to *Zhanshi guojifa yaolun* (戰時國際法要論), 1 page. Author's original preface to *Ri-E zhanzheng guoji shijian yaolun* (日俄戰爭國際事件要論), 3 pages. Preface by Lin Kunxiang (林鵾翔) dated 1908, 3 pages. Preface by Guo Jintao (郭今陶) dated 1908, 4 pages. Introduction by the translators, 2 pages. Explanations by the translators, 2 pages. List of name translation, 12 pages. List of Chinese terminology, 2 pages.
Place of publication: Tokyo
Publisher: Guoji faxue yanjiushe (國際法學研究社)
Later editions and reprints: Not known
Library holdings: Shanghai shekeyuan (P94 G248)
Note: This Chinese publication consists in fact of three different publications, all three translations of publications by the influential Japanese international law professor Takahashi Sakue. Takahashi is the author of 3 major general works on public international law in Japanese; *Senji kokusaihô yôron* (戰時國際法要論), *Senji kokusai kôhô* (戰時國際公法) and *Heiji kokusai kôhô* (平時國際公法) and a

number of publications on more particular issues in international law. The present Chinese translation contains one of his major works, the *Senji kokusaihô yôron* (戰時國際法要論) and two of his publications on more particular issues, the *Nichiro sensô kokusai jiken yôron* (日露戰爭國際事件要論) and *Senji kokusai hôki têyô* (戰時國際法規提要). The *Senji kokusaihô yôron* (戰時國際法要論) and the *Nichiro sensô kokusai jiken yôron* (*Ri-E zhanzheng guoji shijian yaolun* (日俄戰爭國際事件要論) in Chinese) were originally two separate Japanese texts published in 1905, translated into Chinese and combined into one single Chinese publication because of their common authorship and their relevance for the analysis of the recently concluded Japanese-Russian war. In addition a translation of an abstract of legal regulations for warfare, *Senji kokusai hôki têyô*, also initially prepared in Japanese by Takahashi, is appended to these two publications to provide the third part of this Chinese publication. (Sources: Qi Qizhang 2001, *qianyan* 前言 p. 8; Tian Tao 2001, p. 143; *Zhongguo falü tushu zongmu* 1991, p. 744.)

Guoji gongfa 國際公法

Date of first Chinese publication: 1908
Author: Senga Tsurutarou (千賀鶴太郎)
Author's Chinese name:
Translator: Lu Bi (盧弼) and Huang Bingyan (黄炳言)
Original text: Lectures
Imprint Chinese text: Not known
Prefaces etc.: Not known
Place of publication:
Publisher: Zhengzhi jingji she (政治經濟社)
Later editions and reprints: Shanghai: Changming gongsi (昌明公司) 1908
Library holdings: Not known
Note: Lu Bi (1876-1967) studied in Japan for two periods after 1902 and obtained a Chinese degree in politics and law in 1908. He held several prominent positions in the Chinese republican government after 1912. Lu and Huang translated this text while they were studying law in Tokyo. They chose to translate lecture notes from lectures by Senga Tsurutarou (千賀鶴太郎) who had been studying law and living in Berlin for 16 years and at that time served as professor of law at Kyoto teikoku daigaku (京都帝國大學). (Sources: *Zhongguo falü tushu zongmu* 1991, p. 742; Tian Tao 2001, pp. 139-140, 158, 166; Tian Tao & Li Zhuhuan 2000, p. 359; Li Shengping 1989, p. 94)

Guoji gongfa 國際公法

Date of first Chinese publication: 1908
Author: Yang Nian (楊年) (editor)
Author's Chinese name:
Translator:
Original text:
Imprint Chinese text: Not known
Prefaces etc.: Not known
Place of publication: Chengdu
Publisher: Tanyuan gongsi (探源公司)
Later editions and reprints:
Library holdings: Not known
Note: Yang's precise role in the making of this book and the identity of the author(s) are not known. (Sources: *Zhongguo falü tushu zongmu* 1991, p. 746; Tian Tao 2001, p. 144)

Guoji gongfa tigang 國際公法提綱
Date of first Chinese edition: 1910
Author: Thomas Joseph Lawrence (1849-1919)
Author's Chinese name: Luolinsi (羅麟斯)[25]
Translator: Dan Tao (但燾) (1881-1970)
Original text: *The Principles of International Law*. London & New York: Macmillian & Co., 1895.
Imprint Chinese text: 95 pages
Prefaces etc.: Preface by Dan Tao (但燾) dated 1910, 2 pages. *Fanli* (凡例) dated 1910, 1 page.
Place of publication: Shanghai (printed in Japan)
Publisher: Changming gongsi (昌明公司) and Biaomeng gongsi (彪蒙公司)
Later editions and reprints: Not known
Library holdings: Shanghai Cishu chubanshe (341 22), Shanghai shekeyuan (P9 L922)
Note: It appears from the text and his use of name transcriptions that Dan Tao was either altogether unfamiliar with the 1903 translation of Lawrence's *A Handbook of Public International Law* or that he chose to disregard the earlier and by then outdated earlier fashions of translation. Dan Tao, from Puqi (蒲圻) in Hubei province, went to Japan as a foreign student in 1903. He attended a crash-course in Japanese and was accepted at the Kanda dôbun shoin (神田同文書院) in Tokyo in 1904. He was enrolled at the English law department of Chûô University (中央大學) not long after, attending lectures on maritime trade law given by the influential Nakamura Shingo (中村進午) (1870-1939) and where he also worked on his Lawrence translation. Dan Tao also enrolled in the revolutionary Tongmenghui (同盟會) during his years in Japan. He returned to China in December 1911 and was appointed presidential secretary in the preliminary new republican government in 1912. He held several important secretarial posts and other high ranking positions in the republican government in the consecutive years, also after the government of the Republic of China was established on Taiwan after 1949. Dan Tao has also himself written extensively on historical topics. (Sources: Beijing tushuguan 1990, p. 347; Li Shengping 1989, p. 313; Quanguo zong shumu 1935, p. 183; Tian Tao 2001, p. 143; *Zhongguo falü tushu zongmu* 1991, p. 742; Zhou Mian 1999, p. 189.)

A new partial translation by Wang Ding (王鼎) of the sections on neutrality in Lawrence's *The Principles of Internationa*l Law was published by Shanghai Shangwu yinshuguan (商務印書館) in 1914 with the title *Juwai zhongli fajingyi* 局外中立法精義. The entire text was retranslated with the title *Guoji gongfa dagang* (國際公法大綱) by Yang Youjiong (楊幼炯) around 1935.

Lawrence's *A Handbook of Public International Law* (translated into Chinese by Allen and Cai in 1903) had been used as university text book for law students both in Europe and in America. Dan Tao, in the introduction to this 1910 translation, expresses hope that his translation may help promote the study of international law in China, conceivably in the rapidly expanding modern educational system. Dan Tao has found Lawrence's book suitable as a simple and comprehensible introduction to international law in Chinese, seemingly unaware of the long Chinese tradition in international law translations. Lawrence's text of more than 600 pages has been rephrased into 97 pages of Chinese text, keeping the basic textual division and not leaving out any major part of Lawrence's text. The four parts, "The nature and history of international law", "The law of peace", "The law of war" and "The law of neutrality" are retained in Dan Tao's text, while some

[25] Also transcribed Luolinshi (羅麟士).

of the chapters and sub-chapters have been merged. The text proper, however, is heavily abridged and largely rephrased. Dan Tao has sporadically also added his own commentaries on the text (Tao an... 燾案...), occasionally with examples and illustrations from Chinese political history.

Guoji sifa 國際私法
Date of first Chinese edition: 1911
Author: Yamada Saburô (山田三良) (1869-1965)
Author's Chinese name:
Translator: Li Zhuo (李倬)
Original text: A non-identified title by Yamada Saburô
Imprint Chinese text: 252 pages
Prefaces etc.: None
Place of publication: Shanghai
Publisher: Shangwu yinshuguan (商務印書館)
Later editions and reprints: Not known
Library holdings: Shoudu tushuguan (341.9 583)

Pingshi guoji gongfa 平時國際公法
Date of first Chinese edition: 1911
Author: Nakamura Shingo (中村進午) (1870-1939)
Author's Chinese name:
Translator: Chen Shixia (陳時夏)
Original text: A non-identified title by Nakamura Shingo
Imprint Chinese text: 333 pages
Prefaces etc.: None
Place of publication: Shanghai
Publisher: Shangwu yinshuguan (商務印書館)
Later editions and reprints: 5th edition in 1915
Library holdings: 5th edition: Shanghai tushuguan, jindai wenxianbu (224159).

Zhanshi guoji gongfa 戰時國際公法
Date of first Chinese edition: 1911
Author: Nakamura Shingo (中村進午) (1870-1939)
Author's Chinese name:
Translator: Chen Shixia (陳時夏)
Original text: A non-identified title by Nakamura Shingo
Imprint Chinese text: 159 pages
Prefaces etc.: None
Place of publication: Shanghai
Publisher: Shangwu yinshuguan (商務印書館)
Later editions and reprints: 4th edition in 1914
Library holdings: 4th edition: Shanghai tushuguan, jindai wenxianbu (374011). Shoudu tushuguan (341.4 378)

Guoji gongfa; Pingshi zhanshi 國際公法；平時戰時
Date of first Chinese publication: 1911
Author: Xiong Yuanxiang (熊元襄) and Xiong Yuanhan (熊元翰)
Author's Chinese name:
Translator:
Original text:
Imprint Chinese text: Not known

Prefaces etc.: Not known
Place of publication:
Publisher: *Fazheng congshu* (法政叢書) no. 20. Shuntian shibao she (順天時報社)
Later editions and reprints:
Library holdings: Not known
Note: The two Xiong's are referred to as authors of this book. Whether or not this title also contains translations is not clear. (Sources: *Zhongguo falü tushu zongmu* 1991, p. 746; Tian Tao 2001, p. 144)

Guoji gongfa 國際公法

Date of first Chinese publication: 1911
Author: Jin Baokang (金保康) (editor)
Author's Chinese name:
Translator:
Original text:
Imprint Chinese text: Not known
Prefaces etc.: Not known
Place of publication: Tianjin
Publisher: Bingwushe (丙午社)
Later editions and reprints:
Library holdings: Not known
Note: Jin's precise role in the making of this book and the identity of the author(s) are not known. The text may be a reprint of or otherwise related to the 1907 Jin Baokang translations of Nakamura Shingo. (Sources: *Zhongguo falü tushu zongmu* 1991, p. 746; Tian Tao 2001, pp. 144, 166)

Guoji sifa 國際私法

Date of first Chinese publication: 1911
Author: Ren He (仁和) (editor)
Author's Chinese name:
Translator:
Original text:
Imprint Chinese text: Not known
Prefaces etc.: Not known
Place of publication: Shanghai
Publisher: Qunyi shushe (群益書社)
Later editions and reprints:
Library holdings: Not known
Note: Ren's precise role in the making of this book and the identity of the author(s) are not known. (Source: *Zhongguo falü tushu zongmu* 1991, p. 746)

BIBLIOGRAPHY

Allen, Young J. (ed.). *Wanguo gongbao* 萬國公報. *Qingmo Minchu baokan congbian zhi si* 清末民初報刊叢編之四. Vol. 33. Taibei: Huawen shuju 華文書局, 1968.

Angle, Stephen C. *Human Rights and Chinese Thought. A Cross-Cultural Inquiry.* Cambridge: Cambridge University Press, 2002.

Arrighi, Giovanni, Takeshi Hamashita and Mark Selden (eds.). *The Resurgence of East Asia. 500, 150 and 50 years Perspectives.* London and New York: Routledge, 2003.

Barnett, Suzanne Wilson. "Wei Yuan and the Westerners: Notes on the Sources of the Hai-kuo t'u-chih." In *Ch'ing-shih wen-t'i* 2, IV, November 1970, pp. 1-20.

Beijing tushuguan 北京圖書館 (ed.). *Minguo shiqi zong mulu* 民國時期總目錄 (1911-1949), Vol. *Falü* 法律. Beijing: Shumu wenxian chubanshe 書目文獻出版社, 1990.

Beiyang fazheng xuebao 北洋法政學報. Tokyo: 1906-1910.

Bennett, Adrian Arthur. *John Fryer: The Introduction of Western Science and Technology into Nineteenth-Century China.* Harvard East Asian Monographs no. 24. Cambridge, Mass.: Harvard University Press, 1967.

——. *Missionary Journalist in China. Young J. Allen and his Magazines, 1860-1883.* Athens, Georgia: The University of Georgia Press, 1983.

Biggerstaff, Knight (Bi Naide 畢乃德). "Tongwenguan kao" 同文館考. In *Zhongguo jindai xuezhi shiliao* 中國近代學制史料. Volume 1, first part. *Jiaoyu kexue congshu* 教育科學叢書. Shanghai: Huadong shifan daxue chubanshe 華東師範大學出版社, 1983, pp. 197-213.

Bluntschli, J. C. *Das moderne Völkerrecht der civilisierten Staaten als Rechtsbuch dargestellt.* Nördlingen: C.H. Beck'schen Buchhandlung, 1868.

——. *Denkwürdiges aus meinem Leben.* Nördlingen: C.H. Beck'schen Buchhandlung, 1884.

Boorman, Howard L. (ed.). *Biographical Dictionary of Republican China.* New York & London: Columbia University Press, 1967-71.

——. "Wang Ching-wei: A Political Profile". In Hsüeh, Chün-Tu (ed.). *Revolutionary Leaders of Modern China.* New York, London, Toronto: Oxford University Press, 1971, pp. 295-319.

Britton, Roswell S. "Chinese Interstate Intercourse Before 700 B.C." In *The American Journal of International Law.* Vol. 29. Washington & Concord: The American Society of International Law, 1935, pp. 616-635.

——. *The Chinese Periodical Press 1800-1912.* Taipei: Ch'eng-wen Publishing Company, 1966.

Brownlie, Ian. *Principles of Public International Law.* Oxford: Clarendon Press, 1998.

Boucher, David. "Political Theory, International Theory, and the Political Theory of International Relations". Vincent, Andrew (ed.). *Political Theory: Tradition & Diversity.* Cambridge: Cambridge University Press, 1997, pp. 193-213.

Bull, Hedley. "Society and Anarchy in International Relations". In Butterfield, Herbert & Martin Wight (eds.). *Diplomatic Investigations: Essays in the Theory of International Politics.* London: George Allen & Unwin, 1966, pp. 35-50.

——. "The Grotian Conception of International Society". In Butterfield, Herbert & Martin Wight (eds.). *Diplomatic Investigations: Essays in the Theory of International Politics*. London: George Allen & Unwin, 1966, pp. 51-73.

Bull, Hedley & Adam Watson (eds.). *The Expansion of International Society*. Oxford: Clarendon Press, 1992.

Butterfield, H. "The Balance of Power". In Butterfield, Herbert & Martin Wight (eds.). *Diplomatic Investigations: Essays in the Theory of International Politics*. London: George Allen & Unwin, 1966, pp. 132-175.

Cao Nianming 曹念明. "«Geguo lüli» shi Zhongguo zuizao fanyi de guojifa zhuzuo" 《各國律例》是中國最早翻譯的國際法著作 («The law of Nations» is the earliest Chinese translation of a work on international law). *Lishi daguanyuan* 3, 1992, p. 51.

Chang, Hao. *Liang Ch'i Ch'ao and Intellectual Transition in China, 1890-1907*. Cambridge: Harvard University Press, 1971.

——. "Intellectual change and the reform movement, 1890-8". In Fairbank, John K. & Kwang-Ching Liu (eds.). *The Cambridge History of China. Volume 11: Late Ch'ing, 1890-1911, Part 2*. Cambridge: Cambridge University Press, 1980, pp. 274-338.

Chang, Hsi-t'ung. "The Earliest Phase of the Introduction of Western Political Science into China." In *Yenching Journal of Social Studies* V-1950, pp. 1417-1445.

Chen Chi 陳熾. *Yongshu* 庸書. In *Chen Chi ji* 陳熾集. Beijing: Zhonghua shuju 中華書局, 1997.

Chen Guoqing 陳國慶. *Wan Qing xinxue shilun* 晚清新學史論. Xi'an: Sanqin chubanshe 三秦出版社, 2003.

Chen Heng 陳恆 & Fang Yiner 方銀兒 (ed.). *Tao Yuan wenlu waipian* 弢園文錄外篇. Zhengzhou: Zhongzhou guji chubanshe 中州古籍出版社, 1998.

Ch'en, Jerome. *China and the West. Society and Culture 1815-1937*. London: Hutchinson, 1979.

Chen, Vincent. *Sino-Russian Relations in the Seventeenth Century*. The Hague: Martinus Nijhoff, 1966.

Chen Xulu 陳旭麓. *Jindai Zhongguo shehui de xin chen dai xie* 近代中國社會的新陳代謝. Shanghai: Renmin chubanshe 人民出版社, 1998.

Chien, Helen Hsieh (tr.). *The European Diary of Hsieh Fucheng. Envoy Extraordinary of Imperial China*. New York: St Martin's Press, 1993.

Ching, Julia and Willard G. Oxtoby. *Moral Enlightenment: Leibniz and Wolff on China. Monumenta Serica Monograph Series* XXVI. Nettetal: Steyler Verlag, 1992.

Chiu, Hungdah. "The Development of Chinese International Law Terms and the Problem of Their Translation into English." In *The Journal of Asian Studies* 27-1967, pp. 485-501.

——. *The Status of Customary International Law, Treaties, Agreements and Semi-official or Unofficial Agreements in Chinese Law. Occasional Papers/Reprint Series in Contemporary Asia Studies*. No. 2 - 1989 (91). Baltimore Md.: School of Law, University of Maryland, 1989a.

——. *Chinese Attitude Toward International Law of Human Rights in the Post-Mao Era. Occasional Papers/Reprint Series in Contemporary Asia Studies*. No. 5 - 1989 (94). Baltimore Md.: School of Law, University of Maryland, 1989b.

——. *Nationality and International Law in Chinese Perspective. Occasional Papers/Reprint Series in Contemporary Asia Studies*. No. 3 - 1990 (98). Baltimore Md.: School of Law, University of Maryland, 1990.

Chouban yiwu shimo 籌辦夷務始末. Taibei: Tailian guofeng chubanshe 台聯國風出版社, 1972, Vol. 5 (*Tong Zhi chao* 同治朝), pp. *juan* 26:29b-38b, *juan* 27:25a-26b, *juan* 31:4a-5a.
Cohen, Jerome Alan (ed.). *China's Practice of International Law: Some Case Studies*. Cambridge Mass.: Harvard University Press, 1972.
Cohen, Jerome Alan & Hungdah Chiu. *People's China and International Law. A Documentary Study*. Princeton: Princeton University Press, 1974.
Cohen, Paul A. "Wang T'ao's perspective on a Changing World". In Albert Feuerwerker, Rhoads Murphey & Mary C. Wright (eds.). *Approaches to Modern Chinese History*. Berkeley and Los Angeles: University of California Press, 1967, pp. 133-162.
——. *Between Tradition and Modernity: Wang T'ao and Reform in late Ch'ing China*. Cambridge Mass.: Harvard University Press: 1974.
Covell, Ralph. *W.A.P. Martin: Pioneer of Progress in China*. Washington: Christian University Press, 1978.
Desjardins, Arthur. "La Chine et le Droit des Gens". In *Revue des Deux Mondes*. December 1st and 15th 1900. Paris: Bureau de la Revue des Deux Mondes, pp. 522-549, 815-844.
Ding Pingyi 丁平一. *Hunan weixin yundong shi 1895 zhi 1898 nian*. 湖南維新運動史1895至1898年. Taibei: Han-Chung Book Co. Ltd., 2000.
Dudden, Alexis. "Japan's Engagement with International Terms." In Liu, Lydia (ed.). *Tokens of Exchange: The Problem of Translation in Global Circulation*. Durham & London: Duke University Press, 1999, pp. 165-191.
Dunn, John & Ian Harris (eds.). *Grotius*. 2 volumes. *Great Political Thinkers 7*. Cheltenham, UK & Lyme, US: Edward Elgar Publishing Limited, 1997.
Elman, Benjamin A. *On Their Own Terms. Science in China, 1550-1900*. Cambridge, Mass. & London: Harvard University Press, 2005.
Encyclopedia of Public International Law. Amsterdam, New York, Oxford: Elsevier Science Publishers, 1984.
Escarra, Jean. *La Chine et le Droit International*. Paris: A. Pedone, 1931.
——. *Chinese law. Conceptions and evolution, legislative and juridical institutions, science and teaching*. Cambridge: Harvard University, 1961 (1936).
Esherick, Joseph W. *Reform and Revolution in China. The 1911 Revolution in Hunan and Hubei*. Berkeley: University of California Press, 1976.
E'shi jingwen 俄事警聞. Shanghai, 1903-1904.
Fairbank, John King (ed.). *The Chinese World Order. Traditional China's Foreign Relations*. Cambridge Mass.: Harvard University Press, 1968.
Fang Hanqi 方漢奇 (ed.). *Zhongguo xinwen shiye tongshi* 中國新聞事業通史. Beijing: Zhongguo renmin daxue chubanshe 中國人民大學出版社, 1997.
Fang Weigui 方維規. "Lun jin-xiandai Zhongguo "wenming", "wenhua" guan de shanbian" 論近現代中國"文明"、"文化"觀的嬗變. In *Shilin* 史林. Shanghai: Shanghai shehui kexueyuan lishi yanjiusuo 上海社會科學院歷史研究所, 4-1999, pp. 69-83.
Farquhar, Norma. "A Bibliography of the Writings of W.A.P. Martin." In *Papers on China*. Vol. 10, October 1956. Cambridge, Mass.: Harvard University, East Asian Research Centre, 1971, pp. 128-141.
Fass, Josef. "Chinese Newspapers". In Leslie, Donald D., Mackerras, Colin, and Wang Gungwu (eds.). *Essays on the Sources for Chinese History*. Canberra: Australian National University press, 1973, pp. 221-228.
Feng Guifen 馮桂芬. *Xianzhitang ji* 顯志堂集. Taipei: Xuehai chubanshe 學海出版社, (1876) 1967.

Fenwick, Charles G. *International Law*. New York & London: Appleton-Century-Crofts, 1948.

Ferguson, Jan Helenus. *Manual of International Law: For the use of Navies, Colonies and Consulates*. The Hague: M. Nyhoff, and London: W.B. Whittingham and Co., 1884.

——. *Juridiction et exterritorialité en Chine*. Bruxelles: P. Weissenbruch, 1890.

Ferguson, J. W. H. *A Glossary of the Principal Chinese Expressions Occurring in Postal Documents*. Shanghai: Statistical Department of the Inspectorate General of Customs, 1906.

Fitzgerald, C.P. *The Chinese View of their Place in the World*. London: Oxford University Press, 1964.

Gasster, Michael. "Reform and Revolution in China's Political Modernization". In Wright, Mary Clabaugh (ed.). *China in Revolution: The First Phase, 1900-1913*. New Haven and London: Yale University Press, 1968, pp. 67-96.

——. *Chinese Intellectuals and the Revolution of 1911. The Birth of Modern Chinese Radicalism*. Seattle & London: University of Washington Press, 1969.

Ge Shijun 葛士濬 (ed.). *Huangchao jinshiwen xubian* 皇朝經世文續編. Taibei: Guofeng chubanshe 國風出版社, 1964 (1898).

Geng Yunzhi 耿云志 et.al. *Xifang minzhu zai jindai Zhongguo* 西方民主在近代中國. Beijing: Qingnian chubanshe 青年出版本社, 2003.

Gezhi huibian 格致彙編. Shanghai: Gezhi shuyuan 格致書院, 1876-1892.

Gong, Gerrit W. "China's Entry into International Society". In Hedley Bull & Adam Watson (eds.). *The Expansion of International Society*. Oxford: Clarendon Press, 1984, pp. 171-183.

Guo Songtao 郭崧燾. *Lundun yu Bali riji* 倫敦與巴黎日記. In *Zou xiang shijie congshu* 走向世界叢書. Hunan: Yuelu shushe 岳麓書社, 1984 (1891).

Hao, Yen-p'ing & Erh-min Wang. "Changing Chinese views of Western relations, 1840-95". In Fairbank, John K. & Kwang-Ching Liu (eds.). *The Cambridge History of China. Volume 11: Late Ch'ing, 1890-1911, Part 2*. Cambridge: Cambridge University Press, 1980, pp. 142-201.

Hall, William Edward. *A Treatise on International Law*. Oxford: The Clarendon Press, 1895.

Hamashita, Takeshi. "Tribute and Treaties. Maritime Asia and Treaty Port Networks in the Era of Negotiation, 1800-1900". In Arrighi, Giovanni, Takeshi Hamashita and Mark Selden (eds.). *The Resurgence of East Asia. 500, 150 and 50 years Perspectives*. London and New York: Routledge, 2003, pp. 17-50.

Harrell, Paula. *Sowing the Seeds of Change. Japanese Students, Japanese Teachers, 1895-1905*. Stanford, California: Stanford University Press, 1992.

Hershey, Amos Shartle. *The International Law and Diplomacy of the Russo-Japanese War*. New York: Macmillan, 1906.

Holland, Thomas Erskine. *Studies in International Law*. Oxford: Clarendon Press, 1898.

Holzgrefe, J.L. "The Origins of Modern International Relations Theory". In *Review of International Studies*. Vol. 15. Butterworths, 1989, pp. 11-26.

Hsü, Immanuel C. Y. *China's Entrance into the Family of Nations. The Diplomatic Phase 1858-1880*. Cambridge, Mass.: Harvard University Press, 1960.

Hsu, Immanuel. "Late Ch'ing foreign relations, 1866-1905". In Fairbank, John K. & Kwang-Ching Liu (eds.). *The Cambridge History of China. Volume 11: Late Ch'ing, 1890-1911, Part 2*. Cambridge: Cambridge University Press, 1980, pp. 70-141.

Huang, Philip C. *Liang Ch'i-ch'ao and Modern Chinese Liberalism*. Seattle & London: University of Washington Press, 1972.
Huang, Yi. *Der deutsche Einfluß auf die Entwicklung des chinesischen Bildungswesens von 1871 bis 1918: Studien zu den kulturellen Aspekten der deutch-chinesischen Beziehungen in der Ära des deutschen Kaiserreichs. Europäische Hochschulschriften* Series III, vol. 637. Frankfurt am Main: Peter Lang, 1995.
Hughes, E.R. *The Invasion of China by the Western World*. London: Adam and Charles Black, 1968.
Huntington, Samuel P. *The Clash of Civilizations and the Remaking of World Order*. New York: Simon & Schuster, 1996.
Hurrell, Andrew. "Vattel: Pluralism and Its Limits." In Clark, Ian & Iver B. Neumann (eds.). *Classical Theories of International Relations*. Basingstoke: MacMillian Press Ltd., 1996, pp. 233-255.
Iriye, Akira. "Public Opinion and Foreign Policy: The Case of late Ch'ing China". In Albert Feuerwerker, Rhoads Murphey & Mary C. Wright (eds.). *Approaches to Modern Chinese History*. Berkeley and Los Angeles: University of California Press, 1967, pp. 216-238.
Iriye, Keishiro. "The Principles of International Law in the Light of Confucian Doctrine". In *Recueil des cours (Académie de droit international de la Haye)*. Vol. 120. Dordrecht: Martinus Nijhoff Publishers, 1967 (printed 1968), pp. 1-58.
Janku, Andrea. *Nur leere Reden. Politischer Diskurs und die Shanghaier Presse im China des späten 19. Jahrhunderts*. Wiesbaden: Harrassowitz Verlag, 2003.
——. "Der Fall Kang Youwei (1898) und das völkerrechtliche Prinzip der Nichtauslieferung politischer Flüchtlinge in der Shanghaier kommerziellen Presse". Unpublished paper 2004.
——. "Translating genre: How the 'Leading article' became the *shelun*". In Lackner, Michael & Natascha Vittinghoff (eds.). *Mapping Meanings. The Field of New Learning in Late Qing China*. Leiden: Brill, 2004, pp. 329-353.
Jellinek, Georg. "China und das Völkerrecht". In *Deutsche Juristen-Zeitung*. No. 19 October 1900. Berlin: Huber, 1900, pp. 401-404.
Jichengbao 集成報. *Zhongguo jindai qikan huikan* 中國近代期刊彙刊. Beijing: Zhonghua shuju 中華書局, 1991.
Jiangsu 江蘇. *Zhonghua minguo shiliao congbian* 中華民國史料叢編. Taibei: Dangshi shiliao bianzuan weiyuanhui 黨史史料編纂委員會, 1983.
Jiang Tingfu 蔣廷黻. *Jindai Zhongguo waijiaoshi ziliao jiyao* 近代中國外交史資料輯要. Taibei: Taiwan shangwu yinshuguan 臺灣商務印書館, 1982
Jingzhong ribao 警鐘日報 (*Alarming Bell Daily News*). Shanghai, 1904-1905.
Judge, Joan. *Print and Politics. 'Shibao' and the Culture of Reform in Late Imperial China*. Stanford: Stanford University Press, 1996.
——. "Key Words in the Late Qing Reform Discourse: Classical and Contemporary Sources of Authority." (http://www.indiana.edu/~easc/resources/working_paper/noframe_5_all.htm) (5th January 2005)
Kamachi, Noriko. *Reform in China. Huang Tsun-hsien and the Japanese Model*. Cambridge, Mass. & London: Harvard University Press, 1981.
Kang Youwei quanji 康有為全集. Shanghai: Shanghai guji chubanshe 上海古籍出版社, 1992.
Karl, Rebecca E. & Peter Zarrow (eds.). *Rethinking the 1898 Reform Period. Political and Cultural Change in Late Qing China*. Cambridge, Mass. & London: Harvard University Press, 2002.

Katô Shûichi 加藤周一 & Maruyama Masao 丸山真男. "Honyakuno shisô" 翻訳の思想. In *Nihon kindai shiso taikei* 日本近代思想大系 vol. 15. Tokyo: Iwanami shoten 岩波書店, 1996.

Keeton, George W. *The Development of Extraterritoriality in China*. New York: Howard Fertig, 1969.

Kennedy, Melville T., Jr. "Hu Han-min: His Career and Thought". In Hsüeh, Chün-Tu (ed.). *Revolutionary Leaders of Modern China*. New York, London, Toronto: Oxford University Press, 1971, pp. 271-294.

Khayutina, Maria. "Exile and Asylum in Ancient China According to the Data of the Chunqiu Chronicle and the Zuo zhuan Narrative". Unpublished paper 2004.

Lackner, Michael, Iwo Amelung & Joachim Kurtz (eds.). *New Terms for New Ideas. Western Knowledge & Lexical Change in Late Imperial China*. Leiden: Brill, 2001.

Lackner, Michael & Natascha Vittinghoff (eds.). *Mapping Meanings. The Field of New Learning in Late Qing China*. Leiden: Brill, 2004.

Lan Guangce 藍光策. *Chunqiu gongfa biyi fawei* 春秋公法比義發微. Nanyang yinshua guanchang 南洋印刷官廠, 1911.

Laozi zhu 老子注 *in Zhuzi jicheng* 諸子集成, Beijing: Zhonghua shuju 中華書局, 1990.

Lawrence T. J. *The Principles of International Law*. London & New York: Macmillian & co., 1895.

——. *A Handbook of Public International Law*. London: Macmillian & Co., 1898.

——. *War and Neutrality in the Far East*. London: Macmillan and co, 1904.

Levenson, Joseph R. "The Breakdown of Confucianism: Liang Ch'i Ch'ao before Exile – 1873-1898". In *Journal of the History of Ideas*, vol. 11, no. 4, October 1950.

——. *Liang Ch'i Ch'ao and the Mind of Modern China*. Berkeley: University of California Press, 1967.

Li Fengbao 李鳳苞. *Shi De riji* 使德日記. *Zou xiang shijie congshu* 走向世界叢書. Hunan: Renmin chubanshe 人民出版社, 1981.

Li Guilian 李貴連. "Ershi shiji chuqi de Zhongguo faxue" 二十世紀初期的中國法學. In Li Guilian (ed.) *Ershi shiji de Zhongguo faxue* 二十世紀的中國法學. Beijing: Beijing Daxue chubanshe 北京大學出版社, 1998a, pp. 1-65.

——. "Huashuo 'quanli'*f*" 話說"權利". In *Beida falü pinglun* 北大法律評論 1998.1.1. Beijing: Falü chubanshe 法律出版社, 1998b, pp. 115-129.

——. *Zhongguo falü sixiangshi* 中國法律思想史. Beijing: Beijing daxue chubanshe 北京大學出版社, 2000.

Li Shengping 李盛平 (ed.). *Zhongguo jin xiandai renming da cidian* 中國近現代人名大辭典. Beijing: Zhongguo guoji guangbo chubanshe 中國國際廣播出版社, 1989.

Li, Sin-Yang. *Doctrines du Droit Public en Chine antique*. Paris: Les Presses Modernes, 1928.

Li Wenhai 李文海. *Shiji zhi jiao de wan Qing shehui* 世紀之交的晚清社會. Beijing: Zhongguo renmin daxue chubanshe 中國人民大學出版社, 1996.

Li Zhaojie. "How international law was introduced into China". In *Guoji falü wenti yanjiu* 國際法律問題研究. Beijing: Zhongguo zhengfa daxue chubanshe 中國政法大學出版社, 1999, pp. 53-135.

Li Zhongxing 李忠興 (ed.). *Quanxuepian* 勸學篇. Zhengzhou: Zhongzhou guji chubanshe 中州古籍出版社, 1998.

Liang Qichao 梁啟超. "Du Xixueshu fa" 讀西學書法. In *Shenshi jizhai congshu* 慎始基齊叢書. 1896a.

——. "Xixue shumubiao" 西學書目表. In *Shenshi jizhai congshu* 慎始基齊叢書. 1896b.
——. *Yinbingshi heji* 飲冰室合集. Beijing: Zhonghua shuju 中華書局, 1996.
Liszt, Franz von. *Das Völkerrecht: Systematisch Dargestellt*. Berlin: O. Häring, 1898.
Liu Huawen 柳華文. "Cong guojifa jiaodu pingxi 1887 nian Zhong Pu «hehao tongshang tiaoyue»" 從國際法角度評析1887年中葡《和好通商條約》. In *Zhongguo bianjiang shidi yanjiu* 中國邊疆史地研究 2-1999, pp. 81-94.
Liu, Lydia H. *Translingual Practice. Literature, National Culture, and Translated Modernity - China, 1900-1937*. Stanford, California: Stanford University Press, 1995.
——. "Legislating the Universal: The Circulation of International Law in the Nineteenth Century." in Liu, Lydia (ed.). *Tokens of Exchange: The Problem of Translation in Global Circulation*. Durham & London: Duke University Press, 1999, pp. 127-164.
——. *The Clash of Empires*. Cambridge, Mass. & London: Harvard University Press, 2004.
Liu Zhengtan 劉正埮, Gao Mingkai 高名凱, Mai Yongqian 麥永乾 & Shi Youwei 史有為 (eds.). *Hanyu wailaici cidian* 漢語外來辭辭典. Shanghai: Shanghai cishu chubanshe 上海辭書出版社, 1984.
Loewe, Michael (ed.). *Early Chinese Texts. A Bibliographical Guide*. Berkeley: The Society for the Study of Early China, 1993.
Lust, John. "The Supao case". In *Bulletin of the School of Oriental and African Studies*, Vol. XXVII, 1964, pp. 408-429.
Ma Derun 馬德潤. *Zhongguo heyu guoji gongfa lun* 中國合於國際公法論. Shanghai: Shanghai: Shangwu yinshuguan 商務印書館, 1907.
Ma Guangren 馬光仁. *Shanghai xinwenshi* 上海新聞史. Shanghai: Fudan daxue chubanshe 復但大學出版社, 1996.
MacMurray, John V.A. (ed.). *Treaties and Agreements with and concerning China 1894-1919*. New York: Oxford University Press, 1921.
Mai Zhonghua 麥仲華 (ed.). *Huangchao jingshiwen xinbian* 皇朝經世文新編. Taibei: Guofeng chubanshe 國風出版社, 1965 (1898).
Mancall, Mark. *Russia and China: Their Diplomatic Relations to 1728*. Cambridge, Mass.: Harvard University Press, 1971.
Martens, Charles de. *Le guide diplomatique: Precis des droits et des fonctions des agents diplomatiques et consulaires: suivi d'un traite des actes et offices divers qui sont du ressort de la diplomatie, accompagne de piece et documents proposes comme exemples*. 5th edition annotated by M.F.H. Geffcken. Leipzig and Paris: 1866.
Martin, W.A.P. (Ding Weiliang 丁韙良). *Xixue kaolüe* 西學考略. Beijing: Tongwenguan 同文館, 1883.
——. *Hanlin Papers: Second series: Essays on the History, Philosophy, and Religion of the Chinese*. Shanghai: Kelly & Walsh, 1894.
——. *A Cycle of Cathay: or China, South and North with Personal Reminiscences*. New York: Fleming H. Revell Company, 1900 (Republished Taipei: Ch'eng-wen Publishing Company, 1966).
——. *The Lore of Cathay, or the Intellect of China*. New York, Chicago, Toronto: Fleming H. Revell Company, 1901.
——. *The Awakening of China*. New York: Doubleday, Page & Company, 1910.
——. *Tongwenguan timinglu* 同文館題名錄. In *Wanguo gongbao* 萬國公報. Qingmo Minchu baokan congbian 清末民初報刊叢編 no. 4. Taibei: Huawen shuju 華文書局, 1968, vol. 12, pp. 7170-7172, 7224-7226, 7242-7246.

Masini, Federico. *The Formation of Modern Chinese Lexicon and Its Evolution Toward a National Language: The Period from 1840 to 1898. Journal of Chinese Linguistics Monograph Series* no. 6. Rome: Department of Oriental Studies, University of Rome, 1993.

Mateer, A.H. *New Terms for New Ideas. A Study of the Chinese Newspaper*. Shanghai: Presbyterian Mission Press, 1915.

Mengzi zhengyi 孟子正義. Beijing: Zhonghua shuju 中華書局, 1987.

Mengzi zhushu 孟子注疏. In *Shisanjing zhushu* 十三經注疏, Taibei: Dahua shuju 大化書局, 1982.

Michio Nagai. "Herbert Spencer in Early Meiji Japan". In *The Far Eastern Quarterly*. Vol. XIV Nov. 1954, pp. 55-64.

Minbao 民報. Beijing: Kexue chubanshe 科學出版社, 1957.

Mittler, Barbara. *A Newspaper for China. Power, Identity, and Change in Shanghai's News Media, 1872-1912*. Harvard East Asian studies monographs, 226. Cambridge, Mass. & London: Harvard University Press, 2004.

Morse, Hosea Ballou. *The International Relations of the Chinese Empire*. Taipei: Ch'eng wen Publishing Company, 1971 (first published 1918).

Moynier, Gustave et.al. *Les Lois de la Guerre sur Terre. Manuel Publié par L'institut de Droit International*. Genève: Imprimerie Charles Schuchardt, 1880.

Nathan, Andrew J. "The Late Qing Press: Role, Audience and Impact". In *Zhongyang yanjiuyuan guoji hanxue huiyi lunwen ji* 中央研究院國際漢學會議論文集 (Academica Sinica. International Conferences on Sinology). 9 vols. Taibei, 1981, Volume on History and Archaeology, pp. 1281-1308.

Nylan, Michael. *The Five "Confucian" Classics*. New Haven & London: Yale University Press, 2001.

Oppenheim, L. (ed.). *The Collected Papers of John Westlake on Public International Law*. Cambridge: Cambridge University Press, 1914.

Osiander, Andreas. *The States System of Europe, 1640-1990: Peacemaking and the Conditions of International Stability*. Oxford: Clarendon Press, 1994.

Otsuka, Hirohiko. "Japan's Early Encounters with the Concept of the "Law of Nations"". In *The Japanese Annual of International Law*. No. 13. Tokyo: The International Law Association of Japan, 1969.

Paine, S.C.M. *The Sino-Japanese War of 1894-1895. Perceptions, Power, and Primacy*. Cambridge: Cambridge University Press, 2003.

Perdue, Peter C. "A Frontier View of Chineseness". In Arrighi, Giovanni, Takeshi Hamashita and Mark Selden (eds.). *The Resurgence of East Asia. 500, 150 and 50 years Perspectives*. London and New York: Routledge, 2003, pp. 51-77.

Perkins, Franklin. *Leibniz and China. A Commerce of Light*. Cambridge: Cambridge University Press, 2004.

Phillimore, Sir Robert Joseph. *Commentaries upon International Law*. Vol. 1-4. 2nd edition. London: Butterworth, 1871-74.

Pomeranz, Kenneth. *The Great Divergence. China, Europe, and the Making of the Modern World Economy*. Princeton and Oxford: Princeton University Press, 2000.

Pomeranz, Kenneth & Steven Topik. *The World that Trade Created. Society, Culture, and the World Economy 1400 to the Present*. New York: M.E. Sharpe, 2006.

Preisner, Wolfgang. "History of the Law of Nations: Basic Questions and Principles". In *Encyclopedia of International Law*. Amsterdam: Elsevier Science Publishers, 1984, pp. 126-132.

——. "History of the Law of Nations: Ancient Times to 1648". In *Encyclopedia of International Law*. Amsterdam: Elsevier Science Publishers, 1984, pp. 132-160.

Pusey, James Reeve. *China and Charles Darwin*. Cambridge, Mass.: Harvard University Press, 1983.

Qi Qizhang 戚其章. *Guojifa shijiaoxia de Jiawu zhanzheng* 國際法視角下的甲午戰爭. Beijing: Renmin chubanshe 人民出版社, 2001.

Qingyibao 清議報. *Zhongguo jindai qikan huikan* 中國近代期刊匯刊. Beijing: Zhonghua shuju 中華書局, 1991.

Quanguo zong shumu 全國總書目. Shanghai: Shenghuo shudian 生活書店, 1935.

Rankin, Mary Backus. *Early Chinese Revolutionaries. Radical Intellectuals in Shanghai and Chekiang, 1902-1911*. Cambridge: Harvard University Press, 1971.

——. "'Public Opinion' and Political Power: Qingyi in Late Nineteenth Century China". In *The Journal of Asian Studies*, vol. 41, no. 3, May 1982, pp. 453-484.

Robertson, Edmund. "International law" in *Encyclopaedia Britannica*. 9th edition. Edinburgh: Adam and Charles Black, 1875-89.

Saneto Keishu 實藤惠秀. (Translated by Tan Ruqian 譚汝謙 & Lin Qiyan 林啟彥). *Zhongguoren liuxue Riben shi* 中國人留學日本史. Hongkong: Zhongwen daxue chubanshe 中文大學出版社, 1982.

Sang Bing 桑兵. *Wang Qing xuetang xuesheng yu shehui bianqian* 晚清學堂學生與社會變遷. Shanghai: Xuelin chubanshe 學林出版社, 1995.

Scalapino, Robert A. "Prelude to Marxism: The Chinese Student Movement in Japan, 1900-1910". In Albert Feuerwerker, Rhoads Murphey & Mary C. Wright (eds.). *Approaches to Modern Chinese History*. Berkeley and Los Angeles: University of California Press, 1967, pp. 190-215.

Scalapino, Robert A. & Harold Schiffrin. "Early Socialist Currents in the Chinese Revolutionary Movement: Sun Yat-sen versus Liang Ch'i-ch'ao". In *The Journal of Asian Studies*, vol. 18, no. 3, May 1959, pp. 321-342.

Schwartz, Benjamin. *In Search of Wealth and Power. Yen Fu and the West*. Cambridge: Harvard University Press, 1964.

Scupin, Hans-Ulrich. "History of the Law of Nations: 1815 to World War I". In *Encyclopedia of International Law*. Amsterdam: Elsevier Science Publishers, 1984, pp. 179-205.

Shanghai xinbao 上海新報. *Jindai Zhongguo shiliao congkan sanbian* 近代中國史料叢刊三編. Taipei: Wenhai chubanshe 文海出板社, 1990.

Shao Zhitang 邵之棠 (ed.). *Huangchao jingshiwen tongbian* 皇朝經世文統編. Taibei: Wenhai chubanshe 文海出版社, 1972 (1901).

Shenbao 申報. Shanghai: 1872-1949.

Shin, Sung Wook. "Reform Through Study Societies in the Late Ch'ing Period, 1895-1900: The Nan Hsueh-Hui". In Cohen, Paul A. & John E. Schrecker (eds.). *Reform in Nineteenth-Century China*. Cambridge: East Asian Research Center, Harvard University, 1976, pp. 311-316.

Shinmi Kichiji 新見吉治. *Chunqiu shidai guoji gongfa kao* 春秋時代國際公法攷. (Translated from the Japanese by the Hubeixue baoguan 湖北學報館) *Hubei xuebao* 湖北學報, 1903.

Shiwubao 時務報 (*Current Affairs, The Progress*). *Jindai Zhongguo shiliao congkan sanbian* 近代中國史料叢刊三編. Taipei: Wenhai chubanshe 文海出板社 1987.

Shixuebao 實學報. *Zhongguo jindai qikan huikan* 中國近代期刊彙刊. Beijing: Zhonghua shuju 中華書局, 1991.

Shi Yuanhua 石源華 (ed.). *Zhongguo shi waijiaojia* 中國十外交家. Shanghai: Renmin chubanshe 人民出版社, 1999.

Shubao 述報. *Zhongguo shixue congshu* 中國史學叢書. Taibei: Taiwan xuesheng shuju 臺灣學生書局, 1965.

Siebold, Alexander Freiherr von. *Der Eintritt Japans in das europäische Völkerrecht*. Berlin: Verlag von Kisak Tamai, 1900.

Smith, F.E. & N.W. Sibley. *International Law as Interpreted during the Russo-Japanese War*. London: T. Fisher Unwin & William Clowes and sons, 1905.

Spence, Jonathan. *The China Helpers*. London: The Bodley Head, 1969.

Su Jing 蘇精. *Qingji Tongwenguan* 清季同文館. Taibei: 1978.

Stevens, George B. *The Life, Letters, and Journals of the Rev. and Hon. Peter Parker, M.D., Missionary, Physician, Diplomatist, The Father of Medical Missions and Founder of the Ophthalmic Hospital in Canton*. Boston and Chicago: Congregational Sunday-School and Publishing Society, 1896.

Svarverud, Rune. "Jus Gentium Sinense: The Earliest Chinese Translation of International Law with some Considerations regarding the Compilation of *Haiguo tuzhi*." In *Acta Orientalia*. Copenhagen: Munksgard. Vol. 61-2000, pp. 203-237.

——. "The Notions of 'Power' and 'Rights' in Chinese Political Discourse." In Lackner, Michael, Iwo Amelung & Joachim Kurtz (eds.). *New Terms for New Ideas. Western Knowledge & Lexical Change in Late Imperial China*. Leiden: Brill, 2001.

——. "Social Darwinism and China's relationship with Korea and Japan in late 19th and early 20th century". In *International Journal of Korean History* Vol. 2, December 2002, Seoul: Center for Korean History, Institute of Korean Culture, 2002, pp. 99-122.

——. "The formation of a Chinese Lexicon of International Law 1847-1903". In Lackner, Michael & Natascha Vittinghoff (eds.). *Mapping Meanings. The Field of New Learning in Late Qing China*. Leiden: Brill, 2004.

Svensson, Marina. *The Chinese Conception of Human Rights. The Debate on Human Rights in China, 1898-1949*. Lund: Department of East Asian Languages, Lund University, 1996.

Takahashi Sakuyé. "The Application of International Law During the Chino-Japanese War". In *Law Quarterly Review*. Vol. XIV. London: Stevens and Sons, 1898, pp. 405-415.

Takahashi Sakué. *Cases on International Law During the Chino-Japanese War*. Cambridge, Cambridge University Press, 1899.

——. *International Law Applied to the Russo-Japanese War, with the Decisions of the Japanese Prize Courts*. London: Stevens and Sons, 1908.

Tan Ruqian 譚汝謙. *Riben yi Zhongguo shu zonghe mulu* 日本譯中國書綜合目錄. Hong Kong: Zhongwen daxue chubanshe 中文大學出版社, 1981.

Tang Caichang ji 唐才常集. Beijing: Zhonghua shuju 中華書局, 1980.

Teng, Ssu-yü & John K. Fairbank. *China's Response to the West: a Documentary Survey, 1839-1923*. Cambridge, Mass.: Harvard University Press, 1981.

Tian Tao 田濤 & Li Zhuhuan 李祝環. "Qingmo fanyi waiguo faxue shuji pingshu" 清末翻譯外國法學書籍評述. In *Zhongwai faxue* 中外法學 (*Peking University Law Journal*), 3-2000. Beijing: Beijing daxue chubanshe 北京大學出版社, 2000, pp. 355-371.

Tian Tao 田濤. *Guojifa shuru yu wan Qing Zhongguo* 國際法輸入與晚清中國. Jinan: Jinan chubanshe 濟南出版社, 2001.

Toby, Ronald P. *State and Diplomacy in Early Modern Japan. Asia in the Development of the Tokugawa Bakufu*. Stanford: Stanford University Press, 1991.

Tsiang T.F. "Bismarck and the Introduction of International Law into China." In *The Chinese Social and Political Science Review*. Vol. 15. Peking: Chinese Social and Political Science Association, 1931, pp. 98-101.

Tsien, Tsuen-hsuin. "Western Impact on China through Translation". In *The Far Eastern Quarterly*, vol. 13, no. 3, May 1954, pp. 305-327.

Tuck, Richard. *The Rights of War and Peace: Political Thought and the International Order from Grotius to Kant*. Oxford: Oxford University Press, 1999.

Tyau, Min-ch'ien. *The Legal Obligations Arising out of Treaty Relations Between China and Other States*. Taipei: Ch'eng-wen publishing company, 1966.

Vattel, Emmerich de. *Law of Nations; or Principles of the Law of Nature, applied to the Conduct and Affairs of Nations and Sovereigns*. Philadelphia: T. & J.W. Johnson & Co, 1863.

Verzijl, J.H.W. "Western European Influence on the Foundation of International Law". In *International Relations*. 1955. London: Sage, 1955, pp. 137-146.

Verosta, Stephan. "History of the Law of Nations: 1648-1815". In *Encyclopedia of International Law*. Amsterdam: Elsevier Science Publishers, 1984, pp. 160-179.

Vittinghoff, Natascha. "Readers, Publishers and Officials in the Contest for a Public Voice and the Rise of a Modern Press in Late Qing China (1860-1880). In *T'oung Pao – Revue Internationale de Sinologie*, vol. 87 (4/5), 2001, pp. 393-455.

——. "Unity vs. Uniformity: Liang Qichao and the Invention of a "New Journalism" for China". In *Late Imperial China* 23, no. 1, 2002, pp. 91-143.

Waijiaobao huibian 外交報彙編. Taibei: Guangwen shuju 廣文書局, 1964.

Walker, Richard Louis. *The Multi-State System of Ancient China*. Westport, Connecticut: Greenwood Press, 1971.

Wanguo gongbao 萬國公報. *Qingmo Minchu baokan congbian* 清末民初報刊叢編 no. 4. Taibei: Huawen shuju 華文書局, 1968.

Wang Ermin 王爾敏. *Shanghai gezhi shuyuan zhilüe* 上海上格致書院志略. Hongkong: Zhongwen daxue chubanshe 中文大學出版社, 1980.

——. *Wan Qing shangyue waijiao* 晚清商約外交. Hongkong: Zhongwen daxue chubanshe 中文大學出版社, 1998.

Wang Ermin 王爾敏 & Chen Shanwei 陳善偉 (eds.). *Qingmo yiding Zhongwai shangyue jiaoshe* 清末議訂中外商約交涉. Hongkong: Zhongwen daxue chubanshe 中文大學出版社, 1993.

Wang, Gungwu. "Power, Rights, and Duties in Chinese History" In *The Chineseness of China. Selected Essays*. Hongkong: Oxford University Press, 1991, pp. 165-186.

Wang Jian 王健. *Goutong liangge shijie de falü yiyi - Wan Qing xifangfa de shuru yu falü xinci chutan* 溝通兩個世界的法律意義—晚清西方法的輸入與法律新詞初探. Beijing: Zhongguo zhengfa daxue chubanshe 中國政法大學出版社, 2001.

——. "Tansuo Xifang de 'Fayan fayu' – Yi Biligan de 'Faguo lüli' wei xiansuo, jian lun waiguofa de fanyi yu Zhongguo falü jindaihua guanxi 探索西方的「法言法語」—以畢利幹的《法國律例》為線索，兼論外國法的翻譯與中國法律近代化關係. In *Fazhishi yanjiu* 法制史研究. Taibei: *Zhongguo fazhishi xuehui* 中國法制史學會, 4/2003, pp. 95-126.

Wang Lixin 王立新. *Meiguo chuanjiaoshi yu wan Qing Zhongguo xiandaihua* 美國傳教士與晚清中國現代化. Tianjin: Tianjin renmin chubanshe 天津人民出版社, 1997.

Wang Tao 王韜. "Xingyao zhizhang xu" 星軺指掌序. In *Tao Yuan wenlu waibian* 弢園文錄外編. Beijing: Zhonghua shuju 中華書局, 1959 (first published 1897), *juan* 9, pp. 246-247.

——. *Tao Yuan wenlu waipian* 弢園文錄外編. Zhengzhou: Zhongzhou guji chubanshe 中州古籍出版社, 1998.

Wang Tieya 王鐵崖. *Guojifa yinlun* 國際法引論. Beijing: Beijing daxue chubanshe 北京大學出版社, 1998.

——. "Zhongguo yu guojifa – lishi yu dangdai" 中國與國際法一歷史與當代. In *Zhongguo guojifa niankan* 中國國際法年刊. Beijing: Zhongguo duiwai fanyi chubanshe 中國對外翻譯出版社, 1991, pp. 5-115.

Wang Weijian 王維儉. "Lin Zexu fanyi Xifang guojifa zhuzuo kaolüe" 林則徐翻譯西方國際法著作考略. In *Zhongshan daxue xuebao* 中山大學學報 no. 1-1985. Guangzhou: Zhongshan daxue 中山大學, 1985, pp. 58-67.

——. "Dingzheng ruogan Zhong Wai cishu zhong 'Ding Weiliang' cimu sheji de shishi" 訂正若干中外詞書中"丁韙良"詞目涉及的史實. In *Zhongshan daxue xuebao* 中山大學學報 2:1987. Guangzhou: Zhongshan daxue 中山大學, 1987, pp. 68-76.

Wang Xiaoqiu 王曉秋. *Jindai Zhong Ri wenhua jiaoliu shi* 近代中日文化交流史. Beijing: Zhonghua shuju 中華書局, 2000.

Wang Yangzong 王揚宗. "Jiangnan zhizaoju fanyi shumu xinkao" 江南製造局翻譯書目新考. In *Zhongguo keji shiliao* 中國科技史料. Beijing: Zhongguo kexue jishu chubanshe 中國科學技術出版社, 2:1995, pp. 3-18.

——. *Fulanya yu jindai Zhongguo de kexue qimeng* 复蘭雅與近代中國的啟蒙. Beijing: Kexue chubanshe 科學出版社, 2000.

Wang Yiliang 王貽梁 (ed.). *Shengshi weiyan* 盛世危言. Zhengzhou: Zhongzhou guji chubanshe 中州古籍出版社, 1998.

Wang Yongxin 王用心. "'Wanguo gongfa' de jige wenti" 《萬國公法》的幾個問題. In *Beijing daxue xuebao* 北京大學學報 (*Zhexue shehui kexue ban* 哲學社會科學版). Beijing: Beijing daxue 北京大學, 3:2005, pp. 78-86.

Wei Yuan 魏源 (ed.). *Haiguo tuzhi* 海國圖志. 50 vol. edition. Yangzhou: Guweitang 古微堂, 1844. (60 vol. enlarged edition 1847, 100 vol. second enlarged edition 1852, 125 vol. third enlarged edition 1895)

Wei Yuan 魏源 & He Changling 賀長齡 (eds.) *Qing jingshi wenbian* 清經世文編. Beijing: Zhonghua shuju 中華書局, 1992 (1827).

Wheaton, Henry. *Elements of International Law*. 6th edition annotated by William Beach Lawrence. Boston: Little, Brown and Company, 1855.

Wight, Martin. "Why is there No International Theory?". In Butterfield, Herbert & Martin Wight (eds.). *Diplomatic Investigations: Essays in the Theory of International Politics*. London: George Allen & Unwin, 1966, pp. 17-34.

Wills, John E. *Embassies and Illusions. Dutch and Portuguese Envoys to K'ang-hsi, 1666-1687*. Cambridge, Mass., Harvard University Press, 1984.

——. Pepper, Guns, and Parleys. The Dutch East India Company and China, 1662-1681. Los Angeles: Figueroa Press, 2005.

Wong, R. Bin. *China Transformed. Historical Change and the Limits of European Experience*. Ithaca and London: Cornell University Press, 1997.

Woolsey, *Theodore Dwight. Introduction to the study of international law: Designed as an aid in teaching, and in historical studies*. 4th edition. London: Sampson Low, Marston, Low, & Searle, 1875.

Wright, David. "Yan Fu and the task of the translator". In Lackner, Michael, Iwo Amelung & Joachim Kurtz (eds.). *New Terms for New Ideas. Western Knowledge & Lexical Change in Late Imperial China*. Leiden: Brill, 2001, pp. 235-255.

Wu Xuanyi 吳宣易. "Jingshi Tongwenguan lüeshi" 京師同文館略史. In *Zhongguo jindai xuezhi shiliao* 中國近代學制史料. Volume 1, first part. Jiaoyu kexue congshu 教育科學叢書. Shanghai: Huadong shifan daxue chubanshe 華東師範大學出版社, 1983, pp. 189-197.

Xianfa xinwen 憲法新聞. *Qingmo Minchu qikan huibian* 清末民初期刊彙編. Taibei: Jingshi shuju 經世書局, 1985.

Xianzheng zazhi 憲政雜誌. *Qingmo Minchu qikan huibian* 清末民初期刊彙編. Taibei: Jingshi shuju 經世書局, 1985.

Xiangbao 湘報. Beijing: Zhonghua shuju 中華書局, 1965.

Xianggang Zhongguo yuwen xuehui 香港中國語文學會 (ed.). *Jin-Xiandai Hanyu xinci ciyuan* cidian 近現代漢語新辭辭源辭典. Shanghai: Hanyu dacidian chubanshe 漢語大辭典出版社, 2001.

Xiangxue xinbao 湘學新報, *Xiangxue bao* 湘學報. Changsha: 1897-1898

Xinmin congbao 新民叢報 (*Sein min choong bou*). Yokohama: 1902-1907.

Xiong Yuezhi 熊月之. *Xixue dongjian yu wanqing shehui* 西學東漸與晚清社會. Shanghai: Shanghai renmin chubanshe 上海人民出版社, 1994.

——. "*Haiguo tuzhi* zhengyin xishu kaoshi" 〈海國圖志〉徵引西書考釋. Zhonghua wenshi luncong 中華文史論叢 vol. 55-1996. Shanghai: Shanghai guji chubanshe 上海古籍出版社, 1996, pp. 235-259.

——. "'Liberty', 'democracy', 'president': The translation and usage of some political terms in late Qing China". In Lackner, Michael, Iwo Amelung & Joachim Kurtz (eds.). *New Terms for New Ideas. Western Knowledge & Lexical Change in Late Imperial China*. Leiden: Brill, 2001, pp. 69-93.

——. *Zhongguo jindai minzhu sixiangshi* 中國近代民主思想史. Shanghai: Shanghai renmin chubanshe 上海人民出版社, 2002.

Xu Weize 徐維則. *Dongxixue shumu* 東西學書目. 1898/1902.

Yadong shibao 亞東時報. Shanghai: 1898-1900.

Yanabu, Akira. "Shakai, society: Translation by people who had not known 'society'". (http://www.japanlink.co.jp/ol/soc.html) (24th January 2005)

——. "Kenri, right: Ken means right, ken means power". (http://www.japanlink.co.jp/ol/rig.html) (24th January 2005)

——. "Jiyuu, liberty: Repulsion of Yanagida Kunio". (http://www.japanlink.co.jp/ol/lib.html) (24th January 2005)

Yishu huibian 譯書彙編. Tokyo: 1900-1903.

Yu, P.K., Yu-ning Li & Yü-fa Chang (Yu Bingquan 余秉權, Li Youning 李又寧 & Zhang Yufa 張玉法) (eds.). *The Revolutionary Movement During the Late Ch'ing: A Guide to Chinese Periodicals* (清季革命運動期刊敘目選輯). Washington, D.C.: Center for Chinese Research Libraries, 1970.

Zeng Jize 曾紀澤. *Chushi Ying Fa E guo riji* 出使英法俄國日記. *Zou xiang shijie congshu* 走向世界叢書. Hunan: Yuelu shushe 岳麓書社, 1985.

Zhang Haipeng 張海鵬. *Zhuiqiuji: Jindai Zhongguo lishi jincheng de tansuo* 追求集：近代中國歷史進程的探索. Beijing: Shehui kexue wenxian chubanshe 社會科學文獻出版社, 1998.

Zhang, Jingcao. "How Western International Law Was Introduced into China and Its Influence upon China." In Luk, Bernhard H.K. (ed.). *Contacts Between Cultures*. Vol. 4: *Eastern Asia: History and Social Sciences*. Lewiston: Mellen, 1992, pp. 264-270.

Zhang Pufan 張普藩. *Zhongguo falü de chuantong yu jindai zhuanxing* 中國法律的傳統與近代轉型. Beijing: Falü chubanshe 法律出版社, 1997.

Zhejiangchao 浙江潮. *Zhonghua minguo shiliao congbian* 中華民國史料叢編. Taibei: Dangshi shiliao bianzuan weiyuanhui 黨史史料編纂委員會, 1983.

Zhengfa xuebao 政法學報 (*The Tsen fah shui pao, A monthly magazine of political and law works*). Tokyo: 1903-1904.

Zhixinbao 知新報. Shanghai: Aomen jijinhui 澳門基金會, Shanghai shehui kexueyuan chubanshe 上海社會科學院出版社, 1996.

Zhongguo falü tushu zongmu 中國法律圖書總目. Beijing: Zhongguo zhengfa daxue chubanshe 中國政法大學出版社, 1991.

Zhongguo jindai xiandai congshu mulu 中國近代現代叢書目錄. Shanghai: Shanghai tushuguan 上海圖書館, 1979.

Zhou Mian 周棉 (ed.). *Zhongguo liuxuesheng da cidian* 中國留學生大詞典. Nanjing: Nanjing daxue chubanshe 南京大學出版社, 1999.

Zou Zhenhuan 鄒振環. "Jingshi Tongwenguan ji qi yishu jianshu" 京師同文館及其譯書簡述. In *Chuban shiliao* 出版史料 1989-2. Shanghai: Shanghai shudian 上海書店, 1989, pp. 82-87.

——. *Yingxiang Zhongguo jindao shehui de yibai zhong yizuo* 影響中國近代社會的一百種譯作. Beijing: Zhongguo duiwai fanyi chuban gongsi 中國對外翻譯出版公司, 1996.

INDEX